PENGUIN BOOKS

THE MONEY LENDERS

Anthony Sampson began his career in journalism editing *Drum,* the black magazine in South Africa, about which he wrote his first book. He returned to London in 1955, joining the staff of *The Observer,* with which he has been associated ever since. *Anatomy of Britain,* published in 1962, established his reputation as a journalist and was followed by *The New Europeans* in 1968. In *The Sovereign State of ITT,* published in 1973, he broke new ground, describing in detail the political workings of a multinational corporation. This was followed by *The Seven Sisters,* a study of the major oil companies, in 1975, and *The Arms Bazaar,* about the arms corporations, in 1977. In 1979 Mr. Sampson was invited by Willy Brandt to be editorial adviser to the Brandt Commission on North-South relations. Anthony Sampson contributes regularly to *Newsweek* and *The Observer* and lives in London with his wife and two children.

THE
MONEY
LENDERS

ANTHONY SAMPSON

PENGUIN
BOOKS

Penguin Books Ltd, Harmondsworth,
Middlesex, England
Penguin Books, 625 Madison Avenue,
New York, New York 10022, U.S.A.
Penguin Books Australia Ltd, Ringwood,
Victoria, Australia
Penguin Books Canada Limited, 2801 John Street,
Markham, Ontario, Canada L3R 1B4
Penguin Books (N.Z.) Ltd, 182–190 Wairau Road,
Auckland 10, New Zealand

First published in the United States of America
with the subtitle *Bankers and a World in Turmoil*
by The Viking Press 1982
Published in Penguin Books 1983

LIBRARY OF CONGRESS CATALOGING IN PUBLICATION DATA
Sampson, Anthony.
The money lenders.
Includes index.
1. Banks and banking, International. 2. Bankers.
3. Underdeveloped areas—Banks and banking. I. Title.
HG3881.S1827 1983   332.1'5   82-15049
ISBN 0 14 00.6485 0

Printed in the United States of America by
R. R. Donnelley & Sons Company, Harrisonburg, Virginia
Set in Videocomp Optima

Contents

Introduction

This is a book about the relationship between bankers and nations, particularly developing nations—from England in the fourteenth century to the United States in the nineteenth century to the many-colored developing world of the 1980s. I try to show how banks grew up into the huge global organizations that we know today, and how they operate across frontiers in the contemporary world; but I do not attempt to cover the many complex activities of domestic banking and the economic theories that lie behind them. My interest is in the international politics of banking, and the personalities that lie behind them. Many economists have described banking in terms of the interplay of macro-economic forces; but this book tries to show how banks are also affected by the character of their leaders and the problems of particular competition, and I have tried to show how the world looks through the eyes of individual bankers.

In a subject of such huge geographical and historical dimensions, I have had to be very selective, following the fortunes of a few distinctive bankers and providing case histories of significant countries, which show special problems and crises in the relationship. But I have also tried to look at the relationship from the point of view of the nations, and at the wider problems of their development, trade, and prosperity. I have tried to show how the world institutions grew up after the Second World War and how the dispensing of foreign aid raised new hopes followed by disillusion; while in the last chapters the two themes begin to converge, as bankers' problems have overlapped with the problems of aid and the reform of the world economic system.

In writing this book I have not attempted to provide an original economic analysis or to give statistics which are widely available elsewhere. I have concentrated on the political element: I have used the traditional methods of a journalist, talking to a large number of bankers, experts, and politicians, and filling in the background through my travels and reading, with much help from colleagues. Bankers have not normally been a favorite subject for writers and political journalists. Novelists and playwrights, if they deal with bankers at all, have tended to depict them as malign figures in the tradition of Shylock. Trollope, Zola, or Dreiser have been more interested in reckless financiers who soar and fall than in the steadier and more circumscribed lives of bankers who lend other people's money. But I believe there is a special psychological, as well as political, interest in the conjunction of a disciplined and introvert banker—the very quintessence of advanced capitalist civilization—with the chaos and opportunities of an emerging developing country with almost opposite values.

I first became curious about the role of international bankers when I returned from South Africa to London twenty-five years ago, and was struck by the contrast between the erratic world of the black townships and the confident assessments of men behind partners' desks in the City of London assessing the prospects 6,000 miles away: watching the black nations graduating to independence in the fifties and sixties, I saw some of the relationships turning sour. My more recent and practical interest followed logically from my last two books, *The Seven Sisters* about the oil companies and *The Arms Bazaar* about the weapons business, which were part of my growing interest in the multinational corporations. The oil crisis of 1973, which transformed the role of the OPEC countries and brought new opportunities for arms sellers, also created vast surpluses, much of which were deposited in Western banks. The tragic story of the Shah, whom I saw at the peak of his prestige, provided an important case history in the story, first of the oil companies, then of the arms salesmen, and then of the bankers.

My curiosity about the bankers was whetted after I had been invited in 1978 by Willy Brandt to become editorial adviser of the international commission of which he was chairman, which was looking for new solutions to the North-South deadlock. Listening to the discussions and helping to write the final report, I became more aware that the future of many developing countries was interlocked with the problems of the big banks, and that aid could be less important to the poorer nations than changes in the world system which could help them to develop their own resources. In my own talks with members of the commission I began to think that the solutions at the top were less technical and more political than they often appeared from below. With this background I thought it could be useful and interesting to give my own personal account of the critical frontier between bankers and nations; this book is the result.

In writing it, I have tried to give some picture of how the world looks both to international bankers and to the developing countries with which they deal. The reader may sometimes feel that he is being whirled dizzily round the globe without stopping long enough to collect his thoughts. If so, I can only plead that this restless pursuit is not unlike the experience of international bankers themselves, as they rush between their client countries, switching their minds from one complex problem to the next. It is a story which, of its nature, has no ending or neat summing-up. The bankers are among the most cosmopolitan of people; but they are up against all the contradictions and dangers of the contemporary world, and their story can only end honestly with a question mark.

I have many debts to people whose brains I have picked and who have given valuable advice, but many of them might prefer not to be mentioned. I am specially grateful to friends who urged or encouraged me to begin this daunting task: most notably Jerome Levinson, the former chief counsel of Senator Church's subcommittee on multinationals, now of the Inter-American Bank; Karin Lissakers, who worked on the same subcommittee; Joe Saxe of the World Bank; Professor Susan Strange of the London School of Economics, who has helped so many students in this field; Professor Jonathan Aronson, whose own book *Money and Power* gave me useful insights; and John Heimann, the former U.S.

comptroller of the currency. Among bankers discretion must be the better part of gratitude. My reception from the biggest banks varied widely: Citibank and Chase Manhattan were welcoming and cooperative, while Barclays and the Bank of America were less so. But in many banks, including some surprising ones, I must record my appreciation to friends, both old and new, who gave me candid and outspoken views and invaluable information. I have a special debt to many friends on the Brandt Commission who helped to give me different views of the problem as seen from different continents; notably Sonny Ramphal from the Commonwealth Secretariat in London, Peter Peterson from New York, Abdlatif Al-Hamad from Kuwait, L. K. Jha from New Delhi, and Rodrigo Botero from Bogota. I am specially grateful to Robert Cassen, formerly of the Brandt Secretariat, who, with his long experience of development problems, patiently tried to explain some of the economic complexities.

In writing a topical book I have as before had to work at speed, and I am grateful to my publishers and agents for their help and forbearance; particularly to Alan Williams and Alan Gordon Walker, my editors in New York and London; to my agents, Sterling Lord and Michael Sissons; to the staff of Viking Penguin and of Hodder and Stoughton, and of my other publishers in Europe and Japan. I am specially indebted to my assistants, first Maili Brisby and then Alexa Wilson, who saw the book through its various stages of chaos; and as always to my wife, Sally, for enduring the strains of authorship.

THE
MONEY
LENDERS

1
MIDAS AND THE ASS

Bankers are just like anyone else, except richer.

OGDEN NASH

"My name is Ozymandias, king of kings;
Look on my works ye Mighty, and despair!"
Nothing beside remains. Round the decay
Of that colossal wreck, boundless and bare
The lone and level sands stretch far away.

SHELLEY

No convention in Washington is quite so overwhelming as the gathering of four thousand dark-suited men who arrive in the fall, flying in from 140 countries, to take over the Sheraton Washington Hotel. They seethe into the lobbies, lurk round the entrances, and crowd into the garish elevators, impregnating every floor with their intensity. The hotel becomes as self-sufficient and placeless as a liner in mid-ocean; through its intricate system of decks, promenades and underground halls the visitors can spend a whole day without breathing the open air. Most of the world—even China, even Vietnam—have come to set up shop in this temporary financial supermarket. Luxury suites have been converted overnight into miniature embassies, with their own national flunkies, secretaries, and atmospheres. In one suite the Saudis are complaining about their exclusion from the seats of monetary power. In another the boyish South African finance minister, Senator Horwood, is eagerly explaining how gold is indispensable to discipline, and protesting that bankers do not appreciate his country's stability. In the *passagiata* of delegates round the central lobbies you can hear almost every nation's viewpoint except that of the Soviet bloc.

It is extraordinary only in its ordinariness. Only a few delegates
—a West Samoan in a long blue skirt, a minister from Mali in
flowing embroidered green robes—add a dash of color. The rest
are almost uniformly sober-suited, pinstriped, white-shirted, with
cautious ties and shiny shoes. There are scores of Arabs, but not
a single galabea or burnous. They cover the world, but the world
in monochrome. There could be little doubt that this is what it is,
a convention of bankers: the annual meeting of the World Bank
and the International Monetary Fund.

Through the main entrance more bankers are swarming in,
whose roving eyes suggest a very practical purpose. The limousines come and go, ferrying the grandees from the other hotels:
Rockefeller of the Chase, Wilfried Guth of the Deutsche Bank, Sir
Anthony Tuke, the hereditary chairman of Barclays Bank. It is an
odd sight for an ordinary customer who associates bankers with
a sedentary dignity, waiting for the world to come to them cap in
hand. Here—there can be no doubt of it—they are searching out
the world, lingering awkwardly by the elevators, dawdling by the
newsstand, and then suddenly walking—almost running—too fast
for dignity. Across there a pack of Japanese bankers—they seem
to move in sixes—is converging on a finance minister. Along the
corridor a grave-looking French banker, looking very *haute
banque*, looks as if he is in full pursuit of new African prey.
Waiting by the lobby is the gaunt shape of the high mandarin of
London banking, Sir Jeremy Morse, the chairman of Lloyds, who
is said to be one of the few men who really understand what a
Special Drawing Right *is*. "It's just a pity," remarks one of his
rivals, "that they forgot to put blood in his veins."

Everyone is watching everyone else out of the corners of their
eyes, wondering what they're missing, like children playing a
game of sardines. "Do you know who he is? He's *literally* the boss
of Manny Hanny." "You wouldn't think he speaks perfect Japanese—he spent seven years in a Zen temple." "He's got fantastic
contacts in that part of the world—you and he ought to get together." "He's really *very* close to Imelda Marcos in Manila."
Many of them begin to look not so much like bankers as financial

middle men, contact men, or—could it really be?—*salesmen*. As they pursue their prey down the escalators, up the elevators, along the upstairs corridors into the suites, they cannot conceal their anxiety to do business. For these men who look as if they might have been trained to say no from their childhood are actually trying to sell *loans*. "I've got good news for you," I heard one eager contact man telling a group of American bankers; "I think they'll be able to take your money."

In the bowels of the hotel the official delegates are streaming into the brightly lit conference hall to sit behind the nameplates of their 140 countries arrayed like the UN assembly. Up on the high dais the two financial nabobs, Robert McNamara and Jacques de Larosière, sit below the giant emblems of their institutions, the World Bank and the International Monetary Fund.

The opening speech is by this year's chairman, Amir Jamal, the soulful Minister of Finance from Tanzania, one of the poorest and most beautiful countries in the world. Jamal has been a member of the Brandt Commission, which has recently produced its "program for survival," and he insists that the poorer countries should have a greater say in the world's system: "Why assume that the poorest of the world have no interest in world stability?" His own country, he says, has taken an unbearable strain since the price of oil wrecked its terms of trade—"the punishment for the crime of being poor." The World Bank and the IMF tell the poor countries to set their houses in order without realizing their hardships: "What kind of sense is it, when the thatched roof of that house is catching fire, and floods or blizzards are deluging it at the same time?"

He is followed by De Larosière, the compact French managing director of the International Monetary Fund, with bright eyes behind his metal spectacles. He speaks in stern tones—as if he were really the world's bank manager—about the dangers of inflation, the necessity for monetary discipline, but also the need to change his own institution: "It must adapt itself to new realities;

it must respond to the needs and aspirations of its membership."
Then McNamara gets up to deliver the last of the twelve annual
speeches with which he punctuated his career at the World Bank.
In his metallic voice he points once again to the fearful condition
of the 800 million who live in absolute poverty from which they
have no escape, and reproves the Americans and British for their
diminishing aid. The World Bank, he insists, has barely begun to
develop its full potential. He concludes, pausing with emotion,
almost in tears: "We must begin—as the founders of this great
institution began—with vision. With clear, strong, bold vision.
George Bernard Shaw put it perfectly: 'You see things, and say
why? But I dream things that never were, and I say, why not?' "

McNamara is followed by President Carter, who promises
American support for the institutions which reflect "both our
fundamental humanitarian principles and our economic interests." Carter is followed by a succession of the world's ministers
of finance, who go up to the podium, adding gloom to the darkening financial landscape. The ministers from the poorer countries
complain about their desperate need for aid, while Western ministers warn against the rate of inflation. The Iranian minister com-
plains that the freezing of his country's assets has undermined
confidence in the international banks. The German minister en-
dorses the concern of the Brandt Report, that the world's arms
race is diverting money from aid. The Saudi minister, Mohammad
Abal-Khail, speaking in Arabic and representing all the Arab states,
protests about the refusal to admit observers from the Palestine
Liberation Organization.

The Palestinians are the specters at this financial feast; a delegation makes their way into the building, only to be thrown out, and
they hold a press conference in the courtyard outside. But behind
the scenes the Arab delegates have been visiting each other's
hotel suite, determined to assert their common strength, not so
much to champion the Palestinians (who embarrass many of
them) as to insist on a greater say in the IMF and the World Bank.
For money is now the Arabs' specialty, and they see themselves
as the sharp end of the wedge on the Third World. Their encoun-

ters with other delegates in the corridors suggest some new relationships: what has Kuwait got to say to Western Samoa? What have the Saudis to say to the Brazilians? The Arabs seem like a nouveau riche candidate for a conservative club who has been blackballed and calls into question the club's rules. Everyone knows that the control of these financial bodies is in the hands of a few rich nations, headed by the United States, who hold 20 percent of the votes. But the Arabs are increasingly resentful and they insist on aligning themselves with the poorer nations who—impoverished as they are by the high price of oil—are still glad of rich friends.

After the opening speeches the convention hall rapidly empties and the bankers and delegates go back to the hotel lobbies and suites. They have not come here to listen to the usual stuff about inflation or absolute poverty, but to make profitable deals with the ministers and delegates who are now so uniquely and conveniently assembled in one place. ("I've seen ten finance ministers in three days," one banker explained to me, fingering his diary. "It would have taken a month to track them down round the world.") The truth is that, behind all the panoply of global financial statesmanship, this meeting has become the most superior of all salesmen's conventions. "It's a trade fair," as one banker put it, "but we don't give away samples. We just give our visiting cards."

Over the last thirty-five years the commercial bankers have flown in to this jamboree in still greater numbers. They start arriving long before the formal meetings begin, and many of them never go near the conference corridors. The Shoreham Hotel just opposite the Sheraton is full of bankers' suites, dining rooms, and cocktail parties to lure the ministers and delegates across the road. In the Bob Hope suite Walter Wriston and Al Costanzo, the top men of Citibank, preside over a succession of lunches and dinners. ("Will I see Mr. Costanzo at the Sheraton?" I asked his secretary. "Oh, no—he never goes over *there.*") Wriston, who is one of the world's most competitive bankers, surveys the scene with his well-cultivated languor. "Some people like to dream up a conspiracy," he tells me, "but there's less to this than meets the eye."

The princely style of bankers soon eclipses the relative austerity of the officials. As Cadillacs and Mercedes carry them away to their parties, I notice McNamara's stooping frame striding alone down the slope, running across the road, and disappearing behind the shopping block opposite. With the years the bankers' parties have become more competitive and more carefully stylish. The official hosts provide huge and stately parties for delegates. "That's the Western Hemisphere," the hostess explains when I ask about the throng that has taken over half the Shoreham lobby. The exclusive "Group of Thirty," the club of financial experts, provide an elegant gathering at the Phillips Gallery, where the central bankers who know the real secrets exchange knowing glances: the urbane American comptroller of the currency, John Heimann, has a cryptic smile to denote "if you knew what I know." But the commercial bankers' parties overshadow the others as they compete to show their cosmopolitanism, taste, or resources. The Banco di Roma celebrates its hundredth birthday with a dinner party for 600 under a huge tent on the Mall. The First Boston Corporation gives its party with a fife-and-drum band at the Corcoran Gallery. The Shoreham banqueting rooms are filled up with Merrill Lynch or Brown Brothers Harriman. In an upstairs suite the bankers' magazine *Euromoney* dispenses champagne before lunch every day. Lehman Kuhn Loeb, the international investment bank, gives a supper party in a tent in a Georgetown garden, decorated with beautiful women. ("I hope you'll explain to my wife what hard work this all is," says one of the hosts. "I think she imagines it's some kind of jamboree.")

Back in the hotels it becomes easier to distinguish the different tribes of the hunters and hunted, for they wear colored badges stating their business or country. Blue for the governors (the ministers of finance or their deputies); green for the delegates from 140 countries; brown for the guests, who include the top bankers; orange for the 600 journalists; and red for the "visitors," the hordes of ordinary bankers in pursuit of their customers. As they pair off or make huddles it is tempting to play a kind of card game with them, awarding points to different combinations. Greens with blues are common enough; oranges and greens are not surprising. It is the combination of red and blue—a banker who has buttonholed a Minister of Finance—which scores the most points, for here a loan may be clinched, or a deal signed up. The ministers from credit-worthy countries are desperately in demand. "The trouble with this business," as one investment banker explained, "is that there are ten hares chasing each fox. When you get to the minister, your rivals have got there before you." The new Prime Minister of Peru, Dr. Ulloa, is in special demand: five years ago his country seemed almost broke, but now the oil is flowing westward across the Andes pipeline, transforming his balance of payments. "I can hardly face going back to the hotel," he is heard to complain; "there are six different banks waiting for me."

The scenes in the hotel provide a kind of pageant of the world's economic problems. At the core are the official bodies, the World Bank and the IMF, working with the slowness and caution of international bureaucracies. Surrounding them and outnumbering them are the commercial bankers, topped up with Arab money, who are looking to lend money to developing countries, as well as to Western customers. Moving between them are Arab ministers and bankers, still bewildered by their new wealth but flexing their financial muscles. On the edges are the hundred other countries of the Third World who want to borrow money wherever they can. Each group has its own worries and insecurities, and its own view of the world's problems. Bankers see a struggle between their own adventurous free enterprise and the bureaucratic controls of governments and world institutions. Officials see a conflict between the prudence of the rich countries and the reckless demands of poorer countries for a New Order. The poorest countries see a simple problem of their own survival.

But debt makes its own uneasy alliances and the bankers themselves are never as secure as they might look. They have their own private worries about the rapid expansion of internal lending, depending on the surplus funds of the oil producers. There are too many lenders chasing too few borrowers—as the pursuits round the corridors suggest—and too large deposits compared to too little capital. Many of them are looking toward their central bank or to the IMF as their safety net, or their debt collector. The word "default," hardly ever uttered, is still in the back of their mind.

THE BANKERS' BURDEN

Behind all its global responsibility and impersonal style banking is still a "people business," as this gathering makes clear. Economists may talk about the macro-economic functions of the international capital market, but down in the marketplace itself there are real people trying to impress and persuade other people, worrying about their bank's balance sheet and writing off their bad debts. It may be the most personal business of all, for it always depends on the original concept of credit, meaning trust. However complex and mathematical the business has become, it still depends on the assessment of trust by individuals with very human failings.

Bankers come in all shapes—tall ones from America, small ones from Japan, fat ones from Latin America—yet they look more like each other than like other professionals in their own countries. They are nearly all well-tailored, well-organized, controlled: they go through hearty and extrovert motions, but without the riotous back slapping or compulsive drinking of other salesmen's conventions. They seem specially conscious of time, as they look at their watches and their hour-by-hour diaries, always aware that time is money. There is always a sense of restraint and tension. (Is it part of the connection which Freud observed between compulsive neatness, anal eroticism, and interest in money?)

Behind their billions and banquets there is still a kind of monkishness. The Belgian banker Louis Camu, the former chairman of the Banque de Bruxelles, compared bankers to monks who were "practicing chastity"; bankers, he suggested, were practicing giving credit—"which imposes an obligation not unlike chastity: an abstention from certain pleasures."[1] Bankers, Camu explained,

[1]"The Daily Life of a Banker," The Banker (April 1977).

were very different psychologically from financiers: a financier is like an eagle soaring into the sky; while a banker is more like a trout, whose very element is liquid. Are these men submerged in their streams of money as they peer skeptically out at the world?

Their tension is built into their business: they are looking after other people's savings, yet they make their profits from lending them out, which must entail risks. "If we don't take risks, then we're not real bankers," says Tom Clausen, who ran the Bank of America before he took over the World Bank. Bankers often stress that they are merely reacting to external events: like women in Victorian times, they are not required to take initiatives, only to say yes or no. "I'm just trying to deal with a succession of accidents," says Walter Wriston. "It's like surfing," says a partner of Barings, "just waiting for the next wave, and trying to keep upright." Yet the more they compete, the more aggressively they seek to lend. "This bank," says Harold Cleveland, the historian of Citibank, "has a tradition of being very conservative and very aggressive"; and other banks claim the same combination. It sounds contradictory, but it is the bankers' dilemma. A small customer who trusts a bank with his savings may be shocked to learn that his money has been lent aggressively across the world; or that what a bank calls its assets are in fact its loans. But bankers ever since Shylock have been accustomed to being reviled; their long-suffering style assumes that their true value will never be appreciated.

They are not all so long-suffering. There are two kinds of bankers, who can sometimes be distinguished by their look and the pace of their walk. The men from the deposit banks—commercial banks or "clearers," like Citibank, Barclays, or Deutsche Bank—are responsible for millions of bank accounts in hundreds of branches, and they have to look very dependable. The investment bankers (or merchant bankers) make deals between rich individuals or companies which do not involve the small saver, and they are allowed to look more aggressive. They have greater freedom and enterprise, like a taxi compared to a bus: "You live off your deposits," one merchant banker told a deposit banker, "we live off our wits." "I regard the commercial bankers rather as tooth-brush salesmen," one Arab banker put it; "the investment bankers are more like dentists." Commercial banks have made most of their profits from interest, investment banks from fees—though commercial banks have recently become much more interested in fees, too. Investment bankers may be cleverer, but they play a less prominent role on the world scene; they can act as temporary fixers and brokers, but they do not command the billions of deposits which provide the ultimate power.

Not surprisingly, bankers are discreet even between themselves: "I always had the feeling," said one maverick former bank chairman, "that success was measured by the extent one gave nothing away."[2] But discretion is not always distinguishable from dullness, and it is a special gift of many bankers, like David Rocke-feller or Tom Clausen, that they can make the world sound more boring than it seemed before. To use Swift's simile, they are like a dark well, you are never sure whether it is very deep or empty. By the nature of their work, these men must reduce everything to figures: they even describe their committees by their numbers—the Group of Ten, the Group of Twenty-four, the Committee of Twenty. They are made uneasy by factors which cannot be measured.

(It is not misleading or sexist to describe senior bankers as *men;* they maintain a male stronghold. Tens of thousands of women have become tellers, at which they are often quicker than men, and some have excelled at corporate and international finance. "Eventually they realize that a woman can be useful," said one successful woman banker. "After all, *they* can't dance with the heads of central banks." There are some formidable women officials, like Muriel Siebert, the Superintendent of Banking in New York State, or Elizabeth Sam of the Singapore Monetary Authority. But at the top of commercial banking, women are rare. "The men are always playing their own macho game," one woman banker explained. "It's not really the money they want—it's beating

---

[2]Lord Longford, *Five Lives* (London: Hutchinson, 1964), p. 52.

their colleagues by making that extra phone call at night.'')

Big bankers never like to be too far out of line with the rest. ''There's always a kind of herd instinct,'' said Wilson Schwartz of the Manufacturers Hanover Bank. ''There's never anything so good,'' said Frank Reilly of the Chase in London, ''that we want to have a hundred percent of it.'' ''I quite agree with you,'' said a distinguished London banker when I put forward a controversial point, ''but I'd rather not be the first to say it.'' (An attitude which explains why many of the quotations in this book will be anonymous.) They watch each other carefully, to make sure others are following. Yet the history of banking remains the history of individual people each making their own judgment—vulnerable to hopes and fears, flattery and persuasion, moods of optimism and pessimism—and this book will try to trace the effects of some of their judgments as they move round the world.

THE WORLD IN PINSTRIPE

The cosmopolitanism of these global bankers is breathtaking. No other profession can keep pace with their globetrotting and contacts. An assassination in South Korea, a revolution in Nicaragua, a coup in Turkey, reverberate in their boardrooms. Jet travel, telephones, and telex have transformed their business more than any. ''Whether we like it or not,'' says Wriston, ''mankind now has a completely integrated, international financial and informational marketplace capable of moving money and ideas to any place on this planet in minutes.''[3]

This informational marketplace has its limitations. It is bound together by airport lounges, first-class aircraft seats, and the self-contained hotel complexes which (like their Washington venue) are cut off from their cities like castles surrounded by moats. When he ventures into developing countries the banker is no longer in a world of unpredictable adventures and frantic battles with language in disorganized hotels. He is in a world of Intercon-

[3]Speech to the International Monetary Conference, London, June 11, 1979.

tinentals or Hiltons and prestige palaces designed to impress and protect him from the rest of the country—the Cho-Sun in Seoul, the Grand in Taipeh, the Mandarin in Hong Kong—each of them plugged into reassuring news services and telephones and humming with the same air conditioning, creating identical atmospheres whatever the climate. Their comfort and reassurance may never compensate for the loneliness of the long-distance banker, but it ensures that one hotel is much like another. However exotic the destination, he will still find himself sleeping in the same impersonal six-sided room.

The banker must always try to reduce each country to numbers: to political and economic indicators, comparative statistics or differences of ⅛ percent in the interest rate. Each country is neatly classified according to its credit rating as if it were a credit-card customer. Each year two bankers' magazines, *Euromoney* and *Institutional Investor,* compile their own league tables of the world's nations, put together by collating reports from leading banks: and this popularity poll has begun (like the top twenty pop songs) to exert its own power and prestige. According to *Institutional Investor* the most credit-worthy countries in 1980 were the United States, Switzerland, West Germany, and Japan, with most of Western Europe not far behind. Still quite far up the list was the Soviet Union (27), followed by East Germany (32), Czechoslovakia (35), and Hungary (41). In the middle were all kinds of countries which looked stable one moment and perilous the next —like Iraq (42), South Korea (43), and Thailand (51). At the bottom were the countries which most bankers regarded as beyond the pale, like Jamaica (88), Iran (89), Turkey (93), including a string of African countries and ending with "basket cases" like Uganda (97) and Zaire (98), where bankers were still, as the magazine reported, "in a state of shell shock."

These bare ratings may not be very accurate guides to political stability; but they matter to ministers of finance who have to argue with bankers about that extra ⅛ percent on a billion-dollar loan, and whose prestige and machismo is bound up with their place in the list. Commercial bankers are not too much concerned with the ratings or "country risks" of the poorest countries: they will anyway only lend them money for short periods, for specific deals or for projects with effective guarantees—like pawnbrokers who will only lend on the security of a bracelet or overcoat. But in twenty to thirty developing countries they have a much closer interest: for they have lent quite heavily to their governments as well as to companies, and in some of them they can see very little prospect of ever getting back their money, or even their interest. And now at the beginning of the eighties they are specially worried about a few countries which are knee-deep in debt.

What will happen to Brazil? It is the biggest borrower in the history of banking. It owes no less than $60 billion, much of it to American banks. It has borrowed so much that it has acquired its own "Debtor Power." As the saying goes: "If you owe the bank enough money you own it." There are 129 Brazilian delegates at the Washington Conference, compared with 75 Americans. For all its unique dangers, Brazil is part of a continuing story. As a partner of Barings put it: "It looks rather as America looked to us a hundred years ago. It could collapse, but it could become one of the great powers of the world."

And what will happen to South Korea? It has been the most spectacular of the wonder countries of the Far East, a banker's dream, displaying the energy and discipline that the West has lost, repaying its debts with the foreign earnings of its shoes, T-shirts, or transistors. But one dictator has been assassinated and a new one has seized power; it looks much less stable, and its credit-rating has fallen.

And what about Poland? It presents a special dilemma. A decade ago loans to Poland were thought to be opening up Eastern Europe as well as providing good business, backed by all the security of Soviet banking and gold. But the Poles borrowed and borrowed, with few extra exports to show for it, until now Poland owes $25 billion to the West and spends as much on its repayments as it earns from its exports, while strikes and wage increases have created a new crisis with the Soviets. If the Russians were to invade Poland, some bankers are openly asking, would they not provide much greater security for the loans?

MONEY AND RELIGION

And what are the Saudis up to? Of all the oil powers they are by far the richest, but in the world's financial pack they are always the joker. The Western governments want them to lend more to the developing countries; the banks want their deposits; the developing countries petition them for aid. But the old industrial countries are reluctant to share their financial power in the world institutions with these desert parvenus, and the Saudis are developing their own ideas about spending and lending their money.

While the banks were holding their convention in Washington the Saudis were finishing building a very different kind of conference center at breakneck speed at Taif, near Mecca, on top of the escarpment which rises up above the Red Sea plain. It is a weird meeting place: the road to Taif from the coast stretches straight across the desert, past camels and forsaken cars, goats and airstrips, with boulders littered across the sand as if thrown by an angry giant. After seventy miles a sign announces MECCA—MUSLIMS ONLY; but another road is open to infidels, which heads straight for a massive escarpment, a mile high. The wide road slowly zigzags up the side of it, across viaducts which nearly cross over each other, until it reaches the edge of the plateau.

A few miles across a lunar landscape appears the conference center of Taif, with glass and marble walls and a gold onion dome looming up below mountainous rocks. Further on an immense Intercontinental Hotel stands in the desert next door to a group of forty-two identical palaces, each in white marble, each with the same row of arched windows, each with the same chandeliers and huge Persian carpets. The cost of the whole complex was estimated at between a quarter of a billion dollars and two billion. Yet the palaces look oddly temporary, as if they had been dropped intact from the sky.

Here at Taif, four months after the Washington convention, the

Saudis were hosts at the Islamic Summit Conference, attended by delegates from thirty-eight nations, including twenty-eight heads of state. Kings, sheiks and presidents flew into the special airport to be received by King Khaled, who walked out on his stick to meet each one at the gangway. They each heard their own national anthem, inspected the guard of honor, and entered the brand-new terminal with high chandeliers and thick carpets. They were each driven to one of the palaces, each with a chef specially trained in the appropriate gastronomy. On the next day they all went to Mecca along the new four-lane highway, to make their seven perambulations round the holy Kabah and to pray together squatting in their hemless white robes. On the next three days they gathered in the great hexagonal conference chamber to proclaim their unity and common purpose—to establish an independent Palestine, to liberate Jerusalem, and to give economic assistance to their poorer brothers.

The style and pageantry were more like that of sixteenth-century Europe—when monarchs competed in splendor and hospitality—than that of the contemporary West. Even other Arabs were visibly dazed and confused: the Saudis seemed less sophisticated and educated than their neighbors in Lebanon, Jordan, or even the emirates: yet they had the mystique of a tribal people who reminded them of their own origins. While Western bankers were working out intricate formulas for recycling or rescheduling debts, the Saudis were dispensing their billions with a casual and personal largesse, as if they were still Bedouin chiefs giving out favors to their visitors, but multiplying the gifts by a few million. The Taif conference was another reminder of this extraordinary twist to world history: that this huge new source of wealth should be granted to one of the most conservative and proudly tribal people on earth.

They were now hosts to Islamic countries containing a quarter of the world's population. Watching their leaders processing through the conference center in their robes, fezzes, or military uniforms it was difficult to imagine them as a homogeneous group: they looked as diverse and colorful as the bankers in Washington looked uniformly gray. They included Algerians and Moroccans at loggerheads, and Syrians and Jordanians who had come close to war; the Iranians would not come to a conference which included the Iraqis, whom they were fighting. Islam proved no more able to reconcile political disputes than Christianity. They included some of the richest countries, like Kuwait and the emirates, and some of the poorest, like Mali or Bangladesh. The Saudis' combination of puritanism and extravagance gave a bewildering example to the poorer countries. Lunching in one of the lavish restaurants I asked a Bangladeshi waiter about the delicate fresh flowers on the table. "They come from Holland—they come by plane every day," he answered mournfully. "This conference costs too much money."

But these nations were beginning to be bound closer with chains of gold. The summit ceremony was televised by satellite to thirty countries; telephones and telex could transmit overnight what Pakistan had to say about Palestine, or Morocco about Afghanistan. The contrasts between Muslim intellectuals had been increased by the diaspora of Palestinians, Lebanese, and Pakistanis, building up their own networks of radio stations, newspapers, and academic exchanges. The electronic marketplace was not confined to the West. And in the last decade the Muslim members of OPEC had given $3.5 billion to developing countries, mostly within Islam, half of it from Saudi Arabia. The pace of aid was now quickening. At the conference the richer countries— partly prompted by Libya's ambitions toward Chad—approved a promise of a billion dollars to the Sahel countries on the edge of the Sahara. Saudi Arabia proposed a new $3 billion fund to finance projects within Islam. The president of the Islamic Development Bank, Dr. Ahmed Muhammed Ali, explained how he looked forward to creating an Islamic Common Market and strengthening the links between Islam to challenge Western commercial domination. The promises of aid were not received with wholehearted gratitude: Bangladesh had often petitioned its fellow Muslims in OPEC for cheaper oil, which OPEC refused to concede. But the richer members were stepping up their grants, and the Saudis now claimed to be giving away 9 percent of their gross national product. The West was constantly telling developing countries to help each other, which they were now beginning to do in their own way. Would it be a new version of the old religious rivalry, going back to the Crusades? Would the Saudis, with all their conservatism and Islamic confusion about usury, emerge as a major banking power in the world?

The news of the Islamic conference at Taif caused some apprehension to the mandarins of the International Monetary Fund and the bankers who dealt with the Middle East. It seemed to turn their business upside down; it was about the money of religion, not the religion of money. And it raised worrying questions about how far the Saudis would be integrated into their great ''informational marketplace.'' Would the Saudis, who had the kind of capital which the rest of the world desperately needed, prefer to deploy their billions in their own Islamic fashion, establishing their own leadership in a quarter of the developing world?

But what relevance anyway had the pronouncements of bankers and the promises of sheiks to the lives of the 800 million people living in ''absolute poverty''? Even within a few miles of Taif there were people living in wind-blown shacks which were almost untouched by twentieth-century technology. The people in the Sahel in Africa only notice that each year the desert encroaches further, and that they have to lower their buckets still deeper to find water, and travel still further in search of firewood. Whether colonized or decolonized they still have to deal with a distant government which pays them so little for their crops that they can barely survive from one year to the next. Projects for aid get distorted by the bureaucrats and politicians in the towns before they reach the villages. They are unlikely to be impressed by the talk about massive transfers or the brotherhood of Islam, as they confront the harsh elements which have dictated their poverty for as long as anyone can remember.

THE UNBANKABLE WORLD

The bankers' world is still very incomplete, like a sixteenth-century map: it has a few finite regions full of accurate statistics, surrounded by the hinterland of the unknown. The two worlds of the bankable and the unbankable may coexist close together: the orderly management of Singapore a few miles from the jumble of Indonesia; the confusion of Mozambique next to the order of South Africa; the trim little Cayman Islands next to seething Jamaica. But across these red lines people defy organization: telephones don't work, planes don't take off, and precise questions get forgotten in speculation or laughter. There may be the appearance of order and reason at the Intercontinental, where the bell captain still appears while there is rioting and rebellion around the corner; but the real truths lie beyond the hotel lobby. The yardsticks of the bankers' trade are lost in immeasurable problems: productivity means little where countries must employ as many people as possible; the ravages of hunger make nonsense of statistics about manpower; the gross national product is incalculable in a subsistence economy which uses little cash; the high birth rate frustrates all efforts to improve the standard of living.

Most bankers prefer to keep away from the hundred or so countries which lie beyond their red line. Some of them privately give credence to the old idea of Malthus that the growth of population leads to the drastic correctives of nature. "I'm bound to say that when I read about wars and famines in Africa," one of them said, "I begin to think that's a kind of inevitable adjustment." They are glad to leave the problems of poverty to do-gooders and charity mongers, like McNamara, Oxfam, or Brandt.

Yet even the most cold-nosed banker cannot altogether ignore these blurred edges of their ordered universe. Even in immediate commercial terms, there are always some profits to be made from financing trade, even in the least credit-worthy countries, or from advising bankrupt governments how to stave off the demands of their creditors. And a banker who takes a longer-term view of the world has to look beyond the immediate confines of credit: he may regard the talk of "one world" or "planet earth" as part of the rhetoric of doomsday, but he is continually faced with the interdependence of the continents. He cannot ignore the shortages of food and critical resources which affect the world markets and the economies of rich countries as well as poor: he cannot be indifferent to the destruction of forests and vegetation which is steadily diminishing the world's potential. The oil crisis has not only revealed the dependence of every nation on a single indispensable currency: it has also put the richer oil producers in a bargaining position on the bridge between North and South, so that no serious banker can be indifferent to the political attitudes of Kuwait or Saudi Arabia.

Mounting debts have created their own interdependencies between creditors and debtors, who often make odd bedfellows: Polish Communists with American Republican anti-Communists; a dictator in Zaire with a professorial banker from New York; an old Quaker bank lending to a militarist South African government. And when they lend to the developing world, as we will see, bankers often have only a remote prospect of seeing their money back. They protest about the wastage of official aid, but they are often in fact engaged in their own form of aid, on a far bigger scale than traditional assistance, and with its own kind of waste. Cautious and orthodox bankers have found their fortunes interlocked with megalomaniac tyrants or religious zealots in obscure parts of the world. Whether they like it or not they cannot escape.

Much banking is a very technical activity without much political consequence: it "consists essentially of facilitating the movement of money from point A, where it is, to point B, where it is needed," the present Lord Rothschild complained when he worked at the family bank.[4] But bankers acquire a critical political importance when their money crosses frontiers between rich and poor countries, where the choice between points C and D can help to transform the whole life of the country; or as Costanzo of Citibank

[4]Lord Rothschild, *Meditations on a Broomstick* (London: Collins, 1977), p. 17.

puts it, it is a "challenging arena for working out the economic destinies of nations and the human aspirations of their people."[5] They may still insist that their operations are purely technical; but they have unwittingly become actors in the drama of nations.

The encounters of these pinstripes with the ragged edges of the developing world are a recurring theme of this book. It is not a new story. Dispensing money has always been full of hazards and comedy. Midas himself, though he turned everything he touched into gold, ended up with the ears of an ass. The story of bankers' blunders in developing countries goes back—as the next chapter will show—at least as far as the disasters of Italian bankers in fourteenth-century England. Bankers, for all their deadpan style, have always been fallible human beings. But today, when half the world is in debt, and when a new hoard of wealth has accumulated in one of the least predictable regions, bankers have entered the center of the world's political stage. For it is they who make the money go round.

[5] Speech to National Association of Accountants, Birmingham, January 16, 1979.

2
WHO KEEPS THE WORLD?

The process by which banks create money is so simple that the mind is repelled.

J. K. GALBRAITH

Every country, of course, was once a developing country. However formidable their resources and people, most nations depended initially on foreign money and bankers to help them to finance their trade. In medieval Europe the interaction between capital and enterprise began to transform the Continent, and produced the new profession of bankers, as opposed to mere money lenders, who were international in their origins. Medieval laws forbade the practice of usury, and treated money lenders as outcasts; but the merchants who developed into bankers could make profits by dealing between currencies, and could lend money for international expeditions, armies, and trade, which made them indispensable to their rulers.

By the late Middle Ages the expanding European trade, encouraged by the Crusades against Islam, had produced the first international banks. The wool workers in Florence, who imported bales of wool from Spain, England, and even Africa, were financed by Florentine merchants whose savings helped to finance the Renaissance.

To these Italian bankers England was a wild developing country on the edge of their world, a kind of medieval Zaire. Its exports of wool offered prospects of big profits: but with its despotic monarchs, its tribal wars and corrupt courtiers, it had a high country risk. After King Edward I expelled the Jews in 1290 he needed the Italians to finance his wars and the agents of Florentine bankers, the Bardi and Peruzzi, moved to London, lending money

33

to finance the King's wars, to be repaid by the tax on wool exports. But after King Edward III came to the throne in 1327 he was confident that he could compel his own English merchants to finance his wars: he defaulted on his Italian debts, and the banks of Bardi and Peruzzi collapsed. Economic historians still disagree about how far England benefited from these Italian loans: Michael Postan believes that they did little to improve farming or the wool industry, and that by financing wars they helped the King "to unsettle the economic life of the country." But the Italian finance played a critical role in linking England's trade with the rest of Europe, maintaining uniform standards for wool and accounts, and helping to give London merchants their own expertise.[1]

By the mid-fifteenth century Cosimo dei Medici had established an international bank based in Florence, with a much more extensive and sophisticated network. He had branches in Bruges, Avignon, and London, as well as in Italian cities, each run by a manager who shared in the profits; in Rome the Medici bank handled the Pope's account, including his profitable alum monopoly. In Florence it took deposits from rich Florentines, which could be withdrawn on due notice (between three months and a year), and which earned interest of around 10 percent. Cosimo's grandson, Lorenzo the Magnificent, became the most famous of all patrons of the Renaissance, his crooked nose and big jowl looking out from contemporary masterpieces. He was depicted as the very epitome of the Renaissance Man—ruler of Florence, poet, scholar, and patron, as well as banker—and many later bankers were to see themselves with the same kind of magnificence, combining culture with shrewd business. But Lorenzo was both a less enterprising patron than his grandfather and a much more careless banker. He and his chief executive, Sassetti, could not control their branch managers. Lorenzo relied too heavily on borrowed capital, while his overheads mounted; he had to sell his castle at Caffagiolo, outside Florence, to his cousin; and he only avoided

[1] See M. Postan, *Medieval Trade and Finance* (Cambridge University Press, 1973). Also Michael Prestwick, "Italian Merchants in England," in *The Dawn of Modern Banking* (New Haven: Yale University Press, 1979).

bankruptcy by raiding the Florentine funds. His London branch had already lent far too much money to King Edward IV, who was embroiled in the Wars of the Roses, which took him deeper into debt; and after trying to reschedule their debts with the King the Medici bank had to write off 52,000 florins and close their London office. "Rather than refuse deposits," concludes the historian of the bank, "the Medicis succumbed to the temptation of seeking an outlet for surplus cash in making dangerous loans to princes."[2] It was a warning relevant to more recent bankers.

The huge imports of gold from Latin America to Spain in the sixteenth century helped to provide Europe with a reliable common currency which allowed a vast expansion of credit. The fifteenth and sixteenth centuries saw the establishment of the first modern banks, including the Banco di Santo Spirito in Rome, the Monte di Pieta in Naples, and the Bank of Palermo in Sicily, all of which still exist. The old word "bank" or "bench" began to be used in England to describe, first the table on which a money lender did his business, and then the money lender's office. The internationalism of these "bankers," who financed trade all over Europe, allowed them to diversify their risks and make profits between currencies; in Christopher Marlowe's play *The Jew of Malta* the merchant Barabas explains:

> In Florence, Venice, Antwerp, London, Seville,
> Frankfurt, Lubeck, Moscow and where not,
> Have I debts owing; and in most of these,
> Great sums of money lying in the banco . . .

And in *The Merchant of Venice* the money lender Shylock revealed the importance of international intelligence when he assessed the prospects of his client's underwriter, Antonio:

> He is sufficient, yet his means are in supposition: he hath an Argosy bound to Tripoli, another to the Indies, I understand moreover upon the Rialto he hath a third at Mexico, a fourth for England, and other ventures he hath squandered abroad . . . the man is notwith-

[2] Raymond de Roover, *The Medici Bank* (New York: New York University Press, 1948).

standing sufficient, three thousand ducats, I think I may take his bond.

The private loans for trade, governments, or armies formed one ingredient of modern banking. The other was the ability to use other people's money, which became more important as wealth was distributed. "The distinctive function of the banker," as the economist Ricardo described it in 1817, "begins as soon as he uses the money of others." The lending of bank deposits, which is the basis of the contemporary network of credit, is traditionally traced back to the goldsmiths who kept other people's gold and realized that they could safely lend some of it to others. The banker is neatly defined in an Act of 1679, under Charles II of England: "Whereas several persons, Goldsmiths and others, by taking or borrowing great sums of money, and lending out the same again, for extraordinary hire or profit, have gained and acquired to themselves the reputation and name of bankers."

But using other people's money obviously depended both on exceptional trust and on stable currencies, and these were fortified by the invention of national banks, led by the Bank of Sweden in 1674, which issued its own notes. The Bank of England followed in 1694, when a group of merchants agreed to lend £1.2 million to King William III at 8 percent, in return for a monopoly of bank notes and the right to receive deposits. It continued to finance governments through its bonds, thus creating what was called the "national debt"—a model for other national banks, or "central banks," as they were later called. The National Debt grew from a million pounds in 1694 to £800 million in 1815 without the national ruin that many had predicted.

ROTHSCHILDS

The more stable currencies and the greater confidence of depositors provided a much stronger basis for trade between countries. There was now greater scope for anyone who could lend money across the frontiers, allowing merchants to pay for cotton or wool before they were sold; but this business depended on trustworthy networks, with quick communications. In Frankfurt in the middle of the eighteenth century Mayer Amschel Rothschild took the process further. He began dealing in cloth and old coins, and extended his business to money-changing and discounting bills for the hugely rich local ruler, the Landgrave of Hesse-Cassel, who was augmenting his fortune by hiring out his soldiers. Rothschild sent five sons to the financial capitals of Europe—Paris, Vienna, Naples, London, and Frankfurt—and thus laid the foundations of an international banking house under the sign of the five arrows. When Napoleon occupied Hesse-Cassel the Landgrave fled to Denmark, and Rothschild made huge profits by investing his master's fortune, while he was able to circumvent the blockades and shortages of the Napoleonic wars, lending and transferring money across the borders.

In the confused state of the Continent the Rothschilds built up their own supranational intelligence network, with fast packets, agents, carrier pigeons, and couriers, which enabled them to be the first to receive news of the victory of Waterloo. With the return of peace the financial power of the Rothschilds had become overriding: these "vulgar ignorant Jews," Metternich's secretary Gentz explained, were now "the richest people in Europe." In the booming capitals of Europe the five brothers soon eclipsed the staid private bankers with their speed and international intelligence, financing railways, insurance companies, and foreign projects. In London the stout, uncouth figure of Nathan Rothschild, still speaking in a thick German accent, standing alone by his favorite pillar at the stock exchange, was acknowledged as the leading banker in Europe, understanding the interaction of money and politics as no one else. In the headlong pursuit of new bourgeois wealth the Rothschilds were seen as the masters of the new international capitalism. "Money is the god of our time," said the poet-philosopher Heinrich Heine, a banker's son, "and Rothschild is his prophet."

European governments, particularly the British, depended on the Rothschilds for quick supplies of funds in an emergency: they lent money for the relief of the Irish Famine in 1847, for the Crimean War, and to enable the British government to buy its half-share in the Suez Canal from the Khedive of Egypt in 1876; as Disraeli told Queen Victoria with some simplification:

> Four million sterling! and almost immediately. There was only one firm that could do it—Rothschilds. They behaved admirably; advanced the money at a low rate, and the entire interest of the Khedive is now yours, Madam.

The Rothschilds opened up a new dimension in international banking, much more deeply interlocked with politics and diplomacy than the Medici, and acting as the channels and guarantors between the new middle-class wealth and the development of continents, commemorated by Gilbert and Sullivan:

> The shares were a penny, and ever so many
> Were taken by Rothschilds and Barings

Throughout the nineteenth century, they continued to forge new links between European savings and ambitious new projects. In Vienna they founded and controlled the Kreditanstalt Bank, which became the chief deposit bank in Austria-Hungary. The French Rothschilds supported the Nobel brothers in controlling the Russian oilfields which challenged Rockefeller's oil monopoly. The British Rothschilds helped to finance Cecil Rhodes in his diamond and gold mines in South Africa, and lent their support to financiers against the Afrikaners before the Boer War.

By the late nineteenth century the Rothschilds had become less obvious outsiders, much more integrated with the life of each country. In Britain Nathaniel Rothschild became the first Jewish peer, and his children the friends of the Prince of Wales: Lord Rosebery, the Prime Minister, was married to a Rothschild. The Rothschild mansions in Piccadilly or in the Vale of Aylesbury, packed with treasures, became caricatures of the new luxury. In France the Rothschilds became barons, owners of racehorses, vineyards, and huge country estates. In Naples they went out of business when Garibaldi arrived, and in Frankfurt they closed down in 1901; but in Vienna they continued to be indispensable to the Hapsburgs. While each rich branch put down national roots, they still kept their connections. They knew that the success of their banking depended on understanding the world.

THE LONDON BANKER

For a century after the end of the Napoleonic wars in 1815 London was the world's financial center, enriched by growing private fortunes and international trade, which increased with each stage of the Industrial Revolution. As the trade extended, so it transformed the nature of banking. London was not only the richest city, it was also the city which made the most effective use of its money. Its banks were able to attract the savings of the whole country, lending them wherever the profit was greatest, first within Britain, then across the world, carefully attuning the interest rates to the risks. "Thus English capital runs as surely and instantly where it is most wanted," wrote Walter Bagehot in 1873, "and where there is most to be made of it, as water runs to find its own level."[3]

As they became more confident the bankers felt able to lend greater sums compared to their own capital, and foreigners began both to deposit their funds in London banks and to borrow money from them. When in 1873 Bagehot (the editor of *The Economist,* who had also been a practical banker) wrote his classic study of banking, *Lombard Street,* he described London as "by far the greatest combination of economical power and economical delicacy that the world has ever seen." The deposits in London banks were £120 million, compared to only £40 million in New York, £13 million in Paris, and £8 million in Germany.

In the early nineteenth century most international lending came from a few private banks controlled by wealthy families, whose

[3]Bagehot (London: Kegan Paul, 1888), p. 13.

reputation had attracted other rich men. As Bagehot described
it:

> The name "London Banker" had especially a charmed value. He
> was supposed to represent, and often did represent, a certain union
> of pecuniary sagacity and educated refinement which was scarcely
> to be found in any other part of society. . . . The calling is heredi-
> tary; the credit of the bank descends from father to son; this inher-
> ited wealth soon brings inherited refinement. Banking is a watchful,
> but not a laborious trade. A banker, even in large business, can feel
> pretty sure that all his transactions are sound, and yet have much
> spare mind. A certain part of his time, and a considerable part of
> his thoughts, he can readily devote to other pursuits. And a London
> banker can also have the most intellectual society in the world if
> he chooses it. There has probably very rarely ever been so happy
> a position as that of a London private banker; and never perhaps
> a happier.[4]

But in the meantime the new "joint-stock banks," like the Westminster and the National, were taking deposits from the growing
number of small savers, and lending their money cautiously but
profitably. These new banks, owned by anonymous shareholders
and soon run by professional managers, were at first much suspected; they could not, Lord Overstone complained in 1832, "be
guided by so nice a reference to degrees in difference in the
character of responsibility of parties." But they grew and prospered, with the Bank of England as their safeguard, and they soon
eclipsed the old private banks in the scale of their deposits and
domestic loans.

By the late nineteenth century the joint-stock banks—"clearing
banks" or "deposit banks," as they were also later called—had
acquired many of the characteristics that they possess today;
as the socialist writer H. M. Hyndman described them in
1890:

[4]*Ibid.*, p. 269.

> Receiving money on deposit and lending it out again at a profit became so large a part of the bankers' daily business that a banker only considered that he entered fully upon his functions while he was doing this. Business with him is literally an affair of other people's money; his own capital being only a sort of security for the proper conduct of the business, and a reserve in case of a run or a period of continuous lack of confidence.[5]

They were essentially home-grown: they had their origins in provincial banks owned by local landed families, many of them Quakers who as a persecuted minority had established a tradition of mutual trust and financial prudence: the last joint-stock bank to be created, Barclays, was a federation of Quaker banks whose controlling families continued to dominate its board and took turns as chairman. With their local interests and caution they confined their lending to customers within their own region, or their own country; and they left foreign lending to the private banks or "merchant banks."

But the more the depositors, the greater the risk that a temporary panic could cause a run on the bank; and a panic in one capital could quickly spread to another. As early as 1875 Carl Meyer von Rothschild, as he watched stock markets falling everywhere, described how the "whole world has become a city." The dangers of collapse had become greater with the spread of joint-stock banks and the growing scope for speculation: the crash of the respected London firm of Overend Gurney had reverberated through the world, and had compelled the Bank of England to develop into virtually the "lender of last resort," like a modern central bank.

Bagehot in 1873 was specially worried by the secrecy of the big banks, which were facing growing risks with their low cash reserves compared to deposits: "The amount of that cash is so exceedingly small that a bystander almost trembles when he compares its minuteness with the immensity of the credit which rests

---

[5]*Commercial Crises of the Nineteenth Century* (London, 1892; New York: reprinted Augustus M. Kelley, 1967).

upon it." Bagehot has since been misquoted by bankers and others as having said that "we must not let in daylight upon magic";[6] in fact he used that phrase not about banks but about the British monarchy. Nothing was further from Bagehot's thinking about banks. He insisted, on the contrary, that the banking system had to be made safer and more open: "Our great joint stock banks are imprudent in so carefully concealing the details of their government, and in secluding those details from the risk of discussion."[7]

BARINGS

The supremacy of London attracted merchants from all over Europe, like the Rothschilds, Hambros, Kleinworts, or Schroders, who first used their connections with their home country to finance trade and lend money across frontiers, and later became part of the City's financial system. The earliest of these immigrants was Johann Baring, who came from Bremen to Exeter in 1717, becoming a successful cloth merchant while Mayer Rothschild was collecting coins in Frankfurt. His sons John and Francis set up a trading company in London, and Sir Francis emerged as the most influential banker of his time: before his death in 1810 he was said to be worth £7 million, and to be the "First Merchant of Europe."

Like Rothschilds, Barings had access to funds much greater than governments; and when the Bank of England itself was in difficulties after a heavy drain on its resources in 1839, it was Barings that rescued it by organizing a consortium of European banks. In the first decades of the nineteenth century, Barings was seen, together with the upstart Rothschilds, as the secret controller of nations' destinies, the "sixth power of Europe"; in the famous lines of Lord Byron in 1823:

> Who keep the world, both old and new, in pain
> Or pleasure? Who makes politics run glibber all?
> The shade of Bonaparte's noble daring?
> Jew Rothschild and his fellow-Christian, Baring.

[6]See for instance Joseph Wechsberg, *The Merchant Bankers* (London: Weidenfeld & Nicolson, 1967), p. 3.
[7]Bagehot, p. 264.

While Rothschilds was mainly concerned with the old world of Europe, Barings was becoming more interested in the new world of the Americas, and particularly the United States. It had business in America before the Revolution, and it strengthened its connection when Sir Francis's son Alexander married the daughter of the rich Philadelphia businessman William Bingham. When President Jefferson wanted to buy the huge territory of the Mississippi Basin from France, he looked to Barings, which could finance the Louisiana Purchase, even though it provided Napoleon with $15 million at the height of his wars against Britain. Barings lent to the Bank of New York in 1823, to the Planters Association in Louisiana in 1829, and to many state governments. After 1839, when Maryland and Pennsylvania had both defaulted (see next chapter), the City of London was much more wary of lending to this unstable developing nation, but Barings kept its nerve; it began financing American railroads in the early forties, and became increasingly expert in American credit, with its intelligence networks throughout the United States.

By the late 1880s Barings was losing to Rothschilds, but it appeared impregnable in its resources and prudence. The family seemed to represent Bagehot's ideal of the London banker. There were already three separate Baring peerages (Ashburton, Northbrook, and Revelstoke); and the head of the bank, Lord Revelstoke, was regarded as London's leading financier, more thoroughly respectable and British than Lord Rothschild. Barings had helped to finance the Manchester Ship Canal and the launching of the Guinness Brewery as a public company; its credit was accepted all over the world, and it was a symbol of British security. "There was a feeling of satisfaction throughout the country," said H. M. Hyndman, "that a purely English house should stand so high at a time when German Jews held the leading place in nearly every great continental city."

But Barings had become too complacent. Behind its staid exterior it was rash in its lending and investment, particularly in Argentina, which was regarded as its special preserve in Latin America, as Brazil was Rothschilds' preserve. Barings had raised Argentina's first loan in 1824, and even though it defaulted four years later, the bank soon regained confidence in this vast fertile territory with its hoard of resources which seemed like a banker's dream. By the 1880s Buenos Aires was booming as never before, attracting a rush of immigrants and capital from Europe to this gateway to a new America. Barings was leading a succession of loans and investments, but it had not reckoned with the ability of the Argentinians to wreck their own country. The new President Celman filled his government with carpetbagging politicians who plundered the country and debauched the currency, and soon the flagrant corruption undermined the confidence of investors.

By August 1890 the governor of the Bank of England, Lord Lidderdale, warned Barings that it was accepting too many bills from its Argentine agent. By November rumors spread through the City that Barings was in serious trouble. The governor consulted other City grandees, who confirmed the terrible news that Barings had been unable to sell its Argentine securities and might have to stop payments the following week. There was a weekend of studied calm, deliberately misleading the market; the governor took his son to the zoo. Then the Chancellor of the Exchequer called on the governor. They agreed that the Bank of England could not itself rescue Barings, whose liabilities amounted to £21 million compared to the Bank of England's reserves of £10 million. But the consequences of Barings' collapse would be incalculable. The two men agreed that "the great houses must get together and give the necessary guarantees."

The public rumors continued, causing growing alarm. Four days later the government broker John Daniell pleaded with the governor: "Can't you do something, or say something, to relieve people's minds: they have made up their minds that something awful is up, and they are talking of the very highest names—the very highest!"[8] But behind the scenes the governor and the chancellor were organizing other bankers for an international rescue. The chancellor quickly talked to Rothschild, who persuaded the Banque de France to lend the Bank of England gold worth £3.5

[8]Sir John Clapham, *The Bank of England: A History,* Vol. 2 (Cambridge University Press, 1945), p. 156.

million. A special Argentine Committee was set up in London with Lord Rothschild himself as chairman. The Prime Minister promised that the British government would if necessary bear half the losses from Barings' bills. But the governor soon persuaded the biggest merchant banks to contribute to the special fund, including Rothschilds, Glyn Mills, Currie's, even the new American bank of J. S. Morgan, and with more difficulty the British joint-stock banks. Eventually they raised £17 million, which soon averted the crisis, and by the following January the bank rate was down to 3 percent. Barings was reconstructed as a limited company, Lord Revelstoke retired, and four years later the bank had paid off all its obligations. Barings' reputation had been seriously damaged; but the City could congratulate itself on its combined strength. As Ellis Powell described it in 1915: "The Bank is not a single combatant who must fight or retire, but the leader of the most colossal agglomeration of financial power which the world has so far witnessed."[9]

But while the creditors were saved, the debtors suffered heavily. Two years after the crisis H. M. Hyndman wrote: "It is quite possible that, when the circumstances come to be reviewed in the dry light of history, the Baring crisis of 1890, and the way in which it was met, will be cited as an example of the break-down of capitalism in the department of high finance." Certainly the crisis had global repercussions. In London small investors suffered heavily and had to sell off sound securities, including American railroads. In Buenos Aires the Banco Nacional could not meet its obligations, and credit collapsed. Trade with South America went down to a trickle, and the City took years to recover its confidence. In Germany the panic and the run on gold added to the growing depression. The United States had to send gold back to London to pay for British securities, while the tighter money market caused commercial and financial disasters; and a new panic in 1893 brought a sudden demand for gold, which caused a new succession of failures.

The Baring crisis had revealed how rapidly a collapse in one

[9] *The Evolution of the Money Market* (New York: reprinted Augustus M. Kelley, 1966).

country could now affect all the others, and how the development of whole continents could be set back by the mistakes of one bank. The ultimate breakdown had been avoided by the mutual assistance of the bankers, which set a historic precedent for the following decades. But small investors, workers, and foreign debtors had no such safeguards, and they were much more conscious of the narrow base on which their security depended.

THE EUROPEAN SCRAMBLE

The last decade of the nineteenth century continued to be a perilous time for banks and investors. Latin American governments defaulted, American railroads went bankrupt, Australia was set back by drought. The South African gold mines had attracted a rush of British capital but they proved very untrustworthy, surrounded by political hazards; by the end of the century the British government was plunged into the Boer War in South Africa, which dried up funds to other parts of the world, and even at one point compelled the British to borrow money from New York. But by the early twentieth century the confidence of bankers returned, and money flowed out of Europe as never before. The British banks extended their loans and securities into foreign ventures which now seemed more secure; they financed factories as well as governments and railroads, and lent money for trade between other countries.

Other European bankers were now moving more boldly abroad as prosperity and savings increased. The French banks, after recovering from the indemnity imposed by Germany after the war of 1870–71, looked toward Eastern Europe and North Africa, which offered higher interest rates and greater opportunities than metropolitan France. They were more directly influenced by their government than the British, and they paid the price for that relationship in their links with tsarist Russia, which eventually accounted for a quarter of all French foreign investments. It led to the greatest of all banking disasters.

The French government had begun encouraging banks toward

Russia after 1887, when Germany had stopped lending, and French money poured into new Russian industries and the Trans-Siberian railroad. Rothschilds led a syndicate to raise a large loan and then withdrew in protest against the persecution of Russian Jews, whereupon the Credit Lyonnais became the chief agent. The Russian government lured the banks and the public with the help of journalists, bribes, and devious diplomacy, while the banks made large profits by financing Russia's war with Japan. Her defeat in that war almost destroyed Russia's credit abroad, but the French government still persuaded the banks to raise a new loan (with British banks participating) which the revolutionaries bitterly attacked as the instrument of tsarist tyranny. "Every French citizen," said Maxim Gorky, "who buys the loan is an accomplice in the organized murder of a people." The French banks continued to lend, financing armaments and strategic railroads for the Tsar in keeping with the Franco-Russian alliance. The more they lent, the greater was their stake in maintaining the Tsar's government. "Debtor and creditor were firmly bound to each other," as Herbert Feis put it; "but debtor, in this case, was the more exigent and the more aggressive in political plans."[10]

The German banks were at first preoccupied with building up the massive structure of their own industry, over which they exercised unique control. The private banks were soon eclipsed by the deposit banks, which came to dominate the whole spectrum of banking, from savings to foreign loans, led by the "Four D's" (the Deutsche Bank, the Diskonto, the Dresdner, and the Darmstadter). These *Grossbanken,* led by the Deutsche Bank, helped to forge the great industrial combines, putting their directors on the boards and making links with other banks through Europe. When they first ventured abroad in the wake of the British they suffered heavy losses, but by the late nineteenth century their surplus funds encouraged them to expand further. They invested heavily in the Americas and in South African gold mines, and

[10]*Europe, the World's Banker* (Clifton: reprinted Augustus M. Kelley, 1974), p. 223.

working discreetly with their foreign ministry they began developing new spheres of German influence. They moved into critical strategic areas: in China they established a German preserve in Shantung; in Morocco they competed with the French in a dangerous contest backed by military force; and in Turkey the Deutsche Bank financed the crucial Baghdad railway, bringing German interests further into the Middle East. Confronting the ramifications of the British Empire, the German bankers and diplomats were determined to acquire their beachheads of influence.

The spread of capital and communications from Europe throughout the world seemed secure and permanent, and the middle classes were confident that they were bringing progress to the world while profiting from it. As Keynes described it:

> The inhabitant of London could order by telephone, sipping his morning tea in bed, the various products of the whole earth, in such quantity as he might see fit, and reasonably expect their early delivery upon his door-step; he could at the same moment and by the same means adventure his wealth in the natural resources and new enterprises of any quarter of the world, and share, without exertion or even trouble, in their prospective fruits and advantages; or he could decide to couple the security of his fortunes with the good faith of the townspeople of any substantial municipality in any continent that fancy or information might recommend . . .[11]

But to the new Communist ideologues of Europe the global power of the banks represented the parasitism and decay of capitalism in the highest and last stage of imperialism, in which (in Lenin's words) "a handful of exceptionally rich and powerful states plunder the whole world simply by clipping coupons." Writing his study of imperialism in Zurich in 1916, Lenin analyzed the ramifications of the giant banks, particularly in Germany, through which "a handful of monopolists subordinate to their will all the operations, both commercial and industrial, of the whole of capitalist society." He deduced that "the twentieth century

[11]*Economic Consequences of the Peace* (New York: Harcourt Brace, 1920).

marks the turning-point from the old capitalism to the new, from the domination of capital in general to the domination of finance capital." He saw the consequent rivalries between capitalist nations as leading inexorably to war. "The question is: What means other than war could there be under capitalism to overcome the disparity between the development of productive forces and the accumulation of capital on the one side, and the division of colonies and spheres of influence for finance and capital on the other?"[12]

Many bankers, on the contrary, were insistent that war would threaten their whole business; most of all the Rothschilds. In the early nineteenth century, on the rising tide of European nationalism, the Rothschilds were regarded as being *too* dedicated to peace at any price: "It is in the nature of things," complained the young Bismarck, "that the house of Rothschild should do everything to prevent war." The Rothschilds, like many bankers, saw international capital as overriding petty squabbles between nations: "We want peace at any price," said Anthony de Rothschild in 1866. "What do we care about Germany, or Austria or Belgium? That sort of thing is out of date." And in the late nineteenth century Alfred von Rothschild was actively trying to reconcile Anglo-German differences. But individual bankers played a very minor political role compared to the mounting pressures of mass nationalism and demagogy and the economic competition between the imperial nations. The bankers appeared to many observers as possessing almost limitless power, with their supranational command over greater sums than any national leader could provide; but in fact they were becoming much more dependent on governments, and more easily exploitable by them.

They were particularly vulnerable in Bismarck's Second Reich, where Bismarck's banker Bleichröder had risen from being Rothschild's agent to become the richest man in Berlin.[13] Bleichröder

---

[12] *Imperialism, the Highest Stage of Capitalism,* 1917, Chapter VII.
[13] Fritz Stern, *Gold and Iron* (New York: Alfred A. Knopf, 1977). I am indebted to this masterly study in these paragraphs.

was invaluable to Bismarck as his financier or "house Jew," as he called him, yet Bleichröder could not afford to offend his patron, who provided the key to his fortune. Like the Rothschilds he realized the dangers of war; but when Bismarck wanted to go to war with Austria in 1866, and could not get the money from parliament, it was Bleichröder, through a shrewd arrangement with the Cologne-Minden railroad, who provided the necessary funds. Bleichröder was enriched by Bismarck's victories over Austria and France, but Bismarck had his own subtle understanding of the interplay of diplomacy, money, and war, in which he could easily outploy his banker. In his later imperial adventures in Africa Bismarck complained about the timidity of German bankers and investors, compared to the British. The German bankers were usually glad to follow their government's advice (Max Warburg, the Hamburg banker, when he was offered some Japanese loans, did "what every good banker does in such cases: I drove to the Foreign Office in Berlin."[14]) Bleichröder, rather than risk financing colonial ventures, preferred the more profitable and safer business of lending to foreign governments, and practicing the "informal imperialism" in the Middle East or Eastern Europe.

Bleichröder saw himself as a genuine internationalist, seeking to protect the rights of fellow Jews elsewhere; when he negotiated with the Rumanian government to protect the persecuted Rumanian Jews he was acclaimed as a hero of international Jewry. But Bismarck, it turned out, was using the campaign against Rumanian anti-Semitism as a cynical weapon to compel the Rumanians to pay off German creditors; once they had done that, he had no further interest in restraining the persecution, which continued. Bleichröder was all too able to deceive himself about his achievements, and his political blindness prevented him from noticing the growing anti-Semitism in Germany itself, which surrounded his lonely old age.[15]

[14] Ibid., p. 418.
[15] Ibid., p. 393.

REASON AND HUMILIATION

The European bankers were helping to transform the world, but with very diverse results. The more disciplined and well-endowed nations soon built up their own industries and savings, which made them less dependent on loans from London or Berlin. The United States achieved a more stable economy after the panics and defaults of the late nineteenth century, exporting not only grain but manufactures to Europe. Brazil and Argentina once again attracted new loans, and the railroads and ports in Latin America provided the foundations for industrialization.

The most spectacular beneficiary was Japan, which in two decades was transformed into a major industrial power. British banks raised loans to build the Japanese railroads, to equip the Japanese forces, and to finance the Japanese wars against China and Russia, while the British government provided political support. The Japanese were soon able to control and direct their growing industries; they nationalized their railroads and established their own capitalists, while ensuring that Japan remained credit-worthy to attract more loans from abroad. By the beginning of the First World War Japan was already a major world power, classified by Lenin as one of those states that were "plundering the whole world."

Across the sea China represented an almost opposite experience for European bankers, with its weak government spread across a huge territory, torn between the need for foreign loans and intense resentment against the foreign influences, which were rapidly encroaching. The resentment exploded in the ferocious Boxer Rebellion in 1900, which led to a massive indemnity that required still further loans. After the revolution of 1911 the rival bankers, including Russians and Americans, came together to form a "sextuple group," but the harassed Chinese government could never enforce the reforms which the bankers required. "Capital and enterprise require a political and social life fitted to their operation," wrote Herbert Feis in 1930. "Those who seek to command them are either induced to reshape their life in conformity with the necessary standard, or have their life reshaped against their will by the slow movement of events. Such were the alternatives presented to China in 1914; such they remain."[16]

The London bankers had recurring problems with the row of Islamic countries—Egypt, Turkey, Iran—which lay on the route from North Africa to India, regarded as crucial to British interests, all ruled by despots whose extravagance was encouraged by their loans, and whose future was very uncertain. They could never be sure whether they were lending to a country or to a shaky ruler. Each country for a time was virtually ruled by bankers, and each is a problem for them today.

Egypt provided a caricature of the encounters between bankers and the chaotic despotisms of the developing world. Since the early nineteenth century the primitive economy along the Nile had been opened up to European investors, and Egypt attracted a new flow of adventurers in the 1860s, when the building of the Suez Canal and the cotton boom during the American Civil War offered dizzy new prospects. The European bankers enjoyed the privileges of extraterritorial law, which made it easy to exploit the profligate Egyptian ruler, Ismail Pasha,[17] who borrowed vast sums to transform Cairo into a new Paris, complete with an opera house in which to perform *Aida*. To pay for his debts the Khedive ruthlessly taxed his peasants and confiscated their property, and sold his shares in the Suez Canal until he finally went bankrupt and was forced to appoint two controllers, one British and one French. The Khedive was deposed, a new ruler appointed, the controllers insisted on cutting state spending, the peasants revolted, a colonel seized power, Europeans were murdered. Finally in 1883 the British took control, appointing Sir Evelyn Baring, later Lord

---

[16]Feis, p. 455.

[17]The details of bankers' dealings with the Khedive are described and superbly documented by David Landes, *Bankers and Pashas* (London: Heinemann, 1958).

Cromer, from the banking family, as Consul-General. Lord Cromer became known as the maker of modern Egypt: he built roads, canals, hospitals, and railroads while reducing the debt, so that by 1913 the country was regarded as thoroughly credit-worthy. But the Egyptian nationalists were nursing their humiliation; and (in the words of David Landes) "the one thing that had changed little was Egypt itself and its people. There was still the land and the river and the sweating *fellah,* living in filth and poverty unmatched even in India and China."

In Turkey the slow disintegration of the Ottoman Empire encouraged the rival ambitions of the great powers and competing bankers. In 1876 the extravagance of the Sultan led him into default, and the European powers imposed their own international financial control. Turkey became divided between overlapping spheres of interests. The Deutsche Bank, encouraged by its government, financed the railway from Istanbul toward Baghdad, to the alarm of the British, while the French banks financed the railway down to Beirut. For a time the creditors were satisfied, and the Debt Administration became the virtual rulers of the country. But the "Young Turks" who seized power in 1908 became involved in expensive wars with Italy and in the Balkans and could not control their own finances. They borrowed heavily at high interest rates, pledging their revenues to the banks; but the more Turkey borrowed, the more dangerous were her military ambitions.

To the east, Iran (or Persia) provided similar dangers. By the end of the nineteenth century the European bankers were lending rashly to the Shah, who loved foreign travel and had extravagant tastes; the court and civil service were so corrupt that little money was used constructively; but by invoking the fear of the Russians, the Shah was able to keep on borrowing, and the Western powers competed to increase their influence. But the West could not indefinitely underpin the Shah against the growing resentment of his people, and he was eventually overthrown; Teheran was in chaos, and the tribes in the provinces revolted. After the Shah's overthrow the parliament, or Majlis, tried to raise new loans and appointed an American, Morgan Shuster, to reorganize the taxes; but the Russians encouraged anarchy, forced Shuster's resignation and the dismissal of the parliament, and obtained their own concession to build a railroad across the frontier. Iran, without any effective government, was carved up between the rival commercial and military interests.

In these disputed areas the bankers' relations with their home governments were fluctuating and often uncertain. Sometimes governments would directly encourage them, as the Germans urged the Deutsche Bank toward Baghdad, or as the British encouraged Sir Ernest Cassel to set up the National Bank of Turkey. Sometimes the bankers and financiers were able to lure their governments to defend their interests, as they did in South Africa before the Boer War. Sometimes the bankers were so eager to lend money to profligate rulers (as in Egypt or Morocco) that they precipitated a crisis in which the European powers took over. But the bankers' confidence in lending money was always fortified by their knowledge of a powerful imperial government behind them; the enterprise of British banks was underpinned by the maintenance of *Pax Britannica* by the British Army and Navy. The word default had a real meaning, and the idea of a bankrupt nation had some validity; for the creditors were in a position to take control of the assets abroad, as at home. Behind the romantic accounts of bold risks and adventures lay the less romantic truth, that the bankers had their nation's armed forces in the background.

How far did this great flow of capital benefit the developing world? How far did it create tensions and the potential for war? The questions will continue to be disputed endlessly between West and East, North and South. Certainly it left many countries with a lasting legacy in the form of railroads, ports, irrigation schemes, and dams (even today the experts of the World Bank can find themselves following in the track of some British engineer who devised plans fifty years ago). Certainly the bankers' loans helped many countries—including the United States, Russia, and Japan—to achieve enough production and exports to eventually attain economic independence and to compete—sometimes with devastating results—against their former creditors.

But the political costs of that rapid development were heavy, for it was achieved with the backing of all-confident imperial forces which imposed enduring humiliations on the local populations, affronting their own cultures and traditions; and leading to bitter and irrational reactions. As Landes puts it: "It is the resentment aroused by spiritual humiliation that gives rise to an irrational response to rational exploitation. The apparently unreasonable, and certainly unprofitable, resistance of many of the world's underdeveloped countries today to Western business enterprise makes sense only in this context."[18] The conflicts between bankers and their bewildered clients, whether in Egypt, Iran, or China, were only the beginning of the long story of cross purposes between the rich and poor countries which has reached a new climax in our own time.

The war that broke out in 1914 and the Communist revolution in Russia three years later put an end to the hopes of a world united by capital. The confidence of German investors and bankers who had watched their interests spreading eastward was shattered as their country was weighed down by unpayable debts and racked with inflation. The Frenchmen who had bought Russian bonds found their coupons valueless when the Soviets refused to honor their debts. The British were forced to sell off much of their foreign investments to pay for the cost of the war. With extraordinary suddenness, the American banks found themselves lending to Europe and other parts of the world; by the end of the war the United States was no longer a debtor, but a creditor nation owed debts of $14 billion. These wartime loans carried few hopes of enriching the debtors; they "went not to increase the wealth of the world, but to promote its destruction."[19]

[18] Ibid., p. 325.
[19] Madden, Nadler, and Souvain, *America's Experience as a Creditor Nation* (New York: Prentice-Hall, 1937), p. 42.

3
THE BANKERS' DISGRACE

Most commercial nations have found it necessary to institute banks; and they have proved to be the happiest engines that ever were invented for advancing trade.

ALEXANDER HAMILTON, 1781

Banks have done more injury to the religion, morality, tranquility, prosperity and even wealth of the nation than they can have done or ever will do good.

JOHN ADAMS, 1819

From the first years of independence the subject of bankers in the United States was politically explosive, for they were at the heart of the question of how the new nation would be developed. Most of the farmers had a fixed distrust of all bankers and paper money, which they saw as undermining their traditions and property. Thomas Jefferson regarded the expansion of credit not as a virtue but as an evil; in his most fanciful vision of the future he wished the United States "to practice neither commerce nor navigation but to stand, with respect to Europe, precisely on the footing of China."[1] But the merchant class, and particularly the promoters and speculators, saw banks as essential and urgent instruments for extending trade and industry, as propounded by Alexander Hamilton. As American commerce and prosperity increased, the extreme opposition to bankers was defeated, but there were still fundamental arguments about who should control the banks and how they should extend their loans. For banking in America grew up from almost opposite assumptions to those in Britain. It began not with a surplus of capital but with an urgent need for it; and

[1]Bray Hammond, *Banks and Politics in America* (Princeton: Princeton University Press, 1957), p. 121.

it was in the midst of a very unpredictable developing country.

New York, as it began to challenge the financial stronghold of Philadelphia, was the scene of the most highly charged arguments when a handful of banks were first established which were later to play a commanding role on the world stage. The Bank of New York—the oldest surviving bank in America—was set up in 1784 with a constitution written by Hamilton, representing the interests of the rich Federalists, who were exclusive in granting their credit. But in 1799 Hamilton's political opponent Aaron Burr succeeded in establishing the rival Bank of Manhattan, with much bigger capital, on the pretext of financing the city's water supplies: an epidemic of yellow fever had revealed the dangers of New York's filthy water, and Burr and his colleagues, closely linked to the Jeffersonians, undertook to provide a hygienic waterworks. But Burr's company was also permitted to engage in banking, and soon found dealing in money more profitable and politically more useful than dealing in water. The Bank of Manhattan, despite the anti-banking scruples of Jefferson, soon challenged the more aristocratic preserve of the Bank of New York, and opened the way to wider credit. The bitter rivalry between the two banks exacerbated the personal hatred between Hamilton and Burr, which led to the famous duel in 1804 in which Burr killed Hamilton. (The two pistols are still preserved in the offices of the Chase Manhattan Bank, into which Burr's bank was merged 150 years later.)

The competition for banks in New York soon quickened, as businessmen realized the huge benefits of credit in stimulating trade. In 1812 a group of local businessmen established the City Bank of New York, headed by Colonel Samuel Osgood, a close friend of George Washington, and the bank was soon able to prove its respectability and patriotism by raising over a million dollars in loans for the war against Britain. The bank, now known as Citibank,[2] grew rapidly with the prosperity of New York, keep-

[2]In 1865, when it surrendered its state charter, it became the National City Bank of New York and in 1955, after merging with the First National Bank, it was called First National City Bank, later contracted into Citibank. I give it this name throughout.

ing enough reserves to survive the successive panics, so that by the time of the Civil War it was leading a group of New York bankers providing gold to finance Lincoln. In the same year, 1812, a group of rich Federalists who had been stockholders in the Bank of the United States (see below) applied for a charter for the "Bank of America," with capital of $6 million, which would make it the biggest in the States. There was heavy opposition from Republicans and existing banks, and the promoters engaged a group of seedy lobbyists, including an Irish preacher, John Martin, who was later sent to a penitentiary for his bribery. But they eventually got their charter approved, and the Bank of America became a prominent New York institution with a former Secretary of the Treasury, Oliver Wolcott, as its president.[3] Thus the three biggest American banks in the late twentieth century—the Bank of America, Citibank, and the Chase Manhattan—each existed in some form before 1825.

The Jeffersonians were soon glad to gain profits and influence through their own banks, but there remained furious controversy about how credit should be controlled, which raged round the successive attempts to establish a central bank. Alexander Hamilton had succeeded in establishing a Bank of the United States in 1790, roughly modeled on the Bank of England, against angry attacks from the Jeffersonians. It took the deposits of the government and effectively controlled and safeguarded the credit of local banks; but though it was well run it was constantly attacked, both by farmers and businessmen, as the oppressor of local enterprise. By 1812 it was forced to close down, followed by the creation of new state banks. As a result, after the British had raided Washington in 1814, most banks had to suspend their payments in specie, which led to huge variations between states in the value of the dollar, and disruption of trade. Three years later a second Bank of the United States was founded, to be run after 1823 by Nicholas Biddle, one of the most engaging and literary of all central bankers; he wrote in a girl's album:

[3]Hammond, p. 163.

I prefer my last letter from Barings or Hope
To the finest epistles of Pliny or Pope. . . .

But Biddle and his backers could not withstand a new on-slaught, led by President Andrew Jackson, with his rhetoric of popular agrarian fury against privilege and money power. There was much irrational hatred in the Western and Southern states, which were in dire need of the bank's capital. "The West's aversion for the federal bank," as Hammond puts it, "was like the nationalistic resentment in a twentieth-century underdeveloped economy which wants and needs imported capital but growls at the 'imperialism' of the country that is expected to provide it."[4] There was also some cynical exploitation by businessmen disguising themselves as paupers, who wanted to escape the bank's shackles. But the combination of populism and commercial interests was overwhelming, worked up by the President. "Andrew Jackson yet lives," he promised, "to put his foot upon the head of the monster and crush him to the dust." The populists soon succeeded in undermining the bank and by 1834 the government had withdrawn its deposits. The fall of Biddle and his bank marked the end, for the next hundred years, of any effective federal system of credit. To the Europeans its white marble building in Philadelphia stood as a memorial of vanished security. As Dickens described it in 1842, when he looked from his room on the empty, ghostlike building: "I hastened to enquire its name and purpose and then my surprise vanished. It was the Tomb of many fortunes; the Great Catacomb of investment; the memorable United States Bank."

Tocqueville saw the battle over the bank as an archetypal conflict between the aristocratic and democratic passions: "The President attacks the Bank of the United States; the country gets excited and parties are formed; the educated classes in general line up behind the bank, while the people are for the President. Do you suppose that the people could understand the reason for their

[4]*Ibid.,* p. 359.

opinion amid the pitfalls of such a difficult question about which men of experience hesitate? . . . With all the rest of society in motion, the sight of that stable point jars, and the people want to see if they can shake it, like everything else."[5]

The Western suspicion of bankers was deep-rooted: the new states of Iowa, Arkansas, Oregon, and California prohibited banks altogether, and Texas maintained a ban on banking (with a brief interval) until 1904. But the populist hatred of bankers was unable to prevent the accumulation of personal financial power on a scale that would eventually dwarf the European money dynasties, as they competed for the domination of American railroads and industries with little concern for local interests. Indeed, it was the rudimentary condition of state banking which hastened the unprecedented centralization of money power in New York.

In the mid-nineteenth century the United States still looked to London to raise loans and finance its development; but London saw it as a very unreliable developing country, with a black record of embezzlement, fraudulent prospectuses, and default. London investors and bankers, led by Barings, had poured money into American securities and state bonds; but the states' governments, encouraged by the popular resentment of foreign banks, were reluctant to impose taxes to repay the interest. In 1839 there was an economic crisis, followed by the failure of the Union Bank of Mississippi and the suspension of the Bank of the United States. Confidence was sinking when, in the middle of 1842, came the traumatic news that two of the most prosperous states, Maryland and Pennsylvania, were defaulting on their repayments.

Investors in London were outraged by the succession of defaults, including those of Mississippi and Louisiana. The London *Times* blamed the bankers for inducing poor states to contract debts beyond their ability to pay, and for creating an artificial boom. The federal government could not now float any loan abroad, and Rothschilds in Paris warned that the United States could not "borrow a dollar, not a dollar." The chief American

---

[5]*Democracy in America,* trans. George Lawrence (New York: Anchor Books, 1969), p. 178.

agent for loans, the respected George Peabody (see below), was refused admission to the Reform Club because his nation had not paid its debts.[6] Even the poet William Wordsworth was outraged by the defaults, and the witty clergyman Sydney Smith, who had invested a small part of his fortune in Pennsylvania bonds, exploded into a series of famous diatribes with a moral indignation that makes modern criticisms of Zaire or Cuba seem mild. "There really should be lunatic asylums for nations as well as individuals," he wrote in the London *Morning Post*. America, he said, was

> a nation with whom no contract can be made, because none will be kept; unstable in the very foundations of social life, deficient in the elements of good faith, men who prefer any load of infamy, however great, to any pressure of taxation however light.

Whenever he met a Pennsylvanian at a London dinner, he wrote, he felt "a disposition to seize and divide him. . . . How such a man can set himself down at an English table without feeling that he owes two or three pounds to every man in company, I am at a loss to conceive: he has no more right to eat with honest men than a leper has to eat with clean men."[7]

But patiently and secretly Barings, together with Peabody and others, was trying to persuade the states—particularly Pennsylvania, the "greatest sinner"—to restore their good name. They realized the perils of foreign intervention: "The press no doubt is a powerful engine, but it is a dangerous one for foreigners to play with." But they overcame their scruples to organize a campaign of bribery and public relations to encourage newspapers, local worthies, and clergymen to put the case for restoring credit. "Experience shows," said Barings' agent Samuel Ward, "that it is only necessary to present a sufficient *motive* and people *will* tax themselves." In Maryland Barings helped to finance candidates who favored resumption in the forthcoming state elections, and

[6]Ralph Hidy, *The House of Baring in American Trade and Finance* (Cambridge, Mass.: Harvard University Press, 1949), pp. 294–309.
[7]Hesketh Pearson, *The Smith of Smiths* (London: Hamish Hamilton, 1934), p. 295.

warned the directors of the Chesapeake and Ohio Canal Company that they would get no more money until Maryland resumed its payments. In the elections in 1846 the "resumptionists" narrowly won; and soon afterward Maryland raised new taxes, which enabled it to repay its debts. The campaign had cost Barings about $15,000; it was worth it.[8] In Pennsylvania Ward organized a succession of protests which were "followed up like a temperance movement," and which soon took effect; a new bill was passed in 1844 which enabled Barings to be repaid the next year.

But not all investors and bondholders were so easily repaid. Railroads and banks continued to collapse, leaving British shareholders further outraged. The State of Mississippi continued to be the bane of London investors, who by 1868 had formed (with Barings' support) their own Council of Foreign Bondholders, which today still champions their cause. In 1875 Mississippi passed a constitutional amendment disclaiming its obligations, but the council refused to give up its claims to arrears of interest which by 1929 amounted to $32 million. Orthodox London bankers can never quite get over the fact that an American state has remained in permanent default. One director of the council, Douglas Reid, declared that when he died the word "Mississippi" would be found engraved on his heart.[9] And the present director, Michael Gough, even though Mississippi does not answer his letters, still has not abandoned the battle to get compensation for Mississippi bonds, along with Chinese, Mexican, and tsarist Russian bonds.[10]

MORGAN'S

Morgan, Morgan, the Great Financial Gorgon!

POPULAR SONG, 1900

As confidence in American credit increased and savings multiplied, the new American private banks began to acquire their own

[8]Hidy, pp. 314–30.
[9]Ronald Palin, *Rothschild Relish* (London: Cassell, 1970), p. 114.
[10]*Financial Times,* March 22, 1980.

power to finance development, rivaling Barings and Rothschilds. The changing balance was exemplified in the history of the most powerful of them, the House of Morgan. Its basis was laid in the career of George Peabody, a dry-goods clerk from Massachusetts who set up a banking house in London in 1837, just before the great railroad boom. Peabody had begun by buying and selling goods across the Atlantic, and gradually extended into financing other people's deals, thus becoming a banker. He soon became regarded as a kind of financial ambassador in London; he gave a banquet every Fourth of July, and helped to give trust and respectability to the risky business of investing in the United States. He bequeathed part of his fortune to housing the poor (in the Peabody Buildings still visible in Central London), and to education in the Southern United States; and his achievement is commemorated by his statue opposite the Bank of England.

Needing a younger partner, Peabody was recommended a promising young businessman from Hartford, Junius Morgan, whose father had made a fortune in insurance; and in 1854 Junius Morgan arrived in London with his family, including his eldest son, Pierpont, who soon also joined the firm and later became its representative in New York. During the Civil War Peabody and the Morgans struggled to raise loans for the North while most of London was supporting the South; so that after the peace they were well placed to expand their business. When Peabody retired in 1864 Junius Morgan took over the business, changing its name to J. S. Morgan, and was soon able to show the growing power of American capital. When the Germans had crushed the French in the War of 1870, the French government desperately looked for a loan to restore their economy, and invited Junius Morgan to Tours: he put together a "syndicate"—the new American word for an association of subscribers—which provided a bank issue on very stiff terms. With the end of the Franco-German War Morgan made a large profit, and his bank was talked of as a rival to Rothschilds.

But Morgan's concentrated on the United States, where Pierpont had strengthened its position by an alliance with Tony

Drexel, the heir to a powerful Philadelphia bank. The firm of Drexel Morgan established itself in a new marble building with an elevator at 23 Wall Street, which remains today the site of the Morgan headquarters. Morgan and Drexel helped to re-establish the reputation of American loans with British investors after the ravages of the Civil War and made handsome profits from the new flood of money across the Atlantic.

When Junius retired in 1879 his son Pierpont established himself as a power in his own right. A big rugged man, with cold eyes, a bushy mustache, and a huge nose, which became increasingly bulbous, J. P. Morgan soon became a symbol of the growing centralization of American money. In the jungle of new wealth in New York he was relatively an aristocrat, descended from five generations of Morgans who had farmed in Connecticut. He extended his father's collection of paintings, helped to set up the Metropolitan Museum of Art, and pursued a luxurious life-style in his house in Madison Avenue, on his estate on the Hudson, and on his yacht *Corsair*. But he never lost his acquisitive aggression: he appeared, in Moody's phrase, "as if chosen by circumstance and inheritance as the heir to North America." After outmaneuvering Jay Gould and Harriman he eventually controlled nearly half the American railroad system: his managers rationalized and refinanced the scattered small companies through the process of "Morganization," establishing effective cartels through "gentlemen's agreements." His power to raise loans and manipulate money gave him a growing advantage over the industrialists, and in 1901 he was able to raise the unprecedented sum of $1.4 billion to establish the monopoly of United States Steel, based on Andrew Carnegie's Pittsburgh steel mills.

Morgan's resources, far greater than the federal government's, enabled him to survive all the successive panics and manias that afflicted American financiers through the eighties and nineties. He could show his indispensability to President Cleveland in 1895 when he faced a massive run on gold which had depleted the Treasury. Cleveland put his faith in Congress to authorize a popular loan which never materialized; while Morgan put together a syndicate, with August Belmont, Jr., of Rothschilds, to provide $65 billion in gold to be paid for by an issue of bonds; and Cleveland was forced to accept Morgan's terms. Twelve years later Morgan could again show his supremacy. A succession of failures in 1907 had led to the crash of the Knickerbocker Bank and the collapse of the New York stock market, undermining more banks and trust companies. Morgan presided over an all-night meeting of the bankers and arranged with the help of James Stillman of Citibank for the stronger banks to form a committee to safeguard the threatened trust companies, while the banks temporarily restricted their payments to depositors. The panic subsided and the Knickerbocker Trust reopened the next year.

By 1913, six years after the Knickerbocker crisis, the government had established the Federal Reserve System in the chief cities to provide for the first time a reserve of gold in times of financial crisis. But Morgan was still the dominant banking power, on a scale far greater than the Rothschilds in Europe. He was the personification of the forces of commercial reason, against the populist emotionalism across the continent; and when he was questioned by a congressional committee, to defend his money monopoly he presented himself as the stern patriotic moralist. When the attorney Samuel Untermyer asked him, "Commercial credits are based upon the possession of money or property?" he replied firmly, "No, sir: the first thing is character." In his old age, traveling through Europe and Egypt to collect art treasures and reflect among the pyramids, he became a legendary collector: but he preferred to patronize dead artists rather than the living, and he never lost his banker's instincts. "He was accused of not looking at the object when in reality he was looking into the eye of the man who was trying to sell it to him. That was, after all, how he had reached the summit in finance and it had paid off well."[11]

After Pierpont Morgan died in 1913 his son Jack—a less aggressive and forceful character—ran the bank with a team of

[11]Francis Henry Taylor, *Pierpont Morgan* (New York: The Pierpont Morgan Library, 1970), p. 29.

professional managers led by Thomas Lamont, who carefully avoided publicity and exposure. Morgan's appeared less of a personal empire, more an anonymous institution representing the heart of capitalism. With the First World War it assumed a much more international role, and with its long British connections it was committed to the Allied cause, against fierce attacks from the German and Irish lobbies. "Our firm had never for one moment been neutral," said Lamont afterward. "We didn't know how to be."[12] When the Allies looked for an Anglo-French loan to pay for their arms buying, Morgan's undertook to raise £100 million and it was appointed purchasing agent for the Allies until the Americans entered the war. With the great shift of financial power to New York, Morgan's rapidly stretched further overseas: already in 1916 it was leading a group of banks in China to finance its modernization against the threat of Japan. After the war, in the wrecked and debt-ridden Europe of the twenties, Morgan's was an important power, negotiating with the central banks while Washington remained aloof. "The governments of the world," said Secretary of the Treasury Carter Glass in 1919, "must now get out of banking and trade." Morgan's helped to raise $100 million in 1920 to safeguard the French franc against speculation; it raised half of the ill-fated Dawes Loan in 1924 to finance German recovery; and in 1925 we find Thomas Lamont agreeing to finance Mussolini with $150 million in bonds and loans. The balance of debt had tipped decisively from America to Europe, and it was Europe that was to provide new problems of default.

CITIBANK AND CHASE

While Morgan had been building up his private empire in the late nineteenth century the big deposit banks, with the funds of thousands of smaller savers, were beginning to rival his money power. The small New York banks which had taken root

[12]Harold Nicolson, *Dwight Morrow* (London: Constable, 1935), p. 197.

in the early nineteenth century had now grown into giants.

After the Civil War Citibank had extended rapidly under the presidency of an ambitious industrialist, Moses Taylor, who helped to finance the first transatlantic telegraph. But its most spectacular expansion came with the presidency in 1891 of James Stillman, an icy New Englander who became a banker of legendary skills. "Drab of personality, tight-lipped, cold and passionless," as Allan Nevins describes him, "he stood in striking contrast with such men as the imperious many-sided Morgan and the brilliant, dynamic Harriman. Old-fashioned in his methods, never a promoter or a manipulator, he brought to banking a consuming passion, and showed a positively uncanny wisdom and adroitness in making money multiply itself."[13] By 1893 Stillman had made his bank the biggest in the city, with deposits of over $34 million, and five years later it was helping to underwrite $200 million in bonds to finance the United States war against Spain.

Stillman was a close friend of William Rockefeller, the younger brother of the founder of Standard Oil, who was becoming increasingly involved in financial speculation while his brother John concentrated on oil and philanthropy. "I like William," Stillman once commented, "because we don't have to talk. Often we sit fifteen minutes in silence before one of us breaks it!" Oil power and money power were already becoming closely interlinked in New York. With William Rockefeller's help, much of the spare funds of Standard Oil went through Citibank—specially useful during the bad years of 1893–95—so that Citibank soon became known as the Standard Oil bank. In fact, William's dealings were not always approved by his older brother, who retained a suspicion of all bankers, particularly of Stillman, and who believed that money should be used directly for expansion. But Stillman and William were building up their own solid power base, and their friendship was cemented when two of Stillman's daughters each married William's sons. William Rockefeller became a major shareholder in Citibank, and his son Percy, Stillman's son-in-

[13]*John D. Rockefeller,* Vol. 2 (New York: Scribner's, 1940), pp. 439 ff.

law, though a drunkard, became treasurer of Standard Oil.

Stillman stamped his own personality on Citibank, a combination of aggression and conservatism that became its special pride. When he retired in 1914 he was succeeded first by Frank Vanderlip and then by Charles Mitchell, a flamboyant salesman who marketed loans and bonds like any other product, extending Citibank into the suburbs of New York and pioneering personal credits. Mitchell had no large personal holding and he belonged to a new managerial generation, leading an army of managers and high-pressure salesmen. But he pursued his private gain with a recklessness which would lead to his downfall.

In the meantime Citibank was facing an upstart rival. The Chase National Bank had only been chartered in 1877, and had a comical and checkered beginning. It was founded by John Thompson, a seventy-five-year-old former schoolteacher with a bushy white beard who had become an expert on currency values: he named it after the former Secretary of the Treasury Salmon Chase, who had organized the financing of the Union during the Civil War. Thompson himself became its second president at the age of eighty-two but could not keep pace with his rivals; his cashier Isaac White resigned after making rash loans and was later arrested and jailed for not paying his landlady rent. In 1886 the Chase was bought out by a group of more substantial businessmen, led by a former comptroller of the currency, Henry Cannon, who extended the bank outside the city and rapidly increased its profits: he was succeeded by another former comptroller, Barton Hepburn, who continued its respectable progress until he was killed by a New York trolley car.

The spectacular expansion of the Chase began in 1911, under the presidency of Albert Wiggin, a resourceful financier and obsessive poker player. Wiggin was determined to dominate his rivals, including Citibank. He absorbed a succession of other banks; he assembled a board of leading industrialists, including Charles Schwab of Bethlehem Steel and Alfred Sloan of General Motors; and he competed with Citibank's expansion in Latin America. But he was also speculating wildly with his own private companies, including two called the Shermar and Murlyn Corporations after his daughters. The companies participated in dubious stocks, including Harry Sinclair's oil company, and made profits from "selling short" the shares of the Chase Bank itself. Wiggin showed little restraint in his own financial ambitions, and by 1929 his salary of $275,000 from the Chase was generously augmented by many of the fifty-nine other companies of which he was director.

A few New York banks had begun to venture into lending abroad and Citibank was a pioneer, following in the wake of American trade. The Federal Reserve Act of 1913 had allowed national banks to set up branches abroad, and Citibank quickly established its own offices, first in Buenos Aires, then in Rio de Janeiro, São Paulo, Havana, and Montevideo. During the First World War, while the European banks were losing ground, Citibank seized its opportunity and spread through Latin America and Europe. It made the most of the expansion of trade in the twenties, surviving all the economic crises, until by 1930 it had reached a peak of a hundred overseas offices in twenty-three countries and territories—more than any other American bank.

In the twenties many banks began selling Latin American bonds to the American public with thousands of local agents across the country, persuading small savers to invest their money in developing countries: they were more risky, as always, but more profitable. The banks were not farsighted or fastidious in their methods. The Chase built up business in Cuba, where it established close links with the murderous dictator Gerardo Machado (who punished some of his critics by dropping them into the sea, tied by weights, to be eaten by sharks). The Chase continued to extend loans to him, including a personal credit reaching $200,000, and employed his son-in-law in the bank. Citibank, with the investment firm of Seligman's, floated a loan of $50 million to Peru, taking the precaution of paying $450,000 to the son of President Leguia to ensure that the deal would go through[14];

[14]*Stock Exchange Practices Report,* 1934, pp. 220–21.

but soon afterward Leguia was unseated, and Peru defaulted.

American foreign loans poured money into Europe and Latin America; between 1924 and 1928 they averaged $1.3 billion a year, of which half went to Europe. "Whereas in the middle decades of the nineteenth century American promoters had scoured Europe in search of foreign lenders," wrote Cleona Lewis, "in 1925–29 they were searching the world over for foreign borrowers." But the lending had little relationship to any likely increase in production which could help to repay the loans; all too often it simply financed corruption, and the hectic competition between salesmen often produced absurd consequences. At one time in Colombia twenty-nine representatives of financial houses were competing to lend, and one hamlet in Bavaria which was reported by American agents to need $125,000 was eventually persuaded to borrow $3 million.[15] The enthusiasm of American investors was inevitably fitful, for it was linked to the vagaries of the New York market: the future of developing nations became dependent on its day-to-day moods.

BANK OF AMERICA

In California in the meantime a young Italian had approached banking at the beginning of the century from a viewpoint almost opposite to that of the Manhattan merchants. California had banned banks altogether until 1879, but when their opportunity came the bankers played a spectacular role. Amadeo Giannini was the son of an Italian immigrant who had arrived on one of the first Union Pacific trains and had bought a hotel in San Jose, where he was born. His father was shot by a crazy farm worker, and Amadeo started dealing in fruit and vegetables for his stepfather. He soon realized that the self-contained Italian community at North Beach offered special opportunities, and in 1904

[15]See Cleona Lewis, *America's Stake in International Investments* (Washington: Brookings Institution, 1938), p. 377, and Max Winkler, *Foreign Bonds, an Autopsy* (1933), pp. 86–88.

he set up his own little "Bank of Italy" in San Francisco.[16]

Giannini was now a big, extrovert showman who saw himself as the people's banker. He advertised shamelessly for depositors and borrowers, he talked to Italians in their own language and he kept his office door open to visitors. Two years after he founded his bank the San Francisco earthquake destroyed much of the city. According to legend Giannini arrived at his bank just in time to carry away the gold in wagons; nine days after the earthquake, with a showman's instinct he put up a tent on a wharf. While other banks stayed closed he reopened with a plank and a bag of money, proclaiming that San Francisco would soon be rebuilt greater than ever with the help of his loans. It was a dramatic return to medieval origins (when the word *bank* meant a money changer's bench) and Giannini's confidence yielded handsome returns in the subsequent rebuilding. When next year a new financial panic reached California, Giannini was able to display a hoard of gold behind the counter and increased his deposits while other banks were being drained.

He soon realized that California could offer huge scope for a bank that could open branches throughout the state, for it had rich pockets of savings in some cities while the rural areas desperately needed seasonal loans. When California passed a new banking law in 1909, which left the way open for branches, Giannini quickly began buying up local banks beyond San Francisco. His customers now included not just Italian farmers but all kinds of promoters in the great Californian boom; he was soon helping to finance the transformation of Los Angeles, and was lending money for movies with the names of the "bankable" stars as his security. By 1927 he controlled three hundred branches, and his bank was already the third largest in America. He still kept his flamboyant personal style, rushing between his branches and showing himself to his public like a star: he was the "Bull of the West." He believed he could control his bank

---

[16]For the events which followed, see Marquis and Bessie James, *Biography of a Bank* (New York: Harper & Row, 1954), Chapter 2.

through character, not money, and he never made a large fortune out of it. ("No man actually owns a fortune," he once said; "it owns him.")

He was now determined to extend across the United States by getting round the law that restricted banks to one state. He set up a holding company called Bancitaly Corporation and sent out salesmen to sell its shares to Italo-Americans through the West and Midwest. He then invaded New York, buying the staid old Bank of America, which had been founded at the same time as Citibank, which gave him a beachhead onto the much more profitable business of dealing in securities and investments. To consolidate his empire he set up a new superholding company called Transamerica, whose shares were soon boosted by his charismatic reputation. He also bought the New York firm of Blair, which brought in two financial experts: Elisha Walker and his young associate Jean Monnet (later far more famous as the father of the European Common Market). Giannini, now sixty, talked about retiring and leaving Walker and Monnet to run his empire. In twenty-five years the little Italian bank had turned into an apparently formidable financial power—a triumph of populism against the aristocratic principle.

CRASH

All these powerful banks—Morgan's, Citibank, Chase, and the future Bank of America—had grown up from their very different roots to become major financial operators in the boom of 1929. All of them used their deposits to finance shaky investments, and juggled with speculative shares through their interlocked companies. Morgan's heavily backed the fraudulent railroad group of the Van Schwerigen brothers of Cleveland. Giannini's Transamerica rode high on overblown expectations. Charles Mitchell of Citibank defied the warnings of the Federal Reserve Board, of which he was a director, and continued to insist that the economy was "fundamentally sound."

When the first crash came on "Black Thursday," October 24,

the bankers rushed round to Morgan's as they had done in the panic of 1907. Thomas Lamont of Morgan's presided over the meeting, which included Charles Mitchell of Citibank, Albert Wiggin of Chase, but also a significant new presence—George Harrison, governor of the Federal Reserve Bank of New York. The banks agreed to form a pool, as they had done twenty-two years earlier, to stabilize the market by buying stocks, and Lamont reassured reporters with his classic understatement: "There has been a little distress selling." Morgan's suave broker Richard Whitney walked ostentatiously onto the stock market floor to buy large chunks of stock. The market began to rally, and it looked as if Morgan's could once again rescue the country.

When the market plunged again the following Monday, the bankers assembled again, in Morgan's library, with Jack Morgan in the chair. But this time it was Harrison, the government's man from the Federal Reserve, who saved the day. He knew that loans of over $2 billion had already been called in, and that the money market could not survive without intervention. He undertook to buy huge amounts of government bonds from the banks to allow the stock market to stay open, and the banks to take up the loans. The stock market, though it sank still further, was able to stay open in the black weeks that followed, and at last began to rally temporarily in mid-November. The bankers could retain their dignity; Morgan's was able to disguise the bankruptcy of the Van Schwerigen railroads; and Whitney, the Morgan's broker, still appeared the calm savior.

It was not until a year later that the real banking crisis began, when the Bank of the United States—which gave loans to thousands of small Jewish businessmen in New York (no relation to the federal bank of a century earlier)—faced a run of withdrawals. The other New York bankers refused to rescue it, partly, it is alleged, because of their anti-Semitism; and the bank closed its doors—the biggest failure in American history.[17] A panic followed across the

---

[17]See Milton Friedman's account in *Free to Choose* (New York: Harcourt Brace Jovanovich, 1979), Chapter 3.

States, and in one month 325 banks failed. In the spring of 1931 there was another banking crisis, and in 1933 a run of failures set off a new panic just before President Roosevelt's inauguration. Between 1929 and 1933 the number of American banks had shrunk from 25,000 to 18,000.

Two years after the Great Crash had begun, the role of the big banks began to come to light, when Senator Pecora of New York presided over hearings in Washington. Then it emerged that Morgan's had its own preferred list of influential clients; that Albert Wiggin of Chase, operating through his daughters' companies, had been benefiting from the crash by his own secret bear operations; that Charles Mitchell had been paid over a million dollars for his share in Citibank's profits in the first half of 1929, and had then sold some of Citibank stock at a loss to his wife to avoid paying taxes.

Now the casualties were spectacular. Charles Mitchell had to resign from Citibank after his testimony, to be succeeded by a staid and gentlemanly banker, James Perkins. Mitchell soon afterward was tried for and acquitted of tax evasion, but was later successfully sued for a million dollars in taxes. Albert Wiggin of the Chase had retired in apparent dignity after the crash, with a pension of $100,000 a year; but in the meantime the bank, by a circuitous route, had come under the control of the Rockefeller family. Old John D. Rockefeller, despite his aversion to bankers, had eventually been persuaded to obtain more financial expertise for administering the family fortunes, and had bought the Equitable Trust, which rapidly expanded and absorbed other banks through the twenties. In 1930 his son-in-law Winthrop Aldrich became president of the Equitable, which soon made a bid for the Chase. Wiggin remained president, but Aldrich was the powerful vice-president, and when the banking scandals emerged he allowed Wiggin to become the scapegoat: he was publicly disgraced, and eventually deprived of his pension. In the meantime Winthrop Aldrich took over the bank and presented himself— almost alone in Wall Street—as the advocate of major banking reforms.

Giannini seemed at first to be right out of the game. The financial experts he had brought in, Walker and Monnet, had soon decided that the great Transamerica company, absurdly overvalued, had to be rescued. Walker persuaded Giannini to take a two-year holiday in Austria, and himself became president, with Monnet as vice-president; they wrote down the Transamerica assets, refused Giannini a bonus, and set about reorganizing the whole network. But these master bankers had underestimated the power of Giannini, who was now fuming in exile about his loss of power; he had little money of his own, but he still put his faith in his popular appeal. There followed one of the most extraordinary epics in the history of banking. Giannini secretly traveled back via Canada and California—his two years now expired. He consulted with his son in Vancouver and then came out with a public statement denouncing Walker for selling out the assets of Transamerica, and prepared for a proxy fight to recapture control. Walker now claimed to be the biggest shareholder, but Giannini knew that the stock was scattered among 200,000 people, many of them Italians. He raised funds from loyal supporters, advertised, and toured California, attacking the Wall Street interests that had captured and downgraded Transamerica. Walker retorted by revealing Giannini's past blunders and unfounded optimism; but optimism and dividends were what his shareholders wanted, and Giannini could appear as the champion of stockholders' democracy against the power of Wall Street. At the stockholders' meeting in February 1932 Giannini was triumphantly re-elected, and Walker and Monnet resigned. "We had reckoned without the energy and guile of the old warrior," Monnet reflected later; "perhaps we were unlucky, perhaps maladroit."[18] Certainly they had miscalculated the power of populism.

Giannini faced plenty of new problems. The Bank of America (as he had now renamed the Bank of Italy) was loaded with farm mortgages and with the debts of Transamerica; and as the Depression deepened there were great doubts about its soundness. But

[18]*Memoirs* (London: Collins, 1978), p. 108.

Giannini had taken the precaution of supporting Franklin Roosevelt in his campaign of 1932. At his inauguration Roosevelt proclaimed that "the money changers have fled from the high seats in the temple of our civilization"; and two days later he ordered all banks to be closed, promising that only sound banks would be allowed to reopen. He swiftly pushed his Emergency Banking Act through Congress, which allowed the Federal Reserve to give credit to banks against assets which they could define very broadly—the classic method of disguising a bank's insolvency. The Bank of America was a doubtful case and the governor of the Reserve Bank in San Francisco reported that it was "hopelessly insolvent." But Giannini was able to press home the political consequences of closing a bank with so many small depositors, and at the last minute the White House intervened to save it.

In the wake of the Great Crash and the revelations that followed, the bankers lost much political support. The Glass-Steagall Act of 1933 forced the deposit banks to separate themselves from banks selling securities; Morgan's henceforth could not deal with investments, and a quite separate firm, Morgan Stanley (headed by a younger son of the family), now dealt in securities; while Citibank and Chase also divested themselves of their securities affiliates. The next year the Securities Exchange Act, partly basing itself on the British Companies Act, established the Securities and Exchange Commission (SEC) to prevent the manipulation and rigging of the stock market. The following year the Banking Act gave much greater powers to the Federal Reserve Board in Washington, which now dominated the regional reserve banks from its temple in Constitution Avenue.

Economists still argue about the basic causes of the economic collapse. Milton Friedman insists that it was the Federal Reserve System which, by refusing to buy government bonds which would have provided the banks with more cash, precipitated the monetary crisis which led to the economic crisis.[19] But the power and prestige of the American bankers—the "banksters," as New Deal-

[19]Recently re-stated in *Free to Choose*, Chapter 3.

ers in Washington called them—were never to be the same again; for the Great Crash had revealed not only their greed but their incompetence. "The stereotype of bankers as conservative, careful, prudent individuals," said Bernard Baruch, "was shattered in 1929." Or as Professor J. K. Galbraith put it, thirty years later:

> A banker need not be popular; indeed a good banker in a healthy capitalist society should probably be much disliked. People do not wish to trust their money to a hail-fellow-well-met but to a misanthrope who can say no. However, a banker must not seem futile, ineffective, or vaguely foolish. In contrast with the stern power of Morgan in 1907, that was precisely how his successors seemed, or were made to seem, in 1929.[20]

It was an odd sequel that the bank which had grown most rapidly and rashly, and had nearly been closed down, should flourish more than any. Giannini's Bank of America continued to have financial and political problems. In California, after much foreclosing on farm debts, it became one of the biggest landowners in the state, attacked as the heartless agent of big business by journalists and (by implication) by John Steinbeck in *The Grapes of Wrath.* Giannini was in fact desperately trying to avoid bankruptcies—for running farms was an unenviable task—but his political image was now tarnished after the glittering early days in North Beach. Washington still looked suspiciously on his holding company Transamerica, and in 1938 the SEC charged it with making false statements about its financial condition.

But as the economy of California began to recover, the Bank of America had forged ahead again, selling personal loans and auto loans with new aggression, and becoming closely involved with new Californian industries, including aircraft and the movies. Giannini's brother, Doc, financed Walt Disney's *Snow White,* and the bank kept Disney's business ever afterward. (The bank's first million-dollar loan for a movie was for Sam Goldwyn's *The*

[20] *The Great Crash,* paperback ed. (London: Penguin, 1961), p. 136.

Kid from Spain—during its filming Goldwyn's wife said, "Sam, how drawn you look," and Doc Giannini replied, "What she meant was overdrawn.")

Adventurous lending pushed up the profits; and the bank was prepared to lend a higher proportion of its deposits than most others (48 percent in 1942, compared to the American average of 32.5 percent). In terms of deposits it was still only the fourth biggest bank in America in 1939, but in terms of loans it was the biggest of all. It had long ago overtaken Morgan's, approaching the business from the opposite direction. With its thousands of small depositors, its aggressive salesmanship, and its sensitivity to popular politics it was the forerunner of the mass banks of the future.

THE WORLD DEPRESSION

The Great Crash and the Great Depression which followed had long repercussions on the rest of the world. The whole pattern of international trade was disrupted by the falling production and investment from America. Latin American countries which had borrowed from the big New York banks now found themselves unable to pay interest—for they could not increase exports at a time when America was putting up her tariffs—and many of them had to default on their loans. The extension of the Depression to Europe was to lead to global catastrophe.

The end of the First World War had found the European bankers shorn of much of their international network. The Germans had lost most of their foreign holdings. The French loans to tsarist Russia were repudiated. The great merchant banks in London had to play a much more modest foreign role. Barings made a few loans to Brazil and Peru, and participated in a loan to Czechoslovakia; but the Latin American business was now dominated by American banks like Citibank and Chase. The London bankers now concentrated on the safer countries of the Empire, like Australia and Canada. Domestic lending was largely taken over by the deposit banks, which were run by much more cautious bureaucracies under stately chairmen ("These impeccable spinsters," as Maynard Keynes called them), who looked askance on new kinds of lending like hire purchase or building societies. Much of the international negotiation was in the hands of Sir Montagu Norman, who became governor of the Bank of England in 1920, and stayed there for the next twenty years.

The economic ruin of Germany, the post-revolutionary chaos in Russia, and the impoverishment of France and Britain had undermined the structure of European trade and banking. Sir Montagu Norman at the Bank of England and Emile Moreau at the Banque de France and Benjamin Strong of the Federal Reserve Bank of New York were constantly trying to re-establish the pre-war stability of currencies, while the City of London tried to revert to its old international role. But the postwar boom in Britain was soon followed by depression; the reversion to the gold standard in 1925 only worsened the scene; and the attempt to exact reparations from a bankrupt Germany made Europe still less stable.

In this dangerous condition Europe was hit by the Great Depression, which dried up American orders and cut down employment. It was now the turn of the Europeans to see bankers behind every disaster. The Rothschild bank in Vienna, the Kreditanstalt, faced a rush of withdrawals and collapsed, knocking down dominoes all across Europe. The German banks first tried to rescue it, and then themselves faced a panic which caused the Darmstadter, one of the biggest, to collapse. In the aftermath the German banks could not pay their foreign debts, and had to be granted a moratorium. The freezing of German funds then caused a new crisis in Britain: other European countries sold sterling to buy gold from London and the British bankers now insisted that the Labour government must balance the budget and make big cuts in wages. The Labour Party split, and a fragile national government was formed to enforce the austere measures, denounced by the left as a "banker's ramp." Britain, followed by other countries, was forced to go off the gold standard.

Fear and defensiveness only worsened the Depression. Each country tried to protect its own industry by putting up tariffs and competed for capital through higher interest rates; and these "beggar-thy-neighbor" policies further dried up the flows of international trade. Few European bankers dared to make loans; when Victor Rothschild (later Lord Rothschild) briefly worked in the family bank in 1931, he found "the City seemed moribund, boring, rather painful." The economies of Britain and France were weak and vulnerable, while the American banks were preoccupied with their domestic predicament.

Germany was looking toward desperate remedies. The president of the Reichsbank, Hjalmar Schacht, resigned in 1930 in protest against the American Young Plan to exact reparations. He put all his faith in getting Hitler elected; and he helped to persuade other bankers, including the Deutsche Bank and the Dresdner Bank, to finance Hitler's crusade. After Hitler came to power in 1933, Schacht brilliantly supervised the integration of the German banks into the war economy, making Germany increasingly self-sufficient and independent of the rest of Europe. By the time that he became disillusioned with Hitler in 1938 and joined the conspiracy against him, it was too late to stop the financial machine he had created.

The cosmopolitan world of the old German-Jewish banks was finally shattered. Soon after Hitler had invaded Austria in March 1938, the head of the Austrian Rothschilds, Baron Louis von Rothschild, was arrested, imprisoned, and only released after he had given over the family assets in Austria. The interdependent world of international bankers of the nineteenth century was now barely recognizable. And when the British and French economies, and later the American, were revived with full employment, they were based on the preparation for war. The succession of disasters that followed the collapse of the Kreditanstalt still haunts the minds of many older men who look back on it nearly fifty years later. "No one who went through those times," one veteran banker reminded me, "can feel altogether confident when people today say that the world's banking system is fundamentally sound."

4
THE BROTHERHOOD
OF MAN

Prosperity has no fixed limits. It is not a finite substance to be
diminished by division. On the contrary, the more of it that other
nations enjoy, the more each nation will have for itself.

HENRY MORGENTHAU
Bretton Woods, April 1944

It was at the height of the Second World War, when Britain's
prospects seemed most desperate, that the intellectual foundations were laid for a new international economic system. Looking
back on it now, the boldness of that vision looks extraordinary.
Surrounded by the chaos and destruction of war, politicians and
economists were able to start again from scratch—"present at the
creation" in Dean Acheson's phrase—with a decisiveness which
they could never repeat. Both the horrors and the idealism of war
made them determined to create "one world" which would avoid
the catastrophic divisions that caused the disaster. The original
concepts were put forward not by bankers, bureaucrats, or politicians, but by two brilliant academics from right outside the political or banking tradition—a British homosexual and an American
Communist sympathizer, both notorious for their rudeness and
independence of mind.

It was Hitler's initiative in propounding a "New Order" for the
postwar world that induced first the British, then the Americans,
to think out their own plans. The odd way in which it began has
only recently come to light.[1] In November 1940 Harold Nicolson,

[1]*Collected Writings of J. M. Keynes,* Vol. XXV (London: Macmillan, 1980),
pp. 1 ff.

the politician and writer who was then serving in the British Ministry of Information, wrote to his friend Maynard Keynes, the economist who was then unpaid adviser to the Treasury. Nicolson wanted Keynes to launch a campaign to counteract the Nazi propaganda of Dr. Funk, the German banker and finance minister, who was broadcasting to Europe about a postwar New Order; and Nicolson enclosed some German broadcasts with some British government comments making fun of the German promises to abolish the role of gold. Keynes replied, pointing out that he, too, did not believe in the gold standard and that "about three quarters of the German broadcasts would be quite excellent if the name of Great Britain were substituted for Germany or the Axis. . . ." Soon afterward the British ambassador in Washington, Lord Halifax, also asked Keynes to reply to the German promises; and Keynes now began seriously to work out his own ideas for a postwar economic system, based on a new kind of international bank. While Churchill's war cabinet was desperately trying to stave off military defeat in North Africa, Keynes was calmly envisaging the economic problems of the postwar world (in his six volumes of war memoirs Churchill mentions Keynes only once).

Before the war Keynes, preoccupied by Britain's own recovery and planning, had been ambivalent about both world institutions and overseas lending. But he was now determined to avoid the chaos of exchange rates which he had seen after the First World War, and by 1941 he was convinced of the need for global cooperation and what he called "financial disarmament" to prevent the retreat into autarky.[2] He constructed his bold plan for an "International Clearing Union," whose central concept was, as he put it, "to generalise the essential principle of banking as it is exhibited within any closed system." It would in effect be a World Central Bank, providing its own bank notes (which Keynes called Bancor), creating credit from richer countries and allowing overdrafts to needier nations. Keynes was doubtless influenced by Britain's own impending crisis, which would call for large over-

[2]*Ibid.,* p. 195.

drafts; but he had a wider vision of how such a union could assist poorer countries to survive trade cycles or falls in commodity prices, and he foresaw with great clarity the problems that bedeviled the Third World in the following decades. He seized on the unique opportunity to construct a fairer world. "It may be doubted," he wrote, "whether a comprehensive scheme will ever in fact be worked out, unless it can come into existence through a single act of creation, made possible by the unity of purpose and energy of hope for better things to come, springing from the victory of the United Nations, when they had attained it, over immediate evil."

Keynes's clarity of vision was reflected in his simplicity of language, which avoided all jargon and always sought to relate his policies to the situations of ordinary people. "We have to bear it constantly in mind," he explained to Sir Frederick Phillips in the Treasury, "that, in the long run, large economic projects cannot possibly come into existence except with the aid of an instructed and educated public opinion."[3] He retained his homely style, not only in his public speeches and articles for amateurs, but in his communications with the mandarins of finance, including the governor of the Bank of England, Sir Montagu Norman.

The essence of the scheme is very simple indeed (Keynes explained to Norman in December 1941). It is the extension to the international field of the essential principles of *banking* by which, when one chap wants to leave his resources idle, those resources are not therefore withdrawn from circulation but are made available to another chap who is prepared to use them—and to make this possible without the former losing his liquidity and his right to employ his own resources as soon as he chooses to do so. Just as the domestic situation was transmogrified in the eighteenth and nineteenth centuries by the discovery and adoption of the principles of local banking, so (I believe) it is only by extending these same principles to the international field that we can cure the manifest evils of the international economy as it existed between

[3]*Ibid.,* p. 204.

the two wars, after London had lost the position which had allowed her before 1914 to do much the same thing off her own bat.[4]

While Keynes was working on his international bank, Harry Dexter White, the adviser to United States Secretary of the Treasury Henry Morgenthau, was preparing his own blueprint for the postwar world. The son of Lithuanian-Jewish immigrants, White had graduated from Columbia, Stanford, and Harvard to become the expert on international economics at the Treasury. He retained striking freedom of action; he and his wife were surrounded by radical assistants—there were many in Washington—who may well have been Communists; and he was later accused, though without final proof, of passing information to the Russians. As Morgenthau later described him, "He could be disagreeable, quick-tempered, overly ambitious, and power went to his head." Dean Acheson was often, he said, "outraged by Harry White's capacity for rudeness in discussion." But his intellect and influence with Morgenthau gave him a unique authority.

White, like Keynes, had his own experience of the dangerous chaos of currencies: in Latin America he had advised countries how to set up a managed currency system after their silver had been drained by the United States. By the summer of 1941 White was convinced of the need for a new international organization after the war to safeguard the monetary system, to restore foreign trade, and to revive the nations' economies; and he drafted a plan for a "Stabilization Fund" and a "Bank for Reconstruction and Development." The fund, which was the germ of the future International Monetary Fund (IMF), was more conservative and less ambitious than Keynes's proposal. Like Keynes, White advocated an international currency which he called "Unitas"; but the assets of his fund would be limited to the funds voted by each member nation, and it would not be able to expand further without the approval of each nation's taxpayers. It was an agency for distributing money rather than, like Keynes's Clearing Union, a machinery

[4]*Ibid.,* pp. 98–99.

for creating credit. White conceived his fund in conjunction with a more far-reaching international bank, a lending agency which could provide long-term loans for reconstruction, financing trade, or stabilizing the prices of commodities; it would make loans with its own notes, and buy and sell gold and securities like a world central bank.

Keynes's and White's proposals were both published in April 1942, remarkably unscathed by the bureaucrats, each gaining support from his own government. The Americans suspected Keynes of some special pleading for easy loans to Britain, but Keynes insisted that his Clearing Union was based on good banking practice. "It is a piece of highly necessary business mechanism, which is at least as useful to the creditor as to the debtor. A man does not refuse to keep a banking account because his deposits will be employed by the banker to make advances to another person." Keynes was exasperated by the contortions of language in the documents from White and the U.S. Treasury, which he called "Cherokee" as opposed to his own "Christian English": he complained that the first draft was "difficult to understand and almost impossible to read." He was exasperated by White's refusal to grapple with the problem of gold: "He has not seen how to get round the gold standard difficulty and has forgotten all about the useful concept of bank money." But he was excited and encouraged that White had the same underlying attitudes about world institutions and concessions of national sovereignty.[5]

The two men first met in September 1943 in the first of a series of barbed encounters. A contemporary photograph marvelously captures the tension between them: White smiling tightly with his arms crossed in front of him while Keynes leers down at him, with his big teeth, clutching a roll of documents as if it were a club. Keynes complained (to Sir Wilfred Eady) that White was "over-bearing, a bad colleague, always trying to bounce you, with harsh rasping voice, aesthetically oppressive

[5] *Ibid.*, p. 161.

in mind and manner; he has not the faintest conception of how to behave or observe the rules of civilised intercourse." Yet he admitted that he had "a very great respect and even liking for him."[6] White hated Keynes's lordly style, referring to him sarcastically as "your Royal Highness"; he burst out with ungrammatical anger, while Keynes made rapier thrusts with a rudeness which (his friend Roy Harrod commented) "was sometimes carried to an indefensible length."[7]

While Keynes had the more subtle mind, White had the more powerful government, restrained by a Congress which was sure to balk at the apparently unlimited liability of Keynes's world bank. Keynes reluctantly accepted the substance of White's proposed fund, soon renamed the International Monetary Fund, while White's bolder sister body was whittled down. The bank was now to be an investment organization, not a world central bank: it would not compete with private investors, and it would not supply capital to finance foreign trade or stabilize commodities. The idea of an international currency had now disappeared. Even thus watered down it was attacked by the orthodox American bankers: "Where can you loan thirty to fifty billions around the world with any prospects of being repaid?" complained a vice-president of Citibank, Wilbert Ward. *The New York Times* protested that "American taxpayers would make loans to foreign governments whether or not these taxpayers individually considered the loans to be sound."[8]

But the central concept of cooperation was still intact, and delegates on both sides were determined to make the most of this unrepeatable opportunity to reorder the world. As the British economist Dennis Robertson put it in 1943: "Knowing what we know of the centrifugal forces at work among the nations of the world, of the ease with which wills tire and good intentions fade, can we doubt that in this, as in the political field, it would be wise

[6] *Ibid.,* p. 356.
[7] *The Life and Times of John Maynard Keynes* (London: Macmillan, 1951), p. 559.
[8] Robert W. Oliver, *International Economic Co-operation and the World Bank* (London: Macmillan, 1975), p. 160.

to lay the foundations while imaginations are active and hopes are high?"[9]

After preliminary talks between the Americans and the British at Atlantic City, the delegates from forty-four nations met in July 1944 at the New Hampshire resort of Bretton Woods, where over four weeks they thrashed out the postwar economic system. They spent most of their time over the charter for the International Monetary Fund, which had now been hedged in by the restrictions of monetary experts and lawyers ("to judge from results in this lawyer-ridden land," Keynes complained, "the *Mayflower,* when she sailed from Plymouth, must have been entirely filled with lawyers"[10]). But they still allowed some flexibility for the "International Bank for Reconstruction and Development" (IBRD), or the World Bank, as it was soon called—for which its later presidents were grateful. The British wanted it to take greater risks than commercial banks, but the Americans insisted on conservative principles, so it was restricted to lending for specific projects, except in special circumstances. Keynes wanted both institutions to be in London, as the center of international trade, or else in New York. But the Americans insisted on having them in Washington, and since they were putting up far the largest quota they could not be denied.

It was assumed that the United States would remain the dominant partner, and that the dollar would indefinitely remain the world's reserve currency, interchangeable with gold, with sterling in a secondary role. It was hard to imagine the world ever being otherwise. The Soviet Union sent delegates to Bretton Woods, and at the end of the conference Moscow looked like it would join the two bodies. "We march to victory together," said Fred Vinson, later U.S. Secretary of the Treasury; "we move on the path of peace together." India and Latin American countries were also there, but most other developing countries were still colonies and unrepresented. After they became independent they nearly all

[9] *Ibid.,* p. 119.
[10] Harrod, p. 583.

joined the IMF in order to borrow from the World Bank; but they felt no real responsibility for the decisions at Bretton Woods.

In spite of the compromises and resentment of American domination the meeting ended with a historic agreement between forty-four nations determined to build a new kind of world. In his farewell speech Keynes summed up the mood of optimism: "Few believed it possible. If we can continue in a larger task as we have begun in this limited task, there is hope for the world. If we can continue, this nightmare will be over. The brotherhood of man will have become more than a phrase."

Before the agreement was ratified the American bankers mounted a sharp counterattack. Winthrop Aldrich, still the president of the Chase, put forward his own six-point program, giving priority to removing trade barriers, and the American Bankers Association wanted to cut down the powers of the IMF. Eventually a compromise was worked out which restricted the fund's loans to offsetting short-term fluctuations in exchange rates. After long debates the United States Congress ratified the Bretton Woods agreements in July 1945, followed by twenty-seven other nations by the end of the year. The Soviet Union had already hardened its attitude after it had been refused an American loan, and though it continued to send observers, it was clear by the end of 1945 that it would not join. Eighteen months later the Soviets were preparing to establish their own economic bloc, COMECON.

In March 1946, when the Western delegates met again to settle the details at Savannah, they were already confronting a more divided world: it was just after Churchill's speech at Fulton which had warned about the Soviet iron curtain. Russia was now right out, and India took her place as having the fifth biggest quota in the fund. Keynes once again tried to put the fund and the bank in New York; he complained that the salaries of the executive directors of the IMF were too high, and that it needed a strong head, with a minimum of interference. He again urged that both bodies should be based in New York. He argued passionately and excitedly against the Americans, disillusioned with their insensitivity: "I went to Savannah expecting to meet the world, and all I met was a tyrant." But he was very conscious of Britain's dependence on an American loan which was not yet through Congress. He was overruled and exhausted, and on the train back to Washington he had a heart attack.[11]

Keynes, like most others, expected that Harry White himself would be the managing director of the IMF, but in the meantime an extraordinary secret scandal was preventing it. President Truman had just been warned by the FBI that White and other senior civil servants had passed secret information abroad which had then been passed on to the Soviet Union. Truman quickly ensured that White should only be an executive director, surrounded by carefully screened assistants. The top job at the fund passed to a very orthodox Belgian, Camille Gutt, who suffered much interference from the directors; and the tradition was thus accidentally established that the head of the IMF would always be European, and the head of the World Bank an American.

The arguments between Keynes and White were to reverberate over the following decades, with many twists and ironies. While it was White's plan which took shape in the International Monetary Fund, the vast explosion of international credit through the Eurodollar market was to have something in common with Keynes's Clearing Union; but without controls and with galloping debts and inflation, Keynes's dream was "beginning to look more and more like a nightmare."[12]

THE WORLD BANK

In May 1946 the directors of the World Bank met for the first time, in the headquarters on two floors of a new building at 1818 H Street, near the White House, where it has been ever since. The bank was soon an anticlimax. The Europeans resented the Ameri-

[11]*Ibid.,* pp. 632–39.
[12]Martin Mayer, *The Bankers,* paperback ed. (New York: Ballantine, 1976), p. 503.

can domination, and were already negotiating their own bilateral loans; while the Americans found difficulty in choosing a president. At last Truman announced the appointment of Eugene Meyer, the seventy-year-old veteran banker and publisher of *The Washington Post,* who installed himself in his office with an American flag. But Meyer soon resented the liberal influence of the executive directors, who included the American Emilio Collado, the Englishman Sir James Grigg and the Frenchman Pierre Mendès-France. Meyer resigned, and after another awkward interregnum another president was announced, the master lawyer John J. McCloy.

McCloy, who was then fifty-one, was already a shrewd figure on the strategic crossroads between politics, law, and banking; and his durable personality will weave in and out of subsequent chapters. A stocky Irishman, he was born, as he explains, "on the wrong side of the tracks in Philadelphia," rose up through the Harvard Law School, and soon became a prominent lawyer. After Pearl Harbor he became Assistant Secretary of War (in which job he first became concerned with Middle East oil), and in 1945 he joined the powerful law firm of Milbank, Tweed, which had close links with the Rockefellers, the Chase Manhattan (whose building it shares), and the conservative coterie of East Coast bankers.

In the World Bank McCloy's influence was decisive. He saw it as only a temporary institution, until private investors could provide the necessary long-term capital. He brought with him as vice-president Robert Garner, a former treasurer of Guaranty Trust; while the American director Emilio Collado, who was thought to be too liberal, resigned and was replaced by a vice-president of the Chase, Eugene Black. The three Americans all shared an apartment in Washington and effectively excluded the other directors from their decisions. They were skeptical of much of the idealism of Bretton Woods and "Morgenthau and all those clucks," as Garner described them; and they set about organizing an active and orthodox bank, with a fanfare of publicity. They sold bonds through the United States, and soon approved its first loans —$250 million to France (at 3.25 percent plus 1 percent commission), $195 million to the Netherlands, and $40 million to Denmark.[13]

The two lusty twins, as Keynes called them, the IMF and the World Bank, were now safely established. The economic foundations of Bretton Woods would survive unshaken for thirty years. But much of the vision and the idealism was already lost as the cold war divided the world. Originally there was to have been a third body, the International Trade Organization (ITO), which would have been concerned not only with tariffs but with organizing commodity markets, which was of urgent importance to the developing world. The ITO was agreed to at a meeting in Havana in 1948, but Congress would not ratify it, and it was followed by the much less far-reaching organization of GATT (General Agreement on Tariffs and Trade), while the problem of commodity prices was never properly broached.

As for the two founders, they soon disappeared from the scene. Lord Keynes, exhausted by his emotional negotiations, died soon after returning to Britain. Harry White soon found himself a target of the witch-hunt against Communist sympathizers; he had to resign from the fund, and in 1948 he appeared before the House Committee on Un-American Activities, where he was relentlessly questioned by Congressman Richard Nixon and others. He effectively cleared his name with a passionate speech asserting his patriotism and belief in freedom of speech, but he died a few days later.

MARSHALL AID

The modest efforts of the World Bank were soon being eclipsed by a far bolder initiative, compared to which (as McCloy put it) the World Bank was as a rowboat to the *Queen Elizabeth*. The worsening world atmosphere had changed the whole outlook. American economic policy was now closely linked to the cold

[13]See Robert W. Oliver, *International Economic Co-operation and the World Bank* (London: Macmillan, 1975), pp. 238–45.

war: the fear of Soviet expansion had led to the American involvement in Greece and Turkey and put an end to the hopes of "one world." By May 1947 Truman was warning that Europe was economically disintegrating, and the next month his Secretary of State, General Marshall, made his famous speech at Harvard advocating assistance to Europe, with the proviso that the Europeans themselves must take the initiative and organize the program. The proposal was quickly taken up by the Western European foreign ministers, led by Bevin and Bidault, and rejected by the Soviet Union and Eastern Europe. The "Marshall Plan" was under way on the Western side of the iron curtain, and in the following years Congress was to approve funds of $13 billion to reconstruct Western Europe. It was enlightened self-interest; it was designed both to strengthen Europe's resistance to Communism, and to provide markets and trading partners for American industry. In its generosity and farsightedness it exceeded anything before or since, and its success was to transform the economic balance of the world.

With the recovery of Europe the American bankers began crossing the Atlantic. Already before the Marshall Plan they were negotiating their own private loans. In 1945 Chase had led with a loan to the Netherlands and continued to lend money on commercial terms to France, joined by Morgan's. From the Bank of America Giannini flew over to Italy to inspect his subsidiary, the Banca d'America e d'Italia, and began extending credit to other Italian banks. But the Marshall Plan had the bankers built into it, with each European country choosing its own American bank. In the four years from 1948 Chase had the biggest commitments, with $977 million, followed by Citibank. The Bank of America, still specializing in Italy, was at sixth place with $389 million.

The disciplines and structures of the old European banks soon began to reassert themselves, and the old circles of bankers soon re-formed. The French banks, even though nationalized, were still run by many of the same families. The British Labour government nationalized the Bank of England but was never able to control it, and the hereditary bankers still held sway. Nowhere was the recovery of the bankers more spectacular than in Germany. In the first postwar years, the power of the Big Three German banks, the *Grossbanken,* appeared at last to be broken, and the Allies were determined to split them into thirty-three regional components. The chairman of the giant Deutsche Bank, Hermann Abs, who had become a director in Hitler's heyday in 1937, was arrested and detained by the Americans for three months. But the British soon found him indispensable, making him their financial adviser, and the anti-Nazi policies of the Allies were soon overtaken by anti-Communism. By the end of the Allied occupation Abs was already a key figure in Germany's economic revival: a dapper, indestructible man with a trim mustache and a mastery of international finance. The Allies first modified and then abandoned their plans to split up the banks, so that German industry was once again dominated by the Big Three, with Abs as the chairman of the Deutsche Bank, whose biggest corporate customer, Krupps, was also reinstated as a giant corporation. The Deutsche Bank was once again in a position to hire or fire industrial chairmen, to accompany their client firms "from the cradle to the grave."

The recovery of European capitalism in the wake of the Marshall Plan and NATO led to cries from the left, particularly from France, that the Americans were building a "Bankers' Europe." The cries became louder when Jean Monnet—the same Monnet who had been defeated by Giannini in the Bank of America—made the first steps toward a European Community, with strong support from the Americans. It was not a Bankers' Europe in any very literal sense: the recovery had been the result of political decisions by Truman, Acheson, and Marshall. European banks were still quite tightly controlled by their national governments and central banks, and the currencies were not to become convertible until 1958. But it was true that the reconstruction, with the growing stability of the franc and the Deutschmark, was soon to transform the international opportunities of American bankers, rehabilitated after the ignominy of the prewar disasters.

5
THE SUPERBANKERS

Banking is perhaps the most personal of the big businesses.

MARTIN MAYER

In the years after the Second World War New York was the financial capital of the world, and its biggest banks began to take on the characters recognizable today. They competed to attract deposits from customers, and to lend them money with an aggressiveness and visibility which distressed the staid banks of Europe. They embarked on a succession of mergers so that by 1961, according to the Department of Justice, the five biggest banks had 75 percent of all deposits in the state. The Bankers Trust merged with a succession of smaller banks. The Manufacturers merged with the Hanover, to create "Manny Hanny"; Chemical merged first with the Corn Exchange, then with the New York Trust Company.

Even Morgan's merged with the Guaranty Trust, which had been the first American bank to go into the Middle East early in the century, which gave the merged bank a brand-new opportunity. Morgan Guaranty still kept its headquarters in the same low building that J. P. Morgan had put up at 23 Wall Street, but extending into the tall neighboring block in Broad Street. It remained "wholesale," dealing with august corporate clients rather than the vulgar masses; the "gray men of Morgan's" were so discreet that their chairmen were little heard of: 23 Wall Street has no name on its marble façade, and its banking hall looks like the entrance to a vast mansion, with a two-ton chandelier in Louis XV style hanging from the domed ceiling and an ominous portrait of Pierpont Morgan looking down from the wall.

These giant banks had a less personal style than their forebears, and the experience of the Great Crash had made their chairmen both more cautious and more discreet. But the judgment of risk and credit was still a very individual responsibility: a dynamic chairman could still impose his character and drive on a bank, as Giannini or Stillman had done in the past. While economists and model makers were inclined to see all banks as part of an impersonal machinery governed by market forces and laws of supply and demand, the bankers themselves still saw it as a people business with great scope for character. The new master bankers—like Gaylord Freeman of the First Chicago, Serge Semenenko of First Boston, Gabriel Hauge of Manny Hanny, Donald Platten of Chemical—could still change the direction of their banks, and each bank had its own tradition and local conditioning. The two old New York rivals, Chase and Citibank, were headed by men who were determined to make their mark, not just on New York, but on the world.

CHASE MANHATTAN

The Chase now appeared as the aristocrat of the retail banks. Under the long chairmanship of Winthrop Aldrich, the grandson of John D. Rockefeller, it had re-established its respectability after the traumas of the Great Crash. There were frequent comings and goings between the Chase and Washington, including the appointment in 1949 of a former vice-president, Eugene Black, to become president of the World Bank (see next chapter). In 1953 Aldrich himself became ambassador to Britain, and he was succeeded by John J. McCloy, who after leaving the World Bank had become High Commissioner in West Germany, on close terms with the new government of Konrad Adenauer. McCloy's style and upbringing were modest, but he was now in the center of a network of influence. His wife's sister was married to the former ambassador to Britain, Lewis Douglas, McCloy's old friend at Amherst; through his law firm of Milbank, Tweed, he remained close to the Rockefeller interests, and involved with the rapidly expanding interests of the oil companies; while his stints at the World Bank and in Germany had broadened his diplomatic connections. McCloy soon came to appear—as Richard Rovere described him in 1961—as a kind of chairman of the American establishment.

McCloy pushed through the biggest consolidation in the history of American banking. The Chase had long wanted to merge with the oldest New York bank, the Manhattan, which after a succession of mergers had fifty-seven branches in Queens, Brooklyn, and the Bronx, whereas the Chase had only two. When the Chase first tried to buy the Manhattan, its old charter of 1799 appeared to make it impregnable, but McCloy found a neat lawyers' solution: technically the Manhattan would take over the Chase. So in 1955 the Chase Manhattan was born with McCloy as chairman representing the Rockefeller interests.

The Rockefellers, while they carefully avoided any overt involvement with the Standard Oil companies, remained visibly close to the Chase, which wielded a much wider financial power. The total holdings of the children of John D. Rockefeller II in the Chase Manhattan amounted (according to Nelson Rockefeller's testimony in 1974) to only 620,000 shares or 2.54 percent of the total; but this excluded the shares held by Rockefeller Center—which the family effectively controlled—and the Rockefellers could effectively dominate the scattered shareholders of the Chase. Four of the five brothers had done some time in the bank. Nelson had done a spell with the foreign department in 1934; the next brother, Winthrop, had also been a trainee; Laurance spent a few months at the Chase before becoming a director of Rockefeller Center. And in 1946 the youngest brother, David, joined, intending to make his career in it. He was, he liked to explain, "the first member of the family since Grandfather who has done a regular job in a company":[1] and many people assumed that David had been chosen by his Uncle Winthrop as his eventual successor.

[1] Peter Collier and David Horowitz, *The Rockefellers,* paperback ed. (New York: New American Library, 1977), p. 428.

David was the most conventional and industrious of the five brothers. As a shy, podgy boy he had seemed overawed by his glamorous brother Nelson, and at Harvard he was undistinguished except as a collector of beetles, which he still is. (Was it a subconscious attraction to the creature which, as the Egyptian scarab, had marked the earliest money, itself associated with excrement?)[2] He went on to study at the London School of Economics and to take his doctorate at Chicago with a thesis on economic waste. When he joined the Chase he began as assistant manager and arrived by subway, but he was soon promoted to be vice-president for Latin America and by 1956, when McCloy made the merger, he was one of four executive vice-presidents.

With his chubby face, long nose, and fixed smile David was already seen as a totem of the bank, a tireless spokesman both for the Chase and for American free enterprise in general. He had developed an automatic glad-handing style with a pumping handshake and a beaming "Delighted to meet you"—not unlike his brother Nelson's, but with less warmth and energy. He seemed genuinely to like people, to want to help them and spread his goodwill. He seemed driven to extend himself everywhere, to be recognized and accepted as if he were breaking down the isolation of his grandfather's inheritance. When he traveled he kept little black books listing everyone he had ever met before, which ended up with over 40,000 names: as he explained, "If you have a way of saying, Well I remember the last time we met was at such-and-such a place, they are pleased." His colleagues realized the advantages of his surname: "We piggy-back on this introductory knack of David," one vice-president, John Haley, explained. "When I pick up the telephone and call somebody," Rockefeller himself puts it, "they are a little more apt to answer than they might be if they'd never heard my name."[3] But the modesty was

[2]See William H. Desmonde, "On the Anal Origin of Money," in Ernest Borneman, *The Psychoanalysis of Money* (New York: Urizen Books, 1976).
[3]Public Broadcasting System, "The World of David Rockefeller," *Bill Moyers Journal,* February 7, 1980.

misleading. His style soon became princely—always flying in his private plane, entertaining with banquets, insisting on meeting monarchs or presidents in each capital, and causing trouble if he did not—while he still shook thousands of hands with his glad-to-meet-you, glad-to-meet-you.

His colleagues were unsure about his ability. He was slow, ponderous, and not quick with figures: when he made an interesting speech other bankers asked who wrote it. In conversation he was a master of bankers' platitudes. But within the anonymous bureaucracy of the Chase his regal presence filled a vacuum. He was a monarch superimposed on a republic, and he could personify a business that was becoming more deadeningly impersonal—like the British Queen at the head of Whitehall. Was the idea of a giant bank run by computers and statisticians too depressing to face? Certainly many colleagues were glad to portray David Rockefeller as more important in the bank than he was.

By 1960 he was president of the Chase and joint chief executive with George Champion, a veteran employee who was preoccupied with domestic expansion. The Chase had big investments in Manhattan real estate and in the mid-fifties they redeveloped part of the old Wall Street district which was decaying as business moved toward midtown. A sixty-story skyscraper of aluminum and glass rose above the old classical and gothic bankers' palaces: the biggest bank building in the world, with marble concourses, looked onto a Japanese garden and a two-and-a-half-acre Chase Manhattan Plaza, later decorated by a forty-foot fiberglass sculpture by Dubuffet. It was a civic display reminiscent of the great Florentine or Venetian palaces of the Renaissance.

Most of the skyscraper consisted of workaday offices and cubicles, but the seventeenth floor was a spectacular art gallery hung with post-Impressionists and contemporary American painters. At the end of a wide corridor a high glass door slid open and shut automatically; and behind it, surrounded by paintings round a huge square room, sat David Rockefeller. In his setting and style he seemed the very picture of the modern Medici, the magnificent prince and patron as well as banker; I felt that he talked about his

Rothko with more enthusiasm than he talked about his bank. But the comparison with Lorenzo the Magnificent was not altogether reassuring to shareholders, even though the collection soon multiplied its value. For was it not Machiavelli himself, when he chronicled the decline of the Medici bank, who noted the dangers of bankers adopting "the deportment of princes"?[4]

Rockefeller was ambitious in the international arena, and he and his bank had become increasingly closely associated with the Council on Foreign Relations in New York, which in the late forties became less dominated by the Morgan interests and more by the Rockefellers. David's father gave large sums to the council; in 1953 McCloy became chairman of the council at the same time that he took over the Chase, and in 1969–70 David also succeeded to both jobs.[5] David was also a founder in 1954, with Prince Bernhard and others, of the Bilderberg Conferences, which once a year brought together Western politicians, bankers, and businessmen; and in 1972 he initiated the Trilateral Commission, itself closely linked with the council, which brought together leaders in America, Europe, and Japan, with Zbigniew Brzezinski as its secretary. Rockefeller maintained his interest in Latin America, where he constantly stressed the need for expanding free enterprise. During the Vietnam War he joined the Committee for an Effective and Durable Peace in Asia, with two other former Chase men, McCloy and Eugene Black, to drum up financial support for the war; and Chase opened a branch in Saigon, built like a fortress, which Rockefeller himself opened. He remained an unswervingly conservative Republican. President Nixon asked him to be his Secretary of the Treasury; but (it was assumed) he thought himself more influential at the Chase.

With his great private wealth, his surname, his connections and constant exposure, it was hardly surprising that he should be at the center of conspiracy theories about Western capitalism. He was

---

[4]*History of Florence,* Book 8.
[5]For a critical inspection of the council, see Laurence H. Shoup and William Minter, *Imperial Brain Trust* (New York: Monthly Review Press, 1977).

much more visible than McCloy or other business statesmen. His royal tours extended not only to conservative capitals like Pretoria and Brasilia but later to Moscow and Peking, where he opened branches of the Chase. Everywhere he enjoyed access to the leaders as one prince to another. It looked magnificent, but was it really—many colleagues were beginning to wonder—good banking? For while Rockefeller was pursuing his regal career, the Chase was facing much tougher competition from its old rival.

CITIBANK

Citibank too had lived down the disgrace of the Great Crash, and extended itself to compete in the great boom of the fifties. The First National City Bank, as it was formally called, merged with the First National Bank of the City of New York, and the two absurdly similar names became the First National City Bank of New York, later thankfully shortened to Citibank. Like the Chase, it retained a very visible connection with Rockefellers—the "poor Rockefellers," as the younger branch liked to call themselves. While David was moving up through the Chase, Citibank in 1952 chose as president James Stillman Rockefeller, whose name commemorated two money dynasties: one grandfather was William Rockefeller, the other was James Stillman, who had built up Citibank earlier in the century. Stillman Rockefeller perpetuated the bank's tradition of aggression tempered by conservatism: he had a staid style, but flashes of his grandfather's ruthlessness. He expanded through the New York suburbs and moved closer to the ordinary consumer with easier access and loans. While Chase was constructing its palazzo near Wall Street, Citibank built its much less elegant new headquarters on Park Avenue, the new showplace of consumer capitalism.

It might seem odd that while Citibank and Chase were presenting themselves as people's banks they should both proclaim their links with the billionaire family which had been so reviled. But the "poor Rockefellers' " family holdings in Citibank were much less dominating than their rich cousins' in the Chase; and when Stillman Rockefeller moved up from president to chairman he encouraged a new generation of professional bankers to develop Citibank's empire at home and abroad. To plan Citibank's expansion overseas he appointed George Moore, an adventurous banker who later became president and who, it has been said, "did more than anyone else to create the new Citibank: the cold, dazzling, inventive world money machine."[6] Moore's most successful protégé was a young vice-president, Walter Wriston, who became head of the "European district." Moore taught Wriston that intelligent risk-taking was part of the essence of banking. "If we didn't have troubles," he told him, "we wouldn't have any high-price people around to solve them."

Wriston soon made his mark on Citibank as a driving profit-seeker who saw the world as his battleground. He was the son of a historian who became president of Brown University, and young Walter specialized in international law and diplomacy. He was proud of his historical perspective—rare among bankers—and he upstaged his colleagues with sophisticated jokes and quotations. But he was as aggressive as his predecessors, and passionate about free enterprise: "There is no power on earth like the power of the free marketplace," he explained, "and governments hate it, because they cannot control it."

Wriston realized that the big banks in New York were losing corporate business to the U.S. Treasury, which issued bills paying higher interest than the banks were allowed by the Fed; so he devised a new "negotiable certificate of deposit," which could offer competitive interest rates, and which could be bought and sold in the market. The CDs, as they were called, soon attracted billions of dollars back to the banks—particularly to Citibank. Wriston could take much of the credit for the profits which followed.

Wriston saw, too, that American banks were becoming much more interlocked with the rest of the world. "We looked at the problem as a global marketplace," as he later put it, "and not as

6John Brooks in *The New Yorker* (January 5, 1981).

a country trying to export out. And that perspective was and is changing our whole world."[7] In the first postwar decade Citibank had viewed Europe with pessimism, half expecting it to be overrun with Communists; but by the mid-fifties, with the new prosperity, the entrenchment of NATO, and the beginnings of the European Community, it moved further toward Europe, alongside the American multinationals. Under Moore and Wriston it rapidly expanded its offices and services, regaining and increasing the international network that it had lost in the thirties and taking up its old connections. In eight years it grew from 82 to 208 offices, from 27 to 61 countries. It was in the forefront of the American era.

By 1967 Wriston was president, and two years later chairman. He made a sharp contrast with his rival, David Rockefeller: he was lean, austere, and sardonic, disliking the bonhomie and glad-handing of bankers' banquets. He was determined to control his complex corporation through intricate monitoring, attention to profits, and actuarial balancing of risks. He insisted that Citibank was a meritocracy, a collegial group in which his own power was very circumscribed: "People have a very peculiar view about the importance of any single individual in a very complicated society."[8] He did not see the world in terms of princes. "I go and see lots of prime ministers," he explained, "but to go in and talk to one as if you were a government is ridiculous."[9]

Wriston was determined that Citibank should keep on growing, and in 1968 he assured his shareholders that earnings per share would go up by 15 percent a year. It was a vaguer promise than it sounded, for earnings could be differently defined; but it was still rash, for any bank's profits depend on the economic climate; and his rivals warned that it would press him to take too many risks. But at first Wriston could fulfill his promise without much strain, while Citibank raced ahead in New York and overseas. His aggres-

[7]Interview with William Clarke, *Euromoney* (July 1978).
[8]Interview with author, June 13, 1980.
[9]*Euromoney* (July 1978), p. 86.

sive tactics in the old tradition of Stillman and Mitchell were producing high dividends, and by the early seventies "the Citibank syndrome" was making its mark in other banks.

Citibank with its growing profits came to be called "Fat City," but it was a misleading nickname. The bank's style was lean and hungry, with the predatory instincts of its chairman; and the mounting pressures of New York, with too many big banks chasing too few depositors, increased its aggression. Wriston was the subject of endless speculation among rivals. "He's very courageous," said one veteran banker, "but not very subtle: he may go too far." "I often wonder what Walter really thinks will happen," said another; "by forcing free enterprise to its limits, will he force governments to intervene?" He remains the most outspokenly articulate of the big bankers, and his remarks provide a recurring commentary in the following chapters. He likes to play down the political role of the bankers: "There's less in this than meets the eye."

The old competition between Citibank and Chase became tenser with the higher stakes of the world marketplace. David Rockefeller was more interested in high-level diplomacy than in certificates of deposit or detailed bank controls and when he became chairman of the Chase he chose a gentlemanly president, Herbert Patterson, who managed the internal workings of the bank. But the aggressiveness of Citibank—and of other New York banks—was showing worrying results. In terms of total deposits Chase and Citibank had been running closer for the past decade. By 1968 Chase had deposits of $16.7 billion, against $16.6 billion in Citibank. The next year Citibank overtook Chase for the first time. By 1970 Chase had crept up to the lead again, but by 1971 Citibank had leapt ahead with a new inrush of foreign deposits, showing $24.3 billion against $20.4 in Chase; and from then on Citibank maintained its lead. Chase's earnings were still more disappointing to stockholders: in the first six months of 1972 they went up by only 1 percent, against 16 percent for Citibank.

Rockefeller, progressing grandly around the world while his bank's profits declined, was now depicted as a figure of fun by his rivals. "We love David," one Citibanker said; "the longer he stays away the happier we are." By October 1972 something had to be done, and Rockefeller summoned a press conference in the Chase boardroom, where he told an amazed gathering that Patterson would be replaced as president by the young vice-chairman, Willard Butcher. "It was a stunning move by Rockefeller," commented *Business Week,* "indeed a brutal one by the standards of big business and banks, where discarded top managers are allowed to gently fade away." Some critics suggested that it was not Patterson who should have gone but Rockefeller.

CLAUSEN: THE GRANITE HEART?

In the business center of San Francisco a brown granite cliff with zigzag sides had risen up from the banking district, a symbol of the institutional solidity of the Bank of America: a plaque explained that it was dedicated to the philosophy of its founder, A. P. Giannini: "To serve the needs of others—the only legitimate business in the world today." Inside, its lofty spaces were designed to impress the visitor with the bank's wealth and resources; the World Banking Division on the second floor, which receives foreign dignitaries, has a red-carpeted expanse the whole length of the building, the size of a football field, with only a few tiny-looking desks and typists in the way. In the piazza outside the main entrance is a huge sculpture of rounded and polished granite: taxi drivers called it "the bankers' heart."

The bank's citadel turns its brown back on the exuberance of the city outside it, with a more extreme contrast than the Chase or Citibank on Manhattan. While San Francisco and the Coast became wilder and more uncontrollable, attracting Berkeley dropouts, erotic museums, radical radio stations, and far-out art, the Bank of America was unchangingly conservative, constantly preoccupied with the questions of control—budget control, expense control, credit control, people control. It imposed a legendary discipline on its employees, checking on their eight-to-five hours, excluding all oddballs, prohibiting overdrafts. The showy skyscraper was misleading, for in spite of (or because of) its size, the B of A adopted a profile so low that it sometimes seemed to be sinking below the Pacific.

It might seem a paradox that a bank with such publicized and populist beginnings should become so austere, so rigidly controlled, and so secretive. But Giannini's extraordinary adventure, trying to bring order and organization to the rash and hectic promotion of California, called for exceptional discipline. Having grown up as a neighborhood bank it was determined to maintain its principle of "know thy neighbor," while its branches multiplied and its business diversified across the state. After Giannini had retired as chairman in 1945 the bank soon lost any special Italian flavor and was run by committees of bankers from very different backgrounds. The bank settled into a careful anonymity; while its early history under Giannini is lovingly narrated in one of the liveliest bank histories,[10] its subsequent story remains officially unrecorded. It had lost much of its populist appeal, and as a major factor in California's agribusiness and aerospace it was feared by and attacked from the left.

In 1970 a new president and chief executive officer emerged from the enclosed bureaucracy. Tom Clausen was a law graduate from Minnesota who had spent his career inside the bank, working up through the departments. Like a good bank manager he combined a genial style and personal kindness with an ice-cold approach to his business. His profile, too, was low,[11] and his life was encircled by the bank: he was an obsessive worker, a perfectionist obsessed by control. He ruled by committee and talked in sporting terms about the team spirit: even his wife he described as a "good team player." But with his mastery of detail, his

[10]Marquis and Bessie James, Biography of a Bank (New York: Harper & Row, 1954).
[11]He was the only banker, to my regret, who did not feel able to see me for this book. As his PR man Robert Nichols explained on his behalf to me in July 1980: "I have looked at Mr. Clausen's calendar for the remainder of the year, and regret that I find all time available for interviews and meetings with media has been already spoken for."

impassive expression and curt style he could easily overawe his colleagues—particularly in the morning. "All my life it's been difficult for me to say 'Hello' or 'Good morning' until ten o'clock coffee," he once revealed with rare indiscretion, but by late afternoon "I'm very mellow." "If he calls me in the morning," one of his vice-chairmen, Joseph Carrera, admitted, "my secretary tells him I'm not in."[12]

Clausen was aware that the bank's image in San Francisco was not glittering, and by 1977 he approved a new code promising more disclosure and a program to project a corporate character "reflecting reliable performance, credibility, progressiveness, and social responsibility." He explained, "We think we will come across better talking to the press than not talking to the press."[13] But the next year the vice-chairman of the bank, Alvin Rice, abruptly resigned after a row with Clausen and rumors of "conflict of interest." There was a deafening silence from the bank, Rice disappeared—whoops!—through the corporate trapdoor, and the "Rice affair" remained clouded in mystery.

Clausen wanted his bank to extend from local retail banking toward wholesale banking and international lending, but he eschewed Rockefeller's kind of global political exposure and Wriston's race for sheer size and "growth for growth's sake." "While egos may be rewarded by size," he explained, "shareholders are rewarded by earnings and dividends, which are a good deal harder to come by." He could afford to be more relaxed, since his bank was already the biggest in the world; and he had a much more solid base—his "rock of Gibraltar," as he called it—of deposits in a thousand branches which amounted to nearly half of all banking deposits in California. With this security he did not need to compete frenziedly for depositors like the New Yorkers, and by 1977 the Bank of America comfortably overtook Citibank to show the biggest profits—as well as assets—of any American bank.

[12] *The Wall Street Journal,* March 23, 1979.
[13] *The Washington Post,* March 19, 1978.

He remained very competitive. He believed that bankers were too caught up in the herd, and that the secret of success lay in finding business which others overlooked. Like many others he felt hemmed in by the controls which confined banks to their own states and limited their services: "With each financial crisis, it seems, the regulators added a few more bars to our cages." Like the others he expanded rapidly abroad—though more prudently, with an elaborate structure of decentralized "building blocks." He looked southward to Latin America and westward to the Pacific basin, where the Bank of America saw its special destiny, and he established a European regional headquarters in London, near St. Paul's Cathedral, which was to play an important part in future expansion.

In his view of the world, Clausen was conscious of the past hazards and challenges of California. He liked to compare banking to Vince Lombardi's view of football: "Football is two things: it's blocking and tackling." "We have to take risks. That's our business. But if we analyze them properly and price them right, our banks will remain sound. . . ."[14]

He saw that the hectic development of California in the thirties had some resemblance to the present risks in the Third World. He liked to recall how the Bank of America lent money to the young Walt Disney and to Henry Kaiser when he was a fledgling entrepreneur, and how Giannini helped California to become the "fruit and vegetable basket of the nation." "Today similar 'risky' loans are helping farmers develop the resources that will feed tomorrow's generations."[15] As he became more involved with the Third World, he was unexpectedly outspoken about the problems of poverty. "Industrial countries as a group simply have not rallied to the aid of poverty-stricken nations and peoples," he said in Nairobi in 1973. "The poorest nations and the poorest people will be penalized most." His concern became more important when

[14]Speech to the Bank Administration Institute, Los Angeles, November 5, 1979.
[15]Los Angeles Times, March 14, 1976.

he took over as president of the World Bank in 1981 (see page 392).

From his California stronghold Clausen showed a less power-conscious view of the world than Wriston or Rockefeller, but a more measured one; his bank, with the security of its domestic deposits, was to survive the roller-coaster years of the seventies with fewer blunders and traumas than the New Yorkers. Behind his bland style he had his own vision of the opportunities of banking, quoting Lombardi again: "If you aren't *fired* with enthusiasm, you'll be fired with *enthusiasm.*" The view of the developing world as a vast new California might have some advantages for developing countries.

THE HERD

These three giants and their other rivals still made most of their loans within the United States, where they could relatively easily assess the risks of their clients; but even on their home ground they could be surprisingly casual in their lending. In a series of domestic banking fiascos in the sixties the most notorious was the case of the Penn Central Railroad, which had been created by a merger in February 1968. The company soon made heavy losses, and by April next year Citibank led a consortium including the Chemical Bank and Manufacturers Hanover, which provided a revolving credit of $300 million, with very little investigation into the security of the railroad. It was now losing $25 million a month and concealing its losses by selling off real estate, but the banks assumed—as they so often later assumed—that the government would have to rescue an indispensable company if it were in serious trouble. The next year Citibank refused an extra loan, but the Chemical Bank amazingly agreed to lead a new "bridge loan" of $50 million with no real security. Soon afterward the railroad tottered toward bankruptcy. The Nixon Administration tried to save it by arranging a loan from the Navy Department on the grounds of national security. But the Federal Reserve Bank in New York, having looked into the chaos of the company's books, could not authorize any loan, and the railroad collapsed into "the single largest bankruptcy in our nation's history," as Congressman Harley Staggers described it, which had a "major impact on our national economy."[16] In the subsequent outcry, the banks—particularly the "Comical Bank," as it was now dubbed—were castigated for their failure to question the railroad's security. They had shown all their traditional tendency to cling together till the last moment, all making the wrong assumptions about Washington's policies—as they were later to make over New York City itself (see Chapter 9). As Gabriel Hauge of Manny Hanny put it: "The bankers had a herd instinct for trouble."[17]

In the course of the sixties all the big banks began to lend further abroad, projecting a global image with their advertising. The Chase proclaimed itself as "The Bank with the Worldwide Reach"; the Bank of America had its "Man on the Spot" in the capitals of the world; Citibankers were shown against the backgrounds of European ruins: "Historians concentrate on Rome's past. Citibankers concentrate on its busy present and bright future." The Europeans were bewildered by the money salesmen from across the Atlantic who sold loans like cornflakes and crossed frontiers as casually as if they were state lines. The Americans regarded Europe as a single entity much more readily than the Europeans themselves did; they saw it in their own image, as a new kind of United States, and their confidence was rewarded.

But as the herd moved further afield into the developing world they faced far more complex and political troubles than the collapse of a New York railroad. The giant banks found themselves becoming major actors in a different kind of drama, playing a role in new, unformed countries and coming up against emotional governments, ambitious aid projects, and the burgeoning activity of international institutions.

[16]Staff Report of the SEC, "The Financial Collapse of the Penn Central Company" (Washington, 1972), p. 3.
[17]See Martin Mayer, The Bankers, paperback ed. (New York: Ballantine, 1976), p. 320. Chapter 12 gives a vivid account of the domestic problems of American banks at this time.

6
THE OTHER WORLD

Who can now ask where his country will be in a few decades
without asking where the world will be?

Pearson Report, 1969

The World Bank in Washington, after its first conservative years
under Meyer and McCloy, was beginning to acquire a more emphatic character, distinct from that of the East Coast bankers, with
its own cautious blend of commerce and idealism. The decisive
change came in 1949 with the presidency of Eugene Black, who
had previously been the American executive director. Black was
a tall, stylish Southerner from Georgia who had been vice-president of the Chase, and who stuck strictly to orthodox banking
principles, in terms of the bank's charter. The bank could only
lend for specific projects, whose results were tangible, and foreign
governments had to guarantee the repayment of loans—so that
the bank took only a minimal risk. Black was a vain man, very
vulnerable to flattery; when he asked his favorite author, James
Morris, to write a book on the bank, Morris wrote that he "never
seemed to resent, or even perhaps to notice, the sycophancy that
attended him at H Street."[1] He dominated the bank as if it were
his own personal club: making loans was a leisurely and personal
business, and signing was celebrated by a party. Officially the
World Bank was a specialized agency of the UN, "within the
meaning of Article 59 of the charter"; but few people would have
guessed it, looking at the array of American bankers, English ex-
colonial servants, and assorted experts who made up this very
Anglo-American club. Black himself arrived with no special expe-

[1]James Morris, *The World Bank* (London: Faber & Faber, 1963).

rience of the Third World; his attitudes were essentially conservative, and when he retired he became director of several corporations, including ITT.

But Black nevertheless moved the World Bank decisively in
the direction of lending to developing countries, with a determi-
nation which was to have a gathering momentum. The bank was
still officially called the International Bank for Reconstruction
and Development (IBRD); but Marshall Aid had taken over most
of the reconstruction business, and Black saw that the most critical need for development was in the Third World. With all his
banker's prudence, he began lending, not just to "safe" countries like Australia and Canada, but to more doubtful developing
countries, beginning with Colombia and Peru. As the World
Bank began financing dams, ports, and roads in remote countries, Black realized that he needed to know much more about
their backgrounds; and the bank began building up a store of
information about their economic conditions, their debts, inflation, and political problems. Its loans were small compared with
the government loans from Washington, London, and Paris; but
it acquired an importance beyond its resources as the arbiter of
world credit, the provider of advice and technical skills as much
as money.

Black, with his own panache, was able to give a kind of glamour
and prestige to the bank which attracted very able young men. No
one could accuse them of being woolly-minded do-gooders; the
bank never had a bad debt, and it was much more cautious than
the commercial banks, lending no more than its total capital. But
the "Black Man," as he was sometimes jokingly called, generated
a sense of excitement about operating on the frontiers of the
world, and dealing with explosive foreign potentates.

The bank was soon caught up in political problems. Because it
gave multilateral loans, its help was more acceptable to many
developing countries as a more neutral source of funds; but its
neutrality was limited, for the United States was by far its biggest
source of borrowing while Europe was still recovering its own
strength. Congress was constantly complaining, particularly over

projects with heavy diplomatic significance. In 1955 Black agreed to join the American and British governments in financing the Aswan Dam in Egypt, which was intended "to keep the Russians out of Africa"; he promised to lend $200 million at 5 percent. But when the British and Americans withdrew, after Egypt began to move toward Moscow, the World Bank was forced to withdraw too, to the chagrin of Black. For the first time the West had used aid openly as a policy weapon in the developing world;[2] and the withdrawal soon precipitated Egypt's nationalization of the Suez Canal and the subsequent disastrous Suez War.

The World Bank was strictly businesslike in its lending, insisting on commercial interest rates and prompt repayment. But most of the new developing countries were outside the bankers' pale, quite unable to pay the interest or to guarantee the loans. Two of the most populous countries, India and Pakistan, which were politically crucial to the West, were in desperate need of loans, but hopelessly uncredit-worthy by normal bankers' standards. In Washington the Senate was pressing for more lenient loans to save the Third World from Communism; and as a result, the World Bank established in 1960 a new agency, the International Development Association. IDA was run by the World Bank, but it offered "soft" loans requiring interest of only three-quarters percent a year, which could be repaid over fifty years. The funds came from nineteen of the richer countries, led by the United States, and would be lent to over eighty of the poorer countries, with *per capita* incomes of less than $375 a year; in the next twelve years IDA lent $4.4 billion to these countries—over half to India and Pakistan. IDA was the poor man's bank, which could combine businesslike methods with lenient terms; and it relieved the World Bank of its charitable obligations. But its continuity was much more uncertain, for its funds had to be "replenished" every three years with a new vote; and in the harsher years to come Congress became much more hard-nosed, trying to insist that IDA

[2]See Hugh Thomas, *The Suez Affair* (London: Weidenfeld & Nicolson, 1967), p. 25.

must use American goods, and cutting down the World Bank's requests.

AID

The World Bank and IDA were only providing a few drops in the ocean of the developing world; and as the former colonies achieved their independence in the fifties and sixties, the richer countries became increasingly involved in what was vaguely known as "aid." Aid was altogether a new concept, unfamiliar to prewar governments and bankers except in the form of missionary societies, the Red Cross, or occasional generous foreign loans; the word "aid" only became regularly used in the sense of foreign assistance during the Second World War, as in American "aid" to Britain.

But aid was now covering a multitude of different activities and motives—a blend of national self-interest, commercial ambitions, and genuine concern with poverty and starvation. The former imperial powers wanted to maintain their political links and markets, and continued to provide some of the old colonial services. The smaller European nations like the Scandinavians and the Dutch saw an opportunity to make diplomatic and commercial friendships without resentments about domination. West Germany felt the need to extend diplomatic connections as she became again a world industrial power. And the United States saw the need for a network of military and political alliances in its global fight against Communism. But in all the donor countries there was a recurring debate as to how far aid should be disinterested, and how far they should expect commercial returns.

Some of the early expectations of aid and development had tragic outcomes. The propaganda of anticolonialism had encouraged Africans and Asians to believe that they could inherit a new age of plenty with economic as well as political independence, and many new leaders were glad to provide at least the show of new wealth. The first new African nation, Ghana, was the focus of extravagant hopes, not only of Western idealists, but of businessmen and even bankers. Its flamboyant leader, Kwame Nkrumah, became the prophet of "Africanism" and the new "African way of doing things"; he built palaces, a stadium, a new harbor, a dam, and twelve miles of motorway, encouraged by generous loans, grants, bribes, and the prospects for cocoa which depended on the chocolate eaters in the West. But the cocoa price fell, the debts mounted, and Nkrumah became increasingly megalomaniac while his ministers enriched themselves: one of them was soon found to have bought a golden bed from a London store. Within ten years Ghana was virtually bankrupt, in pawn to the bankers, and it never recovered from the weight of its debts. Ghana became a favorite case history for critics of aid, and the golden bed became a symbol of the corruption of the Third World. But the blame for the tragedy of Ghana lay on both sides: it had been caused by corruption and carelessness from Western adventurers, as much as by Ghanaians.

America was far the biggest provider of aid, particularly after the International Development Act of 1950, which promised "to aid the efforts of the people of economically underdeveloped areas to develop their resources and improve their living conditions." In the Kennedy years in the early sixties the American enthusiasm for aid reached its peak. Kennedy was determined that aid should not be linked to short-term security as it had been under Eisenhower and Dulles. "If we undertake this effort in the wrong spirit," he warned, "or for the wrong reasons, or in the wrong way, then any and all financial measures will be in vain"; and he wanted to show that "economic growth and political democracy can develop hand in hand." He reorganized aid in a new Agency for International Development, called AID, whose aims would be divorced from military support. He established the new Peace Corps, run by his brother-in-law Sargent Shriver, which sent thousands of young Americans into the Third World. And the prevailing optimism was reflected by the UN General Assembly, which adopted a historic resolution in 1960, based on the recommendation of the World Council of Churches, proposing that the rich countries should spend at least 1 percent of their national income on grants and concessional loans to the Third World.

Kennedy was inevitably most concerned with Latin America, where Castro's revolution in Cuba and his propaganda through the continent posed a challenge to American capitalism. Eisenhower had already set up the Inter-American Bank along the lines of the World Bank to provide loans for development on a commercial basis; but Kennedy wanted to show that American capital could be accompanied by social progress, and in August 1961 his ambitious new Alliance for Progress was proclaimed at the meeting of Latin American states at Punta del Este in Uruguay. Kennedy's message emphasized that this was a revolutionary program which recognized everyone's rights to progress: "We meet to carry on that revolution to shape the future." At the meeting Douglas Dillon, the former banker who headed the American delegation, was confronted by the Cuban guerrilla leader Che Guevara, who told the Latin Americans that they must thank Cuba for America's sudden generosity, but that being an instrument of imperialism it was bound to fail. But twenty Latin American nations signed the charter of the Alliance for Progress. It promised to stimulate private enterprise and accelerate economic development, but also to strengthen democratic institutions, redistribute land, and provide decent homes. The United States pledged itself to provide most of the $20 billion over ten years.

It was a test case in benevolent capitalism. "No money lender in history has ever evoked greater enthusiasm," Kennedy's aide Morales-Carrión reported to him the next year, adding, "We have yet to see a charismatic banker." But there were soon severe disappointments. The Alliance began just as the prices of commodities were falling—coffee was soon down to 60 percent of its price in 1953—so that much of the new money was needed to balance the payments. The biggest country, Brazil, was in political turmoil under President Goulart, and by 1966 was once again under a military government. American bankers were very skeptical about social reform. Kennedy had asked David Rockefeller, who was very active with his own business, to organize the Business Group for Latin America; but Rockefeller was critical of the "overly ambitious concepts of revolutionary change," and the ideas of the program's organizer, Teodoro Moscoso. Rockefeller wanted the Alliance to concern itself less with social reform and more with furthering business interests; and a year after it was launched a Chase Manhattan report warned that the emphasis on government projects would discourage private incentive. The flow of American investments was already diminishing, as business leaders became more opposed to the program; and the ambitious original plan was soon reduced to a more conventional commercial initiative which (as Rockefeller described it in 1966) "created a climate more attractive to U.S. business."[3] The Alliance achieved some tax reform, more effective planning and economic integration; but it never reached its targets for land reform, education, or literacy, or the expected annual growth rate of 2.5 percent. "Eight years after the signing of the Charter," said the Pearson Report in 1969, "disillusion with the Alliance is widespread."

THE DEVELOPING WORLD

While much of Latin America was becoming economically independent, the vast majority of the world's population lay beyond the pale of any ordinary bankers—too uncredit-worthy to qualify for their loans, too politically unstable, or too shut off from the Western commercial system by the iron curtain. The Communist bloc had its own self-contained trading system known as COMECON, or CMEA, which embraced Eastern Europe and had its own links with Communist China. The components of the European empires—British, French, Dutch, or Portuguese—were gradually emerging into independence, but most of them were too poor to attract commercial loans or to achieve economic independence. They kept links with their former rulers, but tried to

[3]See Collier and Horowitz, *The Rockefellers,* pp. 412–14. Also Arthur Schlesinger, *A Thousand Days* (Boston: Houghton Mifflin, 1965), pp. 652–80.

achieve some independence or "non-alignment" with West and East, in what was becoming known as the Third World. In the climate of the cold war both East and West were concerned with their economic development.

Development was the new word for progress, with the same kind of optimism and ambiguities; and every new nation was now preoccupied with the same ambition. The terminology was very sensitive: the countries which were first described as "backward" or simply "poor" were later called undeveloped, then less developed or "LDCs" or "developing"[4] as opposed to the richer or "developed" nations; and the world was now confusingly classified between developing and developed nations ("developing" was even more awkward in the French *"en voie de développement"*). The division was often misleading: large parts of many "developing" countries, like Brazil, were becoming as rich as many of the "developed" countries in Europe. For other countries the word "developing" was really a euphemism: as Gunnar Myrdal put it in 1968: "By using a term that presupposes that these very poor countries *are* developing, an important question is begged."[5]

Yet the preoccupation with the word *development* reflected a critical change in the world's vision of itself. The new countries were determined to catch up or to narrow the gaps with the industrialized powers, which in turn felt some obligation to help them. And the gaps could be measured, however crudely, by calculating growth rates or gross national product per head. As the world contracted, circumscribed by the rapid communications and common statistics, every part of it was being measured in terms of money. The economists had taken over from anthropologists and missionaries as the experts and interpreters of Africa and Asia, providing their assessments for the World Bank, individual governments, or the expanding "development community." But

[4]The Supplement to the *Oxford English Dictionary* (1972) gives the first use of "developing country" in this sense in 1964, but it was clearly already established by then.

[5]*Asian Drama*, abridged paperback ed. (London: Penguin, 1972), p. 8.

there were still huge imponderables in assessing the future behavior of the developing world, which could not be left to the economists alone. As Gunnar Myrdal lamented:

> It is indeed a remarkable fact, testifying to the damaging compartmentalisation of the social sciences and the insularity of traditional economics, that after the second world war economists could build up a theory of development based solely on physical investment—a theory so incapable of explaining the process of economic growth that a group of them later "discovered" investment in man.[6]

The language of development implied that the whole world was in the process of developing toward the goal of a developed world, and the word *develop* re-echoed like a litany through the speeches. But economists, influenced by Walt Rostow, became less confident that this process could ever be achieved: as the American economist Simon Kuznets said when he received his Nobel Prize in 1973:

> The very magnitudes, as well as some of the basic conditions, are quite different; no country that entered modern economic growth (except Russia) approached the size of India or China, or even of Pakistan and Indonesia; and no currently developed country had to adjust to the very high rates of natural increase of population that have characterised many less developed countries over the last two decades.[7]

The new nations chose various models for their development. Some looked to the United States and Western Europe as the originators of industry and innovation; some to the Soviet Union for massive industrialization by the state; some to Japan as a close-knit network of private corporations interlocked with the

[6]*Ibid.,* p. 299.
[7]Simon Kuznets, "Modern Economic Growth: Findings and Reflections," *American Economic Review,* LXIII, June 1973, p. 255.

state. Each model could be tragically misleading. The earlier industrial nations had grown up in an emptier world of greater opportunity, and the emphasis on industrialization could be disastrous for rural countries depending on agriculture.

India was the biggest question mark of all; and since its independence its prosperity had become a pressing concern for Western governments and the World Bank. Why did most of India remain sunk in poverty and turned in on itself when Japan for instance had leapt so rapidly ahead, exposed to the outside world? Milton Friedman, the zealot of free enterprise, had little doubt about the chief difference: India was committed to central economic planning, on the model of postwar Britain; while Japan had taken off eighty years earlier, by competing globally and encouraging free markets on the model of Victorian Britain. "The real tragedy of India," Friedman said, "is that it remains a sub-continent teeming with desperately poor people when it could, we believe, be a flourishing, vigorous increasingly prosperous and free society."[8]

But could all the complexities of India, with all its ancient religions, traditions and deep self-involvement, be reduced to a simple question of choice between economic policies? For there was always another question: did India really *want* to become part of the Western economic system? Could this vast rural population become rapidly industrialized without wrecking its society? If it really began to export goods on the scale of Japan, could the world accommodate such a vast new flood of textiles or electronics? And was it possible for a democratic country to impose the necessary disciplines? As Mrs. Gandhi put it to me:

It was all right for Japan, with a great deal of American money and help and a population which was basically very disciplined. But we have started off with a political revolution which gave people a lot of political consciousness about rights and nothing about discipline, or responsibility or obligation. In the West you had your industrial revolution first; there was no question of rights of the

[8] *Free to Choose,* p. 81.

workers at that time, they were thoroughly exploited. But we have started at a time when that is the first aspect: you can ignore it a bit, but not much. This is why many of our public sector undertakings have to overspend for housing and other such facilities.[9]

Huge areas of the world had little prospect of becoming "bankable," or linked to the economic system of the West—and specially the countries which the United Nations came to call the "least-developed countries," whose incomes (in 1970) were less than a hundred dollars per head. Most of them were to be found in the two "poverty belts" made up of land-locked countries in Africa and Asia; the African belt stretched from the Sahara in the north to Lake Nyasa in the south; the Asian belt stretched from the two Yemens through Afghanistan to South Asia. The people in these territories, surviving in harsh climates or deserts with minimal crops, were in no position to benefit from the expansion of world trade, from the demand for minerals, or from commercial loans. To international bankers they were the global equivalent of the slums in American cities, which local bankers "redlined" as being uncredit-worthy. There was no alternative to some sort of aid if they were eventually to fend for themselves.

However skeptical the rich countries might be about their prospects, there were powerful economic as well as compassionate reasons for helping these poorest territories. For in their search for fuel and food many tribes were destroying the environment on which they depended, in a vicious circle of poverty leading to still greater poverty. The up-rooted trees and bushes caused the Sahara to encroach, mile upon mile, onto once habitable land, and the floods swept down the Himalayas with still greater fury. As the West became more concerned with conserving the world's resources, and the environmentalists joined with the economists, the needs visibly increased while the aid diminished.

[9]Interview with author, October 1980.

UNITED NATIONS

The hopes of the Third World were centered on the institution only a few blocks away from the headquarters of the New York banks, which represented an almost opposite approach to the world. In the first postwar years the West saw the United Nations primarily as the arena for arguments between the two superpowers, but after a succession of large and small nations had achieved independence, the UN became the chief forum for pressing their views and needs on the rest of the world. The great semicircle of the General Assembly filled up with delegations from African and Asian states with new names, and the delegates' lounge became the social meeting place for the hundreds of new diplomats. None of the founders had foreseen the scale of this proliferation when they established the principle of one nation, one vote.

The UN soon evolved its own intricate language, which was hard for outsiders to decode. Official documents were worded in a dry neutral style acceptable to both capitalist and Communist countries (or "centrally planned economies," as they soon insisted on being called). And the General Assembly became the megaphone for high-flown resolutions attacking the more powerful members but unrelated to likely action. Western diplomats were exasperated to find more and more nations, smaller and smaller islands and enclaves, hurling speeches across the floor which were a compound of Marxism, anticolonialism, and home-grown hyperbole. To the cautious World Bankers in Washington, who were evolving their own coded and muted language to discreetly describe the problems of their client states, these outbursts were anathema.

It was not surprising that the new nations should put such faith in words. Words, after all, had been the artillery of their own liberation, representing ideas which had transformed continents. But the new leaders of independent states faced more intransigent enemies than their colonial oppressors, confronting the harsh facts of world commerce, of unbalanced payments, uncreditworthiness, and mountains of debts. They waged their paper war against the rich nations, bombarding them with salvos of speeches and documents while their arsenals of Xerox machines delivered still more ammunition. The language became more ferocious and strident as the effectiveness became less certain. But the Western finance ministers and bankers who faced this verbal gunfire were increasingly immune; their instructions from their governments were simply to stand firm, and give nothing away:

> Sticks and stones may break my bones,
> But words will never hurt me.

By the late fifties there was already a confrontation between the rich and poor countries. The new nations were coming to believe that their future prosperity would depend less on pleading for aid and more on uniting to achieve fairer terms of trade and higher prices for their raw materials—rather as the labor unions in the last century had turned to collective bargaining. The prophet of the new thinking was an Argentinian economist, Raul Prebisch, who had first made his mark when at only thirty-four he ran the new Central Bank in Buenos Aires, the youngest central banker in the world. After the war he became secretary of the UN's Economic Commission for Latin America, where he propounded his theories that the terms of trade had been moving in favor of the richer countries ever since the late nineteenth century, which could only be reversed by organized pressure. His ideas received a cutting edge after a steep drop in commodity prices, when the UN resolved in 1962 to summon a special conference on trade. It was to be called by the initials UNCT; but the Americans complained that this would imply encouraging East-West trade, and eventually the Indian delegate L. K. Jha suggested it be called the United Nations Conference on Trade and Development, or UNCTAD. (The initials were later given other meanings, including Under No Circumstances Take Any Decision.) The first conference in 1964 resolved to form a permanent secretariat with its headquarters in Geneva, headed by Raul Prebisch.

UNCTAD became the chief forum for resolutions and demands for better terms of trade. The developing countries formed their own majority caucus inside UNCTAD, called the "Group of 77" —which kept that name even after it grew to over a hundred— which became their chief commercial lobby. The group ranged from booming industrial nations in Latin America to barely populated desert territories in Africa, but they were determined—again like the unions—to maintain their unity in their bargaining with the Western industrial nations (the Communist bloc, being more self-contained, played a less important role). They devised carefully negotiated formulas for "remedial arrangements" or "the stabilization of commodity prices at remunerative levels," which they pressed on the West. "Unctalk" was a private language of obscure formulations mixed with strident demands, which reflected all the difficulties of reaching agreement among a hundred nations. But behind it lay the desperate predicament of countries where sudden falls in the prices of coffee, copper, or tea, which meant a few cents or pence in the supermarkets of the West, could make the difference between life and death.

GRAND ASSIZE

By the late sixties many of the high hopes about development and aid were fading. In the United States the idealism of the Kennedy years was overtaken by the Vietnam War; in Britain the Labour government, with its ambitious new Ministry of Overseas Development, had to cut back its plans after Britain's own economic setbacks. Europeans and Americans were becoming more doubtful about the benefits of aid, with the stories about wastage, corruption, and vast inequality; while the relentless growth of population made the Third World look like a bottomless pit. "Like a thief in the night," said Asoka Mehta of the Indian Planning Commission, "population growth can rob us of all that we achieve, day after day, in economic growth."

By 1967 George Woods, who had succeeded Black as president of the World Bank, was sufficiently concerned to propose a "grand assize" to assess the results of twenty years of aid, and to "propose policies which will work better in the future." A year later the World Bank set up a commission chaired by Lester Pearson, the Canadian ex-prime minister, with seven other men (including two bankers) from three continents: Sir Edward Boyle, the British Tory ex-cabinet minister; Roberto Campos, the Brazilian economist and ambassador to Washington; Douglas Dillon, the New York banker; Wilfried Guth, of the Deutsche Bank; Professor Arthur Lewis, the Jamaican economist; Robert Marjolin, the former vice-president of the European Community; and Saburo Okita, the Japanese economist. Arthur Lewis persuaded the others that the problem "could be licked": Dillon was orthodox and bankerlike, but Guth was much more flexible and more concerned with the Third World.

Without too much anguish they managed to agree on a report called *Partners in Development,* which summed up the state of the world at the end of the sixties. The developing countries, they found, had progressed far better than was generally realized. Between 1950 and 1967 they had increased their gross domestic product at a rate of 4.8 percent a year—much faster than Western countries during their nineteenth-century booms (Britain had grown by 2 percent a year between 1790 and 1820, Germany at 2.7 percent between 1850 and 1880. Even Japan had only reached 4 percent between 1876 and 1900). A few countries had grown much faster, led by Taiwan with an annual increase of 9 percent. The richer countries had contributed much aid: "Never before have so many concerned themselves with the task of improving the lot of mankind." But the gap between the richest and poorest countries was still widening. The staggering growth of population, so unforeseen twenty years earlier, showed little sign of subsiding. Much aid had been misdirected, too much had been spent on industry, too little on agriculture; while exports from the Third World, as a proportion of world exports, had actually declined.

And the richer Western countries—the report pointed out—were now spending proportionately less of their income on aid, in a climate which was "heavy with disillusion and distrust." The United States, still far the biggest giver, was now contributing less, disappointed with the results of earlier aid, which had been linked to security or short-term political favors. The Third World was frustrated and impatient; "On all sides," the commissioners reported, "we sense a weariness and a search for new directions." Urgent steps must be taken, not only out of moral obligations, but for reasons of enlightened self-interest. The interdependence of nations and the acceleration of history must change people's concept of national interest. The world was now a village.

The commissioners emphasized the benefits of private enterprise—"dollar for dollar, it may be more effective than official aid"—and they foresaw a time when capital markets and direct investment would take over most development: "It is fundamental to our strategy that the need for aid should eventually subside." But in the meantime private investment was no alternative to public aid. They insisted that proper aid ("official development assistance") should go up from its average 0.39 percent of GNP in 1968 to an average of 0.7 percent by 1975; and this target became the most publicized element in their report. But the first requirement for development, they stressed, was expanding world trade. The richer countries must reduce their import duties, help to finance "buffer stocks" of commodities, and abolish their quotas for manufactures from the Third World.

The Third World welcomed the Pearson Report as a sign that Western leaders were ready to make some serious concessions. But the hopes were soon dashed. The United States was preoccupied with the Vietnam War. The optimism of Kennedy and Johnson was followed by the defensive skepticism of Nixon. All the Western nations except the Scandinavias and Holland fell short of the target for aid.

The developing countries were becoming disillusioned with the West's willingness to help them, and more militant in their demands for fairer terms of trade. And they were asking more fundamental questions about the world economic system that had been set up at Bretton Woods.

THE MONEY MANDARINS

The other pillar of Bretton Woods, the International Monetary Fund, had only gradually become involved with the problems of the Third World. The six purposes of its charter included "the development of the productive resources of all members"; but it was at first mainly preoccupied with Western Europe, particularly France and Britain. It was constructed, in contrast to the UN, as a rich man's club. Its voting rights were roughly proportionate to the quotas (or contributions) that members paid into it, which gave America and Western Europe an overwhelming weight. It was mainly concerned with upholding financial discipline, coordinating national monetary policies, and preventing economic warfare. Its constitution ensured that it followed the principle: "To him that hath, shall be given."

Commercial bankers were inclined to see the IMF as an extending of the discipline and safeguards of the central banks inside each nation. It was to be a "lender of last resort" which could bail out a country in extreme difficulties, but only on tough terms: it should impose strict conditions to make sure that a country put its house in order and should never be confused with aid. The world needed "a combination of financial insurance and political discipline," as Harold Cleveland of Citibank later put it. "If the clarity of the IMF's lender-of-last-resort role is blurred by mixing it up with other kinds of financial intermediation or aid, there may be a serious loss of financial discipline. Lenders and borrowers may come to feel that the IMF will always come to their rescue and so may be led to take risks they should not take."[10]

The first managing director, the Belgian ex-Minister of Finance Camille Gutt, ran the Fund on austere lines, rigorously controlling his own staff's expenses and preaching the importance of stable exchange rates. "He taught us," recalls the monetary expert Irving

[10]Statement to Subcommittee on International Trade, Washington, February 7, 1980.

Friedman (see Chapter 10), "that devaluation was a form of confiscation." It was not assumed that a European should always be in charge, and when Gutt was due to retire in 1951 he was very nearly succeeded by an Indian banker, Sir Chintaman Deshmukh. But when Deshmukh could not take the job, it went to a Swedish banker, Ivar Rooth; then (1956) to a Swedish economist, Per Jacobsson; and then (1963) to a French civil servant, Pierre-Paul Schweitzer. These European managing directors were much more circumscribed than the presidents of the World Bank (or than either Harry White or Keynes had intended); and the Americans through their executive director were dominant. Keynes had insisted that the Fund should not be "one of the minor desks at the U.S. State Department"; but that was often how it looked, particularly to the Third World.

The Fund was unrelentingly strict toward developing countries —particularly toward the Latin Americans, who were going through their customary economic crises in the fifties, while the Eisenhower Administration was insisting that private investment could finance their development. The Fund would lend money to a country only on condition that its government swiftly cut public spending and impose drastic deflation, which forced down wages and increased unemployment. This severity, and the emphasis on private investment, were in ironic contrast to America's own nineteenth-century experience of public investment and improvident finances. As Arthur Schlesinger, the historian who became President Kennedy's Special Assistant, observed:

As for Washington's insistence on fiscal purity, this was perhaps a trifle unseemly on the part of a nation which had financed so much of its own development by inflation, wild-cat paper money and bonds sold to foreign investors and subsequently repudiated. If the criteria of the International Monetary Fund had governed the United States in the nineteenth century, our own economic development would have taken a good deal longer. In preaching fiscal orthodoxy to developing nations, we were somewhat in the position of the prostitute who, having retired on her earnings, believes

128 / THE MONEY LENDERS

that public virtue requires the closing down of the red-light district.[11]

As the ex-colonies became independent they each joined the IMF, putting in their small quotas and receiving their small voting rights in return; but they saw the IMF as an essentially foreign club of rich and mean men. They had not taken part in the original conception; to them it was born in "original sin."[12] The IMF could lend money through its system of *tranches* (or "slices" of credit) which were linked to each country's original quota. The first tranche—which amounted to a quarter of the quota—was lent automatically, but each of the three subsequent tranches became progressively stricter; a system of conditions was devised (bleakly known as "conditionality"), which insisted on the stock IMF remedies of devaluation and deflation. The poorer countries complained bitterly that the Fund was imposing shock treatment to which they could not respond like the rich countries. The Fund replied that they came for help when it was already too late for gentler remedies.

The Fund did make some concessions to developing countries whose income from exporting food or raw materials could suddenly fall through no fault of their own, leaving them destitute. By 1963 the IMF had agreed to open an extra "window," which it called the "compensatory financing facility," which could lend money to tide countries over their loss of exports. Six years later it opened another window, called the "buffer stock financing facility," which could help countries build up stocks of raw materials to protect them against falling prices. But the terms of these loans were so strict that few developing countries ever used them.

By the late sixties some of the Anglo-American confidence was beginning to be undermined, as the dollar's role as a reserve

[11]Schlesinger, p. 158.
[12]Ismail-Sabra Abdalla, "The Inadequacy and Loss of Legitimacy of the IMF." Development Dialogue: Uppsala, 1980: 2, p. 38.

currency was weakening. Many countries were insisting that the Fund must break away from its dependence both on the dollar and on gold, which accounted for most of the world's reserves, and as the dollar weakened the Americans became less interested in the IMF. John Connally, Nixon's Secretary of the Treasury, "seemed to have written off Bretton Woods and the International Monetary Fund as a total loss," as Charles Coombs of the New York Federal Reserve described it, and when he paid his first visit to the Fund he appeared to treat it "as a museum in which anything that wasn't already stuffed ought to be."[13]

Tentatively the IMF was now seeking to be less dependent on the dollar and gold. At their annual meeting in Rio in 1967 the directors of the Fund had finally approved a new kind of currency, with the baffling name of a Special Drawing Right, which could take over some of the functions of gold. Two years later they agreed to make a first issue of SDRs, in proportion to each country's quota, to the value of $9.5 billion. They fixed the value of one SDR against gold at the same rate as the dollar: one thirty-fifth of an ounce of gold.

The SDR was not strictly a currency at all; it was a right to borrow from the IMF which governments or central banks could use to buy currencies. Its hideous name reflected the caution with which the Fund launched it; for many governments, particularly the French, dreaded that it would undermine the ancient discipline of gold and stimulate inflation. The definition of an SDR continued to confuse many politicians, not without reason. You could not touch it, see it, or easily describe it; some people called it "paper gold" or the "money of moneys."

The rich countries devised the SDR without consultation with the Third World, and the first allocation of $9.5 billion was anyway tiny compared to the world's reserves, which had gone up to $104 billion by the end of 1972. Yet it was nevertheless a breakthrough in economic diplomacy. For the first time in history the world had agreed on an international basis for payments

[13] *The Arena of International Finance* (New York: John Wiley, 1976), p. 219.

which did not depend either on gold or on one nation's trade. It was a step toward the kind of global currency that Keynes and White had envisaged thirty years earlier, with "Bancor" and "Unitas." In the following years, as the dollar fell further and international debts mounted, the Third World began to look to this abstruse new form of currency as a chief hope in rescuing it from penury.

But the Fund continued to impose its strict discipline on any country in trouble, without much regard to the political consequences; and its shock treatment was likely to threaten the stability of any democratic government which accepted it. In 1964 the Fund had insisted that the Dominican Republic must impose policies which quickly reduced the worker's standard of living and put thousands more out of work; the next year there were riots and upheavals, and the U.S. government had to intervene. In 1972 the Prime Minister of Ghana, Professor Busia, was already tottering in the face of economic disasters aggravated by the fall in the price of cocoa; when he had to borrow from the Fund the terms were so stringent that they immediately precipitated a military coup which was the end of democracy in Ghana. It was a consequence which worried many British liberals, including the Conservative Prime Minister Ted Heath.

The Fund had become eminently hatable by Third World governments, and seemed almost to play up to the role of the merciless banker foreclosing on innocent victims. Its palatial new headquarters in Washington were much grander, and even more isolated, than the World Bank: with fourteen stories built round a huge atrium like a Hyatt hotel, but strictly excluding the public. Its staff were segregated from ordinary people, with their own country club outside Washington; their ample salaries were tax-free and even secretaries traveled first-class. They were mostly Europeans or Americans from the same backgrounds of economics, business schools, and banks, and when they visited developing countries they lectured their leaders with little understanding of local politics.

BANKSPEAK

While the militants of the Third World developed their own Unc-talk, the economists and lawyers in the IMF produced their own rarefied Bankspeak, which seemed designed to conceal any real meaning from ordinary people. The tortuous Cherokee, as Keynes had called the original jargon, had evolved into an inscrutable private language; simple words like lend, borrow, debt, or money, which described the heart of the business, were carefully avoided in favor of circumlocutions. The Fund, of course, had to appear thoroughly impartial, avoiding any suggestion of blame or moral judgment, which inevitably dried up its style. But the IMF's Bankspeak often betrayed a love of obscurity for its own sake.

Earlier economic writers like Adam Smith or Bagehot had often compared money to water, which could flow, be frozen or diverted; but these watery metaphors had long ago been distorted by such phrases as "liquidity" or "negative flows." Abstract nouns ending with "ity" became a kind of mania in the IMF, with such words as "conditionality" (meaning conditions), "capability," "automaticity," "additionality," "modality," and above all "facility"—a word that could mean anything from a lavatory to an airport, but which in the IMF meant a new fund. Abstract nouns with the passive tense enabled the Fund's managers to portray all their decisions as inevitable and impersonal, removing any suggestion of "who . . . whom." "There are, of course, circumstances in which the application of credit tranche conditionality would not be appropriate," they explained, meaning: "We cannot always impose conditions on new loans."[14]

The science of economics had admittedly become far more specialized and mathematical; yet the Fund's key decisions were still about basic questions of loans, funds, or exports. As the Fund and the bankers became more concerned with their relationships with developing countries, the use of clear language became more

[14]*IMF Survey,* June 1979.

necessary; but the sentences seemed to become more contorted as the problems became more serious—as though trying to conceal their authors' anxiety. Elaborate nouns were the harbingers of more serious trouble ahead. The word "recycling," with its reassuring associations of compost and ecology, was soon to be adopted to describe the perilous process of lending Arab money to uncertain countries. The more bankers worried about countries going broke, the more they talked about renegotiation, rescheduling, or restructuring, or even if necessary moratorium, but never the dread word "default."

The mandarins at the IMF were very aware of their power over developing countries, and they knew more about their secrets than most of their critics; they had seen the world (in the banker's phrase) with its trousers down. They knew that a minister of finance would often ask them to enforce measures which he would have liked to enforce but did not dare to. They were the elected scapegoats of the world community, and they could always say to themselves, like all bankers, "if you knew what we knew." Like the early federal bankers in the United States, they saw themselves as upholding discipline and truth against the wild excesses of populism and demagogy. But this embattled attitude had great dangers. It could easily lead to an arrogance which ignored the political consequences and which assumed that there was only one kind of truth.

7
LONDON AND THE EURODOLLARS

Adventure is the life of commerce, but caution, I had almost said timidity, is the life of banking. . . .

WALTER BAGEHOT, 1873

During the fifties there was little indication that London could again become a world financial center: it seemed to offer a study of banking in decline. The London bankers were much more defensive and somnolent than the Americans, surveying their past more lovingly than their future. "The traditional banks," Jack Hambro explained to me at Hambro's Bank in 1960, "are like the British Empire. There's nothing more to gain, and quite a lot to lose." The war and the vanishing Empire had cut down their overseas interests, and they were retreating into narrower dealings within Britain. The great old merchant banks which could once make or break nations were now busy merging provincial brewers or advising pension funds. They were roughly equivalent to American investment banks, but their social position was grander: they cultivated a haughty style reinforced by heredity. Visiting their mahogany parlors in the late fifties I found myself in a scene of butlers, silver salvers, and old claret which seemed to belong to a Victorian play; most of the cast of military and country-house characters turned out to be interconnected or intermarried, and several were within the nexus of conservative interests which was then becoming known as the Establishment.

The banks' behavior was governed not by government officials and company lawyers but by the unwritten rules of the Bank of England, whose governor operated more like a headmaster than a judge, with a system of frowns, nods, and occasional deadly disapproval; and his authority was reinforced by his "court" of sixteen directors, most of them bankers. The governor during the fifties was Lord Cobbold, the brother-in-law of Sir Charles Hambro and of the Duke of Abercorn, who cultivated extreme secrecy and refused to talk to journalists. ("We are, after all, a bank," he explained, "and nobody wants their bankers to talk too much.") And he was followed—it was hailed as an adventurous choice— by the third Earl of Cromer, one of the five Baring peers.

Most leading merchant banks—the "acceptance houses," as they were called—were intermarried with the landed aristocracy which made the Rockefellers or Stillmans look like parvenus, and they were doggedly defending their territory. "Blood is thicker than water," to quote Jack Hambro again, "and much nastier." Lazards, though descended from French-Jewish traders in New Orleans, was now thoroughly English and Gentile, owned by Lord Cowdray and run by Lord Kindersley, with the help of Lord Brand and his brother Lord Hampden. Morgan Grenfell, with which Lazards worked closely, was still part-owned by Morgan's in New York, but was now run by Lord Bicester, one of the "Financial Smiths" who had been banking in London since the seventeenth century, with the help of a cluster of peers. Lazards and Morgan Grenfell worked closely together—they even shared a box at Covent Garden—and saw themselves as guardians of the City's interests. As Lord Kindersley told the Bank Rate tribunal in 1957: "I do not think Lord Bicester would find it in the least surprising that I should come to him and say to him: 'Look here, Rufie, is it too late to stop this business or not?'"

In this protective atmosphere the bankers saw little need to look outside their large families. Barings was still run by Barings and their sons-in-law (though many had been distracted by their Hampshire estates); Rothschilds was still run by Rothschilds, but their Victorian palazzo at New Court, full of family portraits and relics of Waterloo, looked more like a museum of banking than a bank, and the talk at lunch was likely to turn to rhododendrons or music. With their common backgrounds of Eton, country houses, and St. James's clubs, the merchant bankers were well equipped to close their ranks against outsiders. They showed a special antagonism toward the most aggressive and brilliant intruder, Siegmund Warburg, a refugee from Hamburg, from the famous banking family. As Warburg put it later: "I was not an English newcomer, but a German newcomer, a fellow who has not been educated in British schools, who speaks with a foreign accent . . . I remember some people in very good houses talked very nastily behind my back: 'Do you know this fellow Siegmund Warburg? He starts in the office at *eight o'clock* in the morning!'"[1] Warburg represented the more competitive and cosmopolitan tradition of banking, harking back to the years before 1914, and surveying his London colleagues, he thought (he told me at the time) that "Britain's blood pressure isn't high enough."

Warburg did a good deal to raise the bankers' blood pressure. He first made his name as a master of corporate takeovers and he became famous when he tried to buy British Aluminium on behalf of American clients, Reynolds Metals. Lazards, Hambros, Morgan Grenfell, and others clubbed together to try to stop it "in the national interest" while they hastily fixed up an alternative bid from another American company, Alcoa: Lord Kindersley explained to me, with a twitch of his military mustache, that "there is still honor among thieves, but one bank did not respect it." Warburg eventually won the Aluminium War, and other banks soon began to follow his aggressive tactics. But his wider influence came from his awareness of a world outside with constant new opportunities. He had much closer relationships with Europe than most British bankers, and he pressed continually for Britain's entry into the European Community. As early as 1962 he was convinced of the importance of Japan, when he visited it with a Bank of England delegation, and he persuaded a few rich German friends to invest there.

The British deposit banks were even less competitive in the fifties: the Big Five, whose names alternated along the high streets, offered the same interest with the same reluctance to seek new customers, contemptuous of Californian salesmanship. Each bank

1"The Confessions of Siegmund Warburg," *Institutional Investor* (March 1980).

had its own tribal traditions, with a conservative grandee at the top of an obedient infantry of clerks and managers. The Westminster was headed by Lord Aldenham, the head of the Gibbs dynasty, which had made its Victorian fortune from guano ("from selling turds of foreign birds," as the City rhyme puts it). National Provincial was linked with the "Financial Smiths" and with Coutts, which had been the bankers to every sovereign since George III. The Midland with its industrial background was the most democratic. Lloyds had West Country and Welsh connections, still with Lloyds on the board; and Barclays was still run by a federation of old Quaker families.

The Big Five felt little incentive to take new risks. Their credit was strictly controlled by the Bank of England, and most British workers never went inside any bank: they preferred to put their money into post office savings or building societies. The bankers normally followed the old principle of only lending money to people rich enough not to need it, though they included dignified companies like Rolls-Royce or the British Motor Corporation (later British Leyland) whose prospects were very uncertain. As Lord Franks, then chairman of Lloyds, described it to me: "It was like driving a powerful car at twenty miles an hour. The banks were anesthetized—it was a kind of dream life."

There were some stirrings of life in the late fifties, when the London banks began buying up hire-purchase companies and offering American-type personal loans, with some embarrassment. "It is one of the perversities of fate" (as a Midland pamphlet explained) "that the need to incur some sizable exceptional expenditure. . . ." The Big Five discovered, said Franks, that "they could sit up and even walk," and the merchant banks were competing more seriously for corporate business. But international banking was still limited by the restrictions and uncertainty of sterling. Only a few cosmopolitan operators realized that a new kind of currency was beginning to transform the market. But no one foresaw how rapidly it would break down the frontiers of the bankers' world.

ENTER THE EURODOLLAR

The Eurodollars crept in stealthily. They began (according to one version) back in 1949 when the new Communist government in China, wanting to protect its dollar earnings from the Americans, placed them in a Soviet-owned bank in Paris called the Banque Commerciale pour l'Europe du Nord, whose cable address happened to be "Eurobank." Then the Russians, also worried that the Americans would block their dollars, began likewise keeping them outside America—both in the Paris bank and in the Moscow Narodny Bank in London, which had followed very orthodox practices through all the vagaries of Anglo-Soviet relations. This new refugee currency was soon traded by other European banks, and took the name Eurodollar (it is said) from the cable address in Paris.

It was not the first time a currency had established itself outside national control. In the nineteenth century several foreign countries had traded in sterling deposits. The Maria Theresa dollar, which was first coined in Vienna for the Austro-Hungarian empire, was later minted in London and Rome for use in the Middle East: it is still legal tender in regions around the Red Sea. But these were coins, not credit. The new Eurodollars were soon to become an expatriate currency providing world credit on an unprecedented scale.

In 1958 most Western European countries—though not Britain—agreed to allow their currencies to be convertible into dollars for the first time since the war, which gave new freedom to dealings across frontiers. In the same year the United States moved into deficit, so that dollars were flowing rapidly into Europe. Companies and banks often preferred to keep funds in the form of Eurodollars—which were simply dollars held outside the United States—which could earn higher interest at a time when American interest rates were strictly controlled.

London seemed in many ways an unpromising financial center for this new business. Britain was even more bogged down in her own economic problems after the Suez War, which caused a run on the pound and further cut back the world role of sterling. The atmosphere of London was much less obviously dynamic than that of Frankfurt or Zurich. But international banking has very deep roots; and the small bit of land around Lombard Street, where Italian bankers had first set up counting houses six hundred years earlier, had accumulated the combination of trust and expertise which had survived Britain's industrial decline and the City's somnolent leadership. The London bankers still had very quick communications within their crowded territory, most of them within a stone's throw of the Bank of England; they had skillful foreign exchange dealers, many of them foreigners. There were still the ex-imperial bankers, like Grindlays, Chartered, and Standard, which had their own overseas networks and antennae. London's geographical position had a special global advantage: it allowed a dealer to talk to Tokyo in the morning, New York in the afternoon, and California in the evening.

And London could inspire confidence in foreign visitors. It was a big city with every kind of foreign community, much more fun than Zurich or Frankfurt. Its stock exchange, insurance market, and brokers were highly organized. Its legal background, always crucial to bankers, was uncorrupt and relatively fast-moving. And the banking system, through all its vicissitudes, had survived longer than any. "They've got everything but the money," as one American banker put it, "and every banker knows that money comes to people who know how to handle it."

A few imaginative outsiders in the City could recognize an opportunity when they saw it. One of them was an opinionated self-made banker called Sir George Bolton, who had been the British executive director of the IMF, and who for years had been overseeing exchange controls inside the Bank of England. He left it in 1957 and became chairman of a run-down establishment called the Bank of London and South America. BOLSA had lost most of its Latin American custom after defaults, local restrictions, and the general British withdrawal, but Bolton soon saw a chance to revive it with the help of Eurodollar deposits, which he could lend to Latin American governments. He brought in clever young men, set up a foreign exchange department, and soon linked the bank with the Mellon bank in Pittsburgh. He was not an economist, but he was fascinated by the global movements of money. "Like the ocean, these markets are never at rest," he said in 1964; "and like women never entirely predictable." He embarrassed civil servants and politicians with his rumbustious championing of global free enterprise. "I thought him a reckless adventurer," admitted Sir Frank Lee, the head of the Treasury, who later became his admirer.[2] But most bankers now give Sir George credit for his foresight. Some of the more adventurous banks, like Warburg's, Montagu's, or Kleinwort's, also saw the possibilities of new profits; but those who understood it preferred not to publicize it. As the veteran financial writer Paul Einzig described it, "The Eurodollar market was for years hidden from economists and other readers of the financial press by a remarkable conspiracy of silence . . . I stumbled on its existence by sheer accident in October 1959, and when I embarked on an enquiry about it in London banking circles several bankers emphatically asked me not to write about the new practice."[3] In 1960 the London *Times,* in the first recorded reference to the word, mentioned "the so-called Euro-dollar."

The Eurodollar market rapidly multiplied; it roughly tripled in 1959 and doubled again in 1960, boosted by the European boom and the expansion of American multinational corporations. Then in 1963 President Kennedy, worried by the increasing flow of dollars abroad, announced the Interest Equalization Tax, which made foreign borrowing in America more expensive. It was designed to strengthen the dollar and uphold the Bretton Woods system; while it failed to bolster the dollar it quickly encouraged international borrowers to look to Europe and Eurodollars for their loans. It was the central irony of this story, as aggressive bankers love to point out, that the attempt at controls led to the huge expansion of an uncontrolled market.

A further boost came with the escalating Vietnam War, which increased the American deficit, and the credit squeeze in Wash-

[2] *A Banker's World,* ed. Richard Fry (London: Hutchinson, 1970), p. 7.
[3] *Foreign Dollar Loans in Europe* (New York: St. Martin's, 1965), p. vi.

ington in 1966, which again restricted interest rates inside America. The Chase, Citibank, the Bank of America, and scores of others extended into London to provide loans and services for their multinational clients and to deal in Eurodollars away from the overview of Washington. "By building an apparatus in an amazingly short time for the collection and redistribution of the world's surplus cash and capital resources," said Sir George in 1966, "the commercial banks have produced a unique machinery for serving the financial needs of the whole world, both East and West."[4]

The gathering flood of expatriate money freed from government controls horrified many central bankers, particularly German bankers with their inborn fear of inflation: Hermann Abs, the veteran chairman of the Deutsche Bank, with his long memory of German disasters, preached sermons about the evils of Eurodollars, which he thought could not last. The new currency offended many of the moral laws behind banking; it was "money without a home," which could flit across European frontiers to Caribbean islands, Singapore, and Hong Kong. Economists continued to argue about whether the process of lending and relending could dangerously multiply and create dollars which were not there before.[5] And the more conservative bankers feared that the rash lending of this runaway money, with no "lender of last resort" to support it, could lead to the collapse of a bank which no government could bail out.

But free market enthusiasts welcomed the Eurodollars' triumph over national bigotry and restrictions; and Walter Wriston, who had run Citibank's "European district," was specially thrilled by this liberation, which he had anticipated back in 1957. "National borders are no longer defensible against the invasion of knowledge, ideas or financial data," he explained later. "The Eurocurrency markets are a perfect example. No one designed them, no one authorized them, and no one controlled them. They were fathered by controls, raised by technology and today they are

---

[4] Fry, p. 147.

[5] See for instance Geoffrey Bell, *The Eurodollar Market and the International Financial System* (New York: Macmillan, 1973).

refugees, if you will, from national attempts to allocate credit and capital for reasons which have little or nothing to do with finance and economics. . . ."[6]

The City of London became still more separate from the rest of Britain, like an offshore island in the middle of the capital. Even in the nineteenth century it had been cut off from the growth of British industry in the North: it made its money out of overseas trade rather than domestic investment. Now the moat round the City was wider than ever. The young British bankers and their foreign counterparts earned much higher salaries, augmented with capital gains, than industrial managers in the provinces. The new international markets, together with Britain's own perilous boom, began to transform the style and pace of the City. New skyscrapers shot up between the old classical buildings, dwarfing the familiar skyline topped by St. Paul's Cathedral; even Rothschilds knocked down their palazzo to make way for a functional block.

The old guard of hereditary bankers lost influence as more thrusting young men with international backgrounds moved into the old family banks. Mercedes and Cadillacs competed with the Rolls-Royces; and unpronounceable names of European, Far Eastern, or Arab banks appeared between the fading imperial buildings. The pressure for space within the square mile pushed office rents far above the levels of Manhattan, and equal to Hong Kong. The shiny new offices, with their computers, video screens, and direct-dial telephones—installed much more efficiently than in the rest of Britain—had all the benefits of the new electronic marketplace. It was much easier to communicate with a financial center across the world than with another part of the same country.

American sandwich sessions began to challenge the long London lunch; but international banking had always been associated with gastronomy, at least since the early nineteenth century, when Baron Rothschild employed the greatest chef in Paris, Carême; and Rothschilds were still conscious of culinary dividends. Bankers' dining rooms in London were the settings for wooing and seduction: Hambros and National Westminster competed for the

[6]Speech to the International Monetary Conference, London, June 11, 1979.

most elegant meals; while Warburgs stuck to brisk spartan lunches with beer (sometimes even having two lunches in succession). Americans complained about the strain of bankers' banquets, but they were still vulnerable to the symbols of status. And the more international the market became, the more important were the social impressions.

The rich cosmopolitan life of the City looked more threatened when the Labour government came to power in 1964: office building was stopped; sterling faced a new crisis; the left saw the international bankers or the "gnomes of Zurich" as the villains. But the government saw the Eurodollar boom as too valuable in "invisible earnings" to risk interfering with it. The Bank of England, for all its autocratic appearance, was much more lenient and pragmatic in its regulation than the Fed in Washington; and American bankers found they could obtain permission for new activities in a few minutes which could take months of negotiating with armies of lawyers in Washington.

It looked like a return to the great old days of the London banker before the First World War. Much of the world, it was true, had disappeared behind the iron curtain; the Empire had dissolved; sterling was no longer a world reserve currency. But this new international capital market of the Eurodollar gave the same kind of global scope as sterling in the nineteenth century; it could flow (as Bagehot had put it) like water to where it was most wanted. And London still had its traditional skills and stability in looking after other people's money. As Wriston says: "The Eurodollar market exists in London because people believe that the British government is not about to close it down. That's the basic reason, and that took you a thousand years of history."[7]

The most select part of the Eurodollar market was for foreign bonds, or "Eurobonds," which soon supplemented the traditional issues of bonds in national currencies. Most of these bonds were at first sold to rich individuals who could use them to avoid taxes, and much of the business at first centered on Switzerland, where

[7]Interview with author, June 13, 1980.

Europeans and Latin Americans could deal through their Swiss banks, holding "bearer bonds," which made them still more discreet. The first issue of a Eurobond was said to be in 1957, for the Belgian oil company Petrofina; but in 1963 Siegmund Warburg in London organized a $15 million issue for the Italian *autostrada* which made banking history, and made Eurobonds more acceptable. The merchant banks, including the London offshoots of the big American banks, could make quick profits from selling Eurobonds; and the market became an intense and volatile world of its own, with its own schoolboy language of Swedish bulldogs, Japanese Samurais, and American Yankees, and its own specialized clients, like the legendary "Belgian dentists," who went to Luxemburg to collect their tax-free payments. But these Eurobonds, which carried fixed interest rates and depended on the trust of individual investors, remained a very privileged market: as Stefan Mendelsohn, the authority on Euromarkets, puts it: "The Eurobond market has become one of the world's more exclusive clubs, conferring prestige on banks and borrowers alike."[8] The majority of borrowers of Eurobonds were corporations and institutions within the rich countries and only a few developing countries, including Brazil and Mexico, were later regarded as sufficiently reliable. It was much easier to obtain "Eurocredits"—borrowing from banks, rather than individuals, with a very variable interest rate. And it was this new kind of international lending which was suddenly becoming important to the developing world.

These loans soon escalated in size and became the responsibility not of a single bank but of a whole syndicate sharing the risk. In 1969 an engaging banker called Minos Zombanakis, from Crete, who had begun his career working on the Marshall Aid program for Greece, arrived in London to set up a merchant bank, Manufacturers Hanover Ltd., an offspring of Manny Hanny in New York and Rothschilds in London. Zombanakis was asked to raise an $80 million loan for Iran—the sum seemed huge at the time—and

[8]M. S. Mendelsohn, *Money on the Move* (New York: McGraw-Hill, 1980), p. 137.

decided to try to share it with other banks. He succeeded, and thus put together the first Eurodollar syndicated loan. Later in 1969 he talked to the governor of the Bank of Italy, Guido Carli, who was facing a huge exodus of capital in one of the periodic Italian panics; and he put together a $200 million Eurodollar loan supported by twenty-two banks, to help to tide the Italian government over its crisis. The interest rate was to be three quarters of 1 percent above the prevailing London rate for Eurodollars, known as the Interbank rate or LIBOR; and it was to be revised every six months according to the fluctuations of LIBOR. This system of revising the interest rate every six months, adding the extra margin or "spread" above LIBOR which gave the banks their profit, became characteristic of subsequent Eurodollar loans. Like a fluctuating mortgage it diminished the risks for the banks; but it increased the hazards for the borrowing company or country, which might suddenly find itself paying far higher interest than it had reckoned for.

Putting together these syndicated loans, with one or more banks taking the lead, became the key to this international lending, concentrated on London. It attracted a special coterie of cosmopolitan younger bankers, constantly talking on the international telephones, learning together how to make sophisticated loan agreements, adding clause upon clause. They enjoyed a social world of their own: finance ministers treated them as old friends; they entertained each other lavishly; the final signing of the loan was celebrated with a huge banquet at the Ritz or the Berkeley. The social pressures could often seem more significant than the condition of the borrowing country or company. As one banker described it to me:

When I first started I was amazed how casual it all seemed. When I first signed a loan agreement for twenty million dollars for a country I hardly knew anything about, I thought "we must be crazy." Syndication depends on the personality cult. There's no greater fun than to know that everyone wants to talk to you at cocktail parties and to be part of the world of big BMWs and parties at Annabel's. When an ambassador rings up to suggest you join a loan, you want to be part of it: the Americans are specially vulnerable to flattery. Syndication depends on only about a hundred people in London, and you soon get to know them all. Everyone feels that they're in it together. They hate to be left out.

These syndicated loans were more anonymous and less accountable than the loans of Barings or Rothschilds a century earlier. To most people involved, the end result in Brazil or Korea was as remote as the moon. They were "wholesale" operations divorced from individual investors or shareholders; and they were appropriately commemorated by the bleak "tombstone" advertisements which began fattening the pages of the financial press, each headed with the discouraging words: "This announcement appears as a matter of record only," followed by bare lists of banks which got longer as the years passed.

To the bankers themselves the inscriptions on the tombstones could be fascinating: Who was at the head of the list? Which odd little Midwest banks had come in? Some banks, like Deutsche Bank or Morgan's, would only agree to take part if they were at the top of the tombstone. All the big banks were careful about the company they kept. But to the ordinary observer these formal graveyards made banking seem even further removed from the land of the living. In the old days if a banker were asked by his wife, "What did you do in the City today?" he might be able to reply comprehensibly: "I backed a Japanese shipyard"; or "Argentina defaulted." Today he could only explain that he had joined two hundred other banks in a Eurodollar syndicate for a medium-term loan at three-quarters percent above LIBOR. Yet the political consequences could be equally far-reaching.

In the early years of the Eurodollar the raising of international loans was a sedate and gentlemanly business. The borrower, whether a corporation or a foreign government agency, would approach its customary bank or a specialized bank, which would then arrange the syndicate. But as it became more lucrative and competitive, the loan officers of banks began—around 1970—to solicit business, and to telephone or visit corporations and government agencies on their own initiative.[9] Some of the banks were no longer acting simply as intermediaries between a surplus and shortage of funds: they were now actively selling loans—as they had done in the twenties and earlier.

At first they were lending almost entirely within the industrialized countries, but by the late sixties they were becoming more interested in a few dynamic developing countries which were seeking loans to finance their booming economies. They looked particularly to the two biggest Latin Americans, Mexico and Brazil, which were rapidly expanding their industry and which took up half the total Eurodollar loans to developing countries. But they also began to lend to more uncertain countries, including Korea, the Philippines, Peru, Argentina. They were becoming involved, almost imperceptibly, in relationships with the Third World which would entangle them and which will recur through the rest of this book.

It was in keeping with the historic role of the bankers that they should be seeking out future prospects and returns from uncharted areas, as they had sought them from Japan, Russia, or elsewhere in the late nineteenth century. As the prospects in Europe and America began to look less exciting, they saw opportunities in Latin America or the Pacific Basin, in countries which were producing the new miracles of industrialization, and needed loans to finance them. Even in Eastern Europe the political movement toward détente and the apparent industrial prospects were luring the bankers, particularly to Poland (see Chapter 14). Yet the movement of money toward these more precarious regions did not have quite the same logic as the earlier adventures of Barings or Rothschilds. For though the bankers made good profits from them, the interest rates and fees did not appear to reflect the additional risk above the risk within the older industrial countries; and no banker could be very confident that the loans to Poland (for instance) would be repaid in his lifetime. The herds of bankers appeared to be behaving, in fact, as if there were some kind of safety net; as though they

[9]See Mendelsohn, p. 88.

were working more closely with their governments than appeared to their shareholders or to the public. Yet the relationship between governments and bankers—which varied widely between countries—remained very undefined. And no one could confidently answer the question: Who is responsible if a major nation defaults?

8
THE SECRET HOARD

What the Arabs cleverly have done is to put the New York banks
in the front row of risk. In other words, if Zaire goes kaput, Chase
Manhattan is in trouble.

PAUL ERDMAN[1]

The end-of-the-world syndrome sells a lot of books.

WALTER WRISTON[2]

The supremacy of American bankers was already questioned by
the end of the sixties, as the balance of financial power was
shifting. The world's confidence in the dollar, which lay at the
basis of the Bretton Woods agreement, was undermined by the
Vietnam War. The long boom of the West was faltering, with too
much capacity and too little employment. The pound was devalued in 1968, followed by other currencies, which in turn undermined the strength of the dollar. American manufacturers were
losing out against Europe and Japan; Japanese cars were beginning
to roll into America. The United States showed a deficit for the
first time since 1893. The Nixon Administration tried to hold up
the dollar but by 1971, as Charles Coombs perceived it, they "had
either lost or abandoned any semblance of control of the situation"; and they finally decided to force devaluation on the others.[3] The Western finance ministers at the Smithsonian Institution
in Washington legitimized what the market had already decided,
and devalued the dollar against gold.

During 1972 the Western nations tried to pull themselves out
of recession, at the cost of higher inflation and erratic exchanges.

[1] *Newsweek,* November 28, 1977.
[2] Interview with author, June 13, 1980.
[3] Coombs, p. 215.

One unstable currency affected another. President Nixon said, "I don't give a shit about the lira" (as the Watergate tapes revealed); but he soon found that the run on the lira was unsettling other exchange rates, and indirectly the dollar. By March 1973 Nixon gave up the attempt to fix the dollar to gold. All Western currencies now floated up and down freely. The Bretton Woods system had virtually collapsed. It was in a dazed condition that the bankers faced the biggest shock of all.

THE OIL SHOCK

Wealth was already shifting toward the Middle East in the sixties as the oil revenues were mounting, and Arab money was already making a mark on the world. The Kuwaitis, with huge oil reserves and a tiny population, had been a trading nation before their oil was discovered, when their dhows sailed across the Indian Ocean. They soon realized the importance of deploying their new wealth. They set up their own National Bank of Kuwait as early as 1952, which was to become the biggest in the Middle East; and by 1961 they already had their own Kuwait Fund for Arab Economic Development, partly modeled on the World Bank, which was run by a young Harvard man, Abdlatif Al-Hamad, the son of a Kuwaiti dhow owner.[4] Kuwait was determined to link its prosperity with the Western system, investing very conservatively, influenced by British advice. The Kuwaitis held large funds in London, and dealt in New York through Citibank and Chase. Their movements were already in a position to unsettle the pound.

The Saudis, the biggest oil producers of all, had a far greater potential money power. They too had forged links with the Western capitals. Their central bank, SAMA, passed the oil revenues to the Chase and Morgan's in New York and to the Midland in London, which invested them according to the Saudi instructions. But the Saudis were much less attuned to world trade, through

[4]For an account of the Fund's development, see Robert Stephens, *The Arabs' New Frontier* (London: Temple Smith, 1973), pp. 45–73.

both their tradition and geography, than the Kuwaitis—like Midwesterners compared to New Yorkers. In 1973 the Saudi banks still had no telex machines, which were regarded as a threat to Saudi security;[5] and they were still inhibited, like European money lenders in the Middle Ages, by the religious objections to usury, which were strictly interpreted in this puritanical state. The Koran forbade the practice of *riba,* or usury, and Koranic scholars spent much time arguing as to which banking transactions were *halal,* or sanctioned by Koranic law. The usury laws could be overcome by regarding interest as commission or service charges, but they held back the development of banking through the Arab world; less than 4 percent of Arabs made use of any kind of financial institution. And in Saudi Arabia much of the wealth resided in the personal fortunes of the royal family, which remained wrapped in secrecy.

Beirut was the obvious banking center for the Arab world, with its cosmopolitanism and sophistication, which attracted people and money from all over the Middle East. As the Arab wealth grew, Beirut seemed ideally suited as the entrepôt between the Middle East and the West, with its glossy shops and hotels, its busy airport, and its money souk where visitors could exchange remote Asian or African currencies into dollars or pounds. But Beirut was rent by rival factions and jealousies; it lacked effective regulations and controls, and the one crucial qualification for a banking capital, political stability. Its biggest bank until 1967 had been the Intra Bank, which had been set up in 1951 by a brilliant Palestinian refugee, Yusuf Beidas. He built up a whole network of international assets, including a Fifth Avenue skyscraper, a stretch of the Champs-Elysées, the Londonderry Hotel in Park Lane and a controlling share of Middle East Airways. But Beidas, who was arrogant and also Palestinian, was resented by the old Lebanese bankers. He made the classic mistake of putting too much short-term money into property that was not liquid; and when he got into

[5]See Michael Field, *A Hundred Million Dollars a Day* (New York: Praeger, 1976), p. 99.

difficulties in 1967 the Central Bank allowed him to collapse. Beidas was later charged with embezzlement and fraud before he died in 1969, but many of his investments proved very shrewd. Financial confidence never fully recovered from the crash of the Intra Bank, and many Arab millionaires thereafter preferred to keep their money in Zurich, New York, or London. But Beirut was soon to be overcome by a far worse disaster, when the civil war of 1975 destroyed much of the city and with it any hopes of being the Arab banking capital. The hotels were gutted, the airport closed down, and the souk disappeared. The Lebanese traders dispersed to the Western capitals, and American banks found, with the new speed of communications, that they could dispense with a beachhead. Some Arabs said the war was a deliberate conspiracy to deprive them of their financial stronghold.

The big American banks had long been interlocked with oil money. The two old Rockefeller banks, the Chase and Citibank, had traditional links with the oil companies, and Morgan's had dealings with several of them. At the Chase David Rockefeller and the ex-chairman John McCloy had been pressing Washington to adopt a more pro-Arab foreign policy to safeguard oil supplies; they had both called on President Nixon back in 1968 with a group of oil tycoons.[6] McCloy, who represented all the "Seven Sisters" as a lawyer, was especially active as an intermediary with the Arabs. But neither the Chase nor the other big banks were prepared for what happened in 1973; and few experts took note of James Akins of the State Department when he wrote in *Foreign Affairs* in April 1973: "With the possible exception of Croesus, the world will never have seen anything like the wealth which is flowing and will continue to flow into the Persian Gulf."

When the price of oil was first doubled in October 1973 and two months later doubled again, the change was so sudden that it took some time to comprehend. The OPEC countries would earn an extra $80 billion from their oil exports—about 10 percent of the value of all world exports—and they could only spend a few

[6] Anthony Sampson, *The Seven Sisters* (New York: The Viking Press, 1975), p. 206.

billion of that on more imports. The two richest producers, Saudi Arabia and Kuwait, would receive $37 billion over the year. At this rate (*The Economist* calculated) they would be able to buy all the major companies on the world's stock exchanges in twenty-five years: IBM in seven months, Exxon in four months, and the Bank of America in sixteen days.

In Washington the implications were discussed with alarm but also with paralysis in the poisoned atmosphere of Watergate and the movement to impeach Nixon. For the first year Bill Simon at the Treasury and Henry Kissinger at the State Department pinned their hopes on bringing down the oil price by dividing the OPEC countries. They were encouraged by many economists, including Milton Friedman, who predicted that the cartel would soon break up: when the World Bank's chief economist, Hollis Chenery, argued that the oil price would remain high, it was seen as a kind of treason. The administration was opposed to any move that would appear to accept the OPEC price, and discouraged any plans to recycle or lend the surplus funds to needy countries through the IMF or the World Bank.

The OPEC leaders were equally bewildered by the sudden shift in wealth, and dazed by their sudden success: traveling through the Gulf soon after the price rise, I found Arabs and Iranians awed by the new responsibility. "We thought we were pigmies facing giants," said Al-Hamad of the Kuwait Fund. "Suddenly we found that the Rock of Gibraltar was really made of papier-mâché." The Kuwaitis, with the longest experience of large surplus funds, were eager to buy into Western companies and property; during 1974 they bought, among other things, 15 percent of Daimler Benz, a London property company (St. Martin's), the Tour Manhattan in Paris, and an island off South Carolina.[7] The Iranians were also very active: the Shah bought a quarter of the Krupp steel company and even tried to buy a share in British Leyland. Saudi princes began buying businesses and properties, and Adnan Khashoggi, the arms dealer, started buying banks in California; but there was growing resistance to foreign control. The richest oil countries

[7]Field, pp. 201–6.

were showing a greater appetite for imports than most economists had imagined possible: they planned new towns, hospitals, schools, mosques, and highways to be laid out in the desert, providing bonanzas for Western contractors. They showed a special enthusiasm for the one industry that could expand without limit—the arms industry. The Pentagon's foreign sales of weapons more than doubled in a year, to $8.3 billion in 1974, with almost half the total going to Iran.

But the richest and least populous countries, headed by Saudi Arabia and Kuwait, still could not spend anything like all their surplus, and by the end of the first year it was accepted by most bankers and economists—though not by Milton Friedman—that the oil price was not likely to go down. The OPEC countries would continue to leave most of their money in their banks; and since their own banks were still comparatively undeveloped and local, they deposited their surplus in the Western banks which they knew best, which they had been using for years. These "petrodollars," as they were called, had the same characteristics as Eurodollars, with the same mobility and freedom from national controls, and the same potential to be relent or (in the new jargon) "recycled."[8] The new surpluses brought a huge new opportunity, but also a new uncertainty, to the already thriving Eurodollar market.

To many economists and some bankers the flow of these new billions into the banks appeared fraught with dangers: for most of the money was deposited on a very short term, or could be withdrawn without notice. It added nothing to the capital of the banks, and to lend it to others increased the risk of their exposure. There were many warnings that the banks could not be expected to recycle this money on their own. In January 1975, at the end of the first year of the high oil price, *Foreign Affairs* published an article by a group of experts including the German economist Armin Gutowski, the Japanese economist Saburo Okita and the New York banker Robert Roosa of Brown Brothers Harriman.

[8]The word was already floundering in the financial context before 1973, but it came to be applied increasingly to the relending of OPEC deposits.

The experts agreed that the commercial banks were already overburdened, that they were already "jeopardizing several ratios of deposits and credits to capital," and that as they accumulated more oil money they would become exposed "beyond prudent limits as to individual accounts or currencies." They insisted that OPEC surpluses should be channeled into more secure international institutions, including special OPEC funds, where they could be used for longer-term investment. Their worries were echoed by many other economists, including George Shultz, former Secretary of the Treasury. David Rockefeller himself was concerned about the bank's role in recycling, and wanted a new international facility to take over part of the burden.

But Walter Wriston at Citibank had no such doubts: to him the flood of oil money represented a fundamental challenge for the free enterprise system, and Citibank, as he explained later, was "one of the only financial institutions in the world who said that it could be done. . . . I remember my friend George Shultz came to me and said it was an unmanageable problem, and I said of course it's unmanageable, but that's what markets do." He read Roosa's article in *Foreign Affairs* with indignation: "I called the editor and I said that's a nutty article you got there, Bill[9]—will you run one of mine? And he didn't. . . . They never ran it because the intellectual community had decided that this was the new Watergate. All the big banks were going to go down. It was going to be the story of the century. It didn't happen." Citibank had already increased its expansion to the developing world, but Wriston and his international director, Al Costanzo, sounded completely confident that their bank could safely increase its lending to countries which were now more desperately in need of it. "It was the greatest transfer of wealth in the shortest time frame and with the least casualties in the history of the world," Wriston explained. "I think that is something to be very proud of. . . . It was a terrifically difficult thing to do. We did it. It was also hard to put the guy on the moon. We did that."[10]

[9]William P. Bundy.
[10]Interview with author, June 13, 1980.

MONEY WEAPON?

By early 1975 the flood of Arab funds into American banks was arousing the concern of Capitol Hill—particularly of the Multinationals Subcommittee of the Senate Foreign Relations Committee, which for the previous four years had been investigating the political implications of American investment abroad. Its chairman, Senator Frank Church, with his chief counsel, Jerry Levinson, had investigated first ITT, then the major oil companies, then two aerospace companies, Lockheed and Northrop; in each case uncovering some sensational evidence. They were now—to the bankers' alarm—looking into the political implications of these Arab billions: could they be used as a weapon to influence American foreign policy? But they were confronting the most powerful of all business lobbies.

Senator Church, who was soon briefly to be a candidate for the Presidency, appeared undeterred. He insisted that the banks should disclose the size of their OPEC funds and what happened to them: "We have got to know the impact of these foreign deposits on our own banks, the extent to which they may represent a danger to those banks." And he sent questionnaires to all the major banks asking for details. Half the banks, including the Chemical, the Crocker, and the Mellon, replied to it, but all the very biggest ones refused—including Citibank, Chase, Morgan's, and the Bank of America. Their leaders responded in tones of dignified outrage. "Much of the information you request would involve a break of our obligation to keep confidential the affairs of particular clients," wrote Ellmore Patterson, chairman of Morgan's. "We consider information of the type requested to be highly confidential," wrote Michael Esposito, a vice-president of the Chase, "since its disclosure would be very useful to our competitors."

Church insisted on holding hearings in Washington. The bankers made statements which were calm and bland. Hans Angermueller of Citibank testified that the OPEC customers might well take their business to other countries if the figures were provided

—particularly to Switzerland, where secrecy was inviolable. Boris Berkovitch of Morgan's confirmed that foreign banks would not be required to disclose. Edwin Yeo from the Treasury explained that a move away from American banks would weaken the dollar: "We can finance the American economy without these funds: but it is more difficult." Paul Volcker, then president of the New York Federal Reserve, called it "an extremely dangerous precedent." Thomas Enders from the State Department explained the need to "preserve our banking industry in the face of this massive new shift of ownership resulting from the oil crisis."[11]

The senators on the subcommittee reacted characteristically. Senator Case, who had worked on Wall Street, was worried and skeptical: "I have to be persuaded that this is not a matter that the public is entitled to know about . . . Mr. Volcker talked about presumption of confidentiality. To someone brought up in the banking business and steeped in it, this seems to be sacrosanct and given. To my way of thinking the opposite is sacrosanct and given." Senator Church still insisted that the banks were vulnerable to an embargo. "The OPEC countries are clearly very volatile. . . . They are in basic disagreement with our policy toward Israel. Some of them have already imposed an embargo on us, and at any time they might decide to just pull this money out, and we don't know how much there is. We don't know on what basis it has been deposited, how much of it is short term. . . ." But Senator Symington was wryly skeptical. "I don't see why we have to have this information," he protested; "I know the money is pouring into these banks in New York. And I know they are doing their best to get the money. They are just like locusts, all over the Asian countries and so forth, the representatives of the New York banks. And I know that they are only following what the British have been doing for years. There is nothing new about it. The only thing new is our economy is falling apart, as I see it."[12]

[11]Senate Foreign Relations Committee, *Multinational Hearings,* 1975, Part 15, pp. 29–37.
[12]*Ibid.,* pp. 65–83.

But Senator Percy, whose daughter had married John D. Rockefeller IV (David Rockefeller's nephew), soon revealed the full extent of the bankers' alarm. He mobilized Senator Proxmire, the chairman of the Banking Committee, to oppose the investigations, and he warned the subcommittee: "I think we are dealing with dynamite right now and I think this is the cause of concern for Arthur Burns, for David Rockefeller, for a lot of them." The banks were making sure that only limited amounts of OPEC deposits were available on demand, Percy explained; they were taking care that the Arabs could not pull out the plug. Senator Symington supported Percy, stressing his respect for Burns and Rockefeller: "I would hate to see us rock any boats." Levinson, the chief counsel, still insisted that "those depositors have it in their power . . . to create an extremely serious disturbance in the U.S. financial system." But Percy snapped back: "I think you jeopardize the national interest . . . We know the perilous ground we are on."[13] ("At the time," Levinson commented later, "I did not fully appreciate what a raw nerve we had struck.")

The bankers were now determined to suppress the inquiry, mustering all their lobbying power. David Rockefeller flew down to Washington in his private plane. He breakfasted with Senator Case and warned him that disclosing the banks' figures could bring down the whole Western banking system. He then lunched —"a chance meeting"—with Senator Church at the State Department, repeating the warning of potential catastrophe—made more pointed by the recent revelations that the Chase had had a very bad year (see next chapter). Church felt impelled to accept a compromise: the banks would supply confidential figures to the Fed, which would then release only generalized figures about the deposits and loans of the biggest. The deposits of the individual banks, which Church had first asked for, would remain secret.

These total figures were eventually published in March 1976. They showed that the OPEC deposits were highly concentrated in the six biggest American banks—Bank of America, Citibank, Chase Manhattan, Manufacturers Hanover, Morgan Guaranty,

[13]*Ibid.*, pp. 35–72.

and Chemical. The OPEC countries of the Middle East and North Africa had deposits of $11.3 billion in these six, compared to only $3.2 billion in the next fifteen biggest banks. This $11.3 billion amounted to about 6 percent of the total deposits in the six banks, and about half of it could be withdrawn in less than thirty days. But the Fed insisted in an accompanying memo that if any group of countries were to remove their deposits from American banks, they "would be seriously damaging their relationships with those very banks whom they have selected as best-equipped to hold their funds and would encounter difficulties in acquiring equally attractive assets." In other words, no other banks could take their money.[14]

The bankers had not only succeeded in blocking the investigation; they had dealt a death blow to Senator Church's subcommittee. But the staff continued to worry about the political threat of these billions, and in 1977 Church launched a special staff report on the banks and foreign policy. There had been a revolution, he warned, "that has affected not only the United States but the whole international economic system . . . enormous financial surpluses are concentrated in the hands of a very few countries which cannot spend them for goods and services." The report, which was written by Karin Lissakers, an economist on his subcommittee, analyzed in detail the shift of money power in the previous four years, and repeated the political warnings: "Saudi Arabia did not hesitate to use the oil weapon against the United States in the last Mideast War, despite earlier warm U.S.-Saudi relations; there is no guarantee that next time they won't wield the money weapon, too."[15]

Could the OPEC powers really wield this money weapon? The bankers insisted that the concept was unreal: the oil money was absorbed in a much broader flow of world savings and lending including the huge flow of Eurodollars, and there was no such

[14]*Ibid.*, pp. 128–33.
[15]*International Debt, the Banks and U.S. Foreign Policy,* Washington, August 1977, p. 8.

thing as oil money. Citibank's people were as usual specially emphatic. As their monetary expert Irving Friedman described it: "The demand for funds was not met or made possible by the oil surpluses. The funds were made available by the entire savings-credit mechanism of the Western world . . ."[16] Or, as Wriston put it to me: "If Exxon pays Saudi Arabia $50 million, all that happens is that we debit Exxon and we credit Saudi Arabia. The balance sheet of Citibank remains the same. And if they say they don't like American banks, they'll put it in Credit Suisse, all we do is charge Saudi Arabia and credit Credit Suisse: our balance sheet remains the same. So when people run around waiting for the sky to fall there isn't any way that money can leave the system. It's a closed circuit."

"Sitting here, we were doing what we'd always done," Al Costanzo of Citibank told me. "Looking for loans round the world, with the same credit standards, and then buying the funds. It wasn't the oil expansion that made the difference, but the Euro-dollar market."[17] He had earlier explained to congressmen how the Arab billions caused no special pressure, either toward political change or toward extra lending. "This is very cold-nosed money," as he put it.

> I think the common impression is that somehow the Arabs force money on us, and then we are faced with the problem of what to do with the money. The reality is the other way around. We first go out and make what we consider are credit-worthy loans, and once we have made our loans then we worry about how we fund those loans. . . . This money is jumping around between Citibank and Chase and many others, depending on the bidding for this money that goes on every day in the week. . . .
> These countries have no leverage on us at all, because this money has nowhere to go. It is stuck in the market. This is an interbank market. And I would say, if there is any leverage, it is the

[16] *The Emerging Role of Private Banks in the Developing World* (New York: Citicorp, 1977), p. 45.
[17] Interview with author, March 14, 1980.

other way around. I mean, the people that would have to be concerned are the Arab countries themselves, because they realize all they have is an IOU in a bank account which can be frozen at any time in the United States or in Germany or wherever it is. So if there is leverage here, it is the other way around. It is the depositor who has got a great deal to worry about, and not the American banks.[18]

Many Arabs were likewise inclined to see the deposits as providing a weapon that could be used against *them*. "A reverse embargo by those who hold the deposits is more effective than an embargo by those who own them," Abdlatif Al-Hamad of the Kuwait Development Bank insisted to me. "But if the American banks had refused to accept their funds, OPEC would have been forced to go to the European banks, who would in turn use the American banks—which could not refuse the Europeans without risking the safety of the whole international system. Carried to its ultimate conclusion, such a situation could cause the OPEC countries to scale down their oil production, to avoid creating surpluses —with all the implications that follow."

The big American (and British) banks were soon competing—"like locusts," as Symington put it—to get more and more OPEC deposits, which they never turned away. The flow of Middle Eastern money into the American banks was soon followed, as following chapters will show, by an unprecedented rush of bank lending to some very shaky countries in the Third World. It looked very much like the predicament of the Medici bank five hundred years before: "Rather than refuse deposits, the Medicis succumbed to the temptation of seeking an outlet for surplus cash in making dangerous loans to princes."[19]

[18]House Banking Committee, *International Banking Operations*, Washington, 1977, p. 719.
[19]De Roover, see above, p. 35.

9
THE CRASHES OF '74

When the oil crisis came upon us in October 1973, and stock markets in all the capitals of the OECD countries collapsed like nine pins, that was one moment of truth. The world was, all of a sudden, seen and felt as one interdependent world.

LEE KUAN YEW
Prime Minister of Singapore
October 5, 1978

No warning can save a people determined to grow suddenly rich.

LORD OVERSTONE (1796–1883)

Could the Western banks safely take the strain of this sudden transfer of wealth, to serve as the world's intermediaries between rich and poor? Behind their discretion and apparent confidence there was some cause for genuine concern. The big banks had been increasing their deposits without corresponding increases in capital; and the ratio of loans to capital in some American banks had gone up as high as twenty or thirty to one; they looked more than ever like upside-down pyramids. They were lending not only other people's money but other countries' money; so that the security of banks was increasingly linked with the interdependence of nations.

Already in the boom years before 1973 some of the big banks had become overexposed. Now the oil shock helped to precipitate a succession of banking crises across Europe and America which threw more serious doubts on the system's stability.

LONDON: THE CONTAGION OF FEAR

It was London that suffered the deepest tremors. The British, in spite of their faltering industry, had been indulging in a mood of euphoria approaching mania which the banks had helped to encourage. It had begun in 1971, when Ted Heath's Conservative government had tried to stimulate the economy with cheaper money, while the Bank of England had allowed greater competition between banks by relaxing its control of credit. But very little of the new money supply went into productive industry, and much of it flowed into the hands of property developers, stock market speculators and the new "secondary banks," which mushroomed in the City. The stock market soared by 80 percent in eighteen months: properties were sold and resold at quick profits; while the British economy remained no more productive.

New City financiers made quick fortunes by lending money for property and second mortgages, and in this heady atmosphere many traditional banks were glad to support them. The most famous of them, Jim Slater, began with a group of mutual funds, to which he added his own bank, insurance company, and network of foreign companies. With his youthful dynamism he dazzled many of the older banks, and nearly merged with three of them in turn, Lazards, Warburgs, and Hill Samuel: only a few more skeptical banks like Barings looked askance at him. Slater became the confidant of Tory politicians and the teacher of a school of ambitious young financiers, who learnt how to strip assets, talk up their shares, and play the market.

The spiraling prices with so little behind them had the classic ingredients for a crash; but the Bank of England was slow to see the warnings and the Conservatives remained committed to expansion. By the summer of 1973 the property boom was pushing up house prices far beyond the reach of ordinary buyers, while the British economy was clearly unstable and the flow of Eurodollars was adding to the overlending. Then came the Middle East war and the quadrupling of the oil price. The stock market began falling, a credit squeeze threatened the speculators, and the Treasury and the Bank of England saw a crisis looming up. The Bank had recently acquired a new governor, Gordon Richardson, a former lawyer who did not come from a banking family but who looked groomed for the part, with a gregarious style which could suddenly intimidate. He guarded the bank's traditional secrecy as carefully as if it were the financial arm of MI5. He needed all his discretion, for he soon faced London's biggest banking crisis since 1931 or the crash of Barings in 1890.

By November 1973 the most vulnerable fringe bank, the London and County, was tottering. At the Bank of England Richardson realized that many more fringe banks were becoming insolvent as property shares were sinking. If they collapsed, they would threaten the big banks, which in their eagerness for quick profits had been rashly overlending. The National Westminster (Nat-West) had lent far too much to property companies: its assets were rapidly dwindling as the stock market fell.

Richardson now dreaded what he described as "a widening circle of collapse from the contagion of fear"; and he was convinced that the Bank of England must launch a "lifeboat." He launched it with great speed and the bank now revealed all the advantages of the "old boy net" ("How I envy Gordon," said one American banking official; "all the chairmen just round the corner"). He summoned the chairmen, explained the gravity of the crisis, and quickly persuaded them to provide about $3 billion to rescue twenty-six fringe banks. They secretly propped up their façades from behind so that depositors would not panic, while most City people were quite unaware of how close they were to ruin.

The danger was not over. The winter of 1974 undermined confidence still further, with a miners' strike, a three-day working week, the return of a Labour government, and mounting inflation. Wage claims escalated, the pound fell, the stock market sank still lower. The collapse of banks in Europe and America (see below) extended the danger and the Bank of England now had to add to the loans. Rumors were spreading about impending defaults: the

NatWest took the extraordinary step of publicly stating that it was *not* in difficulties—which did nothing to allay the depositors' fears.

Some members of the Labour government felt that the City should pay for its mistakes with real casualties; but Harold Lever, the financier in the Cabinet, advised leniency, and the governor was emphatic about the need for rescues. "Without the boost to confidence which the lifeboat operation gave," he told MPs later, "some of those rumors would have tended to become self-fulfilling, and would have been translated into fact. If we had had a major established bank which had defaulted—however unlikely that was—I do not know where we would have stopped the course of collapse."

Who should be saved and who should go down? It was the subject of long recriminations later. Many property companies found themselves with negative assets, and were allowed to crash. Jim Slater's empire was taken over by the Bank of England. The oldest British oil company, Burmah, having gambled heavily with tankers, collapsed; and the Labour Cabinet now insisted that Burmah should pay the full price and forfeit its BP shares, which were taken over by the Bank of England. But the bankers who had helped to precipitate the crisis remained relatively unscathed after being rescued by the lifeboat. The NatWest survived, and the secondary banks, which had earned their high interest rates because their loans were risky, were never properly penalized. The relationship between interest rates and risk, which lies at the heart of the bankers' art, was becoming still more blurred.

By the end of 1974 the crash reverberated through the City. Pension funds refused to invest in industry, bringing shares further down; the restaurants and bars of the City were half-empty. The financier James Goldsmith protested about the "Merry-go-round to Hell." In two years seven stockbroking firms were "hammered"—when the bell rings three times on the trading floor—and the number of firms went down from 355 to 244. At its peak in May 1972 the *Financial Times* share index had stood at 543; by September 1974 it was down to 200; and by the Black January of 1975 it had fallen to 146. For London it was a worse collapse than the Great Crash of 1929–31, and the average value of shares (allowing for inflation) was lower than at the worst point of the Second World War, after the evacuation from Dunkirk in 1940.

But behind the scenes there were at last signs of recovery. In November 1974 the governor persuaded Harold Wilson to lift restrictions on commercial rents, which began to revive the property companies. By the end of January the stock exchange had begun the fastest rally in its history, doubling in three months to 300. The restraint of wage claims and the international recovery gradually brought back some confidence, and Britain could now look forward to becoming self-sufficient in oil from the North Sea, which made her more thoroughly credit-worthy abroad.

The City of London emerged from the crisis with relief and some self-congratulation. The Bank of England, with its traditional combination of informality and authority, had been able to avert panic and to prop up major institutions behind the scenes, as it had done with Barings in 1890. The international prestige of the City as the center of the Eurodollar market remained remarkably intact. Yet the bubble itself had been blown up with the Bank of England's permission and even encouragement; and the commercial banks had been carried away by the euphoria.

In the aftermath the Bank and the Treasury devised new banking laws and restraints. The Bank defined more strictly what constituted a bank, and looked more rigorously at the fringe banks and at the foreigners who came to London to escape the oversight of America or the Continent. It had become clear in the course of the crisis that the world's banks had become much more interdependent, and that supervision could not be confined within national frontiers.

HERSTATT

The worst time for the governor in London was in June 1974, when the German bank Herstatt suddenly closed its doors; for at that point the crisis looked as if it might spread round the world, as in 1931. The Bankhaus Herstatt was a respected private bank in Frankfurt, whose owner, Dr. Hans Gerling, also controlled an

166 / THE MONEY LENDERS

important insurance company, which had extensive dealings with foreign banks, including the Chase, which was its clearing agent in New York. The Herstatt had been wildly speculating in foreign exchange, concealing losses in a special account and tampering with its computer. On the morning of June 26, 1974, it owed about $10 million to the British merchant bank Hill Samuel, $10 million to Citibank, $13 million to Morgan's, $12 million to Manny Hanny, and $5 million to the Bank of America. Just when the American banks were beginning their trading (at 10:30 in the morning in New York or 3:30 p.m. in Frankfurt), the Bundesbank ordered the Herstatt bank to close down. It was, as Tom Clausen of the Bank of America later put it, "like putting a hundred-dollar bill on the teller's counter and asking for five twenty-dollar bills —and the phone rings. The teller answers the phone, then hangs up, and closes the window saying, 'I'm sorry, we're closing the window.' "[1] When it was investigated the Herstatt was found to have liabilities of around $840 million, against assets of $380 million.

The sudden collapse of Herstatt caused a panic in a country with bitter memories of bank failures. The president of the Bundesbank quickly promised that the collapse would not threaten other banks, but his precipitate action had unnerved other bankers and investors: the Bundesbank, it later turned out, had been warned of Herstatt's danger several days earlier. The American and British banks were furious at being caught by fraudulent dealings, and shocked by the Bundesbank's lack of responsibility. The memory of Kreditanstalt and the dominoes of 1931 was in many people's minds.

The Herstatt crisis was not, it turned out, a comparable catastrophe: it had been due to rash gambling in currencies, rather than to a failure of the Eurodollar system of credit, and it was relatively easy to restore confidence. A consortium was put together to rescue the remains of the bank, and creditors eventually got most of their money back. The Bundesbank took drastic measures to

[1] See Robert Heller and Noriss Willatt, *Can You Trust Your Bank?* (London: Weidenfeld & Nicolson, 1977), pp. 246 ff.

strengthen its powers, and created a new insurance fund which would compel the big banks to bail out further casualties. The New York banks made new regulations to safeguard their day-to-day foreign transactions.

Most important, the central bankers realized that they must accept much fuller responsibility for their own banks. When eight European central bankers met in Basel in July 1974 at their club, the Bank for International Settlements, they agreed at Richardson's insistence to each support their own country's banks if they were in danger. At the annual meeting of the IMF in September the Americans, Japanese, and others agreed to join in the Basel Concordat; and thereafter the chief bank supervisors met three times a year in Basel (see Chapter 14). But in all the new fluidity of global lending there were still many doubts about the responsibility for foreign subsidiaries and banks based on tax havens: Who were the real "lenders of last resort" to these stateless entities? The central bankers, when they agreed to rescue if necessary their own banks, extracted no bargain in return. The commercial banks were still free, as we will see, to make some remarkably rash loans across the world.

FRANKLIN

New York in the meantime was witnessing its own banking disasters. The Franklin Bank on Long Island had never been very secure; as a tiny bank with four employees in 1934 it had been bought by a young entrepreneur, Arthur Roth, who built it up by lending to customers whom the big Manhattan banks wouldn't accept. By 1951 he had initiated the first bank credit card in history, the Franklin Charge Plan, and by 1964 he had opened a luxurious headquarters in Manhattan. Franklin became the twentieth biggest bank in America, but Roth controlled it rashly and autocratically, and its base was dangerously narrow. In 1971 it announced a loss of $7 million, and at this perilous point it was sold without any apparent objections to Michele Sindona, a quiet and sober-looking Sicilian. With his cosmopolitan charm Sindona had a remarkable ability to impress other bankers; in his complex dealings he worked closely with (among many others) the CIA, the Vatican, the Mafia, Hambros Bank, and the National Westminster in London. His associates included David Kennedy, the former chairman of the Continental Illinois Bank and Secretary of the Treasury. But Sindona proved to be one of the most unscrupulous financial crooks of the twentieth century, and he was able to drain his network of banks to finance his other enterprises and his own private fortune.

When Sindona bought the Franklin he planned to enrich it by speculating in foreign exchange, with the help of two ambitious young dealers; he soon acquired a dubious reputation in Washington, but he was still allowed to open a London branch, widening his scope. The Franklin made risky foreign loans and lost vast sums in its dealings, which Sindona concealed through his other companies, while the oil crisis and the shortage of liquid funds made the bank more vulnerable. By early 1974 it was clearly insolvent, but the comptroller moved slowly, and the Fed was trying desperately to salvage it; Manny Hanny offered to absorb it, but Sindona turned it down. Eventually an expensive rescue was arranged: a group of European banks took it over, renaming it the European-American Bank, while the Federal Deposit Insurance Corporation was left to carry losses of $2 billion on loans and receivables (which were eventually paid off). Soon afterward Sindona's European empire collapsed, leaving large debts to his clients, including the Vatican. Sindona fled to Switzerland, was arrested in New York, and was eventually tried and convicted of fraud and grand larceny. Of all the banking scandals it was the most disturbing, for it raised fundamental doubts about the supervision of the central banks, particularly the Fed. An embezzler and racketeer had been allowed to bring about the biggest failure in American history.

THE CHASE IN TROUBLE

Even some of the biggest American banks were now in difficulties. At the Chase David Rockefeller faced troubles from several directions: from the slump in American real estate, from the uncertain state of several foreign countries including Italy, and from the looming bankruptcy of New York City itself. In each the Chase had been too optimistic in valuing its assets.

The banks had rushed into financing property and building in the heady years of the sixties. New laws in 1960 had allowed them to create Real Estate Investment Trusts (REITs), which enabled small investors to buy shares in property, and American savers, disillusioned with industrial shares, turned more hopefully to investing in land. In four years from 1969 many trusts achieved spectacular returns and capital gains, riding high on the building boom—particularly by financing condominiums in Florida, the favorite territory for land speculation. The biggest trust of all was the Chase Manhattan Mortgage and Realty, whose assets climbed to around a billion dollars, for which the Chase acted profitably as investment adviser. But property values, as in Britain, soon proved to be even more volatile than industrial shares, and the REITs were more vulnerable through the "leverage" which enabled them to multiply their debts against their equity. By the end of 1973 one big apartment developer, Kassuba, had gone bankrupt. In early 1974, as the stock market fell, the real estate trusts sank still further. The Chase Manhattan Mortgage and Realty was plummeting, and as land values dropped borrowers went bankrupt. The Chase was soon assailed by angry stockholders accusing it of self-serving loans and charging excessive fees—which it hastily reduced. By the end of 1975 REIT shares were worth only one-fifth of their value in early 1972. The Chase was left with bad debts and a tarnished reputation.

THE BANKERS' CITY

David Rockefeller was also facing troubles in the home city with which his bank and his family had for so long been identified, which now presented a kind of microcosm of the world's problems. The resplendent Manhattan skyscraper, issuing dignified pronouncements about prudence and discretion, was in the midst of a city which was moving toward bankruptcy. New York was like a microcosm of the world's problems: descending from the marble concourses of Chase Manhattan Plaza to the decaying subway beneath revealed all the contrast between private affluence and public squalor—almost like descending into the Third World. In the following crisis New York appeared to be behaving like an irresponsible banana republic. "We also have our LDCs at home," as Walter Wriston put it; "our least developed cities. . . ."[2]

Under successive mayors, culminating in the rule of John Lindsay, New York City had financed much of its growing welfare by borrowing from the banks, headed by the Chase, which suited both the mayors and the bankers. By 1971 Citibank was giving warnings about the city's fiscal methods, but few other bankers were worried. And the banks themselves had helped to undermine the city's finances, by shifting their investments to less highly taxed areas; as Tom Clausen of the Bank of America explained from California: "Of course the banks played a role in what happened in New York. You know, red-lining is bad, and green-lining is bad. That's what you're talking about."[3]

Bill Simon, the future Secretary of the Treasury, was then selling bonds for Salomon's; he joined the committee to advise on the city's debts, and "at no point during any of these sessions" (he later admitted) "did any one of us seriously question the underlying fiscal condition of New York."[4] When Abraham Beame became mayor he set up a committee of bankers to study financial reforms headed by Ellmore Patterson of Morgan's; but they achieved very little.

In the autumn of 1974 the banks faced their first major shock when they could not off-load a record issue of tax-free bonds, which left them with losses of $50 million. In December the representatives of the biggest banks, including Chase, Citibank, and Morgan's, met secretly with Mayor Beame to warn him that

[2]*Euromoney:* interview with William Clarke, July 1978.
[3]*The Washington Post,* March 19, 1978.
[4]*A Time for Truth,* paperback ed. (New York: Berkley Books, 1979), p. 141.

they could no longer sell city bonds, and that New York must cut back its spending. Beame replied that the banks must support the city more actively and threatened to borrow money from the city's pension funds.[5] Early in the following year the Chase and Bankers Trust discovered that the city lacked the necessary tax receipts, and refused to underwrite a new sale of bonds. When the next month the city offered $900 million worth of tax-free bonds, it could only sell half.

New York was already on the road to default. A bill for $790 million was about to fall due and there was growing evidence of very dubious accounting, which concealed current spending by charging it to the capital account. Mayor Beame promised cuts in spending and jobs, but he could still depict the banks as the scapegoats; he accused them on television of "poisoning our wells," and city workers demonstrated outside Citibank's sky-scraper.

The bankers, led by Patterson, Wriston, and Hauge, were now meeting repeatedly to try to stave off disaster: New York City represented only about 1 percent of their total loans, but a failure would reverberate. At the end of May they came up with a rescue plan: new bonds would be issued by a Municipal Assistance Cor-poration, or "Big Mac," which would be guaranteed by city taxes and administered by New York State. To operate it Governor Carey turned to a politically minded investment banker, Felix Rohatyn, a partner of Lazard's who was expert in intricate deals. But the public was still very skeptical: when the banks first offered Big Mac bonds worth a billion dollars, they had to buy nearly half of them themselves.

David Rockefeller now insisted that they could not sell Mac bonds unless the city drastically cut its costs and froze wages. But how could the bankers control a public borrower with such strong political backing? As a man from Morgan's explained: "In the private sector, you can get audits, you can do things with management. You just can't do this with a public borrower. You

[5]Michael Jensen, *The Financiers* (New York: Weybright & Talley, 1976), p. 139.

can't impose a crisis on a city that has pledged its credit."[6]

In this predicament nearly all the New York bankers, including such champions of free enterprise as Wriston and Patterson, were now appealing to Washington to rescue them with a federal loan: even Tom Clausen from the Bank of America flew to Washington to argue for aid to New York. But Bill Simon, who was now Secretary of the Treasury, was determined to teach a political lesson; "There was no way," he insisted later, "that rational reform could be instituted without some type of default or bankruptcy proceedings, so that the unpayable debt could be extended in time." He portrayed the story of New York as "a terrifying dress rehearsal of the fate that lies ahead of this country if it continues to be guided by the same philosophy of government."[7] But Rohatyn was convinced that a bankruptcy of New York would be disastrous for the banking system, and had icy encounters with Simon. "The only thing we agreed about," he said later, "was what we thought about each other." While the Treasury worried about the "ripple effect" of New York defaulting, Rohatyn warned that banks could sink like a stone: some banks had 20 percent of their paper in the city. Arthur Burns, the chairman of the Fed, proposed a five-year period in which the banks could write off their debts, but Rohatyn insisted that the auditors would not allow it, and Burns eventually had to agree on the need for a loan.

To Simon's anger the New York bankers were trying to make their city a global issue: at the IMF meeting they told foreign bankers that a default by New York would damage the world financial system. The threat was made more credible by the heavy losses incurred by the Chase, reported in October; and at the end of the year Chase was revealed to have lent $400 million to the city, followed by the Chemical with $379 million and Citibank with $340 million. David Rockefeller was trying to use his influence with his brother the vice-president to bail out the city. The bankers' alarm was heightened by their growing dependence on Arab deposits; as Senator Percy put it in Senate hearings in Octo-

[6]*Ibid.*, p. 148.
[7]Simon, pp. 137, 164.

ber: "One of the great ironies is that the city of New York which
is on the precipice of bankruptcy is to a degree dependent upon
the Arab countries keeping their money in the New York banks."[8]

By November, when New York was on the edge of the precipice, the state of New York announced that there must be a
moratorium on short-term notes worth $1.6 billion. The holders
could not claim their money back within three years; they must
either be content with the interest or exchange their notes for the
new Big Mac bonds.

It was close enough to a default to allow Washington to relent,
now that wayward New York had been taught its lesson. President
Ford announced that he would ask Congress to approve a short-
term loan to New York of $2.3 billion, which would be strictly
administered by the Treasury. The bankers' city was saved,
though not before it had shown itself as uncontrollable as any
developing country. "We all spoke the same language," as Wriston described it to me; "everybody knew everybody, and suddenly the management was so bad that we blew it all."[9] But if this
could happen under the bankers' noses, what might not happen
twelve thousand miles away?

DANGER LIST

The Chase's problems were compounded. While it faced losses
from real estate and New York, it had also made loans abroad
which looked much more doubtful after the oil crisis: not just in
developing countries, but also in Italy, to which the Chase was a
big lender. Italy had had to cut back her imports by imposing
special deposits, and the Italian crisis continued throughout 1974.
In September the comptroller of the currency publicly warned the
banks that the state of Italy was "problematical" and examiners
were told to question all short-term loans to Italian government
agencies.

By the end of 1974 the comptroller of the currency in Washing-

[8]*Multinational Hearings,* Part 15, p. 65.
[9]Interview with author, June 1980.

ton was keeping 150 American banks under close scrutiny. Arthur Burns of the Fed explained that "only a very small number of banks can be described as being in trouble," but this was not altogether reassuring. Soon *The Washington Post* and *The New York Times* reported that the comptroller was specially concerned about thirty banks, including both Chase and Citibank, which had insufficient capital to be set against dubious loans: the Chase was blamed for poor management and controls, which had led to $4 billion in "classified loans" that required special oversight. The ratio of loans to deposits at the Chase was alleged to be 97 percent—compared to the recommended ratio of 80 percent.

Rockefeller protested, and the comptroller, to allay the fears of depositors, insisted that the Chase was well managed and in a strong position. But there remained doubts about the valuation of the assets of the Chase, as of other banks. The security of foreign loans, like the value of property at home, was subject to very hazy assessments: who could put a number to the stability of Zaire? Behind all the precise calculations of the bankers—whether about London property, New York bonds, or expectations in Asia—there remained huge question marks. "People think that because balance sheets balance, it's okay," as one New York banker put it. "But in the middle of all their calculations there's often a purely mythical assumption." And these assumptions were now being extended much further round the globe.

10
THE FRONTIERS OF CHAOS

A "sound" banker, alas! is not one who foresees danger and avoids it, but one who, when he is ruined, is ruined in a conventional and orthodox way along with his fellows, so that no one can really blame him.

It is necessarily part of the business of a banker to maintain appearances and to profess a conventional respectability which is more than human. Life-long practices of this kind make them the most romantic and the least realistic of men.

J. M. KEYNES

After the panics and crashes of 1974, the newly rich countries of OPEC were, not surprisingly, more anxious to leave their vast funds only in the safest banks. They concentrated on the familiar American banks—led by the Bank of America, Citibank, Chase Manhattan, and Morgan's—together with a handful of Europeans, including the Big Four in London. The wealth of OPEC was still further separating the giant "money-center banks" from the rest. It was also bringing them into the center of a much more controversial political stage.

For with all their mounting deposits, they were beginning to handle the world's overdraft. The United States was in the midst of a recession and many of their traditional clients—corporations, utilities, or cities—had cut back their expansion. There were some big borrowers in Europe, including Britain and Italy, but Italy was close to its limits. So the banks were now looking farther afield. Already before 1974 they had been lending more to booming developing countries like Mexico, Brazil, and South Korea, whose exports could pay for the interest. But many more countries were now in desperate need of loans to help them pay their far bigger bills for imported oil. The higher the OPEC surplus, the greater were the deficits, not only in Western countries, but in the "non-oil-developing countries" (as they were now bleakly called), which made up more than half the world's population.

Most of these countries in the Third World were too poor or unstable to get any commercial loans. But the banks now regarded about twenty of them as credit-worthy, in varying degrees, and thus promising new customers. They could lend the OPEC deposits to countries which had suffered from OPEC, acting as intermediaries in the process of "recycling." They could earn higher profits because, as a general rule, the poorer the country the higher the interest and charges. In four years between 1972 and 1976 all the big banks rapidly increased the proportion of profits from abroad (see chart, page 178). As a Senate report put it: "While the oil price rise was something close to a disaster for the world economy, it created a bonanza for the banks."[1] Or as one banking expert in London remarked: "It was the easiest money going: you just took 1 percent on the turn, for signing a check for a few million dollars."

The political implications were far-reaching, but they took some time to sink in. In the first place these loans transformed the balance between official and commercial lending to the Third World, overshadowing the resources of the World Bank and the IMF. The "financial markets" which the commercial banks supplied accounted for only 12 percent of external public debt at the end of 1967; but by the end of 1975 they made up 50 percent, or $27.3 billion—and still rapidly increasing.[2]

In the second place the banks were lending to sovereign states rather than to private corporations; by 1974 62 percent of all lending in the financial markets went to governments or to organizations like nationalized industries which governments had guar-

[1] Senate Foreign Relations Committee: *Staff Report,* August 1977. "International Debt, the Banks and U.S. Foreign Policy," p. 3.
[2] Irving Friedman, *The Emerging Role of Private Banks in the Developing World* (New York: Citicorp, 1977).

anteed. The loans were not for specific projects or industries, like loans from the World Bank; even when they were *supposed* to go to a project like a dam or a highway they could easily end up in the coffers of the central government, particularly in the developing world or Communist states. For money, as the bankers say, is fungible: it can easily change places. Whatever their professed purpose, the loans were helping to finance the day-to-day consumption and to redress the imbalance of payments—for which there was no end in sight.

The concept of "sovereign risk," as it was called, was quite different from an ordinary commercial risk. A nation could not go bankrupt like a domestic corporation; the concept of bankruptcy had no real meaning for a nation, for since the days of imperial gunboats the creditors had not been able to seize a nation's assets. If a government could not, or would not, repay the interest, a bank was in a delicate diplomatic position. It could warn the government that it would lose its reputation for credit-worthiness, and that no other banks would touch it. But it could not, as it was to learn in the following years, compel the government to change its economic policies to enable it to repay. The government, on its side, was naturally more careful than a corporation in avoiding bankruptcy or default, for it knew that it would find itself outside the whole system of credit. It was also, at least in theory, always able to repay its debts by taxing its people more heavily, whereas a corporation could not just produce more cars or aircraft to stave off disaster. But the government also knew that if the bank declared a default it could endanger the whole international house of cards, risking panic and mass withdrawals. On both sides it was an intricate game.

The more a bank lent to a country, the more reluctant it would be to declare a default; it would prefer to lend still more, to avert a crisis. Some people suggested that "the big banks may now be so deeply enmeshed in the whole deficit financing process that they cannot afford to say no."[3] The country and the bank were

---

[3] *Staff Report,* 1977, p. 61.

TOTAL, INTERNATIONAL AND DOMESTIC EARNINGS OF 8 LARGE U.S. BANKS FOR 1972 AND 1976

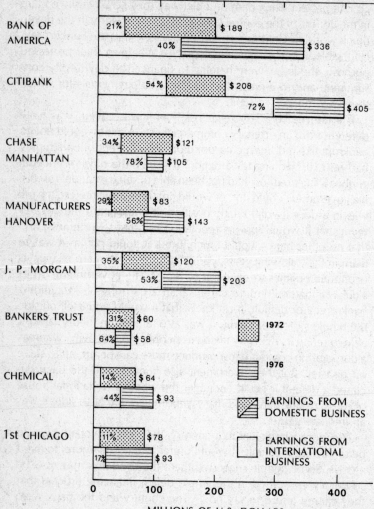

Source: Salomon Bros.

certainly becoming locked into each other, and it was even doubtful whether the bank wanted to escape, so long as it could still
make money from extending the loans. It was a familiar interdependence, and many debtor countries like Canada had quietly
rolled over their debts for decades on end. But the process was
now being repeated by young developing countries where there
were much less certain sanctions. It was like the old stories of the
spendthrift heir and the money lender, who each became dependent on the other. But most of these debtor countries were never
likely to inherit a fortune, and there was now no equivalent to a
debtor's jail.

For the finance ministers in developing countries who faced the
huge bills for importing oil, these bank loans provided relief they
desperately needed. The interest rates were relatively low, in a
time of high inflation; and in "real money" they often turned out
to be negative rates. It might seem surprising, since these countries
were competing to borrow large sums, but compared to total
world savings the demand for loans was relatively slack. The basic
interest rate was still set (see Chapter 7) by LIBOR, the "London
interbank offered rate" for Eurodollars, to which the bank added
the "spread," which made up its profit. In theory the spread
varied according to the risk that the loan might not be repaid. But
as the banks competed more fiercely to lend, so there could often
be a distinction of less than 1 percent between a safe country like
Britain and an unstable one like Zaire. Did this really reflect the
difference in risk? Or had the banks decided that if Zaire defaulted,
someone else would come to their aid? And if so, was not 1
percent too much? They were recurring questions which puzzled
bankers as well as outsiders.

These loans that Citibank or Chase offered to the Third World
were not only relatively cheap; they were also free of many of the
conditions and long negotiations which the official lenders had
insisted on. The World Bank might take three years after the first
application before it finally gave out the money for a dam or a

road. Western governments might insist on using their own companies or experts, with their own political bias. But these commercial bankers, once they had decided a country was credit-worthy, were prepared to lend money for no specific project, with no political strings and with far less delay. Radical politicians in the Third World were surprised to find these capitalists so ready to lend on such easy terms, and began to develop a more relaxed relationship with less fear of dollar diplomacy; while the banks on their side encouraged the idea that they were politically neutral in their global lending. There was an unexpected honeymoon between bankers and developing countries, before the marriage began to show problems.

The banks were desperate to lend, particularly where they saw a chance to establish a close relationship with an expanding nation. It was true that the developing countries, even by 1977, accounted for only 5 percent of their total loans;[4] but this new business was far more profitable: by 1976 Citibank was deriving 13 percent of its worldwide earnings from a single developing country, Brazil, compared to 28 percent from the U.S.[5]

The "lending officers," the money salesmen, now traveled not only through South America—the traditional bankers' back yard —but to the turbulent countries of South Asia, North Africa, or even Zaire. It was odd to come upon a dark-suited, button-collared young man in a sweaty capital of the Third World, trying to make sense of the political jungle from his suite in the Intercontinental. He could be competing anxiously with a rival in the same hotel, trying to sell a loan with some semblance of security, knowing that his salary and promotion depended on his success. The banks had their own systems of credit control and country limits: but the lending officer in the field had wide scope for his own judgment, and the more aggressive the bank, the more important were the salesmen who generated the profits. "It was always tempting to sign up a loan when there was a long grace period

[4]Friedman, p. 34.
[5]Staff Study, 1977, p. 56.

before repayment," as one of them recalled; "by the time the problems began, you'd moved on somewhere else and the chairman had retired."

In Western Europe the ministers of finance were well able to look after themselves. But in the more corrupt countries of the Third World, like Zaire or Indonesia, selling loans was like offering crates of whiskey to an alcoholic. The bankers insisted that they were only responding to the demand, but that was not how it looked to the governments. "I remember how the bankers tried to corner me at conferences, to offer me loans," recalls one Latin American who was then Minister of Finance. "They wouldn't leave me alone. If you're trying to balance your budget, it's terribly tempting to borrow money instead of raising taxes, to put off the agony. These gray hairs of mine are because I resisted that temptation."

CITIBANK'S MARKETPLACE

Citibank was again in the forefront, and Wriston saw the move into the Third World as part of the bank's destiny: "Whether we like it or not, this bank is inextricably involved in world affairs." Citibank had its own complex international network, with 20,000 employees abroad, in branches in over a hundred countries linked by instant communications; it was in many ways better equipped than the governments of superpowers. Wriston sounded confident that the sheer range of his customer countries would cover the risk: "We have some chips in every game in town. . . . In a spectrum of 156 countries there are always going to be three or four in trouble."[6]

In the poorer countries the returns could be much higher; and in 1974 Citibank was earning 40 percent of its total profits from the developing countries, from only 7 percent of its assets. These huge profits came not so much from lending Eurodollars as from operating skillfully within each country, benefiting from the high

[6]*Euromoney* (July 1978).

local interest rates which were often controlled by a local semicartel; so that while profit margins were being driven down by the fierce competition in America, they were staying up in Asia or Latin America. The poorer the country, the higher the profits, and Wriston did not conceal his achievement in making so much money out of poorer countries: "Round here, it's Jakarta that pays the check."[7]

To run the international division at Citibank Wriston had chosen Al Costanzo, the plain-speaking son of an immigrant miner in Alabama. Costanzo had worked his way through college, majoring in economics, helped to run the Marshall Plan in Italy and Greece, and then joined the IMF. He had had long experience of foreign governments—"it's a narrow circle at the top"—and Wriston recruited him to deal with finance ministers and central bankers. Costanzo had his own kind of idealism: "I enjoy nothing more than watching developing countries develop."[8] But his concern had its limits. "I don't feel it's my responsibility to improve the world's economic situation," he told me; "but I believe that good loans help the developing countries."

Wriston and Costanzo built up an elaborate system to ensure effective control of their foreign loans. Every quarter they evaluate the risks in a hundred countries with the help of computerized systems and the economists and statisticians in the Park Avenue skyscraper. The comptroller's division, Costanzo explains, has a "global residency program" through which eight hundred people audit the loans and accounts, and prepare about five thousand detailed reports on the soundness of loans. The bank regulators discuss specific loans in depth with the lending officers, and exhaustively review the information on the credit files. The directors on the fifteenth floor make their judgment of loan limits, but their power is limited. "Twenty years ago a lot of decisions for countries like Jamaica were made off the cuff, in a more personal way," said Costanzo, "but now it's too big for Wriston or Costanzo to

[7]See Sanford Rose, "Why They Call It Fat City," *Fortune*, March 1975.
[8]*Currency Magazine* (New York: Citicorp, February 1977).

override the system. The fifteenth floor can't make the loans—it's the system." But, I asked him, what would have happened to the United States a century ago if the British banks had had this kind of computerized system, to assess such a doubtful risk? Costanzo paused thoughtfully: "We wonder sometimes where the United States might be today."[9]

Wriston insisted that Costanzo and his staff were thoroughly insulated from the commercial pressures to lend: "They have no responsibility whatsoever for budgets and earnings. If they decide to constrict the amount of lending in any one place, it gets constricted."[10] The inrush of OPEC funds, Costanzo says, did not diminish his strict controls of lending: "We never changed the criteria—the flow of OPEC funds made no difference."[11] But the flow of oil money into Citibank nevertheless coincided with a rapid extension of loans to unfamiliar parts of the world.

Citibank's creed, as Wriston and Costanzo proclaimed, promised that international banking would be politically neutral. "I believe we have worked in the whole postwar period to try to live down the accusations of Wall Street imperialism around the world," said Costanzo in 1977. "I think our whole basis for survival in the less-developed countries has been that we do not intervene politically in those countries."[12] The whole impersonal apparatus of computers, credit ratings, and country limits reinforced the concept of neutrality, which made the banks much more attractive to developing countries trying to escape the strings of metropolitan powers. Wriston maintained that "the Eurocurrency market proved conclusively that, although the world may still be divided politically, it is one economically and financially." "International banking," he said in 1979, "is a system designed by fate to exist in a certain state of economic tension with all governments, including the most democratic."[13]

[9] Interview with author, March 14, 1980.
[10] *Euromoney* (July 1978).
[11] Interview with author.
[12] House Banking Committee, *International Banking Operations,* 1977, p. 738.
[13] London, June 11, 1979.

Bankers could certainly show their impartiality in their mounting loans to Poland, Rumania, or Czechoslovakia behind the iron
curtain (see Chapter 14); or by lending both to South Africa and
Nigeria (see Chapter 11). But were they quite so objective, so
politically dispassionate, so unaffected by their home government, as they liked to suggest? How was it that Egypt was regarded
as uncredit-worthy one day, and credit-worthy the next? What
was it that lured the bankers so rapidly into Poland, with all its
pitfalls?

There was little evidence in Washington, it was true, of straightforward pressure on the bankers. The foreign ministries in Bonn
or Paris might exert their influence as they did in the nineteenth
century; but the State Department was more aloof, and could be
subject to pressures in the opposite direction. But there are many
indications, in the stories which follow, of the bankers' herds
being well attuned to the political music from Washington, turning
this way or that as nations went in and out of favor. Wriston
insisted that his bank remained cold and dispassionate: "The ability of anybody to attract credit depends on their management.
Countries that manage their affairs well will always have credit
and those that don't will not."[14] But as the bankers ventured into
the more disorganized regions, were they really so sure about
their sound management?

INDONESIA'S PRIVATE EMPIRE

It was in Indonesia—the fifth most populous country in the world
and one of the most unmanageable, with 140 million people
speaking thirty different languages scattered on 6,000 inhabited
islands—that the bankers were lured into their most dangerous
predicament. Indonesia had attracted many Western adventurers
in the past; its oil had built the fortunes of the Royal Dutch Company before that company merged with Shell. But its corrupt
government and chaotic hinterland provided many traps for the

[14]Interview with author, June 13, 1980.

unwary. In 1967 President Suharto had come to power, welcoming foreign investment and supported by Washington. American and Japanese banks, with Citibank in the lead, had begun financing Indonesian projects, particularly oil.

To run the state oil company, Pertamina, Suharto had appointed a flamboyant medical doctor, General Ibnu Sutowo, who ran it as an autocratic private entrepreneur, reporting only to the President. Sutowo soon had spectacular successes. By 1971 the oilfields were producing over a million barrels a day; he controlled a chain of hotels, fleets of aircraft, and subsidiary companies; and he ran this private empire in his own flashy style, while the rest of Indonesia—whose average income was less than $200 per head—was run by orthodox technocrats. The bankers were never clear which was the real government, but Sutowo was much the most profitable and agreeable to deal with: he was bold and decisive and (as one banker explained) "he seemed wonderfully un-Indonesian."

The general was soon able to borrow huge sums, playing Japanese banks against the Americans, dealing with more and more banks, often without each other's knowledge. He was "an international glamour stock,"[15] as the economic counselor at the American embassy, Erland Heginbotham, described him; with his electric personality, his white Rolls-Royce, and his princely tours of the world, he was able to dazzle and charm bankers into yet more loans, though their purposes were often obscure. Already by 1972 the American embassy was worried that Pertamina was borrowing much more money than the oilfields seemed to require. The IMF—which was asked to renew a "standby" agreement—was anxiously asking several governments how much Indonesia really owed, and warning them that it had borrowed way beyond its limits.[16] Mysterious loans to Pertamina kept on coming to light, and the Indonesia Central Bank was now trying desper-

[15]Senate Foreign Relations Committee, Hearings on "Witteveen Facility," October 6, 1977.
[16]Ibid.

ately to bring Pertamina's borrowing under control. But the bankers were easily able to defy the ceilings and restrictions. As Rachmat Saleh, who became governor of the Central Bank, complained: "It was really very disappointing to see how these banks behaved." Or, as one banker described it: "The banks forced money on Pertamina, and Pertamina ate it."[17]

The oil crisis of October 1973 made Indonesia suddenly much more important to Washington and Tokyo. The Indonesians loyally refused to join in the Arab embargo, and though they made up only 4 percent of OPEC's production, Washington saw them as valuable oil friends. Pertamina was building a new refinery financed by the banks, and had discovered large reserves of natural gas which could supply the West Coast of America. General Sutowo was looking more glamorous than ever.

But by the middle of 1974 the money market was tight, the bankers were alarmed, oil production was below target, and the general was finding it impossible to raise more loans. He tried and failed to raise a large loan direct from the Arabs, but he appeared undeterred. In October 1974 he flew to Gothenburg in Sweden for the launching of a supertanker called *Ibnu,* organized by his financier friend Bruce Rappoport; it was celebrated by the arrival of three golf champions, Arnold Palmer, Gary Player, and Sam Snead, to play golf with the general.

But the bankers were now thoroughly alarmed, particularly since the crashes of Herstatt and Franklin had made the bank examiners stricter. And in February 1975 the crisis broke: Pertamina failed to pay the interest on a relatively small loan of $40 million, made by a syndicate led by a little-known bank, the Republic National Bank of Dallas. The Texan bank had come into Indonesia because of the oil connection, without knowing much about Southeast Asia. It was outraged by Pertamina's behavior and threatened to declare a default and take the company to court to enforce repayment. The threat was serious, because the cross-default clauses in the loan agreements gave the other banks the

---

[17]See *The Billion Dollar Bubble,* ed. Seth Lipsky (Hong Kong: Dow Jones Publishing Company, Asia, 1978), for a vivid account.

right to demand their money as soon as Pertamina missed any payments, which could cause a general collapse of Indonesia's credit. In this tense situation the American embassy tried to calm down the banks, assuring them that Pertamina could be saved, and the diplomats even sent messages through Washington to the bank headquarters.

The governor of the Central Bank, Rachmat Saleh, was now faced with the daunting task of rescuing Pertamina, without even knowing the full extent of its debts to the banks: eventually the total was found to be at least $6.2 billion, of which nearly a billion —nearly two-thirds of Indonesia's reserves—was due for payment in six months. To try to produce some order Saleh then took the bold step of inviting three investment banks which he trusted— Lazard Frères from Paris, Kuhn Loeb from New York, and Warburg's from London—to collaborate as advisers to the government, which they have been ever since. (The group, later called Triad, soon extended its role as country advisers to other parts of the world, setting a new pattern of collaboration between bankers and developing countries; see page 274.) Soon afterward Saleh approached Morgans, which had remained aloof from the Pertamina fiasco, to raise a new loan. After painful negotiations in Jakarta, London, and New York, Morgans put together two syndicates to lend $850 million while the Central Bank spent most of its reserves on the first repayments. The government was now able to begin clearing up Pertamina, cutting down Sutowo's sprawling empire to confine it to oil and gas, until eventually Suharto dismissed Sutowo himself. It was only gradually that the extent of the corruption inside Pertamina was revealed, as Sutowo's promissory notes and personal dealings came to light on scraps of paper. Ibnu's right-hand man, Achmad Thahir, died soon after the bail-out; but in 1980 his widow laid claim to accounts in the Sumitomo Bank in Singapore amounting to $34 million, and Pertamina then charged that Thahir had put away at least $80 million in foreign bank accounts—eleven thousand times his official annual salary.[18]

[18]*Asian Wall Street Journal,* February 3 and February 27, 1980.

By 1977 Indonesia was over the worst of its financial crisis: oil and other commodities were bringing in greater revenues, and Pertamina's plants for liquefied natural gas were coming into production. The Indonesian government had learnt some harsh lessons from the borrowing spree, and it had re-established its credit with the world: by 1980 its reserves were up to $12 billion. But the country had paid heavily for its burden of debt, with far too little to show for it. The bankers' aggressive selling of loans had been a large cause of the crisis, but the bankers had lost nothing from their mistakes. "It was the Indonesian nation that paid the price" (as Seth Lipsky of *The Asian Wall Street Journal* assessed it). "This came with the decision to pay off the banks from hard-won reserves, cut back ambitious development goals, and seek to re-finance those that remain—which, for a nation whose citizens make an average of less than 200 dollars a year, seemed heroic."[19]

THE HEART OF DARKNESS

Even Africa had attractions for the bankers. At the beginning of the seventies the huge land mass of Zaire was being billed as "the Brazil of Africa," with its rich hoard of minerals, including diamonds, a quarter of the world's copper, and more than half its cobalt. The old Belgian Congo, the "heart of darkness," had a long history of exploitation. It had been decimated by King Leopold I of the Belgians with appalling massacres and mutilations, while he was luring Belgian bankers to invest in it; and after its independence in 1960 it had been nearly torn apart by rival tribes fighting for its riches. Now it was dominated by the black dictator President Mobutu, the Founder of the Nation, the Supreme Guide and philosopher of Mobutism—who had drained off much of Zaire's wealth to finance his private palaces and estates, his luxurious journeys to Switzerland, and his mansions in Europe. In neighboring Zambia there was a story that Mobutu went around with a briefcase chained to his wrist containing the gross national prod-

[19]Lipsky, p. 41.

uct. Zaire was not typical of Africa; it was a tragedy that one of its countries richest in resources should be the most corrupt and disorganized.

The American bankers' interest in Zaire had begun in the summer of 1970, when President Mobutu had visited Washington and was warmly received by President Nixon, who made much of Zaire's political importance and economic prospects. Mobutu went on to New York to stimulate business interest: Goodyear was interested in the rubber plantations; Amoco minerals was interested in the copper; the Bankers Trust put together a first general loan of $25 million. As copper went up Zaire lured in more syndicates, successively led by Citibank, the French Société Générale, and the British Morgan Grenfell. By 1974 the rush had become a stampede, with Citibank at the head of it, and with the Japanese banks now joining in. Copper had reached a peak of $1.50 a pound, Zaire had even found some oil, and promised to be the new Eldorado. In the competition, the bankers had lost sight of the risks. "When you're lending to a corporation at home," as one of them reflected afterward, "one of the first questions is: how can it pay the money back? But in Zaire nobody asked that question." The loans helped to finance a series of extravagances, including jumbo aircraft, five hundred British double-decker buses, the world's largest supermarket, and a steelworks. ("Zaire needs a steelworks," as a banker explained, "like it needs central heating.") The commercial bankers were encouraged by official lenders, including the Export-Import Bank in Washington, which financed a thousand miles of power line from the Atlantic to the copper mines—the longest in the world.

But King Copper was always a fickle ruler. After the oil crisis its price collapsed to a third of its peak. The civil war in Angola next door closed the railroad linking Zaire to the Atlantic. Mobutu was diverting much of Zaire's foreign exchange into his own coffers. By June 1975 Zaire had stopped paying interest on most of her debts.

At Citibank's New York headquarters Wriston now had a prestigious new international expert, Irving Friedman, whom he had hired from the World Bank ("I like to stockpile IQs," he explained). Friedman was a white-haired professorial figure with a confident style who came to be called the "Bankers' Kissinger." He had worked in both the World Bank and the IMF, where he had become an international monetary expert. He had limited experience of Third World politics, but he came to Citibank with the authority of a financial statesman, accustomed to patient and delicate negotiations. Zaire was a challenge to his skills; for the country was now, as he put it, "broke, as broke as a country could be." And a formula had to be found to prevent Zaire from default-ing. It was to be a classic demonstration of how bankers conceal a disaster. ("Have you ever watched a rugby football match when one of the players loses his trousers?" said a British politician who was closely observing the banking scene. "They all immediately go into a scrum to make sure that no one can see, while they produce another pair of pants. That's how bankers behave when they see a default.")

Citibank, the chief private lender, was uncomfortably exposed: Zaire owed it about $40 million. It was "not a very exciting number," as Wriston put it, compared for instance to the $120 million that Citibank had written off when the Penn Central went bankrupt. Zaire's total debts to all banks, amounting to $400 million, were small compared to Turkey's or Brazil's. But Wriston knew that if Zaire formally defaulted it would threaten the whole confidence in the international system; and he assembled a spe-cial Zaire working party, including Costanzo and Friedman, to avert the danger. The bankers still hoped that the copper price would turn up, and that they could restrain Mobutu's reckless extravagance. Or, as Friedman hopefully explained it to Congress: "When you had a country which was broke as Zaire but had the real physical capacity and the potential of Zaire, the thing to do was to work with the country to try to re-establish it as a working economy."[20]

The official bodies that had been lending to Zaire—including

[20]Senate Foreign Relations Committee, Hearings on "Witteveen Facility," October 10, 1977.

the World Bank and the Export-Import Bank—tried to reach some kind of accommodation. In June 1976 they met in the Paris Club (the traditional creditors' meeting ground) and agreed to stretch out their loans to reduce the immediate debt; but Zaire promptly failed to make even the first payment. Citibank and others were now more alarmed: they met with the governor of the Zaire Central Bank, and by November 1976 they put together a Memo of Understanding carefully constructed to prevent a default: Zaire would promise to undertake economic reforms, which would prevent its credit rating from dropping still further and entitle it to borrow more from the IMF; and it would pay interest into a special account in Basel. Citibank on its side would use its "best efforts" to raise another $250 million.

The worst seemed to be over. Zaire borrowed another $150 million from the IMF; Mobutu solemnly promised to control government spending; the creditors at the Paris Club were placated. But the country was as chaotic and corrupt as ever, and its accounting was impenetrable. Many of its diamonds, it turned out, were being secretly smuggled across the river to Brazzaville, which explained why Brazzaville was exporting diamonds even though it produced none. And Mobutu's harsh dictatorship was causing growing bitterness among the oppressed tribes, driving the country close to civil war. In March 1977 1,500 "Katanga gendarmes" crossed over from Angola, to try to capture the copper-rich province of Shaba (Katanga), which had tried to secede fifteen years earlier; they pushed back the disorganized Zaire army until a contingent of Moroccan troops was flown in in French planes, and succeeded in beating them back.

In the midst of this chaos, who should arrive in Kinshasa but Irving Friedman, the man from Citibank, accompanied by his wife. He was visiting Zaire for the first time, he explained, for a firsthand assessment of Zaire's new economic program. He had a long talk with Mobutu, who seemed more amenable in the midst of his troubles, and he later pronounced that Zaire's program was "sound and austere," and that Mobutu and his officials were fully committed to it—which caused some amusement to Kinshasa expatriates. Citibank played down the dangers: as the head of the international banking group, George Vojta, put it: "There's not a day gone by without trouble some place."[21]

But the chaos continued. Mobutu soon dismissed the governor of the Central Bank, and stopped paying money into the special account. The IMF insisted that it must have its own man in the Central Bank. Citibank was still using its "best efforts" to put together the new loan, pressing other banks to join it. But just when the loan agreement looked almost ready for signing, Zaire faced a new catastrophe. The invaders from Angola attacked again and reached the copper city of Kolwezi, causing havoc in which forty-four whites were massacred. Mobutu called in French and Belgian troops to restore order, who rescued two thousand whites and routed the invaders, to the relief of Wriston at Citibank: "As an American, I can thank God that the French elections went the way they did."[22] But Mobutu's prestige was still further damaged, and the bankers were still less confident of ever getting their money back. The IMF withdrew its team in despair. When the World Bank sent a mission under a Dutch economist, his house was broken into by soldiers, and his two young daughters raped. The World Bank made no further loans. The greed of Mobutu and his family was insatiable: in September the President's uncle, Citoyen Lito, bought a giant Hercules plane from Lockheed for $13 million in precious foreign currency, for his own extensive commercial operations.

Citibank had now virtually abandoned the "Friedman initiative" to raise a new loan. The IMF was convinced that Zaire's finances had to be reorganized, to stem the corruption and the flow of funds seeping out of the country. To try to pacify his creditors the President had proclaimed his own Plan Mobutu to produce more copper and food, and the bankers seized the chance to commit him to changes. By August 1978 a retired German banker, Erwin Blumental, had arrived in the Central Bank in Kinshasa, as the representative of the IMF, to try to make sense of it. He soon bravely took steps to limit corruption; he issued a directive forbidding any bank from dealing with the most rocky companies, including some of Uncle Lito's. Mobutu tried to protect his family and friends, but Blumental was now in a strong position to control credit.

Mobutu had now virtually accepted the neo-colonizing of his country. He abandoned his strident nationalism, welcomed back Belgians who had once been the hated imperialists to train his army, and leased out a huge territory as a testing ground for the West German missile company OTRAG. But the bankers still could not be confident: by 1979 the total foreign debt of Zaire was $3 billion, inflation was 200 percent a year, and about half the annual exports of diamonds, copper, coffee, and cobalt were now reckoned to go to Mobutu's family and friends. The bankers could see very little prospect of getting their money back.

THE MERRY-GO-ROUND

Zaire and Indonesia were only two extreme examples of the bankers' rash adventures. In many other parts of the Third World —from Peru to the Philippines, from Jamaica to Korea—they were likewise extending their loans. They could make bigger profits, whether from interest rates or from fees, than in the highly organized markets in America and Europe. But how safe was their money, who was really bearing the risk? Some congressmen were baffled and angry that the bankers should prefer these outlandish countries to their home ground in the West. Why, asked Congressman St. Germain of the House Banking Committee, should bankers refuse money to New York and then lend it to Zaire? Why, asked Congressman D'Annunzio, should they reject Italy: "Are we red-lining our friends and our allies who are fighting the battle of Communism?"[23]

[23]House Banking Committee, *International Banking Operations,* March 23, 1977.

By 1977 the bankers themselves were more worried: the developing countries (excluding OPEC) now owed about $75 billion to commercial banks, of which $45 billion was to American banks. "Bank debt to a number of these countries," said David Rockefeller in March 1977, "has been expanding at a rate that should not be—and cannot be—sustained. Lenders will be increasingly selective and cautious in adding such credits to their portfolios. Certainly, that is our posture at Chase."[24] The austere chairman of the Fed, Arthur Burns, issued a more severe warning the next month. "With many countries now heavily burdened with debt," he explained, "bankers generally recognize that prudence demands moderation on their part in providing additional financing for deficit countries. More than one country has recently found that its ability to borrow in the private market has diminished. The fact is that commercial banks generally, and particularly those which have already made extensive loans abroad, are now evaluating risks more closely and more methodically."[25] Which in Bankspeak meant that they had been far too rash, and *should* evaluate their risks more closely.

But many banks were now locked into their developing clients; and once in, it was difficult to get out. Sometimes the only way they could avoid a default, as in Zaire, was by lending still more money—with no end in sight. As the Senate study of 1977 described it:

> The viability of the whole international system is premised on the assumption that all the players stay in the game: that the banks continue lending, and the borrowers keep repaying the interest so that, although the principal may be refinanced or "rolled over" for individual borrowers, the money continues to circulate. The biggest threat to the system lies in the possibility that one of the passengers on this merry-go-round will decide to get off—that one of the large debtors finally decides to repudiate its debt, or one of the lenders says "no more" and calls in the chits.[26]

[24]*American Banker* (March 16, 1977).
[25]Speech at Columbia University, April 12, 1977.
[26]*Staff Report,* 1977, p. 61.

To try to stabilize the merry-go-round after their harrowing experiences some bankers were already beginning to look toward the International Monetary Fund to inform them, to enforce discipline, or to be their ultimate debt collectors. Gabriel Hauge, the chairman of Manny Hanny, proposed that some loans should be jointly financed by the banks and the Fund. But most bankers, including Wriston (see Chapter 18), dreaded any restrictions on their enterprise. They were happy to keep on the merry-go-round, which allowed everyone to keep on making a profit, provided they did not ask for their money back. And even when there was a disaster, as in Zaire and Indonesia, the bankers had the upper hand: it was the people of Zaire and Indonesia who paid for the mistakes, not the bankers. But what then was the sanction against the bankers' rashness? As "Adam Smith" put it: "Imprudent banks are supposed to be punished by the marketplace, by going out of business. But the banks were so interdependent that an imprudent bank could cause the collapse of the System."[27]

Bankers continued to insist that they were behaving strictly commercially. But the whole system of credit, as in the property booms in London or Florida, had mythical assumptions at the heart of it. Everyone had to pretend that Zaire, like an overvalued piece of real estate, was much safer than it really was: all the profits and precise calculations depended on a kind of confidence trick. But Zaire remained very different from a London office block or a Florida condominium; for while these properties were always likely to recover their value, it was much harder to look forward to Zaire being able to repay its debts.

There were very few people who chose to point out that this emperor had no clothes. One of them was Harold Lever, the British Labour cabinet minister who was an acknowledged expert in international finance. He had perceived that, since the oil crisis of 1973, official aid to the Third World was rapidly being eclipsed by the massive loans from the banks, which were, he insisted, really a concealed form of aid, since the bankers were unlikely to get their money back. These large transfers, Lever reckoned, were

[27] *Paper Money* (New York: Summit Books, 1981), p. 254.

essential to rescue developing countries from their predicament since the oil crisis; and they had the advantage that they did not need Parliament's approval. But they could be perilous if they were not properly overseen and controlled. He proposed to his prime minister, Harold Wilson, that the government should monitor the loans more carefully, and bring them into a more organized system; and he went to Washington and New York to discuss the problem with the Treasury and with bankers, including Rockefeller and Wriston. But neither bankers nor politicians were anxious to agree with Lever's theories: the bankers still liked to see themselves as hard-headed men of business, and governments dreaded being too closely responsible for lending abroad. The players still went round and round on their carousel, hoping for dear life that the music would not stop.

11
APARTHEID: THE EYE
OF GOD

Apartheid is morally and economically unacceptable.

ANTHONY TUKE
Chairman of Barclays
April 3, 1974

Many bankers looked with relief toward a country that was both rich and disciplined, run by white men who spoke the same language, with a long tradition of friendship with the West. South Africa was almost a bankers' paradise: a country sitting on gold, with exciting industrial prospects, dynamic entrepreneurs, and workers who could never strike. It was true that its system of apartheid was abhorrent to Western liberals and churches, and to blacks in America: but why should that stir up any more indignation than other autocratic countries, like Brazil, South Korea, or Eastern Europe, where banks were also lending heavily? Could critics really believe that blacks in South Africa had a worse life than blacks in Zaire? As South Africa became more prosperous with the help of the banks, was not the position of the blacks bound to improve?

With such arguments few bankers had serious misgivings about extending their loans to South Africa, and they were irritated and bewildered when they found themselves in the midst of political and moral debates, which even began to damage their business at home. Shareholders and depositors began to challenge their bankers' authority: they made connections between their deposits and the political consequences of loans, and they claimed the right to stop banks lending their money to undesirable regimes. In the ensuing battles they forced bankers to do what they least like to do—to choose.

South Africa had attracted bankers and investors since the late nineteenth century, when diamonds and gold were discovered. Rothschilds in London financed Cecil Rhodes, the British adventurer who created the diamond monopoly of De Beers, built up Consolidated Goldfields in Johannesburg, and annexed Rhodesia as his company's private property. South African gold mines created a vast new source of wealth, most of which at first made its way back to London, through the new breed of gold millionaires. But as South Africa developed and achieved political autonomy after the Union of 1910, the control of its wealth passed into the hands of the South African tycoons, and later of the Afrikaners, who had forged their own nationalism in their wars against the British. As the black population began to assert their nationalism, South Africa looked like a caricature of capitalism, with the workers all painted black, the bosses all white, and gold at the heart of the economy. In spite of their wealth the white South Africans still needed to borrow money and technology from Europe and America to finance their economic expansion and military buildup. The bankers who lent to them found themselves in the front line of a racial conflict with global repercussions.

The first South African banks were corrugated-iron shacks set up for the savings of the early settlers and miners. The Standard Bank of South Africa was founded in 1860, doing business for the British colonial governments; the National Bank was established in 1890, with support from the Afrikaner patriarch President Kruger; and these two competed for the huge growth of local savings after the diamond and gold booms. When in 1925 the National Bank ran into difficulties after competing too rashly, it was bought out by the big British bank, Barclays—which thus came into the midst of the South African political turmoil.

BARCLAYS AND QUAKERS

It was ironic that Barclays should become the most involved in this racial battleground, for it was the most Quaker of all British banks, associated with peace and philanthropy. It had been formed as a joint-stock bank in 1896—the most recent of the big banks—as an alliance of twenty family banks, mostly Quaker and many interrelated, which clubbed together in defense against the other giants. The families were determined to keep their influence, and Barclays remained a group of loosely linked regional banks, with representatives on the main board. "It has always been relatively easy," says one official history, "for a scion of the old Quaker families to reach a high position in Barclays."[1] The families ever since have dominated Barclays, with surprisingly little complaint from other managers; in 1980 the board included a Barclay, a Bevan, a Tuke, a Gurney, and a Tritton—all from old Quaker stock.

The chairman always comes from one of the families. For twelve years until 1962 he was Sir Anthony Tuke, known as the "Iron Tuke," an outspoken conservative who dominated his colleagues. After an interval the job passed in 1973 to Tuke's son, also Anthony, a less confident banker with a rather petulant style who was soon to bear the brunt of the political attacks. (He was in turn succeeded in 1981 by Timothy Bevan, a direct descendant of Silvanus Bevan, who had joined the Barclays family bank in 1767.) The Quaker tradition still shows itself in the public service of some directors like Lord Seebohm, the former deputy chairman who has presided over committees on welfare; but they did not extend their social conscience to business dealings with South Africa.

When Barclays first bought the National Bank in South Africa it became part of the imperial network built up by its offshoot

[1]Sir Julian Crossley and John Blandford, *The DCO Story* (London: Barclays Bank International, 1975), Introduction by Anthony Tuke, p. 229.

Barclays DCO (Dominion, Colonial, and Overseas). It was not until after the Second World War that it faced serious political problems—not with the blacks, but with the Afrikaners, who under Dr. Malan were proclaiming the new doctrine of apartheid. The Afrikaner government encouraged its own banks, including the Volkskas and the Trust Bank, while the two British-owned banks felt threatened and were anxious to please the Afrikaners. The government well understood how to exploit the foreign banks, using their loans, technical skills, and international links without actually nationalizing them (as Hitler had done with the German Big Three). Barclays was proud of its role in helping the Third World. "Few institutions were doing more," says its official history, "towards helping the emerging nations on the road to economic viability." But it was not too concerned with black customers in South Africa. While the blacks were becoming more urbanized, more oppressed, and more politicized, Barclays was actively encouraging white immigration, and its branches remained the visible strongholds of apartheid, where the black "boys" had to line up separately to do business for their masters. (I was working in Johannesburg in the early fifties, surprised at that time to see a British bank so passively accepting the segregation it theoretically condemned.)

Barclays insisted that the South African future was hopeful, and it was much influenced by the most powerful Johannesburg tycoon, Harry Oppenheimer, the chairman of the Anglo-American Corporation and of the De Beers diamond monopoly. Oppenheimer owned 17 percent of Barclays in South Africa, and he sat on the board. He was a shrewd and sensitive financier, a model of the new-style multinational magnate, and he had expanded his gold-and-diamonds business into a giant minerals group extending through black Africa, by pursuing a policy of facing-all-ways. He could do deals with Nyerere in Tanzania or with Kaunda in Zambia, as well as with racist South African governments; he financed both the South African Foundation, which supported apartheid propaganda, and also the Progressive Party, which called for nonracial government.

In private talks Oppenheimer always maintained that growing

prosperity would undermine the barriers of apartheid, because industry would need skilled blacks to work it and the markets of black Africa to sell to. He deplored the cruelties of apartheid, but he warned foreigners that pressure from abroad would only help the Afrikaner extremists. His gentle, self-effacing style combined with his wealth and financial leverage were persuasive. And Barclays was happy to be persuaded that it was benefiting the blacks by its very presence in South Africa.

The first real shock came in 1960, when police attacked peaceful black demonstrators in the township of Sharpeville and killed sixty-nine of them. In the subsequent panic the Johannesburg stock market tumbled, land values slumped, foreign investment almost ceased, the Prime Minister, Dr. Verwoerd, was shot at and nearly killed by a white farmer, and some of the ablest young whites emigrated. Sharpeville was a brutal demonstration that the whites could maintain their domination only by force, and many liberals now hoped that international disapproval could be effective. But South Africa's riches were soon again luring overseas investors and corporations, while Verwoerd was anxious to borrow abroad, not only to relieve the economic crisis, but to forge new links with international finance. In the year after Sharpeville he received welcome support from a new source—David Rockefeller of the Chase Manhattan Bank.

Rockefeller had visited Africa in the year before Sharpeville, when he had opened an office of the Chase in Johannesburg; and the Chase, with Citibank and others, had led a consortium to provide $40 million of "revolving credit" to South Africa. Rockefeller was undeterred by Sharpeville, and saw a chance to get on the inside track with Pretoria by publicly showing his friendship. In 1961 the Chase made a $10 million loan to South Africa, and soon joined a consortium to lend $150 million. Rockefeller's stamp of approval was much publicized, and led to bitter attacks on the immorality of his bank. But the Chase replied: "We believe it would endanger the free world if every large American bank deprived developing countries of the opportunity for economic growth. If one hopes for changes in the Republic of South Africa, or elsewhere, it would do little good to withdraw economic support." Rockefeller continued to show his approval with aggressive support; five years after Sharpeville the Chase bought a 15 percent share in the Standard Bank, Barclays' old rival with 800 branches in South Africa, which was now spreading itself round the world, discreetly shedding the words "of South Africa" from its title.

But the loans were soon arousing opposition from the American civil rights movement, from churches, black organizations, and the United Nations; and in 1966 they launched a campaign against ten American banks that were sharing a revolving loan to South Africa. They bombarded them with letters, delegations, leaflets, and demonstrations: they picketed annual meetings and raised questions to embarrass the chairmen. The Chase was their special target, and at the annual meeting in 1967 picketers displayed signs saying, "Apartheid has a friend at Chase Manhattan." A Philadelphia stockholder proposed a resolution that Chase should withdraw from South Africa, and David Rockefeller read out a careful statement separating morality from economics with the stock bankers' response: "None of us holds any brief for apartheid," he began. "In fact, we regard it as a dangerous and shocking policy." But the withdrawal of the Chase, he went on, would be a setback for blacks: "No matter what one may think about the moral or ethical implications of apartheid, one must acknowledge that the black people of South Africa are far better off economically than the black people anywhere else in the African continent."

The bankers' view of South Africa in the sixties was summed up in a later statement by Joel Stern, the president of Chase Financial Policy: "It was a period of exceptional growth in a highly industrialized and exceptionally productive and efficient society in the utilization of physical and human resources."[2] But the churches' view, as expressed by the World Council of Churches, was: "Apartheid has worked its economic miracle—which now looks increasingly threadbare—by taking away from the black South African his humanity and treating him not as a human being,

[2]Senate Foreign Relations Committee, Subcommittee on African Affairs, Hearings on South Africa, September 9, 1976.

but as an economic abstraction, a unit of production."[3]

The campaign against the American banks began to have some effect: depositors withdrew only about $23 million, but the banks wanted to avoid controversy in the highly charged racial atmosphere, and they knew that apartheid was associated with discrimination at home. By 1969 the ten banks had closed their revolving loan; but other loans continued, and there was a new surge of lending in the early seventies. Citibank was now, as in other parts of the world, overtaking the Chase as the biggest American lender: between 1974 and 1976 it was to participate in loans of $230 million to the South African Iron and Steel Corporation (ISCOR), $230 million to South African Electricity (ESCOM), and $110 million to the government itself; while Citibank's own loans to South Africa rose to over $400 million. The American lending was specially welcome now that the South African government felt itself increasingly isolated: as Professor Steenkamp of the University of South Africa put it: "We have learned that our large international economic relationships are our best shield in a world which has chosen us as scapegoats."[4]

But the campaigners were well aware of this, and kept up the pressure on the banks. The World Council of Churches, made up of 286 member churches, took the lead in a militant spirit. "The fundamental strand which runs through all that the World Council of Churches has written," it insisted, "is that banking and all commercial life—and all of life itself—come under moral judgment, and that there is no place where we may go and hide and say that we have escaped the eye of God."[5] The World Council needed a focus for action, and it found its opportunity in July 1972, when some banking papers called the "Frankfurt Documents" were leaked to an American church group. The documents showed that $200 million had been secretly lent to South Africa by the European-American Bank, a consortium operating in

[3] *World Council of Churches and Bank Loans to South Africa,* WCC, Geneva 1977, p. 7.
[4] *Ibid.,* p. 7.
[5] *Ibid.,* p. 43.

204 / THE MONEY LENDERS

the United States which had close links with the South African diamond trade, owned by six major European banks[6] (which was soon to take over the failing Franklin Bank in New York, see Chapter 9). The World Council asked all six banks to assure them that they would make no further loans, but they all refused. "If we were to allow ourselves to be influenced in our business dealings by political views of this kind," said the Midland, "our international business would rapidly become impossible."[7]

The World Council then withdrew its funds from the six banks, and urged all churches to do the same. In Britain a Methodist minister took up the campaign against the Midland, in which the Methodists held shares, and by April 1976 a formidable group of British shareholders, including the (Anglican) Church Commissioners, the Methodist Church, and the Greater London Council, sponsored a resolution asking the Midland to make no further loans to South Africa. In Holland a well-organized protest group boycotted the Amsterdam-Rotterdam Bank, which at first doggedly refused any concession but then dramatically changed its policy and undertook to make no new loans. In America the general campaign against banks was having some effect, and eight banks promised not to lend any more to South Africa. One of them (Maryland National) was boycotted by black community groups and the United Church of Christ, until it sent a delegation out to Africa: the bank then totally reversed its policy, and even divested itself of existing loans to South Africa.

BARCLAYS' DILEMMA

In Britain the opponents of apartheid concentrated on Barclays. Several other British companies and banks (including the Midland and Hill Samuel) were at least equally friendly with South Africa,

[6]The Deutsche Bank in West Germany, the Midland in Britain, the Société Générale in France, the Société Générale du Banque in Belgium, the Amsterdam-Rotterdam (AMRO) in Holland, and the Kreditanstalt in Austria.
[7]Ibid., p. 26.

but the campaigners preferred a single scapegoat. The annual meetings of Barclays in its headquarters in Lombard Street soon became a regular festival for protesters, who submerged other shareholders' questions: the fifty deadpan directors sat on the stage in front of the blue Barclays symbol, with the main board in the front row, like ninepins waiting to face the questions hurled at them.

In 1969 the antiapartheid campaigners had discovered that Barclays was involved in an international consortium to build a huge dam at Cabora Bassa in Mozambique, conceived by the Portuguese as part of the strengthening of their colonial rule: it would attract Portuguese farmers to settle, help defeat the black nationalist rebels, and provide cheap electricity for both Mozambique and South Africa. The Anglo-American Corporation in Johannesburg had a contract to build roads on the site, and Barclays, as their regular bankers, guaranteed the contract. The antiapartheid forces and black African states seized on this to persecute Barclays. Lord Seebohm, then chairman of Barclays DCO, insisted that the dam was of "immense value to all races" and, after visiting Mozambique, remarked: "The Africans seem to me to get on very well; even in the most expensive hotels you will find Africans at the same table."

Barclays was also under fire for underpaying its black workers. It had accepted in 1971 the principle of equal pay for equal work; but when the Select Committee of the House of Commons investigated wages in 1973, they found that nearly all the 1,600 black workers in Barclays were cleaners, messengers, and tea maids, and that many of the cleaners in rural areas were paid well below the "poverty datum line" (PDL). "A cleaner at Barclays National Bank at Ladysmith," reported the Select Committee, "would require ten years of service to reach the poverty datum line. . . . This did not appear to square with Barclays' statement that a family man should be paid considerably more than the PDL."[8] There-

[8]Fifth Report of Expenditure Committee 1973–74, House of Commons Paper 1116.

after Barclays increased its black wages, employed more blacks as clerks, and promised that it would try to reform apartheid from within; by 1979 it had achieved a breakthrough (as Anthony Tuke described it) by putting some blacks in charge of whites.[9] But there was not much evidence of the promised reforms from within: in 1980 Barclays was reported by the British Labour attaché in Pretoria to be still paying some of its cleaners below the Poverty Datum Line.[10]

The more militant critics called for Barclays' complete withdrawal from South Africa. In 1972 Anthony Tuke insisted that if Barclays withdrew "all that would have happened would be that Barclays, who are recognized as a liberal and international organization, would have given way to a South African-owned company, possibly with a narrower outlook." The critics replied that Barclays had not shown itself any more enlightened than South African employers (particularly than Oppenheimer, who would probably take over if it withdrew); and that Barclays' ownership gave political, financial, and psychological support to the white rulers.

It was a familiar trap for multinational companies: Barclays was trying to straddle nations with opposite political philosophies with a foot in each camp; and as the gap widened it was doing splits. The gap was still more visible in Rhodesia after 1965, where the white minority had declared their independence while the British tried to impose sanctions. Barclays, which had a chain of banks in the rebel colony as well as in black states to the north, was thoroughly evasive. "It was hard to say where DCO stood," says the Barclays official history. "Legally our offices in Rhodesia, over eighty in number, were and still are part of the bank. . . . Fortunately the Rhodesian section of DCO was already virtually autonomous. . . . The UDI had in effect been anticipated and made no change in the administration of the bank's affairs save that London could no longer approve or reject proposals put forward by Salisbury."[11]

[9]Annual General Meeting, May 1980.
[10]*The Observer,* June 8, 1980.
[11]*DCO Story,* pp. 250–52.

Barclays in fact stood both everywhere and nowhere. In Rhodesia it could exchange funds freely with its South African branches and advertised that "a Bank that operates in over forty countries must have their finger on the pulse of international trade"; while in London it could disclaim any control over its Rhodesian branches while it was making good profits out of the transfer of Rhodesian funds through South Africa.

SOWETO AND AFTER

In the early seventies the Pretoria government was pushing through massive investments, many of them linked to its military buildup to make it independent of the West; and after the gold price collapsed in 1974 it had to borrow more urgently. In the words of a U.S. Senate report: "International credit provided the margin of funds needed by South Africa in the 1974–76 years to increase its economic and strategic self-sufficiency."[12] White South Africans were feeling much less secure after the victories of black nationalists in Mozambique and Angola and the spreading civil war in Rhodesia. But the banks were glad to lend to a country with such rich resources and gold reserves. Between 1972 and 1974 South Africa borrowed about $6 billion from the international capital markets, most of it going to the government, public corporations, or local authorities which were part of the iron structure of apartheid.

Ever since Sharpeville the police had tightened their control over the black townships, with the help of fiercer legislation against protests and demonstrations, bans on the two main black parties, and more systematic use of torture. They had taken special precautions in Soweto, the sprawling black township outside Johannesburg, which housed most of the city's black workers, with its rows of tiny box-houses and its strategic police stations.

[12]Senate Foreign Relations Committee, *U.S. Corporate Interests in South Africa,* Washington, 1978, p. 22.

Soweto was the underside of white South Africa's prosperity, which very few foreign businessmen ever visited. And it was in Soweto, in June 1976, that black schoolchildren began demonstrating against the enforced use of the Afrikaans language in their schools. Police moved in and began shooting, and in the subsequent riots hundreds of blacks were killed. Shops were looted, gangsters roamed the streets, and a local Barclays subbranch was set ablaze. The Soweto riots were followed by a new wave of police terror; and a year later the most effective black leader, Steve Biko, was arrested, kept naked and in chains, interrogated and tortured, and finally beaten to death by the police.

The schoolchildren of Soweto provoked a more serious economic crisis than Sharpeville. South Africa had already been feeling the harsh winds of the world depression; now the world's confidence in the permanence of white rule seemed to evaporate. South African gold shares dropped further. Land values collapsed, bankrupting property companies and threatening the banks which financed them. European and American companies soon began selling off their South African subsidiaries. Money was flowing out as rapidly as it flowed in. The Pretoria government had to impose import controls, and strict measures to save fuel. And it again looked to foreign bankers, as it had after Sharpeville, to provide not only loans but international support in its time of isolation.

But the banks were now much less confident about South Africa's stability, and very conscious of the glare of world publicity. Even the Swiss bankers were now in retreat. Robert Studer, senior vice-president of the Union Bank of Switzerland, told a South African conference that there was now serious concern that apartheid could produce revolution, civil war, or underground warfare, and even open war between West and East. "The very existence of these incalculable risks," he warned the South Africans, "would result in the decline of the flood of foreign capital in the future, or in it drying up completely. . . ."[13]

Barclays in London could no longer altogether disclaim respon-

[13] *Africa Contemporary Record,* 1977–78, p. B876.

sibility for Barclays in South Africa. Soon after Soweto its chief executive in South Africa, Bob Aldworth, made some remarks about the difficulties of raising loans which drew a sharp rebuke from the government, and he quickly tried to make amends by investing in £15 million worth of Defence Bonds, which the government had recently launched without much success. He publicly explained that this was to show the bank's social responsibility, both to South Africa and to members of the staff who were doing military service: "We do have a large number of our boys called up continually. We stand behind them." Barclays in London hastily explained that this was "a decision made in South Africa by a South African board."[14] But this commitment to the South African forces outraged British shareholders, all the more coming from an old Quaker bank. Institutions protested, the Prime Minister condemned the investment as "insensitive," and a new uproar broke out at Barclays' next annual meeting in London. The chairman, Sir Anthony Tuke, still insisted that he could not interfere with his subsidiary: "We're not permitted by the British revenue authorities to give them instructions." But when pressed he explained: "I have suggested to the South African board that these bonds will be . . . er . . . should be sold as soon as it is permitted to do so." And he now spelt out more clearly his opposition to Pretoria's policies: "In order to buy arms from abroad South Africa needs foreign currency and it remains our policy here in London not to lend currency to the South African government."[15]

Barclays was now getting the worst of both worlds. The directors in South Africa resented having their hands forced, and Pretoria was indignant at this overt interference; while the British shareholders were still unsatisfied, because Barclays still had loans outstanding to South African public corporations. The black African states were also furious that Barclays was financing the South African army, and demanded that Barclays cease lending altogether.

[14]London *Times,* December 15, 1976; *Financial Times,* December 16, 1976.
[15]Annual General Meeting, April 6, 1977.

The most formidable pressure was from Nigeria—the most populous black nation of all, whose new oil wealth now made it a more important trading partner to Britain than South Africa. Nigeria warned "double-dealers" that they would have to choose between Nigeria and South Africa; and Barclays had a chain of branches in Nigeria, 40 percent owned by the London parent. By March 1978 the Nigerians were insisting that Barclays withdraw from South Africa. When Tuke restated that Barclays would stay there, the Nigerian government ordered the withdrawal of all its deposits.[16] Barclays' patchwork of black and white investments was beginning to split at the seams. Yet despite all these pressures Barclays still proved more resistant to making concessions than the American banks, which now faced more highly organized protests.

In the United States the atrocities of Soweto and the murder of Steve Biko had set off a new wave of campaigning, which forced the bankers to declare their positions more openly. There were significant differences in their responses. The Chase was under fire, not only from shareholders and depositors, but from some of its own senior executives and directors, including Father Theodore Hesburgh, the president of Notre Dame University, who sat on its main board. "The arguments about South Africa run right through this building," one executive in the Chase headquarters said wearily. In 1977 David Rockefeller felt compelled to announce a new Code of Ethics, which promised "strict attention to the legal, moral and social implications of all loan and investment decisions on a global basis": it specifically excluded any loans to South Africa "that, in our judgment, tend to support the apartheid policies of the South African government or reinforce discriminatory business practices." The Bank of America carefully avoided any moral commitment, but explained its position in 1979 in a classic example of Bankspeak: "In South Africa the consequences of the apartheid policy create social unrest that adversely affects the country-risk rating of that nation. Hence, the Corporation's

[16]*Africa Contemporary Record,* 1977–78, p. B749; *The Guardian,* March 23, 1978.

lending activities in South Africa are restrained and will continue to be so." Morgan's was under fire from several institutions, including Harvard and Yale, which showed their disapproval by selling their Morgan bonds. But Morgan's remained noncommittal: in a proxy statement in 1978 it insisted that extending credit did not imply political approval, and that refusal to lend "could work considerable hardship on all the people of that country, most especially on those who suffer the greatest disadvantage under apartheid."

The Chemical Bank was specially sensitive to criticism, as the chief bankers to the UN headquarters, a few blocks down the street; there had been several tense meetings between its management and top UN officials, and its chairman, Donald Platten, publicly voiced his moral abhorrence. "Chemical Bank is strongly opposed to apartheid," said a policy statement in 1978, "and consequently has a policy prohibiting any loan transactions with the government of South Africa. Chemical has not made any term commitments to the government or to government-controlled instrumentalities since 1974."

The most unrepentant was Citibank, the biggest single lender to South Africa, which was responsible for nearly a quarter of all American bank lending. Citibank was now the chief target for protesters, wearing buttons saying CITIBANK FINANCES APARTHEID. George Vojta, Citibank's executive vice-president, explained to the U.S. Senate after the Soweto massacre that "Citibank regards its corporate mission as bringing the provision of a full range of financial services everywhere in the world where it can legally operate at a profit." It would be improper, he insisted, for a private business institution to make an explicit political judgment about South Africa; it likewise made no judgment on the Soviet Union, where it also operated. The rule for all multinational corporations round the world must be "hands off!"[17] Vojta insisted that Citibank's presence in South Africa benefited all its people, and "contributes to the development of a more pluralistic social system."

[17]Senate Foreign Relations Committee: *U.S. Corporate Interests in South Africa,* Washington, 1978, p. 226.

His assessment was quickly contradicted by Tim Smith, the director of the Interfaith Center on Corporate Responsibility, and a leading campaigner: American firms, he insisted, were promoting the pro-white position, while the gap between black and white wages had widened. At Citibank's annual meeting in 1977, Dr. Richard Ernst of the Southern Presbyterian Church, leading a large group of shareholders, took up the charge. "Citibank," he said, "is viewed around the world as one of the major props for their regime."

"The governments on the left always get a better press than those on the right," Wriston complained to me. "I guess shooting people with those kind of liberal bullets is better than the other kind. I don't know—I'm not too impressed with that argument frankly." But shareholders forced even Citibank to make some concessions. In 1978 it announced that it was no longer lending to the South African government or state corporations. "We regard apartheid as having a negative effect on South Africa's economic viability," it told shareholders in a special mailed statement, "and so long as this is the case we will continue to moderate our business involvement in the country. . . . Citicorp is limiting its credit, selectively, to constructive private sector activities that create jobs and which benefit all South Africans." Citibank still stopped short of any moral condemnation of apartheid, and would not promise not to resume lending to the government if the "economic viability" improved. It still lent to private organizations in South Africa, and several American church organizations withdrew accounts worth over $60 million.

In the meantime the money mandarins at the International Monetary Fund remained impervious to the political and military implications of apartheid. Just before Soweto, South Africa had already asked the IMF in January 1976 for a loan of $93 million, together with a standby arrangement, to tide it over its economic crisis, which (as an IMF study made clear) had been largely caused by military spending. The Belgian director, Jacques de Groote (who also represented Austria, Luxemburg, and Turkey), pointed out that South Africa deliberately restricted sales of gold to keep up the price. The director from Upper Volta, Antoine Yameogo, representing seventeen black states, insisted that South Africa's falling exports were due to its treatment of black workers. But the British representative, Peter Bull, explained that the standby arrangement would give the South African authorities "some feeling of international support, which they deserve"; and the loan to Pretoria duly went through.

Five months after Soweto, when the gold price was falling further, South Africa asked the IMF for a new loan of $186 million through the "compensatory financing facility"; the fund which had been planned to protect poorer countries against falling commodity prices was now invoked to help their rich enemy. When the IMF executive board heard the request in November 1976, they did not discuss arms spending or Soweto. The Italian director, Lamberto Dini, supported the loan, explaining that South Africa had cooperated fully with the Fund and that her difficulties were partly due to "political uncertainties at home." The West German director, Eckhard Pieske, was concerned about the high inflation in South Africa, but not with the spending. Thomas Leddy, the American director, insisted that the fall in exports was "due to factors largely beyond South Africa's control."[18]

The loan duly went through. During 1976 the IMF had lent South Africa a total of $464 million, and the next year it lent another $107 million. In those two critical years, in the midst of all the world protest and pressure, South Africa had received from the Fund more than any country except Britain and Mexico, and more than the rest of Africa together. The IMF loans, as it happened, almost exactly corresponded to the increase in South Africa's arms spending during that time.[19]

[18] IMF Confidential Document: "Minutes of Executive Board Meeting," November 10, 1976; January 21, 1976.

[19] James Morrell and David Gisselquist, How the IMF Slipped $464 Millions to South Africa (Washington: Center for International Policy, January 1978).

APARTHEID AND ISOLATION

Three years after Soweto the South Africans, with all their reserves and gold mines, were becoming painfully aware of the difficulty of borrowing money. "It is no secret," complained the chubby Minister of Finance, Owen Horwood, in 1979, "that there is not one foreign bank that talks to us that does not say that if they looked at this country from an economic point of view there is no reason why terms and conditions should not be better."[20] It was specially galling in contrast to black Africa: in late 1978 the South African government found it could only borrow Eurodollars at 1.5 percent above the standard rate for only five years; while soon afterward the Bank of America lent $12 million at the same rate for ten years to the national airline of Tanzania, one of the poorest countries in Africa. Swiss and German banks continued to make profitable loans at the high interest rates; the Deutsche Bank, indifferent to protesters, became Pretoria's chief banking ally, and in 1980 it appeared publicly at the top of a tombstone announcing a big South African loan. But most British and American banks had now stopped lending to the government or public corporations. The few lenders preferred to deal secretly, without tombstones.

South African businessmen, including Oppenheimer, still argued that economic pressure would only force the Afrikaner government to become more intransigent and retreat "into the laager." "Those who seek to bring about change in South Africa's racial attitudes and policies by cutting us off from the capital markets of the world," Oppenheimer told a bankers' meeting in a forceful speech in Mexico in 1978, "should understand clearly that in practice, if not in intent, they are aiming at change by violence."[21] But black leaders were equally convinced that loans would only support the white regime. "If Washington wants to contribute to the development of a just society in South Africa,"

---

[20]*Euromoney* (June 1979).
[21]London *Times,* May 24, 1978.

Steve Biko said before he died in July 1977, "it must discourage investment in South Africa. We blacks are quite willing to suffer the consequences. We are quite accustomed to suffering." Dr. Motlana, the unofficial black leader in Soweto, who took over part of Biko's leadership, was equally emphatic, and the victory of Robert Mugabe in Zimbabwe only reinforced the black leaders' belief.

In fact South African policy was now showing some outward signs of change, clearly influenced by foreign pressure—thus apparently confuting Oppenheimer's argument. When the new Prime Minister, P. W. Botha, took over from John Vorster in 1978, he was aware of the dangers of South Africa's isolation; he was determined to improve his country's image with the West and with black Africa, and he initiated some relaxations of apartheid which, however cosmetic, marked a major change of policy. When in 1979 I encountered a South African trade delegation visiting Britain—including Gerry Muller, the exuberant general manager of Nedbank, a stronghold of Afrikaner finance—they made no secret of their desperate desire to restore trading and banking relations. They admitted freely that apartheid had been modified in response to pressures from abroad; "We can only reform," one delegate stressed, "if there's pressure from abroad. You must keep it up."

Many bankers still maintained that loans for productive projects were really nonpolitical, since they would benefit whichever group was in power. Sir Anthony Tuke pointed to the Cabora Bassa Dam, which was bitterly criticized for helping the Portuguese settlers but was now a source of energy for the black government of Mozambique: "We took the view the dam was a good thing for everybody." On the same grounds Tuke defended Barclays' investment in the South African oil-from-coal process, SASOL, which was extended after the Iranian crisis of 1979. "I find it difficult to understand," he said in reply to a shareholder in 1980, "why it should be good for countries in the Western world to develop alternative energy sources . . . but that it's bad for South Africa to do precisely the same thing." But the black leaders saw SASOL as building up the government's resistance to oil boycotts and international pressure, and in 1980 SASOL became literally explosive. The existing plant was blown up by guerrillas of the banned African National Congress, and the dust from the explosion settled ominously over the white suburbs of Johannesburg.

In their lending to South Africa the bankers had revealed all their shortsightedness and reluctance to change. They resisted any commitment to give a moral condemnation of apartheid, or to make a public statement of policy until they had to—when it was too late for them to gain much political advantage. They were more concerned with the obligations of the past than the scope of the future; and they were repeatedly overtaken by the pace of political change.

Their passive attitudes made it easy for a strong-willed and authoritarian government to manipulate them, as Bismarck or the tsar had manipulated bankers in the nineteenth century, and to use the savings of British or American customers to finance their military preparations. It needed organized protests from depositors and shareholders to make the point that the bankers had a responsibility beyond short-term profit, and that there was a link between the small customer at the counter and the large loan at the other end of the world. The bankers would only show public concern with morality if they were forced to; and they needed external pressure, not only to ram home their responsibility, but to point out the political hazards of their loans.

In June 1981 the Study Commission on U.S. Policy toward Southern Africa, which was funded by the Rockefeller Foundation and which included Costanzo of Citibank among its three advisers, recommended as the first objective of both corporations and government: "To make clear the fundamental and continuing opposition of the U.S. government and people to the system of apartheid." But had that really been the effect of the lending by American banks?

12
THE SUPERCOMPETITORS

No nation was ever ruined by trade.

BENJAMIN FRANKLIN

The crux of the problem is whether leaders in both industrial and developing countries have adjusted intellectually and emotionally to this being one interdependent world.

LEE KUAN YEW
Prime Minister of Singapore
October 1978

As the banks ventured farther abroad they looked naturally toward the countries whose economies were growing most rapidly, which needed to borrow money and showed prospects of being able to repay it. The combination of banking and enterprise was still changing the economic map of the world, continuing the old process in which the Bardi or the Medici had lent to medieval English monarchs, hoping to get their money back from the proceeds of exporting wool; or the Barings and Rothschilds had lent to America and Japan, expecting their returns from cotton or coal. The bankers were passive participants, but their role was indispensable. The concept of the developing world was constantly changing, as more countries were drawn into the commercial system, and during the sixties the economic map was becoming almost unrecognizable compared with the prewar years.

Nowhere was the new pace of industrial activity more spectacular than in the young nations of East Asia. Japan was already an established major industrial power, and as Japan moved into more advanced products, cars and electronics, so the more ambitious nations along the Pacific turned to making the products that the Japanese had outgrown—particularly textiles, the industry that had transformed so many nations in the past six centuries. The boom of the sixties gave new opportunities to nations that had the organization and incentive to provide Europe and America with cheap shoes, shirts, and dresses.

Twenty years ago these countries were seen as colonial outposts. Now each has made its mark on the West, whether in textiles, electronics, or banking itself. During the sixties South Korea and Taiwan grew at an annual rate of 17 percent, and Singapore at 13 percent: and they had grown without increasing inequality, as had often happened in Latin America.[1] The old "invisible hand" of Adam Smith was stretching out across the globe, to find still cheaper supplies to respond to the demand. But they needed to borrow to expand fast enough, and the bankers were thus drawn into this new Pacific challenge. Four countries in particular, sometimes known later as "the Supercompetitors" or the "Gang of Four," stood out as ambitious newcomers in the contest for trade: Taiwan, South Korea, Hong Kong, and Singapore. They all raised difficult political questions as they came closer into the world system. Would their industrial progress bring with it an extension of democracy? Could the West continue to open its markets to their exports, as the Western boom collapsed and unemployment increased? Was there room for everybody in the global marketplace?

This Pacific coastline looked vaguely like an upside-down version of Western Europe, with the same filigree patterns of islands, peninsulas, and bays, contrasted with the huge hinterland of Asia; and the traffic between the countries was more hectic than in Europe. The modernizing of East Asia looked in some ways like a replay of the industrialization of Western Europe a century earlier, with the same rush to the cities, the confusion of identities and desperate competition for markets. Europeans had grown to see their industrial achievement as part of their special discipline or white superiority, which they exported to the United States, Canada, and Australia; but this discipline was now more evident along the Pacific than the Atlantic.

[1] See Armatya Sen, *Levels of Poverty: Policy and Change,* World Bank Staff Working Paper No. 401, July 1980, pp. 32ff.

These "termite people," whom the Europeans used to mock, now appeared to be much more coordinated and synchronized than the gangling Westerners, wired up, switched on, and plugged into the new circuitry of electronic communications: their neat fingers designed to work pocket calculators, their small houses in proportion to tiny TV sets. Their ability to submerge their individuality in the team was constantly impressing Western investors and bankers. "The philosophy is built into their social system," explained James Wiesler, the head of the Asia division of the Bank of America, in October 1980. "It involves the belief that personal goals must take second place to the needs of the nation." To underline its confidence in the Pacific, the Bank of America held its 1980 annual meeting in Hong Kong, from which its president, Tom Clausen, went on to Peking to sign an agreement of cooperation; and it later bought half of a forty-story skyscraper in central Hong Kong, which it renamed Bank of America Tower.

What suddenly woke up these four countries from the deep sleep of Asia? What gave them the fire of Prometheus or the ambition of Faust to master their environment? The economists have their own explanations for their takeoff, including the role of education, land reform, savings, and access to markets. Certainly each country had some kind of head start, with aid or equipment that enabled them to ride high on the boom of the sixties, with enough momentum to survive the setbacks of the seventies. Yet their economic backgrounds were very diverse, and many territories with similar ingredients continued to slumber. Their dynamism was the result of their attitudes and psychological experience at least as much as their economic conditions. "The success is almost entirely due to good policies and the ability of the people," one distinguished economist concluded, "—scarcely at all to favorable circumstances or a good start."[2] Traveling through these countries I had the feeling of being inside a kind of time

[2]I. M. D. Little, "The Experience and Causes of Rapid Labour-Intensive Development in Korea, Taiwan, Hong Kong and Singapore, and the Possibilities of Emulation," *ILO Working Paper*, Bangkok, 1979.

machine which took me back to an earlier era in the West, of
optimism, diligence, and mercantile patriotism. "Is it true," one
young Korean asked me, "that the British used to have an empire
on which they said the sun never set?"

Taiwan was perhaps the most spectacular. Thirty years ago it was
a quiet agricultural island, with rice fields sloping up to the mountainous interior and few natural resources. Then the army from the
mainland arrived under General Chiang Kai-shek (whose son still
rules as President). With the help of massive American aid the
economy was transformed; first the farms were subdivided and
improved, with rice fields filling every patch of spare land, so that
agricultural incomes tripled in a decade; then a succession of
four-year plans transformed the economy. Factories shot up, first
making shirts or shoes, then cars, radios, and TV sets, then increasingly complex electronics and machinery. By 1965, when
the aid came to an end, Taiwan could grow on its own feet,
attracting investors and bankers, building new factories and highways out of its own savings, and borrowing only cautiously for its
major projects. The capital city of Taipeh became a jumble of
different eras—luxury hotels towering above the rows of shack
shops, girls in high heels kneeling in front of the Buddhist temple,
factory chimneys looming above the slum suburbs, farm workers
in coolie hats alongside commuters in dark suits.

In the seventies the Taiwanese suffered a succession of new
setbacks. The oil shock upset their whole balance of trade; the
recognition of mainland China made them leave all international
organizations; and the second shock tipped the balance even
more. Yet they responded with a new burst of energy, redirecting
their exports and buying nuclear power stations, and their exclusion from the world community only stimulated them further. Like
Israel, this island state saw itself surrounded by enemies and dangers; it was one of the club of outsiders who had to find friends
where they could. And the Taiwanese felt themselves constantly
challenged to show that theirs was the real and enduring Chinese

revolution as opposed to the temporary Marxist revolution on the mainland.

They showed few doubts about the root of their success; it was sheer necessity. I asked K. T. Li, the veteran cabinet minister who was a scientist in Cambridge (England) before he helped to organize Taiwan's economic planning. "Only adversity," he said, "can build a nation." They had, he explained, to choose the right policy at the right time, moving from agriculture to industry to electronics. "Now we must be like Switzerland—we must concentrate on high technology." It was not just the Communist ideology, he conceded, that made the mainland Chinese so different, it was their lack of exposure to the world's economic challenges: "The interior makes people introvert; the coast makes them extrovert." "If we don't work hard, we can't survive," said Robert Chien of the Central Bank of Taiwan; "not just economically, but politically. The big nations like India know that the other powers will have to help them, but we can never assume that: we're like the poor kid who just has to work hard."

KOREA AND DEMOCRACY

The South Koreans achieved their industrial success on a much larger scale, with nearly 40 million people, three times Taiwan's population, on their mountainous peninsula sticking out from the Chinese mainland. But their phenomenal organization raised more worrying questions about the relationship between industrialization, political freedom, and Western financial support.

Three decades ago their prospects looked unusually hopeless. They emerged after the Second World War from a forty-year Japanese occupation, first to be partitioned, then to be wrecked and brutalized by a fratricidal civil war. South Korea had been almost defeated before the UN troops fought back to the previous partition line; and most of the industry was in the Communist north.

The South Koreans, like the Taiwanese, received generous American aid and military protection. They were highly literate, as the legacy of the Japanese occupation, and they could push through land reform, which brought about a new social revolution. They had the motivations of misery: the rubble of the war forced them to look to the future, for they could not look back. They were challenged—like the West Germans, but without their industrial experience—to outdo their Communist cousins across the border. And they were equally determined to catch up with the Japanese, with whom they had a complex love-hate relationship. They had felt humiliated by the Japanese occupation, while they despised the Japanese as cultural barbarians; yet the Japanese had taught them the importance of modern disciplines—of punctuality, practical education, and industrial organization. In the fifties the Japanese were building up their own investments in South Korea, and selling their cast-off textile machinery as they moved ahead. The Koreans felt impelled, in the words of their proverb, to "dance to the music of their neighbors"; but they were determined eventually to out-dance them, and to play their own music.

To this common challenge the Koreans soon produced a common response. When their dictator President Park succeeded Syngman Rhee in 1960, he was able to achieve some kind of consensus for a policy of headlong industrialization, organized by a group of zealous economists, newly returned from Harvard, Stanford, and Yale. They saw their country as an economic laboratory with workers, capital, and technology flowing into the brand-new apparatus and more and more sophisticated exports flowing out. The Koreans soon built up their own trading conglomerates, like the Japanese *zaibatsu,* headed by entrepreneurs who became expert in perceiving the changes in worldwide demand. With their cheap, disciplined workers in vast spotless new factories, they could quickly undercut American companies. The buyers from Sears, Roebuck flew into Korea to get the very latest track suits and sports shoes made to their specifications at a fraction of American prices. The bankers saw that Korea was in a strong position to repay its loans. Already in 1967 the Chase had led the way into Korea, followed by the Bank of Tokyo, Citibank, Mitsubishi, the Bank of America, and the rest.

To the bankers the Korean miracle appeared as a welcome contrast to the lethargy and strikes in the West. The Koreans were the hardest workers in the world, with a military discipline and homogeneous background which encouraged teamwork. They transformed Seoul into a skyscraper city with wide avenues, elaborate hotel complexes, and flyovers concealing the slums below them. Their technocrats talked as if the whole world were a do-it-yourself supermarket in which they could buy parts of a steel factory here, a hotel complex there, and build them on green fields without any troubles from labor unions.

When the oil shock of 1974 hit the Far East the Koreans seemed among the most vulnerable people of all; but they soon responded by exporting their own workers. They flew jumbo loads out to Saudi Arabia to build roads and palaces in the grueling heat of the desert, and the foreign exchange which they sent home to their families came close to balancing the extra cost of the oil. Koreans were still bankers' favorites; after the oil shock they were quickly able to borrow $1.5 billion, and they were scrupulous in repaying like clockwork. In 1978 South Korea seemed on the way to becoming a major industrial state: its shipyards were competing with Europe and America, its "pony" cars were being exported to Europe, its TV sets were spreading round the world.

But then in the summer of 1979 the second oil shock brought a huge new increase in the import bill and a new world recession. Rapid inflation pushed up the Koreans' wages higher than their competitors'. Several big industries including cars were in trouble. President Park, surrounded by corrupt tycoons who had been enriched by government contracts, had lost much of his magic. The Korean consensus, which depended on satisfying growing expectations, already looked fragile. Then in December the President was assassinated by his own intelligence chief.

This sent shock waves through the banks. On the day after the assassination the Chase held an emergency meeting and downgraded South Korea's credit rating; in the next weeks scores of international bankers flew into Seoul to inspect the political damage. The new President Choi was a much weaker man and the

Korean technocrats were confused and bewildered, waiting for orders which did not come. In the first euphoria the workers expected higher wages and the students looked for new freedom. The opposition leader, Kim Dae Jung, who had earlier been kidnapped by Park's police from Japan, became again a focus for new hopes of freedom until he was once again jailed. In May the students demonstrated in Kwangju, and were ruthlessly suppressed by the police. The bankers were now thoroughly alarmed and made no new loans to South Korea.

Behind the scenes a power struggle was now taking place in the military. A new leader, General Chun, emerged victorious; and by mid-August he had peacefully deposed the President and established himself as the successor. Chun was determined to reimpose authority on a more puritanical and "purified" basis—ordering tycoons to repay their profits, and executives to go jogging and attend evening classes. He quickly ordered the trial of Kim Dae Jung, which turned out to be a travesty of justice, ending with his death sentence, later commuted.

South Korea had borrowed the West's money and technology, without borrowing its democracy. But bankers were reassured by the return of a strong man to the top; the day after Kim was found guilty, David Rockefeller paid a courtesy call on General Chun. By the autumn South Korea was again established as a prime credit, and the Korean Development Bank was able to borrow $600 million from a syndicate led by Bankers Trust.

Bankers still anxiously watched South Korea, for it was now less certain that they would get their money back. In 1980 their growth rate was estimated at minus 2 percent, and when I asked one of the chief technocrats about the prospects for this newly industrializing country, he replied with a wry laugh: "You mean a newly de-industrializing country?" They knew that they had to return to high growth in order to keep the people loyal to the new President, but growth was increasingly uncertain. The Koreans had invested too much in heavy industries, and the Western countries were now threatening to close their doors against more shoes or TV sets. "You are the teachers who taught us free trade," a minister complained. "Now that we succeed, you turn your backs on us." The Koreans saw themselves as the misunderstood late-comers on the world's stage. "They are acutely conscious of the image of themselves as a historical misfit in a postindustrial age, where capitalism has become an intellectual *bête noire,*" said their ambassador-at-large, Dr. Hahm Pyong-Choon, in October 1980. "The need for national discipline and work ethic is a matter of dead seriousness for Koreans. But it sounds menacingly 'authoritarian' or at best oddly anachronistic to the European ears."[3]

Would industry and prosperity bring more democracy in their wake, as they had in the West in the nineteenth century? "Once our gross national product is more than $4,000 per head," one technocrat told me, "we can afford to give people more freedom." Yet the experience of twenty years had not been encouraging. Much of the dynamic and unity seemed to depend on the military challenge from the north, which General Chun was playing up further. The organization of industry, with its close-knit conglomerates, its technical training and discipline, all revolved around strong central leadership.

Bankers and investors who put money into South Korea were back with the familiar problem of an economy built round a dictator; but this was a dictatorship supported by the most up-to-date technology, promising continued high growth provided the workers stayed obedient and the intellectuals silent. There was little sign of these new capitalist countries providing greater political liberty as they became more prosperous. Without liberty, the stability was still very uncertain.

THE HONG KONG FACTOR

Of all the attractions for Western bankers and investors in the Far East, Hong Kong was the most fascinating. It had long been a freak place which broke all the rules: a capitalist enclave on the edge

[3]Speech to Diplomatic and Commonwealth Writers Association of Britain, October 3, 1980.

of Communist China; a British colony which no one wanted to decolonize; a city-state which could compete with large nations; a last bastion of unrestrained free enterprise. This overcrowded city of 5 million Chinese could look like a throwback to the nineteenth-century jungle of Dickensian London, but with much more mobility and opportunity: a Chinese refugee might swim in from the mainland and become a millionaire ten years later. The sweatshops and tiny upstairs factories could adapt themselves to the changing world markets with a speed which baffled Western visitors, as they switched overnight from toys to digital watches, from wigs to fountain pens.

The British colonial governor maintained a policy of "positive non-interventionism" and laissez-faire much more like Victorian Britain than the contemporary welfare state, which made Hong Kong the hero country of economists like Milton Friedman. "It's like a one-legged man," Friedman said, "winning a two-legged race." The two old British trading companies or "hongs"—Jardines and Swires—each with its network of interests through the Far East, remained (just) controlled by British managers and shareholders. But they were increasingly interlocked with local capital; and Chinese financiers, traders, and bankers, each with their own connections with Peking and the mainland, were increasingly dominating Hong Kong's economy.

One of the most powerful is Sir Y. K. Pao, chairman of the World Wide Shipping Corporation and vice-chairman of the Hong Kong and Shanghai Bank, which has an interest in his large fleet and tracts of land. A genial man with a disarming smile, Pao personifies the confidence of Hong Kong. "Five years ago," he told me, "when a Chinese family sent their son to study overseas, he didn't want to come back. Now the son comes back to help the older generation, bringing new ideas and technology with him. Hong Kong will always survive: it's the gateway to Asia." He looks sadly at Britain, which he admires. "I think something happened after the Second World War; if you have too good a life, you don't want to work. It's very difficult for my good friend"—he points to a photograph of himself with Mrs. Thatcher—"to change it."

The chief manifestation of the financial power of Hong Kong is the Hong Kong and Shanghai Bank, known by old colonial hands as the "Honkers and Shankers," whose stone skyscraper (soon to be demolished) is depicted on many of the bank notes. Its colonial history covers much of the old China trade; it was set up by British merchants in the 1860s, and after being enriched by the opium and tea trade it helped to finance the first Chinese railways and introduced modern banking to much of the Far East, including Japan. In the Second World War it was seized by the Japanese, and its manager died in a Japanese prison camp. When China went Communist it lost all its mainland business, except the branch in Shanghai, which the Communists wanted to keep open as their discreet link with the West. But in Hong Kong it expanded with the industrial boom and helped to finance new industries, services, and shipping—including the empire of Sir Y. K. Pao— while its British public-school managers slowly became diluted with local Chinese.

"The Bank," as it is called in Hong Kong, had a semimonopoly which enabled it to deal roughly with American intruders like Citibank. It controlled more than half the colony's deposits so that it had to look elsewhere to expand, buying the old Mercantile Bank in India and the British Bank of the Middle East. In 1977 a restless new chairman took over, Michael Sandberg, an ex-Indian army officer with an entrepreneurial flair. He quickly pushed through a bid (with the help of Jim Wolfinsohn of Salomon Brothers) for an ailing bank in New York, the Marine Midland, the thirteenth biggest in the United States. The New York bankers, led by Citibank, which had felt done down in Hong Kong, resented this Eastern intruder, and the bid set off an epic battle. The New York State banking superintendent, the combative Muriel Siebert, disputed the need for a foreign owner and insisted on investigating the Hong Kong bank, with its network of 380 companies in forty countries and inner reserves which were kept strictly secret. Eventually the dispute was taken to the comptroller of the currency in Washington, John Heimann, who let the big deal go through. "Here comes the Yellow Peril," Sandberg joked when he met the managers of the Marine Midland, and he celebrated the merger with a banquet in New York in 1980.

It was a dramatic reversal of roles—an old colonial bank from a Chinese outpost becoming a major actor in the American money market. The Hong Kong bank, with its American subsidiary, now had a special lure for American industrialists; it could jangle its special keys to business with Peking or (as it now carefully called it) Beijing. It had never, even in the worst days of the Cultural Revolution, lost its links with Shanghai and the mainland, which were maintained through all kinds of family and business relationships. The First Chicago claimed in October 1980 to be the first American bank with a representative office in Peking; but the Honkers and Shankers boasted "the broadest representation of any foreign bank in China."

There were still many frustrations and setbacks between Peking and the financial capitals of the West, as prospects were overestimated and orders were canceled. But as China was admitted into the IMF and the World Bank and looked further toward Western technology, the bankers could still perceive thrilling opportunities behind the frenzied activity of the Pacific coastline, in the great hinterland of the Middle Kingdom.

SINGAPORE AND THE WORLD GRID

It is no accident that many of the banking centers of the world—from Hong Kong to Manhattan, from Singapore to Grand Bahama—should be found on islands; for islands provide both the detachment from the mainland and the easy access to world trade which are crucial to banking. Singapore is a vulnerable little island between two jealous neighbors—Malaysia to the north and Indonesia to the south. In the last twenty years it has become almost unrecognizable, except for the unchanging old colonial meeting place, the Raffles Hotel. The coastline itself is transformed, with reclaimed land stretching way beyond the beach road and a new container port pushing out to sea. The skyline is punctuated with the towers of hotels and government housing, and the old colonial monuments are dwarfed by office complexes with air-conditioned arcades which defy the equatorial climate. A new highway has become a miniature Wall Street, with all the familiar international banks arrayed along it—the Chase Manhattan, Bank of America, Sumitomo, Indosuez—which have chosen Singapore as their headquarters for Southeast Asia and which have been enriched by floating funds, refugee money, and bribe money from its less stable neighbors. Singapore has built up its own powerful banks, each controlled by a single Chinese entrepreneur—the Overseas Chinese (OCBC), the Overseas Union (OUB), and the United Overseas (UOB)—all now looking abroad, particularly to America, to widen their base. From the tops of these banking towers you can see clearly the closest islands of Indonesia, which begin only five miles—an easy small-boat journey—away. The proximity underlines the contrast between the chaos of Indonesia and the discipline of Singapore, which has become an object of admiration to so many bankers. "Take a country like Singapore," says Walter Wriston, "with a racial problem times two, and no natural resources: the management of that country is such that it had the confidence of the world." The more the old centers of the West appear to be losing their dynamism or drive, the more interesting becomes the question: "How did Singapore do it?"

Ever since it was taken over in 1819 by Sir Stamford Raffles, Singapore has seen itself as being the crossroads of the East, an indispensable harbor for refueling and later a major naval base, which gave the Chinese and Malays the opportunity to be trained in the dockyard, and to become expert traders. When the Singaporeans became independent they realized both their danger and their opportunities. They built on the skills which they had picked up, turning the naval base into a commercial dock. They developed the old colonial air service into one of the most successful airlines in the Third World, attracting Australians and Americans to this new crossroads of the airlanes. To provide jobs they attracted the multinational corporations, which were looking for cheaper and more disciplined workers than Europeans or Americans, and Singapore became a factory city for European and American giants—making Rolleiflex cameras, Swiss watches, and Beecham's penicillin.

Singapore combined international capitalism with domestic socialism, in a philosophy almost opposite to Hong Kong's. It became a bourgeois little island; and while other ex-British colonies, like Jamaica or Ghana, let the old colonial houses crumble and the gardens run wild, Singapore became still more like an English Surrey suburb, with neat little roundabouts, road signs, and newly mown grass verges. It lost much of its Eastern mystique, for there is nothing like American bankers or Australian tourists for dispelling the magic of the Orient. To more socialist countries Singapore appeared a caricature of neo-colonialism—the creature of the multinationals, the pawn of capitalists and bankers. But to most Singaporeans it was the triumph of pragmatism over outdated ideology; and that was the emphatic view of their durable Prime Minister, Lee Kuan Yew.

To many ambitious Asians Lee Kuan Yew, or "Harry Lee," became a symbol not only of Singapore's success but of the potential of the Third World. ("He's far too big a man for such a small country," one Korean technocrat said to me. "He should be put up for auction, to run the country which paid most for him.") With his aggressive and autocratic style he relished the role of *enfant terrible*, baiting Indians, Australians, or his domestic opponents. He began as a fiery socialist law student in London, but by the time Singapore became independent he was thoroughly pragmatic. "The question was how to make a living," he explained. "How to survive. This was not a theoretical problem in the economics of development. It was a matter of life and death for two million people . . . How this was to be achieved, by socialism or free enterprise, was a secondary matter. The answer turned out to be free enterprise, tempered with the socialist philosophy of equal opportunities for education, jobs, health, and housing."

Lee insisted that Singapore, to survive, must have a single social discipline; he was intolerant of dissidents or rebels, whether they criticized his regime or wore long hair. Like the city-states of Renaissance Italy (though without their cultural flowering) the Singaporeans saw their commercial and political future as one. Lee saw that the common danger could help to forge Singapore's unity. "It muted the rivalries between our different people," he told me, "and we could take advantage of it to pull people together." And he was determined that Singapore should learn from the rest of the world. "It's not that we're superior," he told me. "It's that our approach is right. You have to learn how to succeed, to see who performs better, and then copy them. You have to go back to first principles: how do you start developing? There will be no unique and distinctive life forms in the future; it will be one interrelated and integrated world."[4]

Lee had the same kind of view of the global marketplace as the international bankers, like Wriston or Rockefeller, with whom he could make a natural alliance; and he saw himself as a pacesetter for the rest of the Third World. "Our development would not have been possible if Singapore had not been able to plug into the world grid of industrial power houses in America, Europe, and Japan. Other developing countries should be encouraged and helped to plug into this grid. How soon and how effectively they can tap this world grid depends upon them, upon how realistic and pragmatic their governments are in their policies, so as to strike a bargain with those who have the capital, technology and management. . . ."[5]

CHOPSTICKS AND PATRIOTISM

What were the common ingredients of these four supercompetitors that distinguished them from the rest of Asia? There was an obvious ethnic factor: three of them were dominated by overseas Chinese, while the Koreans were closely related to the Chinese

[4] Interview with author, October 17, 1980.
[5] Lecture to International Chamber of Commerce, Orlando, Florida, October 5, 1978.

and their culture. The industry of Chinese exiles has been familiar enough, whether in the Chinatowns of New York, San Francisco, or London, or in other Far Eastern countries like Indonesia or Malaysia, where the Chinese minority wield financial power. The Chinese and Japanese share many cultural traditions, from chopsticks to Confucius; and they frequently explain how the legacy of Confucius encourages discipline, saving, and *diligence*—the Victorian word that has almost gone out of use in the West. Yet Confucius, with his respect for settled hierarchies and old men, for scholarship rather than commerce, could just as well be invoked *against* industrialization; the restless materialism of the young in Hong Kong would make Confucius turn in his grave. And the legacy of Confucius appears very different in mainland China itself.

No one has been more interested in the secrets of the super-competitors than the new rulers in Peking, who have been discreetly investigating their methods. For decades the mainland Chinese have been puzzled by the achievement of Hong Kong, which inspired the modernizer Sun Yat-Sen to his revolution in 1911. "How was it that foreigners could do so much as they had done with the barren rock of Hong Kong within seventy or eighty years" (he said later) "while in four thousand years China had no place like Hong Kong?"[6] The present Peking leaders are well aware of one overriding difference between mainland China and these challengers: the difference of size. They have tried to decentralize and to give more power and flexibility to their local managers; they have given special concessions to two regions close to Hong Kong, making them in effect rival free-trade zones. But they know that they cannot separate their future from the rest of their billion. When the Chinese Vice-Premier Deng Xiaoping visited Singapore he was heard to remark: "If only I just had Shanghai."

But it was not just the compactness of the four that gave them their dynamism. Each of them had experienced a common danger

[6]Maurice Collis, *Wayfoong, The Hong Kong and Shanghai Banking Corporation* (London: Faber & Faber, 1965), p. 117.

which had forced them into common action. The Chinese army which took refuge in Taiwan; the South Koreans who faced the North across the rubble of the civil war; the refugees who crossed from mainland China into Hong Kong; even the Singaporeans, the most privileged of the four, who were split off from Malaysia and looked across to a hostile Indonesia: they were all compelled to break with their past and to work together if they were to survive. Whatever hardships and uprootings that industrialization brought, it was a response to a more wretched alternative, a much greater danger. It was not the economic incentive that first woke them from their sleep; they had already been tipped out of bed. Even if they wanted to turn back, there was not much to turn back to. These countries, with their eyes so firmly fixed on the future, so enthusiastic for change and technology and so acutely aware of their opportunities and markets round the world, were a reminder to the West of what their own countries had lost—a common sense of pride and commercial patriotism which could evoke envy as well as apprehension.

THE PASSAGE TO INDIA

What lessons have these dynamic countries for the rest of the developing world? Their success has depended on their links with the bankers and buyers in the rich countries of the West: their factories are dependent on the shoppers in Bloomingdale's or Selfridges. But the great majority of people in the Third World have no such connections or opportunities: they are turned inward, into their own problems which seem timeless and limitless. To travel from Singapore to India, with three hundred times the population, is to pass into a world of different values and priorities, where time and space have different meanings. If Singapore is plugged into the world grid, then India seems emphatically plugged *out*. It is off the map of ordinary bankers, like the red-lined areas in American cities; when Western businessmen talk about Asia, they don't usually include the subcontinent. India's mass poverty and unemployment impose their own imperatives, which contradict all bankers' calculations about productivity and competitiveness. Indian projects favor manual workers over machines, so that a thousand workers will build a road which could be done by a few bulldozers. The whole of India produces only forty thousand cars a year. And the vast bureaucracy makes its own work with its slow apparatus of form filling, triple checking, and overseeing.

Does Singapore have any lessons for a country like India? Inside the subcontinent, the question seems as impertinent as asking an old philosopher what he can learn from his grandchild who has gone into business: it gets lost in the vastness and the variety of 600 million people. Yet it is a question that many Indian leaders have been asking themselves. "If you could separate Bombay from the rest of India," said one government economist in Delhi, "of course it could do as well as Singapore. If the Punjab seceded, it could do as well as Korea. But they can't: they're part of India." "I admire the way Lee has given Singapore a social discipline," said one of India's chief planners. "But we can't impose that, because we're a democracy. All our planning is subject to sudden changes which come with democratic elections. It's hard to borrow money from foreign banks if you can't promise long-term plans."

"You can never separate economics from politics," said another economist. "The Koreans have obedient workers because they shoot some of them. The problems of East Asia are much wider than those of city-states. But it's true that the newly industrializing countries have made other people realize that something can be done, and they've done it without increasing inequality. They have a better sense of what they can learn from the world —and they've benefited from the inwardness of India and China. We missed out on the trade boom of the sixties. It's not really to do with Confucius or religion. People may say that India is being held back by Karma; but when eventually she takes off, they'll say it's because of Karma."

Lee Kuan Yew in Singapore and Mrs. Gandhi in Delhi represent two almost opposite views of the world, but Lee has enjoyed making the comparison, and pointing out to Indians the benefits of becoming part of the international capitalist system. I put the question to Mrs. Gandhi, of whether India could learn anything from Singapore. "Of course Singapore is quite different," she said. "It has a strategic position. And although in theory it's democratic, in practice Lee is very much a chief there. Our geographical position is such that for sheer survival we have to be self-reliant. We started off with a political revolution which gave people a lot of political consciousness about events, and nothing about discipline or obligation or responsibility. In the West you had your Industrial Revolution first: there was no question then about the rights of the workers."

But Mrs. Gandhi conceded that India has been hampered by the kind of bureaucratic controls that the new industrial countries have avoided, and that she had failed to push through the necessary land reform. "I have no objection to learning from other countries. But you have to be rooted in something; you can't be blown off with the wind. You have to link the outside with what is happening inside: in today's changing world, you cannot afford not to be looking out. We don't want to hang on to traditions which are obsolete; but many traditions are not."[7]

With all its tangled bureaucracy, its introversion and democratic confusion, India is beginning to look farther outward, at least on its edges. Indian workers travel to the Middle East to build roads or palaces in the Arab countries; Indian machine tools are beginning to compete with Korea or Taiwan; the Indian government is beginning to look to the international banks to finance ambitious new projects. For years India avoided foreign borrowing, preferring the cheaper World Bank loans or export credits from Western governments. But now the higher cost of oil has threatened a balance of payments crisis, while India has retained a high credit rating, and has been—as one banker put it—"overtaken on the negative side" by the instability of Middle Eastern countries or Korea.[8] Western bankers were beginning to see India, with all its frustrations, as being more reliable than some of their high-flying

[7]Interview with author, October 22, 1980.
[8]*Financial Times,* January 19, 1981.

customers, like Iran or Korea. Indian financial experts, including I. G. Patel, at the Central Bank, and L. K. Jha, the governor of Kashmir, pressed for greater borrowing for projects which could provide foreign currency; and in 1981 India made its first major approach to the international capital market, borrowing $680 million to finance a new aluminum project in the state of Orissa.

"Mrs. Gandhi insists that there's always an Indian way of doing things," a Singapore politician complained to me, "and she insists on keeping the spinning wheels. But at the same time she wants to have Jaguar fighters. If she wants the Jaguars, in the end she'll have to drop the spinning wheels." But India, with its intricate history and religions, and its population greater than that of all the industrialized nations, will not readily follow their path, or plug itself into the international grid. Whatever political changes and military ambitions and enclaves of industrial activity, the Indian way of doing things will still keep the bankers at arm's length.

THE DRAWBRIDGE

The four supercompetitors were only the advance guard of the procession of newly industrializing countries which were trying to compete in the markets of the rich; altogether twenty-three countries, including such giants as Brazil and India, are classified as NICS. As the Koreans or Taiwanese earned higher wages and turned to high fashion or advanced electronics, so new producers with cheaper labor like Indonesia or the Philippines took over making jeans or tennis shoes. All of them were increasingly worried about being shut out of the markets on which they were dependent. In the boom years their access was relatively easy; but as more Western workers lost their jobs they insisted on more restrictions and quotas for imports, which were now negotiated on a continental scale: the NICS had to bargain with the United States, the European Community, and Japan to reach complex agreements like the Multi-Fibers Arrangement of 1977. Whatever the achievements of individual companies and free enterprise, it was these intricate global engagements, where armies of bureaucrats and lobbyists clashed with their weaponry of statistics, that were determining the future patterns of world trade.

The international banks had their own vital interest in the outcome; for they had to be sure that these new nations could maintain their exports, to enable them to pay the interest if not the whole debt. The global bankers were almost by definition opposed to protection. "The Chase has been opposed to protection for the last forty years," David Rockefeller assured me. "In a world of growing interdependence the last thing we want is protection." Bankers argued that protection would only damage the Western countries in the long run; statistics showed that the NICS provided more jobs through their trade with the West than they took away through their competition. And the bankers had some common interest with the Western consumers, who welcomed the invasion of cheaper goods, without which their cost of living would be still higher. But workers who were laid off could see all too clearly how these foreign goods in the department stores were losing them their jobs. The theory of the international division of labor assumed that while new industrial countries took over producing cheaper goods, the older ones would move into making more sophisticated products. But it was never so easy in practice as in theory; even forward-looking countries like Sweden, which retrained and retrained their workers to prepare them for more advanced industries, found diminishing opportunities as the competition intensified.

The supercompetitors made their plans to cross over new walls which were being built up against them, and they hoped to increase the value of their exports by making more sophisticated shoes or electronics while keeping inside their quotas. "Our whole industrial policy," said Lee in Singapore, "depends on avoiding protection." Ironically, the higher barriers gave them more incentive to improve their quality than many of the sleepier old industrial countries. Hong Kong or Korea moved on to more expensive *haute couture,* leaving antiquated British factories to make cheap jeans. The newcomers knew that they must keep upgrading their products or collapse.

It was the latest act in that long saga of textiles and industrialization which had begun in the wool markets of medieval Florence, and the banks had been in the midst of it from the beginning, and still were. Their loans had helped to launch these new Asian countries into the global marketplace, and they now had the most powerful motive for keeping their debtors in business; if they couldn't sell their goods, they couldn't repay. But the East Asians were latecomers in a much more crowded and competitive world, and their survival depended on selling their goods while the barriers were going up. They looked to the bankers, with their long commitment to free trade, to help them in their predicament; but the bankers had their own conflicts of interest. They were worried about American Chrysler or Ford, as well as the Korean car industry, and they were reluctant to stick their necks out, to prevent their foreign clients' goods from being stopped at the tariff barriers. While the bankers had been extending themselves round the world the politicians in the West were very conscious of a new mood by the late seventies, with symptoms of withdrawal behind national frontiers and growing disillusion with developing countries.

13
MONEY MACHINES

Anywhere you see our name is home.

VISA advertisement, 1980

The style of a bank had changed since medieval money lenders counted coins on a bench, or the Italians lent gold to English kings. It was much harder now to trace the money from the beginning to the end—from the small saver leaving a few dollars in his local bank to the billion-dollar Eurodollar loans raised by a syndicate of two hundred banks to finance a country in the Far East. The banker who spent his time telephoning or traveling between New York and Tokyo had little in common with the teller who took dollar bills over the counter; the movements of billions of Eurodollars had long ago lost contact with any ordinary depositor, or even a government. The language of the global bankers—about financial services, corporate finance, recycling, rescheduling, or restructuring—suggested activities quite different from money lending for profit. Yet the business was still basically the same as the Medicis' or Shylock's; and the further the world went into debt, the more bankers prospered.

While the big banks were making new profits from relending the OPEC billions, they still depended on their "retail" business for an important part of their profits. As they became less certain about their Arab depositors and their borrowers in the Third World, and as the global competition intensified, many bankers began to pay more attention to where their business had first begun—with their savers and borrowers at home.

WRISTON'S TRILLION

Citibank here again was setting the pace. Ever since Wriston had first committed the bank to an annual growth of 15 percent, the target had been elusive; and in 1977 earnings actually fell for the first time since 1961. Wriston knew that he could not increase his profits from corporate banking, for the industrial corporations were themselves becoming more like banks, and their sophisticated treasurers were determined to earn as much as possible from their own funds, switching restlessly between currencies. Much of the new money power in the world now resided in the treasurers' or financial directors' suites of IBM in Armonk, of Unilever in London, of Volkswagen in Wolfsburg. Other kinds of companies were also providing "financial services" which trespassed on the banker's domain. Merrill Lynch, the mass brokerage firm headed by Donald Regan, later to be Reagan's Secretary of the Treasury, was providing money-market accounts for clients which allowed them to write checks. Sears, Roebuck, with its 26 million credit-card customers, was ready to sell debentures along with dresses and sofas. These giants were not confined like the banks to collecting deposits from their own state: they had customers all across America.

In New York the competition for customers was specially intense, and Wriston was determined that Citibank must extend its territory. "The demand deposits in the City of New York," he complained to me, "haven't increased a single dollar in nominal terms in five years. . . . Unless you get your hands on the $1.2 trillion of personal savings in this country, there's no way." Wriston seemed obsessed by this magic hoard. "Willie Sutton said he robbed banks because that's where the money is," he told *Fortune.* "I see that $1.2 trillion out there and I don't see any number that looks like that anywhere else."[1]

Already in 1974 Wriston had decided to spend $200 million on

[1] *Fortune,* March 24, 1980.

a "consumer strategy" to compete for small savings; he appointed John Reed, an aggressive young management expert who had already reorganized the Operations Department with a team of automation experts, to run a new consumer-business unit. Reed reckoned that he could make much bigger profits with more dynamic management and mechanization, and by 1977 Citibank was beginning to install automated banking centers across New York. Cranes lowered prefabricated white kiosks on strategic positions in the suburbs, containing automated little banks without any tellers, which could take deposits and give out cash all round the clock. Citibank's headquarters on Park Avenue became a showplace for mechanized banking: inside the building, robot trolleys steered their own way through corridors, bleeping as they went, delivering the mail. In the banking halls, customers lined up to insert their Citicards and commune silently with chatty machines which displayed their advice on the screen: "If you make a mistake on the keyboard, just press 'clear'. . . . Oops! You pressed too many keys. Please try again." The customers, Citibankers assured me, were delighted with this new relationship. Citibank, John Brooks of *The New Yorker* suggested, was "exploring a new dimension of that profound and little-explored psychological relationship—the one between people and money."[2]

Citibankers presented themselves as the forerunners of a relaxed and impersonal style of consumer banking, proclaiming each move with a salvo of publicity; like Mobil among the oil companies, they were compulsive communicators. They had already extended their commercial scope back in 1968 by creating a holding company called Citicorp, which allowed them to extend into other financial activities. To display their corporate character more flamboyantly, they put up a shimmering Citicorp Center with a diagonal top in Lexington Avenue, next door to their Park Avenue skyscraper: it was held up by four great stilts rising up eight stories, with a covered market including restaurants, shops, and free Citicorp entertainment. It was a spectacular tribute to the

[2]*The New Yorker,* January 4, 1981.

New York consumer, but its name was misleading; the bank's headquarters remained in the undistinguished Park Avenue building, and with its automated techniques Citibank had no need for more space for itself. The Midas syndrome decreed that the bankers, having built the proud palaces that bore their name, would find that they could make more money from renting them to other people.

The New York competition reached a new crescendo as the banks tried to lure more customers. Citibank precipitated a new wave in 1980, when it offered bonuses to anyone who brought in a friend; and the banking halls which had looked like temples now looked like small department stores, cluttered with TV sets and household gadgets. The Bankers Trust decided to retreat altogether from this retail battlefield and sold its Manhattan sites, to give more attention to the wholesale business. Morgan's retained its stately style, concentrating on its rich corporate customers; its high, empty banking halls looked more like tombs than temples and its big business went on in office blocks and private dining rooms adjoining its palace at 23 Wall Street. But the four big retail banks competed shamelessly for mass deposits; the Chemical and the Manny Hanny stared at each other across Park Avenue, watching to undercut each bargain in interest rates.

The Chase had now virtually abandoned its old aristocratic style, and its president, Willard Butcher, who would succeed Rockefeller as chairman in 1981, was a much more down-to-earth figurehead. A bland, hearty man from a conservative Scarsdale background, Butcher had gone into banking with a straightforward zeal: "I'm sort of an evangelist for the market system." He was inexhaustible in his traveling and devotion to statistics, and he could fill in the figures about which Rockefeller was vague. But he showed few signs of a feel for world politics, and he baffled foreigners with his slow clichés and stock football metaphors ("We're going to play Vince Lombardi ball") as if he saw the world as a sports field. Butcher's chairmanship coincided with the intense domestic competition, and the Rockefeller era of princely meetings and high statesmanship would soon fade into history.

All the big New York banks were now waiting impatiently to stretch out for customers across the United States. Certainly it looked increasingly odd that these giants which had built up branches round the world could not, in terms of the McFadden Act, take money in next-door New Jersey or Connecticut. In California eleven of the twenty-one biggest banks were foreign-owned, including the Crocker Bank, now owned by the British Midland. "It becomes increasingly ridiculous," Walter Wriston said in September 1980, "to say that Midland Bank can buy Crocker but Citibank can't. We both speak English."[3] The restriction had already been partly undermined when the Edge Act of 1919 had allowed banks to finance exports through subsidiaries outside their own state; and in 1978 a new International Banking Act allowed these subsidiaries to be merged. The biggest banks, like Citibank and Bank of America, already had thousands of employees in other states. "It's absolutely ridiculous for us to say we don't have nationwide banking," complained Wriston, "when the Bank of America has got three thousand people on Wall Street." By 1980 it appeared that the McFadden Act and the state laws would soon be amended to allow banks to cross the state lines. The giants from New York, California, and Chicago prepared themselves for a coast-to-coast competition which would certainly gobble up many of the 14,000 smaller banks across the country. The old resistance to the central money power, from the days of Jefferson and Jackson, was making its last stand.

How would the internal expansion affect the global marketplace? The bankers' confinement to their own state had pressed them, both commercially and psychologically, to spurt overseas in the fifties and sixties. But now they saw the prospect of borrowers in Arizona or Kentucky who all spoke the same language, with no country risk, no danger of revolution or default. Would the wave of internationalism which had swept them up over the last decade give way to a thankful retreat into the security of their own country?

[3] *International Herald Tribune,* September 25, 1980.

PLASTIC LOANS

The bankers had already discovered a new way to cross frontiers through the extraordinary development of the credit card, which was now providing still greater opportunities. It had begun modestly in February 1950, when the manager of a small loan company, Frank McNamara, established the Diners Club, which provided select members with credit at twenty-two restaurants in New York, and collected a commission in return for paying bills promptly. Then in 1958 American Express, which already had a world network through its tourist services and traveler's checks, began selling its green-and-white card as a prestigious open-sesame to hotels, restaurants, shops, and airlines all through America and across the world. The company made handsome profits from its charges (or "discount rate") to the shopowners or hoteliers, and from the cost of the card. It was not strictly a credit card, but a "travel and entertainment" (T&E) card: it insisted on its customers paying their bills within thirty days, after which it bombarded them with increasingly menacing computerized letters, culminating in angry telegrams and threats from its debt collectors. There were many bad debts and some spectacular excesses—one Korean businessman built a whole apartment block on one card. But by 1980 American Express had about 10.5 million card holders across the world, far outstripping its rivals—Diners Club (4 million) and Carte Blanche (about 1.5 million)—both of which are now owned by Citicorp. American Express had already expanded into a major international bank, and it was now planning to offer a range of financial services direct to the home through new cable systems.

In the meantime the banks themselves were moving into credit cards. They were not so concerned with the charges to shops as with the interest they could collect if card holders did not pay promptly; while American Express threatened its wayward customers, the banks were much more relaxed and simply totted up the interest. The first banker to try it was Arthur Roth, of the ill-fated Franklin Bank on Long Island (see Chapter 9), in 1951; but in 1958 his local effort was eclipsed by the Bank of America and the Chase, which both issued their own cards. Chase lost millions of dollars and gave up four years later; but Bank of America, with its better management, expanded more easily through the shops and hotels of California.

The pace then quickened. The Chicago banks set up their own Midwest Card, which they sent out to millions of addresses, including dead people and dogs, with disastrous losses and frauds. Four Californian banks invented the Mastercharge card, which they too mailed out indiscriminately; Mastercharge was taken over by a group called Interbank, headed by the Marine Midland, which set up an elaborate computer system in St. Louis, providing a nationwide service. The Bank of America gave up the control of its card to a separate company, owned by a group of banks including the Chase, which could thus deploy the card all over the States, and the card's name was changed to Visa, a word with the same friendly connotation in every country. The operation was run by a zealous banker with the marvelous name of Dee Hock, who proclaimed his card in high-flown literary language as the solution to the Americans' "crisis of identity," which would give them recognition as well as currency wherever they traveled.[4]

At Citibank Wriston now saw that Visa gave him the opportunity to increase lending and to escape from the usury laws that limited interest rates in New York. Citibank sent out 26 million letters offering Visa cards, which led to 5 million acceptances. They included some very seedy customers, leaving big losses, but Wriston persevered, desperately wanting to break into new markets in other states. "For a bank to say that you can't come in my market with a Visa card," he said in 1978, "means that no one ever read the Sherman Act. There isn't any such thing as 'my market' here in American law. So that we are already en-

---

[4]See Terry Galanoy, *Charge It!* (New York: Putnam, 1980), for an entertaining account of Hock's progress.

gaged, in my opinion, in the greatest revolution in the financial service business."[5]

Visa and Mastercharge were now competing across the world, challenging the traditional territory of American Express. By 1979 Visa represented a network of 13,000 banks, including Barclays in Britain, the Carte Bleu group of 130 French banks, and a link with the Sumitomo Bank in Japan. In Germany Visa ran into fierce competition from the rival Eurocheque system with its own Euro-card, which in 1978 was bought up by a powerful European group headed by the Deutsche Bank. The Eurocard had forged its own links with Mastercharge in America and with the Access cards owned by a group of British banks. But Visa was more far-flung and versatile, offering bank loans as well as credit in shops or restaurants, and by 1980 it was planning to open its own card center in West Germany.

It was a triumph for the computer. The huge Visa network of outlets and cardholders was run by only three hundred people, most of them in the headquarters outside San Francisco. The computers sorted out the millions of credits and debits and passed them on to the individual banks; the cost of a shirt bought in Milwaukee in the afternoon could be debited to an account in Barclays in Northampton the next morning. The appeals for custom, the reminders of interest, the stern demands for payment were all chattered out by machines pretending to be people. The cards and computers allowed the bankers to lend money without ever having to see a customer or to employ an extra teller; by 1978 Barclays alone was making an extra profit of over $20 million from Visa loans, and it was soon sternly criticized by the British Monopolies Commission for its cozy agreements with the other British card, Access. The expansion of credit cards and electronic banking was bound to favor the biggest banks, which could now operate much more freely across the globe. Dee Hock depicted Visa as a multinational enterprise which had escaped geographical limits, offering customers a "reservoir of value" throughout the world.

[5] *Euromoney* (July 1978).

The controllers of this empire of credit cards had given great benefits to those citizens who were inside the system of credit, while automatically rejecting those who were not: the whole concept of trust which underlay credit had been taken over by machines. It was now marvelously easy for an individual to borrow and postpone repayment, but harder to make sure that he would have the money available. It was, as Samuel Brittan has remarked, a kind of parallel to the growth of the Eurodollar: whether for an individual or a country, "domestic monetary policies have to be tighter than they otherwise need be."[6]

The bankers still yearned for more automation, and they saw their credit cards as only one stage in the development of Electronic Funds Transfer (EFT), which could bypass people altogether with the help of an ATM (automatic teller machine), an OLTT (on-line teller terminal), and a POS (point-of-sale terminal). Their ambition was to build a system which would allow a customer to make his purchase through a point-of-sale terminal in a shop which would instantly debit his account in New York, or reject him if he had no money or credit. It was a thrilling prospect. There were political complaints of course about Big Brother; but President Ford appointed a national commission on Electronic Funds Transfer which reported in 1977 that the system would benefit consumers by stimulating competition, providing more outlets, and reducing costs, and which was confident that there could be effective safeguards to prevent snooping.

Nagging doubts still remained about the threat to the freedom of the individual. Already the credit card, when used for renting cars or hotel rooms, has proved an invaluable device for discreet surveillance by authoritarian governments like South Africa's which wish to keep track of people's movements without being seen to do so. Point-of-sale terminals, once linked up to a police computer, could tell the police where an individual was to be

[6]David F. Lomax and P. T. G. Guttman, *The Euromarkets and International Financial Policies.* Introduction by Samuel Brittan (London: Macmillan, 1981), p. xiv.

found at that very instant. In 1971 a group of experts on computers and surveillance were brought together in Washington and confronted with this hypothetical problem: "Suppose you are given the assignment of designing a system for the surveillance of all citizens and visitors within the boundaries of the Soviet Union. The system is not to be too obtrusive or obvious. What would be your decision?" After two days, the group of experts decided that they could not conceive anything better than Electronic Funds Transfer.[7]

[7]See Senate Judiciary Committee, *Committee Print: Surveillance Technology*, Washington, 1976, pp. 1157–60.

14
THE GLOBAL MARKETPLACE

Never before in the history of banking has so much been owed by
so few to so few.

The Economist, June 10, 1978

In a room high above Lombard Street in London a group of young
men and one woman are sitting around a ten-sided table, each
with two telephones. They swivel a turntable full of directories
and reference books, and look up at television screens which can
instantly summon up the prices offered by banks in Tokyo, Frankfurt, Singapore, or Bahrain. This foreign exchange dealing room,
one of them explained, is the real heart of the bank: here the
global marketplace takes on flesh and blood and you can sense
the excitement of the market. From the table you can imagine the
sun rising and setting round the world; in the morning the Tokyo
exchanges have just closed; by the early afternoon New York is
becoming active; by later afternoon California has come to life.
There are about eight thousand of these dealers across the world,
from twenty different nationalities, nearly all of them under forty:
the strain is too much for older men, and there is talk of break-
downs, broken marriages, and psychosomatic complaints. The
sense of power and knowledge can be heady. It is exciting to feel
able to influence the fate of a world currency; a few dealers can
affect the market in dollars for a few days.

Since the currencies began floating freely, the rises and falls
have been a constant temptation for speculators, which led to
some of the banking disasters of 1974. In the five months after
February 1973 the dollar fell over 40 percent against the Deutschmark, and sometimes went up or down by 10 percent in a week.

The fluctuations still continue, and in April 1980 the Deutschmark rose by 5 percent in one day against the dollar. In New York the currency transactions were averaging $23 billion a day.[1]

Across the telephone or telex the dialogue is spare; "small" is the code word for less than a million dollars and "cable" means the dollar-sterling exchange rate between dollars and sterling. It always opens with the global greeting, HI HI FRIENDS:

HI HI FRIENDS HOW IS CABLE DOLLARS SPOT
HI THERE MOMENT
PLEASE. . . . 05 20 SPOT CABLE. QUICK REPLY
OK WE BUY 3 MILLION STERLING AT 236 20
OK FRIENDS WILL BE DONE OUR DOLLARS TO NORTHERN TRUST
INTERNATIONAL NEW YORK PLEASE
OK AGREED. THANKS AND BI BI FOR NOW.

The bleak dialogue can conceal dramas, when currencies suddenly fluctuate and the dealers speculate about the outcome; on the open line to Hamburg you can overhear hectic discussion between the Germans. Oil is the crucial currency: whenever an oil shortage is imminent the bank quickly sells yen and buys sterling. Most sudden changes in currencies are not due to any political event but to technical factors: a multinational corporation, like Volkswagen or Exxon, may switch a huge sum from dollars into Deutschmarks, bringing down the dollar rate. (When a dealer gets a huge order for, say, a $100 million, he has a chance of a quick profit; he can first buy $50 million for his own bank, before he buys the $100 million for his client, which will push up the dollars.)

But there are still big deals between currencies which are surrounded by mystery and speculation. Who is buying? Who is selling? Are the Arabs coming in? Is the Swiss Bank Corporation buying on behalf of its Saudi friends? If the Saudis are moving from

[1] See Geoffrey Bell, "Developments in the International Monetary System since Floating," *Schroders International* (November 1980).

yen to dollars or from dollars to sterling, the rumblings can reverberate through every international bank. In this electronic marketplace, for all its instant interchange, the most powerful client is still
shrouded; and the fate of currency can still depend on the whims
of a few sheiks.

The mobility of money was encouraging all the big banks to
become more international. By the late seventies they were breaking across national boundaries to invade each other's territory,
buying up foreign networks and offering worldwide financial services. Park Avenue now had the Fuji Bank, the Banque Nationale
de Paris, the Banco di Sicilia, and the European-American Bank
alongside the skyscrapers of Citibank and the Chemical. Lombard
Street, the ancient center of London bankers, offered banks from
thirty different capitals. Citibank was looking for corporate customers all over Europe, and setting up its mechanized money
shops in the high streets; in Britain it was now the sixth biggest
bank. Each global bank advertised its own warm personality—the
Bank with a Heart (Dai-Ichi), the Bank with Imagination (Dresdner), the Listening Bank (Midland), the Universal Bank (Deutsche),
All Roads Lead to Banco di Roma. But they were all increasingly
impersonal.

This global freedom gave many bankers an exciting new sense
of their power. "International banking is a system designed by
fate," explained Wriston, "to exist in a certain state of economic
tension with all governments, including the most democratic." But
many politicians were less enthusiastic. "With the enormous rise
of cosmopolitan banking since the war," Lord Kaldor (the former
economic adviser to the British Labour government) told the
House of Lords in June 1980, "there was a vast increase in mobile
funds of incredible dimensions which were the result of uncontrolled international credit creation in the world market, which is
of this planet but which is not really under any country's rules or
jurisdictions. Those vast funds could be quickly switched from
one currency to another, and that made every country in the
world—not excluding the United States, not excluding even countries behind the Iron Curtain, but only excluding in recent years

the OPEC oil producers—highly dependent on the goodwill, or rather the good opinion, of bankers."

THE WORLD LEAGUE

The power of oil and the fall of the dollar, together with the restrictions on banking between states, were helping to diminish the role of the American banks compared with their rivals in Europe and Japan. "Ten years ago all the ten largest banks in the world were American," Wriston complained in 1980. "This year there were only two of them. The power of the banks—whatever that is, if it ever existed—is getting smaller every morning."

The size of banks can be variously defined, whether by assets (i.e., loans), deposits, or capital; and countries require different methods of consolidating accounts. These were the world leaders in 1979, judged by their assets (deducting *contra* accounts—acceptances, letters of credit, or customers' securities), as reckoned by *The Banker* of London, in its annual list of the Top 500. "It is designed not so much as a league table" (the editor warned) "but more as a convenient and practical framework for showing in broad terms the relative size of the world's largest banks. . . ."[2] But it is inevitably regarded as a league table, and it gives a broad idea of the international competition, with French, German, and Japanese banks jostling with the Americans for top place. Each country's banks—as this chapter will suggest—have their own national attitudes and their own relationships with their government. The rivalries between both the bankers and the governments added to the insecurity of the global scene.

LA BANQUE VERTE

Many American bankers were surprised to see at the top of the list a French farmers' bank with its headquarters divided between Paris and the tourist town of Avignon—bigger even than the other

[2] *The Banker* (June 1980).

Bank and Head Office	Assets less contra accounts	Total deposits	Capital and reserve	Pre-tax earnings	Capital assets ratio (%)
		(in millions of dollars)			
1 Crédit Agricole, Paris	104,997	85,560	6,024		5.74
2 Bank America Corp., San Francisco	103,919	84,985	3,462	948	3.33
3 Citicorp, New York	102,742	70,291	3,598	871	3.50
4 Banque Nationale de Paris, Paris	98,859	97,383	1,386	145	1.40
5 Deutsche Bank, Frankfurt	91,188	61,825	2,924	634	3.23
6 Crédit Lyonnais, Paris	91,085	89,820	1,115	229	1.22
7 Société Générale, Paris	84,914	76,809	1,402	282	1.65
8 Dresdner Bank, Frankfurt	70,331	66,715	1,981	307	2.82
9 Barclays Group, London	67,474	58,504	3,906	1,178	5.79
10 Dai-Ichi Kangyo Bank, Tokyo	66,581	51,863	2,517		3.78
11 National Westminster Bank, London	64,393	59,043	4,175	982	6.48
12 Chase Manhattan Corp., New York	61,975	48,456	2,027	550	3.27
13 Westdeutsche Landesbank Girozentrale, Dusseldorf	60,080	57,787	1,906		3.17
14 Fuji Bank, Tokyo	59,833	47,597	2,485		4.15
15 Commerzbank, Dusseldorf	58,271	44,658	1,442	193	2.47
16 Sumitomo Bank, Tokyo	58,022	47,196	2,438		4.20
17 Mitsubishi Bank, Tokyo	57,344	44,776	2,307		4.02
18 Sanwa Bank, Osaka	55,301	43,601	2,084		3.77
19 Norinchukin Bank, Tokyo	53,663	39,902	203	55	0.40
20 Banco do Brasil, Brasilia	49,130	16,037	3,262	485	6.64

"cow bank" in California. But it is a tribute, not so much to dynamic French banking as to the power of the French farmers' lobby. The branches of the Crédit Agricole can be seen in small towns all over rural France; it takes a quarter of all French savings, of which only a tiny proportion are in Paris. Its friends see the "Green Bank" as the champion of the small farmer, its enemies as a symbol of the pampered protection of French agriculture.

Ever since it was set up as a cooperative in 1892, the Crédit Agricole has had privileges which have infuriated other banks, including exemption from corporate taxes and subsidized credit. As small holdings turned into agribusiness, the bank's power grew; and as French agriculture became more international, it began lending abroad, financing silos in America or canneries in the Ivory Coast. Its managing director is Jacques Lallement, a farmer's son who became one of the inspecteurs des finances, the élite of the French Civil Service; and he insists that his bank must now finance not just farming, but the agricultural environment and housing in general. The Crédit Agricole is now closely linked with farmers in the rest of the European Community, through joint ventures with five other European banks; and Lallement wants the CA to become a "truly international bank with a special role in financing agribusiness."[3]

The wealth of the Green Bank exasperates other French bankers. In May 1978, after it had announced reserves of $60 billion and a surplus for the previous year of $280 million, the big banks persuaded the French Finance Minister to cut back its privileges. But the farmers swiftly mobilized heavy parliamentary support, relying on the traditional suspicion of the small towns against the centralization of Paris; the Crédit Agricole eventually agreed to pay higher taxes, but it was now allowed to operate in bigger towns, and to extend its loans to wider activities. It could present itself as the champion of decentralized and democratic banking, administered by the French for the French, in contrast to the strongholds of bourgeois banking in Paris.

[3] See *The Banker* (May 1979).

It seems remarkable that four of the ten biggest banks in the world should be French, accounting for $380 billion out of the $880 billion assets of the big ten; but French banks are allowed to have a relatively low ratio (less than 2 percent) of capital to loans—because they are nationalized, with the guarantee of the State behind them. They were taken over after the Second World War at the insistence of the French left, though they continued to be run by the same kind of people. Only the Crédit Commercial Français (CCF) among the commercial banks escaped being nationalized by selling off shares to foreign banks beforehand, and it retains a special dynamism. The biggest commercial bank, the Banque Nationale de Paris, was created by a merger in 1966 at the bidding of the French Finance Minister, Michel Debré, who wanted to strengthen the foreign role of the banks abroad. They are all influenced by their government's policy; much of their foreign lending has gone to former French colonies; and they have moved with the tide of French diplomacy, for instance in lending to Eastern Europe. As the world market extended they lent more adventurously, joining the global syndicates to follow profit as much as policy; and the more ambitious bankers like Maurice Armand of the Crédit Lyonnais have become part of the international club. But the fact that they are nationalized is a source of continual resentment to other bankers. For it allows them to lend more in relation to their capital and thus to work with smaller profit margins or spreads, undercutting their rivals and lowering all other spreads. And other bankers are never quite sure where the true power lies—with the bankers or with the government.

THE DEUTSCHE BANK

The German giants were now again playing a world role, as they had before the First World War. The "Big Three"—the Deutsche, the Dresdner, and the Commerzbank—were still led by the Deutsche Bank, which had survived Bismarck, the Kaiser, and Hitler. The bristling personality of Hermann Abs, who had rebuilt it from the postwar ruins, still cast a long shadow. His omnipresence on

German boards provoked frequent attacks from the German left: in 1968 the Deutsche Bank had forced Alfred Krupp to give up his private empire and turn Krupps into a public company, whereupon Abs, who had just retired from the bank, emerged as the chairman of the new Krupps. His spider's web had led to a special law known as Lex Abs, which limited the number of directorships that any one man could hold; but that was mainly window dressing (one executive in the Deutsche Bank assured me), because bankers do not need directorships to exert their power.

Abs remained the *éminence grise* of the Deutsche Bank: he was succeeded as "spokesman" (as the head is discreetly called) by his protégé Dr. Ulrich, who followed the same conservative policies; and Ulrich was duly succeeded by two of *his* protégés, who now jointly rule the bank. Wilhelm Christians, a smooth lawyer-banker who has specialized in international stock markets, runs its domestic operations, in a much more modest style than Abs. "This bank is one of the most democratic institutions I have got to know," he has insisted. "We are fully conscious how vulnerable our reputation for power is."[4] The international side is run by Dr. Wilfried Guth, the banker-statesman who was a member of the Pearson Commission on the Third World, whose speeches on the problems of world banking reveal a rare candor.

The Deutsche had been slow to spread itself abroad again. Abs had seen its overseas branches expropriated after two world wars, and he was wary of moving too soon: he saw Eurodollars as a threat to national controls and a stimulus to inflation. "Abs was going around saying that he was the world's greatest banker," Wriston recalled to me, "that the Eurodollar market was evil, was transitory, and would go away." During the sixties the Deutsche Bank helped to set up the banking club EBIC, which led it into joint ventures abroad, including the European-American Bank in the United States. But it was the Dresdner Bank which was more aggressively international, setting up branches abroad to serve

---

[4] *Financial Times,* April 1, 1980.

German industry and soon competing in the global market for loans; its international head, Manfred Meier-Preschany, now looks forward to the time when the Dresdner's shareholders will be spread among all countries in which they operate. The Deutsche Bank was deserted in 1974 by its most cosmopolitan director, Walter Siepp, who went to the Westdeutsche Landesbank, the biggest of the regional banks, and then took over as the chief executive of the Commerzbank, the weakest of the Big Three.

It was not till 1976 that the Deutsche Bank established a branch in London, and the next year in Paris. But with its resources it was still able to command a unique authority: its name at the top of a tombstone, like Morgan's, was enough to ennoble a loan, and like Morgan's it could take an attitude of take-it-or-leave-it, for other banks dreaded being left out in the cold. It was much less vulnerable to shareholders' protests than American or British banks, and when it lent to South Africa, first clandestinely and then openly, it did not worry about complaints from churchmen or radicals. The Deutsche Bank still had its links with government, though the relationship remained mysterious to foreigners; when Bonn urged it to lend to Poland or Turkey (see Chapter 18), what kind of understanding lay behind it? How far was there an unwritten assumption that the government would if necessary come to the bank's help?

THE UNBANKED BRITISH

By 1979 the most profitable bank in the world was Barclays in Britain, with profits before tax of $1.18 billion, more than Citibank's or the Bank of America's, and twice the profits of Chase. But like the expansion of the Crédit Agricole, the profits of British banks were a tribute to their government's indulgence, rather than their own vigorous enterprise; and the record profits during 1979 produced an uproar not only from the left but even from the bankers' own paper, the *Financial Times,* which called them "not obscene, but ill-deserved." "Something is seriously wrong with Britain's retail banking system," warned Michael Lafferty of the

Financial Times. "It is class-based, diverse, and sleepy. . . . It is a system badly in need of a shake-up."[5] High interest rates had given a huge bonanza to banks which could make money from the current accounts of their small customers, on which they themselves paid no interest. No other countries' banks could so easily get richer by lending other people's money. During 1980, when factories were closing down and businesses going bankrupt, the British banks were declaring record profits: it looked like a return to a preindustrial economy, dominated by money lenders. But even British bankers could not feel secure as they faced more global competition, and Citibank and other foreigners were encroaching with their aggressive tactics and money machines.

The Big Four English banks—Barclays, National Westminster, Midland, and Lloyds—remain very tribal, rooted in the class system. The bank clerks slowly work their way up toward the goal of branch manager, while their boards of outside directors, including elderly peers and elderly ex-civil servants, come to a long lunch once a month. The chairmen likewise come from outside the bank, except for the Barclays' hereditary chairmen (see Chapter 11): the National Westminster is headed by a barrister and landowner, Robin Leigh-Pemberton; at the Midland the former head of the Civil Service, Lord Armstrong, was succeeded by the former British head of Shell, Sir David Barran; while Lloyds is headed by the most mandarin of bankers, Sir Jeremy Morse, with a rarefied intellect and a habit of literally talking over people's heads (if bankers are monks, then he is the abbot). With their detached directors and limited competition it was not altogether surprising that the big English banks were slow to attract the savings of ordinary workers; in 1980 less than 60 percent of Englishmen had bank accounts, and most factory workers would not go near them. "The real challenge to us over the next few years," said Sir Anthony Tuke of Barclays in 1980, "will be our ability to create the necessary modern banking systems and facilities to attract profitably the 11 million wage and salary

[5]*Ibid.,* May 3, 1980.

earners who today have no active clearing bank accounts."

The tribal and centralized structure of British banks had great advantages in providing quick communication and control at a time of crisis, as in the crash of 1974; the governor of the Bank of England as the monarch could quickly bring pressure on his chieftains. But as banking became more international these close domestic relationships were soon challenged. The British banks were more adventurous abroad than they had been at home, and all the Big Four bought up American banks to give them beach-heads across the Atlantic. But they were much less keen on allow-ing easy entry at home, and the crunch came in 1981 over the fifth biggest bank in Britain, the Royal Bank of Scotland—which though its history was different had become part of the same tribal system. The first bidder to buy up the Scottish bank was Standard Chartered, the merger of two ex-colonial banks which, although its business was scattered through Africa and Asia, was still firmly British-owned and therefore considered acceptable. But its bid was soon rivaled by the Hong Kong and Shanghai Bank, a more unwelcome intruder. For this remarkable new giant, though it claimed to be thoroughly British, was unmistakably foreign. In Hong Kong its interests were now (see Chapter 12) interlocked with the Chinese community; it had moved into the Middle East and had bought the Marine Midland in New York; and when it bought a British merchant bank, Antony Gibbs, it was firmly ejected from the club of "Acceptance Houses" on the grounds of its foreignness. Now that it had the effrontery to bid for the fifth British bank, the tribe quickly closed its ranks against the invader. But it raised the embarrassing question: how far could the London bankers continue their international purchases, without making concessions—as New York had so frequently made—in their home territory?

THE WORRIED SWISS GNOMES

The insecurity of banks was even spreading to Switzerland, their traditional stronghold. Ever since the Huguenots from France took refuge in Geneva in 1685 the country had been regarded as almost synonymous with banking, the subject of timeless jokes. ("If you see a Swiss banker jumping out of a window, jump after him," said Voltaire; "there's bound to be money in it.") The bankers' self-discipline merged with Calvinism to encourage veneration of money, while national laws upheld extreme secrecy. Sons followed their fathers in the national dedication without apparent resentment; with all their wealth the Swiss sent less than 7 percent of their children to university, where they seemed almost untouched by the rebellions which shook most colleges in 1968. The traditional neutrality of the Swiss could offer greater stability than anywhere in Europe, and their secretive banks were a refuge, not only for corrupt dictators in the Third World, but for bourgeois savers in next-door France and Italy.

The Swiss banks could not rate among the biggest world lenders: the big three—the Swiss Bank Corporation, the Union Bank, and Credit Suisse—rated twenty-eighth, thirty-first, and forty-sixth in terms of assets in 1979 in *The Banker*'s world league. But they controlled big investment funds and fiduciary deposits which were outside their balance sheets, and Switzerland had far more bank assets in proportion to its population than any other country. While other Europeans tried to underpin their nervous currencies and to fend off economic crises in the sixties, the Swiss could profitably speculate between them while their Swiss franc climbed upward. In Britain Harold Wilson attacked the "Gnomes of Zurich"[6] as a convenient scapegoat for the fall of the pound, while the Italians complained about *"i gnomi"* who were speculating against the lira.

But by the late seventies even the Swiss bankers were facing a less secure future. They had their share of bank scandals in 1974, but they were more worried in 1977, when the Credit Suisse had to write off $700 million after embezzlement and fraud in its branch in Chiasso. It was an indication of its vast hidden reserves

[6]The Supplement to the *Oxford English Dictionary* gives the first use in *The New Statesman* in 1964.

that the Credit Suisse still showed no difficulty in maintaining its next dividend; but this enormous loss threw doubt on the legendary Swiss prudence. At the same time agencies in Washington and other capitals were becoming much more impatient of the Swiss refusal to reveal the secrets of foreign deposits, suspecting them of harboring criminal funds from the Mafia and elsewhere. But still more disturbing was the threat to the social consensus that had underpinned the success of Swiss banking. In the summer of 1980 a group of young Swiss students were infuriated when they were refused money for a youth center in Zurich while the grant for the Opera House was increased; and their subsequent demonstrations shook the complacency of the bankers' headquarters. Students marched naked through the city and broke the windows of the gnomes' temples in the Bahnhofstrasse, which had to be barricaded, while the police counterattacked with tear gas. Was a new generation finally rejecting the long tradition of joyless discipline and self-denial?

The Swiss were still the most successful nation of bankers, but since the huge expansion of the Eurodollar market they were no longer so uniquely well placed. All multinational corporations and all major banks were now gnomes, buying and selling currencies to safeguard their holdings; and remote islands across the world, to which money could be instantly transferred, could provide still greater secrecy.

JAPAN: WOLVES WITH A BONE

The worries of the Europeans were increased by the arrivals of the Japanese, moving in groups, slipping in and out of the capitals of the Third World, one moment undercutting the margins, the next moment stopping lending altogether. What were their real relationships with their government, and with each other? The Japanese added their national discretion to the professional bankers' discretion. "I didn't really understand them," as one English banker explained, "until I was told their proverb: All trouble comes from the mouth."

The Japanese banks had always of course been interlocked with industrial corporations, with their government somewhere in the background. Since British bankers had first financed their steelworks, ship building and railroads in the nineteenth century, the Japanese had established their own business empires or *zaibatsu,* which dominated their economy, each with a bank at the center. The Japanese banks were credited with the same kind of legendary power as the German *Grossbanken;*[7] and during the Second World War the Americans regarded the *zaibatsu* as the engines of industrial militarism. General Douglas MacArthur, as military governor, insisted that they be dissolved; but like the German groups they soon re-formed themselves—though without their old names or controlling families. The Big Four banks again dominated the scene—Fuji, Sumitomo, Sanwa, and Mitsubishi—and before long they accompanied their many companies abroad, to finance their export trade and their search for resources. The biggest, the Fuji Bank, played a powerful coordinating role over the fifty corporations called the Fuyo group, which together accounted for nearly 10 percent of Japan's GNP —including Nissan motors, the Marubeni trading corporation, Canon cameras, the Hitachi engineering company, and the Yasuda insurance companies.

The oldest national bank, the Dai-Ichi ("first"), was established in 1873—before Barclays or the Chase—and after mergers and unmergers it joined with two smaller banks in 1971 to create the biggest Japanese bank of all, called Dai-Ichi Kangyo, or DKB. It is now the tenth biggest bank in the world, but it cultivates the paternal image of "the bank with a heart," with an emblem of a white heart on a red background, a Heart Foundation to promote social welfare, and a "small Kindness Movement," which its staff are encouraged to join. The DKB is proud of being detached from any of the *zaibatsu,* with no dominant shareholding or close industrial connection, so that it can be neutral and serve any

[7]But their role in building up industry has since been questioned, and Japanese industry owed much to entrepreneurs. See Kozo Yamamura, "Japan 1868–1930, a Revised View," in *Banking and Economic Development,* ed. Rondo Cameron (New York: Oxford University Press, 1972).

industry. But the top executives of the bank are not seen to be very different from their rivals—the same golfing economists from Tokyo or Keio universities, the same banking families, the same close links with government. For all the Japanese banks are subject to the mysterious "window guidance" from their Ministry of Finance.

The ministry gives special privileges to the Bank of Tokyo, which handles much of its business abroad, including most overseas aid; and in return the bank provides the government with inside information about foreign countries, as a kind of shadow ministry and intelligence service. It began in 1880 as the Yokohama Specie Bank; half the shares were owned by the emperor and it was the government's chosen instrument for foreign exchange. MacArthur forced the emperor to get rid of his holdings, and it was shorn of much of its influence. But as the Japanese spread abroad again, the Bank of Tokyo reasserted its special role, acting as an advance guard to advise industrialists where to sell. It soon had a wide foreign network, with subsidiaries in America, including the California First Bank in San Francisco. Its top men were smooth and polyglot, many of them coming from the Ministry of Finance and retaining discreet influence and inside information; it prides itself on expert assessments of country risk, and has been in the forefront of the move into China. The current president, Yusuke Kashiwagi, the son of a former president, grew up in New York and spent most of his career in the ministry before he moved to the bank. It is never easy to know where the Bank of Tokyo ends and the Ministry of Finance begins. But its closeness to government has not restrained the bank's aggressive search for profits; and all the Japanese banks, with the security of their government behind them, have been able to operate at lower margins than the Americans.

As the Japanese built up their surplus in the sixties their banks began lending more heavily abroad, and moving into the Third World; and their search for resources and trade led them into some very uncertain developing countries, including Zaire and Indonesia, where Japan had an interest in copper and oil. The competition between Japanese and Americans quickened the headlong rush of loans into the coffers of President Mobutu in Zaire and General Sutowo in Indonesia (see Chapter 10). But the Japanese interest in lending to the Third World was, it turned out, very fitful. After the oil shock and the banking crises of 1974 the banks in Tokyo were soon in retreat; or, as the Dai-Ichi put it: "The undermining of the functions of the Eurodollar market has led the Japanese banks to reflect on their policy for expansion of international operations." The Ministry of Finance insisted that they sharply cut back their overseas lending; and while the Americans were taking greater risks abroad, the Japanese were rapidly withdrawing.

By 1977 Japan was again amassing a huge surplus and the banks were again restless to lend. The ministry lifted its ban, and the bankers went abroad again, to countries ranging from Venezuela to Singapore, from Brazil to the Philippines; by 1979 they were making new loans worth a billion dollars a month. The Japanese lending officers from Fuji, Sumitomo, or the Bank of Tokyo seemed desperate to get rid of their money, flying over from Tokyo at the merest hint of a loan; and their American and European rivals complained that they were beating down the already narrow margins to the point of dumping. "There are so many dogs and wolves," explained Koei Narusawa of the Bank of Tokyo, "fighting over the same bone." When the Sumitomo Bank led a loan of $500 million to the British Electricity Council, at only 0.50 percent above the standard rate of LIBOR, the other banks were infuriated; but Brazil or the Philippines was glad enough to get this new flow of cheap money.

Then came the next crisis: the Iranian revolution, the new oil shortage, the prospect of another recession. The ministry was anxious again. In July the bankers met for their monthly meeting with government officials—the "second Wednesday club" at the Bankers' Association in Tokyo. The international expert from the ministry, Tsuneo Fujita, walked in, bowed to the bankers, sat at the head of the table, and quietly explained the dangers of their lending policies: they were too heavily involved in foreign syndicates, they were lending too much foreign currency compared to their own capital, they were not attending enough to country risk.[8] Three months later the ministry clamped down on new foreign loans unless they helped Japan's own exports and energy needs, and prepared new rules to ensure more prudent lending.

The developing countries were disconcerted by these sudden reverses: most of all Brazil, which was trying to attract new lenders when the Japanese pulled back. Other bankers were also put out: before they were complaining about the Japanese dumping money; now they found it harder to put together syndicates without them in the uncertain months after the Iranian and Afghanistan crises. The Japanese government saw the retreat as natural prudence, to protect their own banks and currency. But other countries' bankers saw it as a threat to the continuity of the international capital market. It was an apparent paradox that the Japanese banks, which were more closely influenced by their government than others, should be the most inconsistent, even irresponsible, in their lending: but that reflected a system that was both more competitive and cautious. And all central bankers were becoming more concerned about the exposure of their biggest banks, particularly in the Third World.

THE GAME OF CHICKEN

All these global banks from Japan, Europe, and America, with their very different relationships with their governments, had become increasingly interlocked, and the world's economic system depended on the safety of individual banks. This chain which encircled the world was as strong as its weakest link.

The memory of the crashes of 1974, with the collapse of Herstatt and Franklin and the perils of the bigger banks, was still green. Since then the central bankers had agreed that they must each be responsible for their own banks, and they had tightened up their own systems of control. The German Bundesbank, which was heavily criticized for allowing the Herstatt fiasco, began supervising more strictly. The Bank of England, after the failures of the "fringe banks" in 1974, scrutinized their activities much more

[8]For a description of the meeting see *Euromoney* (September 1979).

carefully and set up a new system of licenses which distinguished between proper banks and "licensed deposit takers." In Washington the office of the comptroller of the currency, who supervises the banks, became more important under its new incumbent, John Heimann, who was appointed by President Carter in 1977 and who soon showed his independence by pursuing the investigation of Carter's banker colleague, Bert Lance, who had to leave the government. Heimann was determined to prevent further disasters like Franklin, and to cooperate more closely with foreign supervisors. When in 1980 the First Pennsylvania—the twenty-third biggest bank-holding company in America—was approaching bankruptcy, he was able to negotiate its rescue with no show of panic. The comptroller's computer in Washington keeps intricate cross checks on the exposure of all the 14,000 American banks, breaking down their loans by countries, commodities, and corporations, and the bank examiners watch for any crack in the chain.

Every four months the bank supervisors from eleven countries meet in Basel, at the headquarters of the Bank for International Settlements, to compare notes on international lending. They are formally called the Committee on Banking Regulation and Supervisory Practices, but generally known as the Cooke Committee, after Peter Cooke from the Bank of England, who is chairman. Their formal business is to coordinate their supervision over very different systems of accounting, and to strengthen the "prudential control" over the world's banks; but the more useful conversations are over meals or drinks when they can tip each other off about secret worries and shady bankers. They were inevitably concerned with the Eurodollar market, which had proliferated with so little control. "At first it seemed to us like Cloud Nine," one of them said; "but as we looked into the banks' accounting we found we could keep track of most of the Eurodollars." They still could not be altogether confident of this new and volatile currency. The bank supervisors are very conscious of the precedents of panic, like the fearful collapse of the Kreditanstalt in 1931, and they know that there could be a crack in the chain where it is least expected. "You only know afterward where it went wrong," said another member of the committee. "And you know that next time it will be somewhere quite different."

They carefully watch the problem countries—like Brazil, Poland, Turkey, the Philippines, South Korea—to make sure that no single bank is too heavily exposed; the collapse of one would affect all the others. But while they can anticipate a rational crisis, they can never be sure that a country, or even a bank, would not behave irrationally; a demagogue in a developing country might decide to default, like Castro in Cuba, and could threaten the whole house of cards. The international system could survive a shock like the revolution in Iran; but it was still very vulnerable to the mistakes of individual banks. The established banking countries, like the United States, Britain, and Germany, had learnt lessons from their past traumas. The Swiss banks, though they remained opaque to foreigners, had to bare their secrets and hidden reserves to their banking commissioner. The nationalized French banks were rigorously inspected. But what about the Italians, who had been so permissive toward Sindona and other crooked bankers? What about Spain? Supposing—it was the supervisors' job to suppose—that an Italian bank got into serious difficulties and the central bank, for political reasons, would not rescue it; and supposing other countries began pulling their money out of all Italian banks, which then crashed, spreading the contagion of fear across the world, as happened in 1931?

Supposing that three big debtor countries, like Brazil, Korea, and Turkey, were all at the same time unable to make their repayments? "I've learnt that the banking system is remarkably robust and very flexible when it comes to rescheduling," said one of the committee members; "but three countries could strain their resources of people to the limit." And what about banks which are based on the "Secrecy Countries," like Luxemburg or Bermuda or Grand Cayman, which owes much of its success (see Chapter 16) to its total secrecy?

And what about the secrets of Saudi Arabia? The uncertainty about Arab funds was still uncomfortable. The supervisors were reasonably confident that they were keeping track of the main movements of oil billions between the Arab states and Western banks, but what happened when an oil prince put a billion dollars into Germany or Switzerland which was then transferred to New York? Supposing the Saudis lost all faith in the future of the dollar? Supposing there were to be a major political upheaval in Riyadh? The international banking system, like an unfinished jigsaw, still had pieces that would not fit in the middle. There was still a growing discrepancy between the lenders and owners of money. The Western banks had nearly all increased their loans in proportion to their own capital—in some American banks the ratio was as high as thirty to one—while the Saudis had plenty of spare capital but little machinery for lending it, except through their short-term deposits in foreign banks. Many Arab countries were building up their own banks, with huge resources: the Arab Banking Corporation was set up in 1980 by Kuwait, Libya, and Abu Dhabi with capital of a billion dollars—which had taken Western banks a century to accumulate. But they had their own ideas about spending or lending. They were looking not only toward the Western banking system but toward their friends and dependents in Islam.

I found the bank supervisors more interesting and more philosophical people than their titles suggested, or than many of the bankers they supervised. Perhaps that was not surprising; for as they looked into the banks' secrets and surveyed the whole world, their questions went far beyond any formal notions of accounting. They were faced with the fundamental nature of credit or trust, and with unanswerable questions like "What is the real value of Zaire?" And at the heart of their business was the problem sometimes called "the moral hazard": how to have a system safe enough to rescue the banks from collapse, but not so visibly safe that it encouraged banks to be rash and imposed no sanction upon them? "Is it," I asked one of the supervisors, "like a gigantic game of chicken?" "Yes, you could call it that—but with a lot of other games too. The funny thing about banking is that at the top it's very metaphysical."

15
GRAY EMINENCES

Bankers needed a political sense, a second vision, just as sailors need a meteorological sense.

FRITZ STERN[1]

Where in this world of mechanized banking was there a place for the individualist with a personal flair? The old merchant banks in Britain, the *banques d'affaires* in France, or the investment banks in New York, whose partners had played such a powerful world role in the nineteenth century, were now relatively minor actors in the international dramas. The resources of a few rich men had long ago been overtaken by the expansion of the popular banks. The investment banks did not have access to the deposits from millions of savers or from the OPEC nations which lay behind the syndicated loans. But they could still serve as brokers between the giants, helping to put together the big deals; as one of them put it, "We're very good at leading lambs to the slaughter." And they offered more exciting opportunities to financial operators as middle men and entrepreneurs. They were the cavalry of banking, cleverer, quicker, and more mobile than the giants. The deposit banks made most of the profits from the interest on their lending, while the investment banks made them from their fees (for which they invented elaborate euphemisms—compensation, remuneration, advice, or even "close personal relationship," meaning very high fees. British merchant bankers took their delicacy to the point of not mentioning fees until they sent their huge bill). The distinction was becoming more blurred as the deposit banks formed their own merchant banking subsidiaries and increased their earnings

[1]*Gold and Iron,* p. 305.

from fees; but the merchant banks still offered much wider scope for individuals.

It is these smaller banks that show the full force of the profit motive, whether in extracting fees, juggling with investments, or conceiving complex deals. At their worst the investment bankers can develop an obsessive fascination with the arts of money which cuts them off from any sensitivity to political and social consequences. "You can see them being sucked into the vortex of money," as one colleague described them. At their best they have the clearest understanding of the real effects of money on the world, looking over the trees, away from the herd.

The legendary old merchant banks still survived as family firms. Barings in London was still run by Barings, now owned by the family foundation. After the crash of 1890, it was scrupulously cautious: it survived the Great Depression almost unscathed, and it was one of the few British banks that were not overexcited by the go-go years of the sixties. Barings still specialized in Latin America and extended its custom to Africa, particularly Nigeria. It achieved a coup when the Saudis asked it, together with Merrill Lynch, to advise their central bank, SAMA, to which it seconded discreet staff. Rothschilds was still run by Rothschilds, infused by the arrival of the sixth generation in the shape of Jacob Rothschild, whose single-minded competitiveness and moneymaking seemed like a throwback. But Jacob was at loggerheads with his cousin Evelyn de Rothschild, a much more orthodox banker, who was also chairman of *The Economist* and who had a bigger share of the bank. For a time Jacob's father, Lord Rothschild, came back to the bank to serve as mediator, but the tensions remained irreconcilable, until in 1980 Jacob left the bank to concentrate on running his own adventurous investment trust; Jacob was the eagle, Evelyn was the trout.[2] Rothschilds Bank still has its international network, maintaining its links with the Paris bank run by Baron Guy de Rothschild and playing a role in many countries like Brazil where it was powerful a century earlier. But it could not

[2]See Louis Camu's distinction, Chapter 1.

hope to wield the same influence as the giants like Citibank or the Deutsche Bank.

Merchant banks can still be dominated and transformed by a single individual. In London the biggest of them, Hill Samuel, had been the result of an ambitious merger by Kenneth Keith, later Lord Keith. The stately old Morgan Grenfell Bank (partly owned by Morgan's in New York until 1981) was invigorated by a competitive new chairman, Bill Mackworth-Young, who extended its international operations, including arranging a $3.5-billion loan for a steelworks in Brazil. Sir Siegmund Warburg, though nominally retired in Switzerland, still retained his personal influence over his bank in London and its prosperous offshoot in New York, with which he was constantly in touch. He had put together a consortium with Paribas in France and with Becker in Chicago to extend his international scope, and he had his own close relationships with bankers and rich men all over Europe, America, and Japan. As he explained: "If the Deutsche Bank puts away $2 million in a big issue among ten clients, it's very nice. But if we can put two clients in at $2 million each, that also has advantages."[3] Warburg insisted that his banks must remain compact, and never be imprisoned in their bureaucracies; he looked at the herd instincts of the giants with distress.

In Paris likewise a few of the old *banques d'affaires* retained a significant world role, guided by strong individuals. The Banque de Paris et des Pays-Bas, known as Paribas, which was founded in 1872 and which once financed railroads in Spain, Algeria, Egypt, and China, became again more cosmopolitan, helped by its links with Warburg and Becker; and it has important investments in Canada and Hong Kong as well as America. Much of its internationalism comes from its president, Pierre Moussa, who began his career as an inspecteur des finances specializing in French colonies, went on to run the Africa desk for the World Bank, and is still concerned with the problems of the Third World.

The hereditary tradition is also powerful in France. The senior

[3] *Institutional Investor* (March 1980).

partner of Lazard Frères, in both Paris and New York, is Michel David-Weill, whose great-grandfather Alexandre Weill joined the firm of Lazard Frères in San Francisco in 1857; and the firm has maintained the French-American connection. (The British Lazards now has looser links: it is part of the huge Pearson conglomerate, including the *Financial Times* and half *The Economist,* Penguin and Viking books, Madame Tussaud's, and large American interests.) In Paris Lazard Frères likes to see itself as a boutique among supermarkets. In fact, it is part of the French empire of the holding company Eurafrance, which controls insurance companies, property companies, television rentals, and other banks; but David-Weill now spends most of his time in New York, where the Lazard connections are even more wide-ranging.

The prizes for an individual banker in New York are still glittering. When a young Frenchman, André Meyer, arrived in Lazards in New York in 1940, it was little more than a branch of Lazards in London and Paris. Thirty years later he had turned it into a global moneymaker, handling the investments of the superrich, including the Agnellis in Italy, the Pearsons in England, the Boels in Belgium; and helping to build up conglomerates like ITT. Meyer was always a legendary loner, with his uncompromising French accent, his brusque decisions, his laconic early-morning telephone conversations with Europe; he was like an old nut in a bowl of fruit. ("I am not as extreme," said his successor David-Weill; "I do not get distressed if I am not telephoned every two hours.") Meyer's most brilliant protégé in Lazards, Felix Rohatyn, appears almost his opposite, publicly involved in salvaging New York (see Chapter 9) and openly engaged in Democratic politics; but he too is a loner, and Lazards has remained deliberately compact in its offices on the top of Rockefeller Center.

Other New York investment banks have much larger bureaucracies, but they are still heavily influenced by their boss. Morgan Stanley (which has no connection with the giant Morgan's except its joint ancestry) is dominated by its tireless president, Robert Baldwin, who built its staff up from 270 to 1,700 in a decade. Baldwin has reinforced its disdainful and formal style; it will never appear on a "tombstone" unless it is at the top of it. But the stuffiness conceals a relentless pursuit of profits, concentrated in securities and underwriting inside the United States, and the sixty-four managing directors make more than $100,000 a year each. Salomons is likewise driven hard by John Guttfreund, a master trader who requires his senior employees to be "Salomonized." He finds it hard to accommodate individualists like the young Australian banker Jim Wolfinsohn, who was involved in the rescue of Chrysler, who left in 1981 to set up his own firm.

Perhaps the most politically minded of the New York investment banks is Lehman Brothers Kuhn Loeb, the result of a merger in 1977. The chairman, Peter Peterson, was a former marketing expert who became Nixon's Secretary of Commerce and who played an important role in the Brandt Commission (see Chapter 20). He moves around the world like a whirlwind, hardly touching ground between air travel and telephones, calling up colleagues at unearthly hours, but always retaining his Greek instinct as a master bargainer who can push through a big deal. His personality and politics contrast sharply with those of the senior partner, George Ball, the outspoken Democrat and former Ambassador to the UN, who now mixes banking with attacking American policy toward Israel, Iran, and the Philippines, to his colleagues' embarrassment. But Lehman's political and diplomatic connections have given it advantages and access.

COUNTRY ADVISERS

The investment bankers could never compete with the financial resources of Citibank, Barclays, or the Deutsche Bank, but they had independence and skills which were useful to foreign companies and governments in the Third World. As the giants began lending more to developing countries, their central banks looked for more disinterested advice—whether to manage their reserves, to reschedule their debts, or to negotiate with the big banks. A few investment bankers discovered a new opportunity to make profits, as "country advisers."

It began in Indonesia, after the reckless lending of the big banks to the oil company Pertamina had precipitated a financial crisis (see Chapter 10), when the Central Bank turned to the three investment banks—Lehman Kuhn Loeb, Lazard Frères, and Warburgs—to advise them on the reconstruction. The three banks, having been thrown together in this difficult task, saw the opportunity to sell their services elsewhere, and they formed their own consortium called Triad, providing advice to a succession of developing countries, including Zaire, Gabon, Sri Lanka, Panama, and Turkey. In Zaire, as in Indonesia, they had to deal with the mountains of debts which the big banks had helped to build up, and to construct some kind of order out of the surrounding chaos and corruption.

The expatriates who flew in and out of these financial jungles from Paris, New York, or London had the advantage of greater detachment than local government officials or the commercial bankers. They were insulated from corruption and could seek information without being suspected for their political motives. They carefully cultivated (as Paul Fabra described it in Le Monde) the role of gray eminence beside their political masters.[4] Their financial interest was not in extending loans but only in getting their (large) fees. "Our chief problem," one of them explained, "is whether our advice can justify the fee."

Other bankers were also selling their expensive expertise to the Third World. Barings already had the richest of all developing clients, Saudi Arabia. Morgan Grenfell advised Sudan and Oman. Schroders set up a "reserve management service" under its monetary expert, Geoffrey Bell, which advised central banks in richer developing countries like Venezuela and Trinidad about how to diversify their reserves. Merrill Lynch advised several Latin American and Asian central banks.

Other bankers were disapproving or envious. "They're really acting as Ministers of Finance," one complained, "but without the ultimate responsibility. The poorer countries really can't afford them." "It's an ideal business for them," said another, "high

---

[4]See Chapter 20 and Le Monde, February 10, 1981.

commissions and no risks.'' Multinational corporations sometimes found these country advisers on the other side of the negotiating table, acting (as they complained) as financial mercenaries. But in a world caught up in a web of credit and debt no country, however rich or poor, could do without bankers. If countries were ruined by their debts to the big banks, they had to be rescued by advice from the smaller ones. It was an odd twist of history that the merchant banks which were once seen as extensions of British or American imperial power were now advising ex-colonies how to hold their own against the financial powers. They could at least offer some reassurance that Western banks were not all in the same herd.

16
AN ISLAND IN THE SUN

No man is an island, entire of itself; every man is a piece of the continent, a part of the main. . . .

JOHN DONNE, 1625

The billions of expatriate Eurodollars which slipped in and out of the world's financial centers created their own eccentric map of the world. They concentrated not only in London, Frankfurt, and Zurich, but in exotic islands which could provide bankers with secrecy and security without tax or controls. Bankers have always favored islands detached from the politics of the mainland, like Manhattan, Hong Kong, Singapore, or Bahrain. But the most remote havens are the handful of Caribbean islands which began in the sixties to attract these refugee dollars. The impact of international banking on these tiny communities provides an odd sidelight on the relationship of money and politics.

A passing visitor to the island of Grand Cayman, coming ashore from a cruise ship from Miami, could easily take it for an old-fashioned colonial island making its living out of tourism. The boats from the liners come into the little harbor of Georgetown, facing a quayside of bright little gingerbread buildings which look almost too quaint and pretty to be true—churches with comic shaped towers and green corrugated gables, sea captains' houses with rough-hewn pillars holding up decorated balconies, warehouses picked out with bright colors and little fishing boats chugging in and out of the harbor. The shops along the waterfront—the English Shoppe Ltd., the antique store selling English silver, the Viking art gallery, the picturesque pub called the Cayman Arms—seem to play up to the description which used to be given to Grand Cayman, "the island which time forgot." The Caymanian people, whether dark- or light-skinned, appear handsome, easygoing, and welcoming, like an advertisement for the Caribbean in the fifties. It is hard to remember that this island is only two hundred miles away from the turmoil of Jamaica, to which it used to belong.

To the north of Georgetown, along the west coast, the island still appears preoccupied with tourists, of the more prosperous and sophisticated kind. Avenues of royal palms and rows of Australian pine trees, swaying above the scrub, lead up to discreet little villas and clubs where visiting families stay along the seaside; and even the Holiday Inn forgoes its garish lettering and adopts a low profile, with palm-thatched sunshades leading down to the beach. The Seven Mile Beach itself, with its bright white sand and blue sea, has an atmosphere of timeless and placeless leisure, with few signs of transistors, or even newspapers; and the most purposeful tourists are the skindivers with masks, snorkels, and fins, who disappear to explore the brilliant coral reefs and wrecks in the still more remote world under the sea. In the slow pace of the beach life there is only an occasional disturbance, a sudden snatch of brisk dialogue about Eurodollars or flight times, suggesting something more than pure escapism.

It is only the center of Georgetown, behind the façade of the quayside, that reveals a more mysterious activity. Between the old British colonial relics—the government buildings, the post office, the 1919 peace memorial, with their rugged classical shapes—there is a cluster of big white slabs, four or five stories high, with neat rectangles and glass fronts, which look as if they might have been dropped ready-made from the sky. They stare at each other, with their functional glass walls, across the two main streets of the town. Above their entrances are blazoned their names—the Bank of America, the Royal Bank of Canada, Barclays Bank, the Bank of Nova Scotia, side by side with more unfamiliar names, like the Cayman National Bank and Trust Company. And inside their entrance halls are the names of far more banks on big brass plates on the walls—nearly three hundred of them, including most of the famous New York and London banks. Also on the walls, displayed in small white plastic letters, are the names of hundreds of companies. Some of them are familiar multinational names, but most of them are names which seem to be vying with each other in vagueness or exoticism:

> BARRACUDA
> BETTER TIMES
> CREATIVE MANAGEMENT
> CONGO INVESTMENT
> LILLIPUT INVESTMENTS
> GAR
> WHIRLWIND SECURITIES
> GREAT EXPECTATIONS

There are, it turns out, more than 11,000 of these companies now registered in Grand Cayman. The island contains (excluding expatriates) only about 10,000 people, so that it has more companies than inhabitants. But the identity of the companies is wrapped in secrecy. "We know who owns the banks," the governor explained to me in 1980, "but not even the registrar knows who owns the companies."

It is the shadowy presence of these companies and banks on the island, much more than its tourist charms, that accounts for the world's special interest in Grand Cayman in the last few years. It is an island of capitalism which stands out in abrupt contrast to its immediate Caribbean neighbors, Jamaica to the east and Cuba to the north. It insists on remaining a crown colony of Great Britain, apparently invulnerable to the political pressures all round it. And it has claimed to be the world's fastest-growing tax haven or, as it prefers to call itself, "international financial center."

The idea of a tax-free and neutral island has an irresistible appeal to multinational bankers. Tom Clausen, of the Bank of America, looked forward to "an international corporation that has shed all national identity";[1] Carl Gerstacker, the former head of

[1] A. W. Clausen, "The International Corporation: An Executive's View," *Annals of the American Academy of Political and Social Science* (September 1972).

Dow Chemicals, once explained: "I have long dreamed of buying an island owned by no nation and of putting the World Headquarters of the Dow Company on the truly neutral ground of such an island, beholden to no nation or society."[2] Grand Cayman seems to promise just such an island paradise, without taxes, without political troubles, and with money flowing in and out without interruption or surveillance.

Grand Cayman has always been isolated, and some of the inhabitants like to suggest that it has a continuous tradition of buccaneering activity. There is even a legend—without much evidence—that it was the original of Robert Louis Stevenson's *Treasure Island*. Certainly its history was more insular than its Caribbean neighbors'. There are altogether three Cayman Islands —Grand Cayman, Little Cayman, and Cayman Brac—of which Grand Cayman is much the biggest. They were discovered by Columbus on his fourth and last voyage in 1503, and they were noticed by many sixteenth-century voyagers. In 1586 Sir Francis Drake noted that he had "passed by the islands of Caymanas, which are not inhabited. There are on the land great serpents called Caymanas like large lizards, which are edible." But the Cayman Islands remained largely uninhabited, except by occasional castaways, pirates, deserters, and turtles, and the first record of permanent settlement was in 1734, when three families were given grants to land.

The islands became British, together with Jamaica and other Caribbean islands, under the Treaty of Madrid in 1670. They were governed as part of Jamaica, but the British settlers evidently had a more easygoing attitude than those in Jamaica; the relations between slaveowners and slaves were much more relaxed, producing a large proportion of families with mixed blood. A report on the Caymans in 1887 said that they were "a fairly well-to-do, self-reliant and loyal community," and that the tax-collectors "took only what was brought to them." Many of the Caymanians became seamen on American ships, and thus

---

[2]White House Conference on the Industrial World Ahead, February 7, 1972.

came to know more about America or Europe than about the rest of the Caribbean.

Much of the island of Grand Cayman, which is thin and L-shaped, only twenty-two miles across, is still almost untouched by recent history. The flat of the interior still runs wild, with mangrove swamps covering a third of the territory; the highest point is a sixty-foot hill. Along the coastline are little Caymanian villages with tiny houses with green and red corrugated roofs and gimcrack shops with grand names like The Emporium or Godfrey's Enterprise; and the leisurely life of the villagers seems unaffected by the world of banking or tourism. The Caymanians do not show signs of the grinding poverty that can be seen in Jamaica; they talk a precise and articulate English, handed down from Scots missionary schools. There is not much indication of great financial ambition; there is a small business school on the island, but a student there, who turned out to be Nigerian, complained to me that the Caymanians were too lazy to seize their opportunities, and a sociology teacher discovered that all her students came from Jamaica.

In the years after the Second World War, while the rest of the Caribbean was caught up in anticolonialist movements, the Caymanians were already moving toward being a kind of Caribbean Switzerland. They had no real political organizations, they followed individuals rather than parties, and they were overwhelmingly conservative. At the end of the fifties they faced their first decisive choice. When Jamaica was excitedly preparing for independence the Caymanians, led by Dr. Roy McTaggart, determined to break away from the Kingston government and to remain a British crown colony, with their own constitution, governor, and executive council, leaving their defense and foreign policy to London. "It wasn't that we moved away from the Caribbean," one of the local politicians explained, "the Caribbean moved away from us." While other colonies went through all the high expectations and disappointments of independence, and while Cubans experienced the Castro revolution, the Cayman Islands continued to be loyal to Britain, surviving off seamen's remittances and some tourist revenues, as if nothing much was happening. Georgetown was still very cut off from the outside world. When William Walker, now a prominent lawyer, arrived there in 1963, as he recalls it, "there were cows wandering through Georgetown, only one bank, only one paved road, and no telephones."

By the mid-sixties a few businessmen on the island were looking with envy at the Bahamas to the north, also a British colony, which was attracting many big companies and banks by providing exemption from tax. The Caymanians sought the advice of a British tax expert called Milton Grundy, who was well known in the Bahamas, and he helped them to draft a new trust law which would make the Cayman Islands even more attractive than the Bahamas to foreign companies and individuals. One keen supporter of the scheme was the young Treasurer of the island, Vassel Johnson, a very able ex-Jamaican Indian with a long face and a wry smile, who is now Financial Secretary. He was pessimistic about the rest of the Caribbean, and saw the chance to branch out. "We decided to create the right atmosphere," he recalls, "and 1966 was the takeoff."

In 1966 three things happened in quick succession. Georgetown airport was enlarged to take jet aircraft; the island was linked to the international telephone system; the new trust law was passed. Soon afterward Lynden Pindling became Prime Minister of the Bahamas, which were then moving toward independence, causing a wave of panic among businessmen in Nassau. Before long there was a rush of companies and banks wanting to register in Grand Cayman. "We should have put up a golden statue to Pindling," said one lawyer in Georgetown. "It wasn't that Pindling said or did anything to damage the banks," recalls Milton Grundy, "it was just that he was black."

The first rush of business was mainly from rich Englishmen, for whom the Cayman laws provided a way of exploiting a loophole in British tax law. The British Labour government soon closed the loophole, but the Caymans could still provide tax-free benefits to companies and individuals all around the world, particularly in the

United States and Latin America. Grand Cayman was well placed, for it was on the same time zone as New York, and it was in easy reach of Miami, Panama, and other Latin American centers—so that it became part of the classic escape route of money from South to North America. Before long most of the big North American banks were setting up offices in Georgetown, or putting up a brass plate and arranging for a representative to do business.

From the beginning—the Financial Secretary assured me—the Cayman government was determined to remain a "clean spot." They looked with disapproval at Nassau with its casinos, which were often suspected of laundering "dirty" money from Miami or Latin America. But there was a general agreement, as one Cayman banker put it, that "you can't have a proper tax haven if you won't accept cash"; and the government introduced secrecy laws more stringent than those of the Bahamas. "There are really two things about tax havens," explained Peter Leggatt, the manager of the Royal Bank of Canada; "there is sophisticated management of tax avoidance, and there are people trying to evade taxes. Sometimes it's hard to tell the difference."

The bank managers and lawyers I talked to insisted that they did not accept cash without rigorous questioning and references, but they each agreed that others were less conscientious, and each had stories of mysterious visitors arriving with a few million dollars in suitcases. Cash is an important part of their business, much of which is with relatively small customers. "Most of my clients are individuals like American doctors and dentists," one lawyer explained, "who come here with fifty or a hundred thousand dollars in cash to invest; it's more secure than working for a few multinational corporations, who could suddenly leave you."

The rush of money to Grand Cayman soon provided handsome opportunities for a handful of expatriate attorneys and accountants on the island. "A lawyer gets $1,000 for each registration," one bank manager explained, "and he should be able to earn $150,000—tax-free of course—for doing not very much." William Walker is now the doyen of the attorneys, and his firm holds the record—about 1,400—for the number of registered companies, whose names cover the passage outside his office. Walker has an old-fashioned gentlemanly style, with fair hair and blue eyes. His family lived in the Caribbean for three centuries; when he left Barbados after it became independent he settled with relief in Cayman. "We are directors of about five hundred of them," he explained, "and most of them don't require too much work—just signing occasional documents and perhaps holding two meetings a year." He is reticent about the nature of his clients, but he explains: "We funnel a lot of money from Central and South America. . . . Most of the money coming out of Latin America, of course, is in breach of their governments' exchange control regulations."

The lawyers and bankers in Georgetown are accustomed to being criticized abroad for tax evasion, which they regard with amusement. Ten years ago the chairman of the London-based company Lonrho, Lord Duncan-Sandys, was revealed to be receiving an extra $100,000 a year tax-free through the Cayman Islands, and the then British Prime Minister, Ted Heath, referred to it as the "unpleasant and unacceptable face of capitalism." "We had some good jokes about it," said one lawyer. "It may have been unacceptable to Mr. Heath, but it certainly wasn't illegal."

The new business also benefited the small Caymanian middle class, a tightly knit group: a high proportion of them are called either Bodden or Ebank, and some of the Bodden family like to claim descent from a deserter from Cromwell's army who is said to have settled on the island in the mid-seventeenth century. Three out of the seven members of the Cayman Cabinet, or "executive council," are Boddens; and of the eight other members of the legislature one is a Bodden and three are Ebanks. Some of them are only distantly related, but Caymanians often use "the Boddens" to describe the interlocked business interests. The most prominent Caymanian lawyer is Truman Bodden, a slender and very courteous man with a shy smile, who inhabits a paneled office decorated with certificates and a portrait of the Queen. He sounds confident that the continuing conservatism of his people will allow his business to thrive. "Most Caymanians are home-owners, sir," he told me, "and most of them have been to sea. They know how quickly a country can be wrecked, and that if they do anything stupid they'll lose. We mustn't kill the goose that lays the golden egg."

But the really big business of the Cayman Islands goes on inside the banks; and here we are in the most nebulous and secretive regions of global finance, in the midst of Cloud Nine. A few of the banks like Barclays of London or the Royal Bank of Canada have a reassuring physical presence, with a real banking hall and tellers behind counters who will take deposits from ordinary people. But this is misleading; for the really important transactions go on in upstairs offices which have no truck with small customers. When I telephoned the manager of the Bank of America he told me he did not wish to discuss his bank's activities. "We keep a very low profile here" (a description which seemed inaccurate, I pointed out, since Bank of America was proclaimed across the top of the building). Inquiries elsewhere soon suggested that the bank has a staff of about thirty people dealing extensively in Eurodollars. "They've got a massive operation," one lawyer told me. "They move billions of Eurodollars, mostly out of Latin America." Some of the banks are actually based on Grand Cayman, where the secrecy protects them from the oversight of supervisors; including the remarkable Bank of Credit and Commerce International, which is jointly based between here and Luxemburg.

Eurodollars lie behind much of the financial activity of Grand Cayman, but no one on the island, of course, has ever actually seen one. The Eurodollars which flow in and out are not controlled by an islander but by bankers and dealers who keep their own "Cayman book" in London or New York and telex instructions to the island. To obtain the tax advantages of Grand Cayman, a foreign bank only needs a minimal presence on the island —a brass plate, and the use of a secretary, a lawyer and a telex (the Caymans claim to have the highest proportion of telex machines per head—one to a hundred—of any country in the world). "I doubt whether anyone in the Caymans," said one London expert, "knows what the Eurodollar market really is." But so long as Eurodollars are "booked" or "parked" in the island (banks talk of them as if they were cars) they can accumulate interest or capital gains without paying tax to any government. And the attraction is so great that by 1980 there were about 30 billion Eurodollars booked in Grand Cayman—about 3 percent of the total world's supply—with perhaps another 30 billion in the accounts of insurance and other companies in the island.

The specific whereabouts of these billions puzzles many people who deal with them. "Some of my clients get very worried," one lawyer told me. "They insist on a special clause to compensate them if Castro invaded the island. I have to explain that Castro wouldn't find any Eurodollars in the safe; they're all *really* held in New York or London." But their technical presence on the island is enough to ensure their freedom from tax or supervision. This is a matter of periodic concern to central banks, particularly the Federal Reserve; for they are beyond their control, and they deprive the treasuries of large revenues. "The United States tried to inspect the bank books here four years ago," Vassel Johnson, the Financial Secretary, recalled in 1980, "but we asked the British government to oppose their request. The Americans were furious that the little Caymans were resisting them." Soon after this incident the Cayman government passed a new Confidential Relationships (Preservation) Law, which stipulated that "no information relating to a customer or client account with any institution within the local financial community can be disclosed to anyone."

The Caymanians are very aware that they face constant competition in the tax-haven business. In 1980 they were reckoned to be roughly equal to Hong Kong and Bahrain in the numbers of Eurodollars, and way ahead of the British Virgin Islands. The Bahamas are still in a different league, with about three times as many Eurodollars; but the Caymanians have made rapid strides, and they put great faith in their political stability and compactness. Many of the international banks keep only a "shell" in Georgetown; but the Caymanians seem confident that they regard this as their ultimate haven, to which banks and companies can retreat when things get too hot in the Bahamas or Panama. At the same time all these islands are worried that New York, the nicest island of all, will establish its own tax haven with the same advantages, depriving them of much of their *raison d'être*.

How far has this rarefied business affected the ordinary life of the island? Is it possible to benefit from the revenue without being spoilt by it? The actual banks employ a few hundred people and bring in a relatively small revenue; but the growth of the tax haven, it soon emerges, is closely linked to the expansion of employment, construction, and tourism: "A lot of men who arrive in brightly colored shirts with their wives," one government official explained, "turn out to have come over for an annual general meeting, having some fun at the same time." The Cayman Islands have been attracting leisurely tourists, snorklers, and escapists for some years; but in October 1978 a new air route was inaugurated between Houston and Georgetown, which soon quickened the pace of development. The chief promoter of this Texan connection was Jim Bodden, the Minister for Tourism and representative for Bodden Town, who is also the island's most prominent and controversial businessman. A big man with swept-back gray hair and sideburns, he lived for sixteen years in Texas and Florida, and his style is thoroughly Americanized. He runs the Cayman Development Corporation from a long low building behind the Seven Mile Beach, which looks as if it might have been ordered from Texas. Inside there is fake paneling and a long green carpet leading up to Jim Bodden's open door; when I called the lobby was loud with American voices discussing deals: "We're ready to close"—"get the lawyers"—"He'll be coming down the runway any moment"—"We can always split up the site." Jim Bodden explained to me quietly the huge benefits that tourism and building will bring to the island, constantly interrupted by brisk telephone calls ("The sonofabitch . . . what happened? . . . I'll look after him"). "We're pretty important to the free world," he insisted to me, "we were solid behind the United States when Castro came in . . . This is one haven of peace that remains in the world."

The haven was clearly becoming less peaceful. Jim Bodden's

lobby displayed plans for clusters of Florida-type condominiums, and along the Seven Mile Beach the concrete skeletons of long buildings were already sticking up above the palms. The Texan connection was already visible and audible: hotels and restaurants displayed a special yellow book in which Houstonians were invited to write their names, in order to be invited to a frolicking annual Houston-Cayman reunion. On the north shore more sedate houses have been developed for Americans who retire on the island (the Cayman government gives them a six-month trial period, after which, if approved, they can stay forever). Rows of neat, well-gardened villas stretch along the coast, surrounded by oleanders and grapevines, each with the name and home state of its owner hanging outside on a rustic board. ("They're always hoping that someone from their own state will call on them," explained a British expatriate, "so that they can tell them just how much they enjoy being away from it all.") The life of the "expats" may not be quite as idyllic as the setting: the residents look less relaxed and healthy than the tourists, and their conversation suggests a tendency toward feuds, circular gossip, and other islanders' neuroses.

Grand Cayman cannot remain "the island which time forgot" when it is also the island which bankers discovered. As the businessmen follow the tourists the wealth of the island begins to take on more visible forms. "These Texans seem to buy condominiums," the governor remarked, "the way you and I could buy suits." Since the Houston flights began, several Texan corporations have set up subsidiaries on the island, and there are rumors of large Texan holdings in one or two Cayman banks. Already there are some doubts about the social consequences of Jim Bodden's open-door policy toward foreign investment and tourism. "It will make this island into a nation of maids," one Caymanian complained. But the majority of islanders seem content to enjoy the immediate benefits—higher wages for construction workers and servants, more jobs with companies, and more lawyer's fees.

In the midst of all this thrusting commercial development the Cayman islanders insist more than ever on remaining a British crown colony, complete with the old colonial trappings, including policemen in white topees, an annual parade for the Queen's Birthday, and a governor who presides over the executive council and every year makes the Speech from the Throne. The present governor, His Excellency Thomas Russell, is a quiet Scotsman who has spent much of his career on Pacific islands, where he contributed archaeological articles to the *Journal of Polynesian Studies.* He still has a hint of that aloof, slightly pained expression which used to be almost obligatory for colonial governors, but he clearly enjoys the role of supervising this commercial little community with its salesmanship and showmanship. He is quite prepared to open a beauty competition or to put on a Texan hat, but for formal occasions he still wears the extraordinary nineteenth-century uniform of his job—a white suit with gold epaulettes and a high white topee with feathers hanging from it.

"I'm the last pensionable governor from the old British colonial service," he told me in his office in the elegant glass-and-aluminum government building in Georgetown, which is regarded as a symbol of the Caymans' go-ahead attitudes. "It's a pleasantly compact government—all my cabinet are on the same floor. People here are very critical of independence; they think it causes troubles like Jamaica's. They're very conservative: they won't look at the welfare state—to them it means socialism, which means Communism. It's true they're beginning to complain about some things, like access to beaches; but most of them are too busy getting rich to be very worried. When I came here six years ago in the midst of a world recession I was surprised to find the Caymans were doing very well: their offshore banking and tourism seemed unaffected. My job here is really a kind of combination of ombudsman and business consultant. I don't need to interfere very much, and the British government leaves us very much alone —largely no doubt because we don't need any kind of grant."

The Caymans' refusal to become independent caused concern at the UN, particularly within the Committee on Decolonization, which paid a special visit to the islands in 1977 to look for evidence of oppression and imperialist domination; and later two representatives from the Cayman Islands went up to New York to give evidence. "We told them we didn't want to be decolonized," said Truman Bodden, who was one of them. "It was the first case like that they'd had for a long time. But we take the approach, sir, that if there's something good, you mustn't change it. We notice that other Caribbean countries may have political independence, but don't have economic independence. If they do what we do, they could have success too. So long as Britain is responsible for our foreign policy and defense, we can rest quite well. We must be thankful to the Lord, sir, for leading us in the right direction. If we keep people in the government who have a lot to lose, we should be all right."

Not all the islanders are as confident as Truman Bodden about the future. "This is really a very backward island," another Caymanian lawyer, Steve McField, complained. "All they can do is make money, and money is destroying the family life; I never thought to see an Old Folks' Home in Cayman—it used to be an honor to look after parents. There's no real intellectual life here; the only rebellion among young people is smoking Ganja. But we can't stay separate from the rest of the Third World; we're not self-sufficient. What happens when resources get really scarce?" Yet it is hard to find signs of much radicalism or revolt on the island. The most outspoken opposition comes from a scandal sheet called *The Voice,* which revels in uncovering the business interests of the Boddens and other businessmen; but *The Voice* does not represent any organized group. There is little discussion about closer links with Jamaica or other Caribbean islands with all their political problems. "I was regarded as seditious," one journalist in Georgetown complained, "just for saying that Cayman is part of the Caribbean."

Can Grand Cayman remain a haven, both from taxes and political troubles? To many Third World countries, including its immediate neighbors, its isolation and selfishness seem intolerable. The Jamaicans, with their mounting debts, unemployment, and violent political conflicts, think it outrageous that the island which once belonged to them should turn its back, refuse to let in more

Jamaican immigrants, and devote itself to helping rich men to evade their taxes. But the Cayman leaders see their island as part of a quite different world. "The advantage of being an island," one of them explained, "is that you can choose your own neighbors. We've chosen Miami instead of Jamaica."

The islanders see themselves as part of the global financial system on which all free nations, whether they like it or not, must depend. As the rest of the Caribbean becomes less stable—they anticipate—so their haven will become still more attractive as the safe, neutral island which bankers and businessmen need. Vassel Johnson, the Financial Secretary, insisted: "Bad times always send more money down here." "You can't try to define the nationality of capital," William Walker said. "If you try to make laws all-embracing, you'll just shut down international trade." But the Caymans' future remains very uncertain. For as New York has been allowed since 1981 to have its own International Banking Facilities (IBF), freed from domestic requirements for reserves and controls over interest rates, it will be able to offer many of the advantages of the Caribbean, in the same time zone; and Manhattan will be able to become its own offshore island.

The Caymans and other islands could still offer exceptional secrecy, as a refuge for international capital which did not wish to be examined too closely. But however much confidence the bankers put in these secretive and isolated islands, they could not in the end escape from world politics; for both their loans and their deposits were dependent on countries, whether in the Middle East or elsewhere, which were politically explosive. And the idea that capital was neutral, and had no nationality, would receive some rude shocks.

17
IRAN AND THE
"GREAT SATAN"

Never ask of money spent
Where the spender thinks it went.

ROBERT FROST

It was hardly surprising that David Rockefeller should become a
personal friend of the Shah as Iran became more important to
American interests. Rockefeller, as the uncrowned king of the
bankers, had made it his business to befriend monarchs and potentates; and the Shah was a prince among princes, who was able
to turn the key to much banking business. Rockefeller was not, he
explained, "a good friend" of the Shah: he saw him about twelve
times over twenty years, and had six to eight man-to-man discussions about the world. "He was one of the best-informed people
about world events that I've ever met." Rockefeller later realized
(he said later) that the Shah was becoming cut off from his own
people, but he didn't feel it was his job to warn him. He talked
to him as a banker, and if he had mentioned torture or the police
state, "the next time I wanted to see him, he wouldn't have been
available."[1] It was a personal friendship between men who respected each other. But the consequences were to precipitate a
major crisis between the United States and Iran, and to send
shocks through the international banking system.

Western bankers were naturally attracted to the Peacock
Throne, which seemed all the more glamorous after 1971, when

[1] "The World of David Rockefeller," *Bill Moyers Journal,* Public Broadcasting
Service, February 7, 1980.

the Shah staged his extravagant coronation in Persepolis to com-
memorate 2,500 years of the Iranian monarchy. Among the few
American guests were two bankers who knew the Shah well, who
were to play opposite roles: one was Jack McCloy, the former
head of the Chase Manhattan and the World Bank, and adviser
to successive administrations since Roosevelt's. The other was
George Ball, the former Undersecretary of State, who was then
senior partner of Lehman Brothers in New York. The coronation
was seen as a provocative insult by the Mullahs and Islamic leaders in Iran, to whom Persepolis represented the pre-Islamic era of
Darius and Cyrus; but it had a magical effect on American bankers, who were beginning to move into Iran at that time. "They're
like children," complained one Middle Eastern banker who was
approached to join several syndicates at this time; "they're dazzled by that kind of show."

There was nothing new about bankers supporting a corrupt and
precarious shah. Eighty years earlier (see Chapter 2) an earlier
shah had enriched himself with loans from European bankers,
with a profligacy which led to his overthrow. The present Shah
—whose father had taken over the throne with British support—
was very conscious of his country's erratic past. "Maybe I am
lonely," he said to me in 1974, "but maybe that is my strength.
You could be much weaker sometimes if you were not like that."
He went on to explain, "We had four periods of grandeur and
glory, maybe the biggest in the history of the whole world, the
biggest empire but also four periods of decadence. Now I try to
make it steady."[2] He was never confident that his dynasty was
secure; his network of personal investments all over the world
reflected pessimism as well as greed.

It was in the late sixties, as the oil revenues grew and the Shah
extended his ambitions, that the American banks became more
seriously interested in Iran. The Bank of America, the Guaranty
(merged into Morgan Guaranty), and the Chase already had connections with the Shah, including a very affable vice-president in
Teheran, James Thackeray, who played tennis regularly with the

Shah. In 1968 Citibank, in the course of its rapid expansion over-seas, bought a 35 percent share in the local Bank Iranian, with the reluctant approval of the Shah. A specially active banker was Minos Zombanakis, representing the Manufacturers Hanover (Manny Hanny), who put together the first major syndicated loan (see Chapter 7) of $80 million for the Iranians.

David Rockefeller flew in and out of Teheran, staying at the Hilton with his large entourage and impressing the Shah with his influence and his benign concern: on one visit he presented the Shah with a hunting rifle, on another he bought a whole collection of paintings by Iranian artists. It was a friendship of mutual interest. Rockefeller enjoyed the reassurance of a fellow prince, as well as the prospect of business; and the Shah saw Rockefeller as a key to American support—with all the mystique of his name, his foundations, and his international connections, personifying the traditional links between the Chase and the oil industry. Before long the Chase had bought a 35 percent share in the Industrial Credit Bank of Iran; but more important, its New York headquarters was receiving growing deposits from the National Iranian Oil Company—whose dealings (like those of so many oil companies) were kept very secret from others, including the Iranian Central Bank.

After the increases in the oil price in 1973, in which the Shah himself had taken the lead,[3] the financial importance of Iran became far greater. At first the Iranian government used the huge new oil revenues to repay many of its debts; but already by 1975 the Shah was beginning to borrow again, to pay for his immense projects and arms buying. In the next two years Teheran became a magnet for bankers from all over the world, establishing themselves at the Intercontinental and the Hilton, frantically grappling with the erratic telephones and traffic jams, competing furiously to lend more and more to Iran in bigger and bigger syndicates, while the profit margins or spreads narrowed as the competition increased.

It was one of the biggest bonanzas in the history of banking. Iran

[3] *The Seven Sisters,* pp. 257–59.

was not only a huge borrower; it also had the security of the oil revenues and deposits, so that it was a "prime credit." The lending officers competed to offer loans, not only through the major syndicates, but to private companies and organizations. The Citibank salesmen were specially aggressive and relentless in selling private loans, including loans to the Shah's family; the Central Bank, having been bypassed by Citibank, strongly protested until Citibank withdrew some of its men.

But it was the Chase, with Rockefeller's help, which was now established as the leading American bank in Iran, enjoying the special confidence of the Shah and his highest officials. Early in 1977 the Chase took the lead in raising a record loan, which was to have long repercussions. It provided no less than $500 million for the imperial government to balance its budget, which was now suffering from the pace of arms buying and other projects. It was raised by eleven banks, including the Chase, the Bank of America, and Citibank, two Swiss banks, a Canadian (Toronto Dominion), and one British bank (NatWest) which enjoyed special links with the Chase. In making this and other subsequent loans, the Chase with other banks ignored an important article (No. 25) in the Iranian constitution which stipulated that all state loans required the approval of parliament—apparently believing that the Shah's own approval was enough. Their legal adviser in Teheran, Mehran Tavakoli, warned the Chase that these loans might prove to be unenforceable under Article 25,[4] but in the end Chase was reassured by the finance ministry and by other counsel and it went ahead.

The banks were also competing to lend to the Shah and his family, and the frontiers between government and monarchy were blurred. The Shah's family—particularly his demanding twin sister, Ashraf—were well placed to take advantage of foreign banks. The Shah had his own personal bank, the Bank Omran; the word means "development" but the bank was mainly engaged in developing the Shah's fortune; it was wholly owned by the Pah-

[4]*The Wall Street Journal,* March 28, 1980.

levi Foundation which, though presented as a charitable organization, was really the chief vehicle for the family's finances. The
banks were glad to lend money to build the Pahlevi Foundation
skyscraper in New York. "It was an offer," the former head of the
Central Bank explained to me, "that they couldn't very well refuse."

By lending to the Shah's family the banks found it easier to get
other business; but the responsibility for these loans was later the
subject of bitter recrimination. "All the banks knew that the Bank
Omran was the Shah's personal repository for his pocket money,"
the present governor of the Central Bank, Ali-Reza Nobari, complained. "But they went on lending to Bank Omran. Citibank lent,
for example, $55 million to Princess Ashraf for a housing project.
On the site of the housing project she built a palace. And yet
Citibank debits our account for it."[5]

Documents later found in Teheran gave some clues to the
channels through which the Shah's family extracted funds from
the national government and oil company funds, which they
filtered through banks in Switzerland and New York—including
Chase, Citibank, and smaller banks—into their own extensive
private properties, including hotels in Teheran, houses in Manhattan, Beverly Hills, Acapulco, and Switzerland, islands in the Sey-
chelles, a stud in Surrey. American and European companies were
glad to connive in various forms of corruption in their haste to
expand their business. The Chase, which was seen as the Shah's
private banker (which Rockefeller denies having been), was to be
regarded with special suspicion by later revolutionaries.

Two men were especially responsible for the Shah's private
fortune. One was Houshang Ansari, the Minister of Finance from
1974 to 1978, and former Ambassador to Washington. Ansari
was very close to the Shah, whom he sometimes telephoned six
times a day; he also saw a lot of the Western bankers, particularly
from Chase, and his influence was crucial for approval for loans.
The other was Mohammed Behbehanian, who ran the Shah's

[5] *Euromoney* (January 1980), p. 28.

huge estates and had an office in Switzerland; he was also believed to be close to Rockefeller. He looked like a comic-opera
count, a jovial roly-poly man with a tall, bossy Swiss secretary (I
met him once in St. Moritz, when I was waiting to see the Shah).
After the fall of the Shah he disappeared with her and several
million dollars; his wife and children did not hear from
him.

In the euphoria of their massive lending the bankers, like the
diplomats, were slow to see signs of the Shah's political instability.
Already by the end of 1976 there were ominous indications,
including the murder of American technicians by "Islamic Marxists": but they hardly affected the bankers' enthusiasm. A few
Middle Eastern banks which had contacts in the bazaars were
aware of growing resentment; and some individual bankers including George Ball had become very skeptical about the Shah's
future. But most bankers held together in making still more loans.
"There's a comfort in being one of the herd," a man from Chemical Bank explained. "There's always a temptation to hold on too
long—you don't want to bow out, in case you were wrong."
"When Iran indicated that it wanted to borrow," said Al Costanzo
of Citibank, "everyone wanted to be getting in. No one thought
that the Shah was a real risk; we were all caught by surprise—
there were no signals from the embassy, but I should have been
more observant."[6]

It was not until early in 1978, after riots in Qum and Isfahan and
mass support for the Mullahs, that the bankers became seriously
worried about the Shah's fortune and began to reduce Iran's credit
rating. But their huge loans had already locked them into the
country—as the Shah had meant them to. As the exiled Ayatollah
Khomeini extended his influence from Paris, the bankers saw little
prospect of changing their allegiance. "It's not the role of the
bank," David Rockefeller said to me, "to be in touch with opposition parties."[7]

[6]Interview with author, March 14, 1980.
[7]Interview with author, March 12, 1980.

As late as September, when many observers saw the Shah's position as hopeless, the banks were still competing to make new loans at low margins to the Agricultural Development Bank, whose security depended on the Shah's support. When the world's bankers met in Washington in early October for the annual jamboree of the IMF, they still showed little sign of concern about Iran. When the Chase signed its last loan in November the country was in chaos, and the Shah was isolated; when he had tried to impose order through a military government he soon found he could not rely on his army, while the Islamic militants and students were showing their strength all around him.

In early December George Ball presented a report to President Carter, now not as a banker, but as the special adviser. Ball gave a devastating account of how the crisis had come about; how the United States had made the Shah what he had become, nurtured his love of the grandiose and sold him weapons to indulge his fantasies. The outbreaks of violence had irreparably damaged the Shah's position; the banking system had collapsed. A military government would only be able to enforce order with ferocious brutality and torture, and would be unlikely to last more than two years. The only hope of saving the Shah was to persuade him through the ambassador, William Sullivan, to become a constitutional monarch with a council of notables to restore order. President Carter discussed the report with Ball and Brzezinski, who at first wanted to fly out himself to bolster the Shah. In Teheran Ambassador Sullivan found the Shah in no mood to accept realities, and Carter's support now only embarrassed him further. Few notables were prepared to risk involvement in such a precarious regime, and many were leaving the country.

Finally, after much hovering, the Shah flew out of the country on January 16, 1979, in his private Boeing 707, leaving Iran in the uncertain hands of the Prime Minister, Bakhtiar, who was soon eclipsed by the return of the Ayatollah Khomeini. The financial system of the country was now in chaos. Billions of dollars of defense contracts were soon canceled, projects abandoned, palaces deserted. The new Islamic rulers regarded the banks—and particularly the Chase—as the hated agents of the Shah who had corrupted their country and stolen their money, and as the instruments of the "Great Satan" of American capitalism.

THE CHASE LOBBY

The forced exile of the Shah confronted the Chase with the recurring problem of bankers in unstable countries. Were they lending to a ruler, or to a country? "We never feel we're dealing primarily with a ruler," the chairman, David Rockefeller, insisted to me, "though you can't overlook it. We try to make loans that are sound for the country—that the successor regime will find comfortable."[8] But Rockefeller's personal association with the Shah had been very visible, going beyond a professional banker's relationship. The Chase had become a symbol of American support and international capitalism. One Arab banker said to me: "The Chase isn't really a bank, it's an army."

The Shah's exile was an obvious embarrassment to the Western governments which had been his former allies. In Washington the Carter Administration soon wanted to establish some kind of relationship with the Ayatollah and the revolutionary government, and in the following months they even allowed some supplies of weapons to the Ayatollah's regime. In Britain the Foreign Office resisted pressure from conservatives to allow the Shah in; but the State Department in Washington was at first prepared to admit the Shah into the United States, and Henry Kissinger was asked to help to find him a suitable home. Kissinger, like Rockefeller, did not regard himself as a great friend of the Shah. "I met him only eight or nine times," he told me; "he was not a great friend, like Sadat." But he felt a strong loyalty to the man who (as he saw it) had been a bulwark of Western defense for the past twenty years. Kissinger had no machinery for finding large houses, so he turned to David Rockefeller, as an old friend. Kissinger was also employed by the Chase, as chairman of its advisory board; but that,

[8]Interview with author, March 12, 1980.

he insists, was irrelevant to his concern for the Shah.[9]

Rockefeller was in a dilemma. He felt a personal loyalty to the Shah, and there was no doubt that the Chase had benefited from the relationship; but he realized that open identification with him could damage the prospects of the Chase in Iran and elsewhere. So he declined to give assistance and Kissinger instead turned to David's brother Nelson—who had so often helped Kissinger financially in the past, and was also a friend of the Shah. Nelson soon found an appropriate refuge for the Shah in the Beverly Hills estate of Walter Annenberg, the former American ambassador to London, and he also provided the Shah with an American aide, a public-relations man called Robert Armao, who had earlier been the official greeter for New York City. Soon afterward Nelson Rockefeller died, and David was now pressed further to look after the Shah. David assigned Joseph Reed, a vice-president of the Chase who had organized his chairman's journeys around the world, to provide diplomatic assistance, and Reed was thereafter frequently involved in the Shah's affairs.

When the Shah had finally escaped from Iran on January 16 in his private 707, he still hoped that he might soon be able to return to his country. He decided not to go to America, but flew first to Egypt, and then to Morocco, to remain close to his country. But his prospects in Iran were rapidly deteriorating. The Ayatollah returned, denounced Prime Minister Bakhtiar, and nominated a new one, Bazargan. The Islamic revolutionaries were escalating their attacks on America and insisting that the Shah be tried.

Washington was now worried about the consequences of letting the Shah into America, which would encourage suspicions of intrigue and counterrevolution. The State Department asked Kissinger (according to his own account) to try to dissuade the Shah from applying for a visa, and Secretary Vance asked Sullivan, the former ambassador, to press Kissinger to the same end. But Kissinger refused (as he put it) "with some indignation." The State Department then approached David Rockefeller, who also

[9]Interview with author, June 20, 1980.

refused to dissuade the Shah. Kissinger was now publicly outraged that an American government was not trying to find an asylum for the Shah, who was "a flying Dutchman looking for a port of call."[10] And at that time (Kissinger insists) the Shah could have been admitted without risk of reprisals.

One person who was activated by Kissinger's speech, when he read it in *The New York Times,* was Jack McCloy, the former chairman of the Chase and master of *realpolitik,* who was still firmly loyal to the Shah. McCloy quickly called up Kissinger to express his concern, and offered to help the Shah; McCloy, said Kissinger, was "protesting the conscience of American honor" (the word "honor" recurs frequently in Kissinger's account). McCloy was now eighty-four, with a modest and self-effacing style ("Why should you want to come and see an old man like me?" he asked when I once interviewed him); but he was a formidable lobbyist, with countless powerful friends after his four decades' moving between government and business, and he quickly began pressing the Shah's case in Washington.

Kissinger, by his own account, approached the government five times, including two talks with Secretary Vance, and he and Rockefeller eventually enlisted the help of the British government to find a temporary refuge for the Shah in the Bahamas, that traditional refuge of the rich. Then Kissinger used his influence with the government of Mexico (which he and Rockefeller were at that time advising, after the breakdown of Carter's relationship) and persuaded the Mexicans to admit the Shah to live in his private mansion there. David Rockefeller, with the help of Joseph Reed and McCloy, also arranged through David Newsom, the Undersecretary for Political Affairs at the State Department, for the Shah's children to be allowed into America for schooling. But the Rockefeller group were exasperated by the reluctance of the State Department to accept the Shah himself.

All this lobbying, Kissinger insisted, was simply the work of a few private individuals who felt it their duty to support an old

[10] *The Washington Post,* November 29, 1979.

friend and America's honor. "It had to be made clear that some Americans were standing by America's friends," he said to me. "A few telephone calls can hardly be described as a conspiracy; it's not honorable to suggest that a few private individuals can bring effective pressure on the government; the government should take responsibility for its own actions."[11]

But it looked very different to the government in Teheran. They had sentenced the Shah to death, and they demanded that he be extradited. They accused him of having stolen billions from the country, and they saw him as a constant threat to their security. To them Rockefeller, Kissinger, and McCloy did not look at all like private individuals: they were all closely connected with the Chase, which had been very visible under the Shah's regime; and they had all been closely associated with earlier American administrations and had links with the Carter Administration (Kissinger and Brzezinski were rivals, but Brzezinski had been brought into the field of diplomacy by Rockefeller, who had invited him to become secretary of his Trilateral Commission).

The revolutionary government was determined to discover the extent of the Shah's fortune and the role of his principal banker, the Chase. Reporters who inspected records at the Central Bank found a confused trail of payments into a multiplicity of banks, and the exact sums were never established; but it was clear that the Chase and other banks had been the channels for many millions of the Shah's fortune abroad.

During the summer the White House and the State Department were still perplexed by the question of whether to admit the Shah. Brzezinski was firmly in favor, while Carter had grave doubts. When Brzezinski persisted, Carter (as he later recalled) blew up. "Blank the Shah! I'm not going to welcome him when he has other places to go." In July the State Department warned their chargé d'affaires in Teheran, Bruce Laingen, about growing pressure to allow the Shah a visa. On July 26 Secretary Vance sent a cable (secret 194732) to the Teheran embassy asking them to evaluate

[11]Interview with author, June 20, 1980.

"the effect of such a move on the safety of Americans in Iran (especially the official Americans in the compound) as well as on our relations with the government of Iran. . . ."[12] Laingen replied that Teheran was very unstable, that the embassy was inadequately protected, and that it would be unwise to admit the Shah to America; the embassy had new steel doors and thirteen Marines to protect it, but the Iranian guards assigned to guard the embassy were a mixed bag, including a religious group and racketeers. The expert on Iran at the State Department, Henry Precht, wrote a secret memo (later found in the embassy) stressing that "we should make no move toward admitting the Shah until we have obtained and tested a new substantially more effective guard force for the embassy."[13]

The relations between Washington and Teheran remained perilous. The Iranians were still demanding the extradition of the Shah, and early in October Vance, with David Newsom and others, had tense talks in New York with the Iranian Foreign Minister, Ibrahim Yazdi, about America's attitudes. Then a few days later the State Department received unwelcome news from Joseph Reed, David Rockefeller's aide. He had just visited the Shah in a hospital in Mexico; the Shah was seriously ill, and Rockefeller had sent Dr. Benjamin Kean, a specialist in tropical medicine, to see him. Kean had reported that the Shah was suffering from lymph-gland cancer, which needed treatment within a few weeks. But Carter was told (he recalls) that the Shah was "at the point of death" and must be treated in New York. Kissinger at this time was away in Europe; when Reed told him the news about the Shah's illness he merely advised him (he says) to forward the information to the State Department. He was not consulted by the State Department or informed of the threats of reprisals.

The State Department consulted through their embassy with the Iranian Prime Minister, Bazargan; he was clearly unhappy about the Shah coming to New York, and he asked for an Iranian doctor to confirm that it was necessary; but he undertook to protect the

[12] The New York Times Magazine, May 24, 1981.
[13] London Times, November 21, 1979.

American diplomats in the embassy. Many State Department officials were still concerned about the dangers of admitting the Shah,
for the authority of Bazargan was already doubtful in the face of
the fierce anti-Americanism of the Ayatollah and the militants. But
at this point both Vance and President Carter agreed with Brzezinski that the Shah should be allowed into New York, provided he
did not engage in political activities. The Rockefeller organization
now moved in to fly the Shah by private plane to New York,
where Rockefeller aides took him into the hospital by the side
entrance, giving him the pseudonym (absurdly enough) of David
Newsom—as if to advertise that Rockefeller was providing his
own state department. The Shah and the American doctors
refused to allow an Iranian doctor to examine him, thus adding
to the Iranian suspicions.

In Teheran the Ayatollah and the militant students were now
working themselves up into a new anti-American frenzy, preparing for a mass demonstration on November 4, the anniversary of
the attack on the universities by the Shah's police. At this point
Bazargan made a rash move: visiting Algeria for its independence celebrations he talked there with Brzezinski—to the fury
of the militants, who associated Brzezinski both with American
imperialism and with Rockefeller. In Teheran a preliminary demonstration marched through the streets, past the American embassy; and the next day the Ayatollah called on the militants to
step up their attacks on the United States. But the diplomats
remained in their embassy, and on November 4, the day of the
proclaimed demonstration, a mob of thousands attacked the
embassy and took the diplomats as hostages. The Ayatollah gave
his support to the students, and Bazargan, back from Algiers,
was now powerless to protect the hostages. The long siege,
which was to dominate American diplomacy for the next
months, had begun.

Kissinger insisted that the final decision to admit the Shah,
which had such devastating consequences, was the responsibility
of the President and his two chief advisers; but Kissinger, at a time
when his support for SALT II was much needed, had some political leverage. "I think they took the correct decision to admit the

Shah,'' Kissinger said later, ''but they made the mistake of relying on the government and not realizing the power of Khomeini. If I'd been consulted I would probably have recommended they reduce the staff in the embassy. . . . What exactly had we done? Just a few phone calls. After all, they have proved pretty resistant to my suggestions in the past.''[14]

For anyone inclined toward conspiracy theories, the story of the Rockefeller-Kissinger lobby provided a caricature of global capitalism at work. In Paris, for instance, Le Monde gave a vivid description of how the Chase, on the verge of bankruptcy, was interlocked with the network of giant corporations, oil companies, and the CIA, all involved with the Shah.[15] But the truth was more personal, and less sinister. In fact many bankers, including Chase men, were worried about the visible lobbying by the Chase, which was damaging the image of bankers' neutrality all over the world. Rockefeller and Kissinger had their own motives for rashly identifying themselves with an exiled monarch, which were not really in keeping with the interests of the global bank. And the world crisis which was set off by the Shah's arrival in New York soon caused serious upheavals in the international banking system.

FREEZE AND DEFAULT

The taking of the American hostages by the Iranian militants, though a diplomatic outrage, did not present an immediate danger to most American banks. While relations with Iran had been deteriorating, the Iranian Central Bank had been scrupulous in paying interest, and only a few private loans, including some to the Shah's family, were in doubt. In their lending to Iran the bankers had observed their golden rule: only to lend money to those who have money already. The huge deposits of Iranian funds in New York and London, which had accumulated from the oil revenues, more than balanced the total loans to Iran.

[14]Interview with author, June 20, 1980.
[15]Le Monde, June 20, 1980.

But a few individual banks had become concerned about their exposure since the revolution; and some had as much as 10 percent of their loans in Iran. The revolutionary government had been moving large sums out of some of the American banks, particularly the hated Chase Manhattan; and they now favored the Bank of America, which had characteristically kept a much lower political profile: its London branch, the biggest money center in the world, held $2.8 billion of Iranian deposits in November 1979. Morgan's bank, which held only $27 million in Iranian deposits in November, had also been concerned about its vulnerability; and soon after the Iranian revolution a year earlier it had made plans with its lawyers to freeze if necessary the Iranian government's share of Krupps in West Germany, if its own loans were threatened. Both Chase and Citibank had worries about the security of their Iranian loans. Chase, as the Shah's banker, was the obvious target for political attack, and Citibank was thought to have special cause for concern after its aggressive loans to private companies and to the Shah's family back in 1977.

At Citibank Wriston had often talked about the political impartiality of the international capital market; but he had firm views about revolutionary regimes and he was much influenced by the example of Castro, who back in 1960 had nationalized Citibank's banks in Cuba. Citibank had promptly "offset" Cuba's deposits in New York—or taken them in reprisal—so that Castro never cost it a dollar; and it later won its case against Cuba in the Supreme Court. Wriston regarded the Ayatollah's regime as beyond the pale: "I don't think anybody with experience in international politics would call that a responsible government in the international community." He saw the taking of the hostages as the ultimate proof of their irresponsibility: "Anyone who thinks they are entitled, with fifty American hostages, to the niceties of the international law shouldn't be walking the streets by himself."[16]

[16]Interview with author, June 13, 1980.

After the Iranians took their hostages Wriston and other bankers had urgent talks with officials in Washington and New York about the possibility of freezing Iranian assets. Officials at the New York Federal Reserve discreetly consulted executives at Bankers Trust about the Cuban precedent, and the bankers, suspecting what was in the wind, decided swiftly to freeze the Iranian assets in their own bank. The Treasury in the meantime hastily looked up the old documents about freezing Cuban assets and amended them, substituting Iran for Cuba.

Nine days after the taking of the hostages Bani-Sadr, who was then acting Foreign Minister in Teheran, announced at a press conference that Iran would withdraw its deposits from American banks which, he said, were worth $12 billion. There was some doubt about the seriousness of the Iranian threat, but it was enough to alarm the bankers. "How does one ever know?" said Rockefeller. "But how could you not take it seriously?"[17]

To some officials at the U.S. Treasury it seemed like a nightmare scene from Paul Erdman's thriller *The Crash of '79*: the mad act of a foreign government could bring some of the smaller banks toppling, in turn threatening the big ones. "It was the first twenty-four hours which were worrying," said one official; "given time the system can always adjust." The Treasury heard the news at 4 A.M. Washington time, and officials were summoned to work before dawn to finalize the arrangements to freeze the Iranian deposits. They made their plans without much discussion of detail. "We acted knowing it would have adverse side effects," explained one official, "but there was little else we could do." They would freeze all Iranian deposits in American banks, whether they were held in the United States or abroad, but few officials then understood the full repercussions. President Carter signed the order at 8:10 A.M.; he himself made the announcement, and Secretary of the Treasury William Miller stressed at a

[17]Interview with author, March 12, 1980.

press briefing in the White House that the move was "purely in response to the Iranian announcement that it was going to withdraw its deposits from U.S. banks, and not because of the takeover of the U.S. embassy in Teheran." Later evidence gave no reason to doubt Miller's statement; there was no indication at this stage that the administration wanted to use the Iranian deposits as a critical bargaining counter for the release of the hostages—which they later became. There was no attempt to take the deposits under government charge. The bankers were left firmly in control of the Iranian funds, and the bankers remained the key to any future negotiation.

Would Iranian withdrawals really be a threat to the American economy? Before the freeze the size and exact whereabouts of the Iranian deposits were unknown, even to the U.S. Treasury; the banks had maintained their secrecy since the Senate hearings four years earlier (see Chapter 8). But now, in the aftermath of the freeze, the curtains were suddenly drawn. They revealed a total, not of $12 billion as the Iranians had threatened, but of $8 billion, including $6 billion in bank deposits, much more than the total American loans to Iran, and certainly not a grave threat to the American economy. But they showed that the Iranians now had far more money in the London branches of American banks than in New York (excluding the large deposits of gold and dollars in the New York Fed); and they also showed that some banks, including the Chase and Citibank, might soon be short of Iranian deposits to offset their loans to Iran. The system itself was not vulnerable, but individual banks were. As Wilson Schwartz, the economic adviser to Manny Hanny, put it: "You have to distinguish between forests and trees: the forest is safe, but trees can be hurt."

Four years earlier, when senators had asked bankers about the threat of a "money weapon," bankers had assured them that the withdrawal of oil deposits would not seriously affect the economy (see Chapter 8)—particularly since most of the money was in "time deposits" which could not be withdrawn immediately: of the $6 billion of Iranian deposits, it later emerged, only about

$1 billion was "call money." Moreover, the bankers had constantly explained that if money was taken out of the Eurodollar system, it would simply find its way back into it, because there was nowhere else for it to go. "It's a closed system," as Wriston put it; "there is no way they can take a dollar out." It was "cold-nosed money," Costanzo had explained; the big banks were acting simply as intermediaries for the effective transfer of wealth.

So why did the President now insist that this was a threat to national security? The nose began to look much less cold. In the first place there was a clamor for some punitive action, to counter the seizure of the hostages. In the second place several big banks were determined to safeguard their loans by "offsetting" their deposits. Wriston at Citibank responded immediately by offsetting all Iranian deposits in Citibank against its loans to Iran. "It's the oldest device in banking," as he put it. "Just the way you would offset against a bankrupt country, city, or company. . . . It wasn't a question of being worried about debts being dishonored," he explained, "it was a question of priority of claim."[18] Citibank's immediate seizure set off a chain reaction, as other banks moved to make sure of their share of Iranian funds.

Many bankers, both in Europe and America, were shocked by the freeze and the precipitate reaction of Citibank. "We got a lot of conversation from other banks," Wriston said, "that this was the wrong thing to do." The terms of the presidential order itself were controversial, for it froze not only the deposits inside the United States but in American banks abroad—particularly in London, where the great bulk of Iranian money was held, including the $2.8 billion in the Bank of America. But the jurisdiction of American courts over these expatriate dollars was very doubtful; indeed, that very uncertainty was part of London's advantage as a home for international money. The freezing of the deposits precipitated a huge legal wrangle, unprecedented in the history of banking; by late November the Iranian Central Bank had issued writs against five American banks in London, including Chase and

---

[18]Interview with author, June 13, 1980.

Citibank, demanding the repayment of $3 billion in deposits. But it was much more than a legal argument. To freeze money abroad, for apparently political reasons, went against the whole conception of the "oceanic freedom" of international capital. Were these billions of Eurodollars, after all, to be part of dollar diplomacy?

DEFAULT

While Wriston was going it alone, David Rockefeller and his colleagues at the Chase were more vulnerable, not only to Iran, but to other banks. On the day of the freeze a whole army of lawyers arrived in the elegant reception rooms on the sixteenth floor at Chase Manhattan Plaza. The Chase had lent about $350 million to Iran; and though this was less than 1 percent of its total loan book of $37 billion, it was still worrying in the context of other global risks. Moreover, the Chase, unlike Citibank, had been the leader of several big syndicated loans to Iran, which involved it heavily with other banks.

A special uncertainty surrounded the half-billion loan which the Chase had led in 1977—on which the Iranians were due to pay interest, as it happened, on the day after the freeze. In fact the Iranian Central Bank had instructed Chase to transfer the interest of $4 million from its London branch on November 5, but while this transaction was going through, the freeze by Carter had intervened; so that by the deadline for repayment—10 A.M. New York time on November 15—the funds were available, but frozen. The Chase cabled the Central Bank in Teheran that it was "unable to comply with the request" to pay the interest out of the Iranian deposits in London, because of the freezing order.

The Chase then made a historic move. It promptly sent a telex to the ten other members of the syndicate, informing them that the Iranians had defaulted and asking them to decide whether the loan should be "accelerated"—the bankers' euphemism for demanding all the money back. The European members of the syndicate were appalled by this precipitate action; but most of the lenders were American banks, so that the Chase soon had a majority of votes in favor of acceleration. The Chase then demanded the repayment of the principal and interest, amounting to a total of $110 million—a repayment which of course was not made. The Iranian government was thus formally declared in default.

The word "default," as we have seen, carried a special dread for the bankers. Since the revolution in Cuba and the vast expansion of the international capital market, no nation had ever actually defaulted. Bankers had gone to great lengths to avoid declaring a default—whether in Zaire, or in Peru, or in New York itself. They preferred to adopt all kinds of other devices or forms of words—rescheduling, rolling-over, or at worst "moratorium"—to avoid taking a step which would not only put a country outside the pale, but would damage the whole delicate structure of confidence in world banking. Yet now a conservative international bank was declaring a default against a country which had tried to pay the due interest but which had been prevented because its money had been frozen.

The Europeans reckoned that the American banks could quite easily have got their interest from Iran by letting Iran pay through deposits which were not frozen—in Deutschmarks for instance, or yen. Other syndicates, which were not led by Chase, soon had little difficulty in obtaining their interest. The Europeans were increasingly indignant that they were caught up in a political conflict of which they had a very different perspective. As one Swiss banker said: "The financial consequences to the world could do more harm than the deaths of forty-nine people."[19] But most American bankers did not agree. "The U.S. and the world are confronted in Iran with forces that deny everything the West stands for," said *Fortune* magazine in January 1980. "Under these circumstances, the disruption caused in financial markets is by no means the greatest of imaginable calamities."

There were now moves and countermoves through the bankers' world. The Chase default quickly set off others, through the

[19]*Euromoney* (January 1980).

"cross default" clauses in other loans. The gray men of Morgan's emerged briefly from their obscurity, to put into action their long-planned retaliation, freezing the Iranians' quarter share in Krupps in Germany, as the safeguard of their own loans. The Krupps management at Essen were furious at this intrusion, and the Germans complained of the "Wild West tactics" of American banks. The West German Finance Minister, Hans Matthoefer, protested that foreign companies were interfering "in matters that affect our national policy." The directors of the Dresdner Bank, meeting on November 29, announced that they would not declare Iranian loans in default, and warned that the economic warfare between America and Iran could damage the international lending market quite unnecessarily. The U.S. Secretary of the Treasury, William Miller, had said immediately after the freeze that "the action we're taking is not action that should create any kind of disruption at all." But he now toured through Europe to try to explain the decision, and admitted that there were some legal doubts about American control of deposits in London.

The bankers awaited the upshot of the mass of court cases which the lawyers were preparing; there was enough litigation, as Wriston said, to provide "a guaranteed income for the legal profession, their children, and their grandchildren." The judgments would be crucial, not only in deciding whether the Americans could legally freeze deposits abroad, but in seeking to define the whole character of the Eurodollar market. Were these dollars-in-exile, which had been building up since the Russians and the Chinese first hoarded them in Paris to escape from American control, really under the jurisdiction of the American government? Was there after all such a thing as the nationality of money in this global marketplace?

In the first month many European bankers were dreading that the freeze and defaults would undermine confidence in the international markets; that Arabs and other big depositors would prefer to buy gold or to keep their oil under the ground, rather than risk leaving their money where it could be suddenly frozen; and that Western bankers would be much more reluctant to lend money to the Third World, with the threat of default in the air. Their nervousness increased after the Soviet invasion of Afghanistan, which raised fears that Americans would try to use the "credit weapon" as sanction against Moscow or Eastern Europe. Gradually some of the fears subsided, as the laws of the market again asserted themselves. The money had to be deposited and had to be lent.

But the misgivings remained. Seven months after the freeze, when two hundred of the world's bankers met in New Orleans for the annual International Monetary Conference, Wilfried Guth, the respected joint chief executive of the Deutsche Bank—perhaps the most influential of all the Europeans—made a very significant speech: "As to the lessons we can and should draw from the recent Iran experience" he said in appropriate Bankspeak, "I suggest that it is mainly the need for the closest contact and coordination among international banks which has been underscored. In my view, the principle must be upheld even if our governments see no other choice but to take unilateral action. For an international bank, the departure from the international stage in order to assume temporarily a pure national role is not compatible with the degree of interdependence reached in the Eurocredit market. Such attitudes would ultimately lead to a situation in which practical and legal reasons would dictate that only national, instead of international, syndicates be formed—clearly a severe setback for the world financial system."[20] Which translated meant: "If Chase or Citibank try to pursue their own national policies, in Iran or anywhere else, they could break up the whole fragile global system."

THE BARGAIN

As the hostages remained in captivity both the administration and the bankers began to realize that the frozen assets could be the crucial bargaining counter in trying to achieve their release. At

[20]*International Herald Tribune,* June 16, 1980.

Citibank Hans Angermueller, the senior executive (who is tipped to be Wriston's successor), took responsibility for dealings with Iran, and the "initial litigation skirmishes," as he put it, "began to settle down to the long, expensive, and tedious phase of trench warfare."[21] He had many discussions with Citibank's lawyer, John Hoffman, of the New York firm of Shearman and Sterling; they were both very conscious of the legal complexities of past defaulters, such as Cuba and China, with which Citibank was still litigating. They hoped that some kind of deal could be made between the hostages and the frozen deposits, but this would mean releasing all the assets "in one sure, fail-safe step, tightly timed to the return of the hostages." They kept in touch with Washington, discussing various ideas for a deal with Robert Carswell, the Deputy Secretary of the Treasury.

It was not until May 1980 that the Iranians showed sign of movement: Citibank's counsel in West Germany rang John Hoffman in New York to say that Iran's German lawyer had proposed top-secret talks about a possible settlement. Hoffman quickly got the approval, first of Wriston at Citibank, and then of Carswell at the Treasury, and was soon able to meet the German lawyers for Iran in a small town outside Frankfurt. Two weeks later Hoffman had another meeting in Kronberg, in Germany, where he put forward his Plan C, which proposed using the frozen assets to pay off Iran's debts to the banks; and for the next six months he met every few weeks with Iran's lawyers, in Paris, London, Bermuda, Germany, New York, and his home in Chappaqua. It seemed often, he explained later, "like trying to push a pool of water uphill."[22]

Through all the worsening relations between Washington and Teheran the lawyers and bankers kept on talking to each other—even after the fiasco of the rescue attempt. Money had its own logic. The war with Iraq put a greater strain on Iran's resources, and in September the Ayatollah Khomeini first indicated that he

[21]Testimony to Senate Banking Committee, February 19, 1981.
[22]Ibid.

would consider releasing the hostages—though only in return for about $24 billion of alleged Iranian money, including the private fortune of the Shah. At least there was some basis for diplomatic negotiation, and Warren Christopher from the State Department flew to Algiers with the American proposal, with a far lower figure but including the unfreezing of Iranian deposits in American banks abroad. But in mid-November Iran's lawyers came back from Teheran to Dusseldorf, to tell Citibank that the Iranians had now decided *not* to pay off all their debts to the banks, as outlined in Plan C.

Hoffman now had to start over again with a Plan D, which arranged to pay the interest from the Iranian deposits and to continue the loans under strict guarantees—involving much more difficult negotiations with twelve American banks. The London lawyer for the Iranian Central Bank, Roger Brown of Stephenson Harwood, held meetings with each of the banks to agree on the interest to be paid, with Citibank's London lawyers Coward Chance representing the American banks. The prospects for releasing the hostages were now looking more hopeful, and by early January the Iranians showed signs of wanting to settle before Reagan took office. By January 10, 1981, the lawyers seemed close to agreement on Plan D, but the next day the Iranians suddenly announced that Plan D was completely unacceptable, and the meeting broke up in despair.

Warren Christopher and the diplomats were now negotiating their side of the deal in Algiers, and the bankers waited nervously in New York and London, stressing to the Iranians that there could be no deal without their approval. Then on January 15 the Algerians brought amazing news for the bankers: the Iranians now agreed to the original Plan C, by which they would repay all the banks' debts—evidently wanting to break any commercial links with the "Great Satan." The relief among the bankers, particularly in the Chase, was intense, but they still haggled over the amount of interest they owed to the Iranians; and the next day the State Department summoned them to Washington. They still argued, with the Bank of America taking the toughest line, but at last they agreed on a rate of 17 percent. Over the weekend the bankers in

Washington and London worked out the elaborate arrangements for transferring the assets; they would use the Bank of England, which was trusted by both sides, to hold funds in escrow, until their release was jointly agreed. By January 19, when the Iranians had received the final documents, they complained that the banks had added an appendix in an "underhand maneuver" which prevented the Iranians making any additional claims, and they delayed signing it: but at last on January 20 the deal was agreed on. The bankers released $5.5 billion from their overseas branches, and arranged to release another $4 billion from their domestic deposits over the next year. The U.S. Treasury transferred gold to the Bank of England, which already had two of its senior men in Algiers. The next day the hostages were released. It was an exchange of people and money unparalleled in the history of ransoms.

The bankers had been at the center of the bargaining from the beginning, negotiating as if they were an independent state. They had argued skillfully and tenaciously, and they had achieved everything they wanted. They had got back a hundred cents to the dollar from Iran at a time when (as *The Economist* pointed out) the Chrysler company in their own country was only offering them repayments of 15 percent. Other American companies which were owed large sums by the Iranians saw little hope of getting it all back, and they were understandably bitter at the success of the banks, which had risked little from the start.

The banks had not emerged altogether unscathed from the Iranian crisis. Alexander Vagliano from Morgan's assured the Senate Banking Committee on February 19 that American banks had retained their competitive situation; but he hoped that the freeze would not be a precedent and stressed that he would have preferred collaborative action with other nations. In fact, there were already signs that other OPEC countries were looking in other directions—toward Europe and the Far East—for their deposits and investments. And the European bankers made it clear that they would be quite happy to take over lending to Iran in the future.

As for the Chase, it could congratulate itself on not having lost a cent over its Iranian business; but it could also reflect that, if it had not insisted on the Shah coming to New York, the crisis of the hostages would not have occurred in the first place. "I hope you don't think of me as the spider in the center of a web of international intrigue," Rockefeller said to journalists in April 1981; but the Chase had certainly behaved like its caricature, as the chief instrument of international capitalism. Rockefeller had appeared as the Shah's banker one moment, and as a world statesman the next, while distracting the bank and its shareholders from their more lasting interests. And he associated his bank with an exiled monarch in a way that was inevitably seen as a counterrevolutionary conspiracy.

18
COUNTRY RISK

If I owe a million dollars, then I am lost. But if I owe fifty billions, the bankers are lost.

CELSO MING
Brazilian economist, 1980

The revolution in Iran had taken nearly everyone by surprise, and it brought a new urgency to an old question: how do you measure the political risks in a foreign country? With some prompting from governments and central banks, bankers began trying to assess more seriously the hazards of their operations. They turned not only to economists but to diplomats, political scientists, and intelligence experts to advise them in the fashionable new science called "country risk."

The problem was as old as banking, but the American banks had become more concerned since the late sixties, when the influence of their own government over developing countries was visibly waning. "It really began in 1967," according to one political scientist, Stephen Blank of Multinational Strategies Inc., "when Occidental Petroleum did their deal with the Libyan government, which undermined the power of the big oil companies. In the next six years it became clear that American companies had lost the capacity to tell countries what to do; they had to begin studying what countries would do to *them.* By 1973, with the new power of OPEC, the transition was over." The unpredicted success of OPEC had certainly undermined much of the confidence in the projections of economists. When the futurologist Herman Kahn had written his book *The Year 2000* in 1967 the words "oil," "energy," and "Saudi Arabia" did not appear in the index, and after the price increases which changed the balance of the world

317

many economists still insisted that the price must come down. As the bankers lent more money to unstable countries like Zaire or Indonesia, they began to feel the need for political as well as economic assessments; and the collapse of the Shah revealed all the shortcomings of their information.

There was something inherently comic about this attempt to measure the immeasurable, to award credit ratings to countries as if they were hire-purchase customers. The spectacle of bankers, with all their zeal for precision and objectivity, giving marks to nations for good behavior could never be altogether convincing. What could they learn from their hotel suites of the gossip in the bazaars, the mutterings of revolution in the back alleys? How could these immaculate men wander inconspicuously in the souks of the Middle East or drink in the shebeens of Johannesburg? How could they calculate whether Bangladesh or Sri Lanka was the more ripe for revolution? They might think that they were establishing rational systems and yardsticks to measure the world; but they were always deeply influenced, directly or indirectly, by the assumptions of their foreign ministries and governments. They were still following some kind of flag.

While each bank made its own assessment of country risk, the market revealed its own consensus in terms of the length and profit margins of the loans (the maturity and the spread). The magazine *Euromoney* compiles its own "league table" of country risk, based on its statistical analysis of syndicated loans, grading sixty-six borrowing countries in order, and awarding them stars from seven to one. In 1979 the list began with three seven-star countries, France, China, and Britain, and ended with six one-star countries (Gabon, Ethiopia, Guyana, Madagascar, Niger, and Pakistan). It had some remarkable juxtapositions: the six-star countries included five Communist countries—Russia, Czechoslovakia, Hungary, Bulgaria, and East Germany—alongside Western countries like Italy and Canada and newly industrialized countries like Korea and Colombia. In the roll call of three-star countries, white South Africa was sandwiched between black nations like Malawi, the Cameroons, and Tanzania.

The market revealed no color bar, no ideological bias.[1]

"I think I can say I was the inventor of the whole subject called country risk analysis," said Irving Friedman, with characteristic modesty; and it was true that Citibank, after Friedman joined it in 1974, set up a more formalized and self-conscious study of risks than other banks, as we saw in Chapter 10. As Citibank began lending more to the Third World, Wriston built up a team to assess credit risks, led by Friedman and the vice-chairman, Al Costanzo, and he insisted that they had independent powers to defy any pressure to lend.

Other American banks took their own steps to strengthen their political analysis. "We're much more sophisticated on the economics side than on the politics," admitted the senior international economist at Morgan's, Rimmer de Vries;[2] and in 1980 Morgan's tried to establish its own careful rating of countries, so that it could compare them with its ratings of American companies in the same system. "But we have to be very security-minded," one man in Morgan's explained to me; "once a country discovers that it's got a low credit rating, there's hell to pay."

The Bank of America was determined to set up a specially thorough system after the mistakes of Iran. As Richard Puz, the head of the World Banking division, expressed it to me in California: "In Iran our predictive capacity was weak: at that time the visibility of non-quantifiable factors was secondary to hard numbers. We didn't realize how rapidly American support would disappear." The Bank of America devised a classification to make full use of its worldwide staff and decentralized offices. It was unlikely, as their chief international economist Robert Heller explained, "that all relevant information can be compressed into just one single number";[3] so they gave countries a three-point rating, in the form (for instance) of 82AC.

The first number, ranging from 1 to 100, expresses the "debt

---

[1] *Institutional Investor* produces a rival grading; see Chapter 1.
[2] *Euromoney* (July 1980).
[3] "Bank of America's New Country Evaluation System," Euromoney Conference on Country Risk Assessment, New York, October 30, 1980.

service capacity index," based on an international data bank covering eighty countries. The first letter represents the "judgmental economic indicator" based on questionnaires sent out to the bank's country or regional managers, which are then checked at headquarters "for global consistency." The second letter expresses the "judgmental political indicator," which focuses on three areas—governmental control, potential for social unrest, and external factors, assembled from replies from "on-site knowledgeable officers" and revised by senior managers in San Francisco. "The country manager," as Puz explains, "can get so close he can't see the wood for the trees." But the difficulty with such classifications (it seems to me) is that they can't see the trees for the wood. An indicator like 82AC might describe a country like South Africa, with excellent economic statistics and prospects but high potential for social unrest. But once the AC goes down to AE, the E can quickly cancel out all the benefits of the A.

The Chase characteristically turned to ex-diplomats and ex-CIA officers to provide its political intelligence. David Rockefeller had already set up an International Advisory Group, which included Henry Kissinger, meeting four times a year; as the Chase moved deeper into doubtful countries, it took on more political scientists and economists, with beards and mustaches which stood out among the clean-shaven orthodox bankers. It even prepared a special new service to clients called Chase World Outlook, full of computerized calculations about country risks; but it was soon clear that Chase could not say candidly what it thought about (for instance) Saudi Arabia, whose deposits were crucial to the bank; after spending three quarters of a million dollars it abandoned the project. Rockefeller's personal influence still prevailed. In 1980 he set up a three-man Country Risk Management Group, with their own patrician approval, headed by the former head of the Western Hemisphere division, Francis Mason, and including Archie Roosevelt, a former CIA officer, and Ridgway Knight, the ex-ambassador who had often accompanied Rockefeller on his journeys.

"If you sat in on a meeting of the country risk committee," said the Chase's chief economist, Robert Slighton, who also once worked for the CIA, "I think you'd be impressed by how much they knew, but appalled by the difficulty of transferring that knowledge into policies for loans. We can't afford to go into a country when it looks good, and pull out when it looks bad. . . . In retrospect, we overloaned in the seventies; there's a much more hostile environment projected for the eighties."

"Operational banking" (Slighton continued) "consists of a constant war, a continuous adversary process between credit officers and loan officers—it takes place at every level, and it can be very bloody. In assessing the country risk, the most critical questions are, first, the likelihood that the political consensus will be intact; second, can economic policies respond to a sudden shock? A country that doesn't redistribute its wealth is a bad risk; if a loan helps a country to redistribute, that's desirable. In general, we'd rather lend to a country that's *had* its revolution."[4]

Why did the banks, with all their different systems and attitudes, still reach the same conclusion about so many countries, even when they were all wrong? Why did they still behave like starlings or lemmings? In the nineteenth century banks would take their own risks in lending to unreliable countries, as Barings backed the United States. But they were now much more reluctant to get out of line with each other. "There's no opportunity so good," as one Chase man explained, "that we want 100 percent of it."

"Facts make their own decisions," Wriston told me at Citibank when I complained about this uniformity. "If you all look at the same facts it would not be unusual to come up with the same answer. . . . In those days Mr. Rothschild made his fortune by getting carrier pigeons to tell him who won the battle of Waterloo. Now today, when the President frowns in the Rose Garden, it is in the rate of the dollar in thirty seconds. The information explosion puts the facts at everyone's command." But others are more worried by the sameness of view. "I have a medicine-man the-

---

[4]Interview with author, March 12, 1980.

ory," Wilson Schwartz explained to me at the Chemical Bank. "Every institution feels the need to have someone to foretell the future; the Indians looked to their medicine men, and the institutions looked to their economists; but while economists may explain *why* things happen, they can't predict *when* they'll happen; so the banks tend to flock together. And they look more and more toward the IMF—which has both special information, and special authority to enforce their opinion—like the Catholic Church in the Middle Ages."

The Iranian revolution had sent shock waves through the American banks, not only because none of them had predicted it, but because it revealed the full impotence of Washington to protect American interests. It was much less useful to consult the State Department if it had so little ability to influence events, and the oil crisis had brought home the vulnerability of the United States to any oil-producing country. "I can tell you that as a U.S. bank in Mexico we get treated like dirt by the Mexican authorities," Francis Mason said in 1980. "It is nothing personal against Chase Manhattan Bank. I think they take a particular delight in making certain that the British banks or the Canadian banks or the European banks get the business that we do not."[5]

The American bankers, as they worried more about country risk, were turning less to the State Department for advice and more to the World Bank and the IMF (see Chapter 21), which were gradually relaxing their discretion about their nation-clients. "It was like the dance of the seven veils," one banker observed; "each time they'd reveal a little more."

European bankers liked to make fun of the Americans' elaborate calculations of country risk compared to their own personal judgments and hunches. "They like to fool themselves that they're strictly objective," said a British banker, "but they're always influenced by the political atmosphere in Washington. A new fashion can change their judgment like waving a wand." "Why did the Americans all regard Egypt in 1973 as uncredit-worthy one

[5] *Euromoney* (July 1980).

moment, and credit-worthy the next?'' asked one Arab banker. ''It was because Kissinger told them to.'' Yet the Europeans could also be more influenced by their governments' attitudes than they realized. The herds of German bankers had their own stampedes toward Poland, encouraged by guarantees from Bonn. The French banks, nearly all nationalized, could never separate themselves from the changing moods of the Quai d'Orsay. The British banks had a long tradition of being more distinct from their governments; but the Big Four deposit banks, which were now responsible for most of the loans, were much less adventurous than the old merchant bankers like Barings and Rothschilds, and their executives followed in well-worn tracks (like Barclays in South Africa) or simply followed the American herd (like NatWest in Iran). As for the Japanese, they worked more closely with their Ministry of Finance than anyone. Whenever all these nationalities came together in a big syndicate they were easily persuaded to play follow-the-leader.

Who was the real leader, and who was taking the risk? It was an obvious question, but curiously difficult to answer. It was complicated, as we have noted, by the fact that foreign countries could never really go bankrupt like domestic companies and that bankers could no longer seize their assets by sending in gunboats. ''The trouble is,'' as one senior Chase executive said, ''that we aren't used to the idea of a foreign default.'' By rescheduling or restructuring their loans, as in Zaire, the bankers could keep on postponing the moment of truth.

The question was specially serious in three countries with huge mounting debts which each represented a different kind of political risk: Brazil, Turkey, Poland. Each of them showed little prospect of paying back the money, each had a very checkered political history, each was attracting still more loans. But who was really responsible for the risk?

BANKING ON BRAZIL

For over a century Brazil had been the object of great expectations and extreme uncertainties. In the mid-nineteenth century both Brazil and Argentina had been talked of as a "new America," luring entrepreneurs, capital, and immigrants from Europe. While bankers eventually gave up hope that the Argentinians could ever run their country sensibly, they continued to look to Brazil with optimism. But in the meantime it had accumulated the biggest debt in history.

By 1980 Brazil owed no less than $60 billion, much of it to commercial banks, headed by Citibank. That might seem small compared to loans inside the United States: it was the cost, for instance, of only four subway systems on the scale of Washington's. It seemed manageable compared to the size of the Brazilian economy. Brazil was the colossus among developing countries, with a land mass bigger than that of the United States, half the total area of South America. Its population, now 120 million, had been doubling every twenty-five years; its gross national product was the tenth biggest in the world; it produced the world's biggest coffee crop, a harvest of soybeans second only to America's, and a third of the world's iron ore. It had a team of forceful and expert technocrats and managers. It was a kind of microcosm of world development, with pockets of extreme riches and poverty. By many standards it was absurd to call it a developing country.

But Brazil's foreign debts could be repaid only by exports which earned foreign currency; and by 1979 more than three quarters of those exports went to servicing its debt—a "debt-service ratio" which banks normally regard as dangerously high. Brazil, unlike its rival debtor Mexico, had little oil of her own; each time the oil price went up, the prospects of repaying the debt were more distant.

It was a matter of critical interest to American banks, and particularly to Citibank, which had put many of its eggs into the Brazilian basket over the last six decades. Wriston regarded Brazil as a triumphant example of how Citibank had not behaved like the herd. "I know lots of people who have been waiting to invest in Brazil for thirty years," he explained: "Their judgment is that it is a land of tomorrow and tomorrow is not here. Our judgment in 1914 was that today is here, and we've been there ever since. . . . Our view is that it has a lot of problems, but they are all going to work out and we are not at all upset about them—that's a very great difference of view between other banks."[6] Citibank had built up a large domestic banking business inside Brazil, including a half-share of an important finance company, the Banco Crefisul de Investimento. The more the other banks kept away from Brazil, the more lucrative was Citibank's business, and Brazil contributed an important share of its global profits: in 1976 as much as 20 percent. "Citibank will continue to benefit from a relatively high-yielding portfolio," said its *Financial Review* in mid-1978, "for several years to come."

Brazil's most recent boom had dated from 1964, when the populist government of President Goulart had been overthrown by military leaders dedicated to rapid expansion. They appointed as economic overlord the academic economist Roberto Campos, who cut back the runaway inflation and invented the idea of "indexation" to link wages to inflation. He was succeeded by his protégé Delfim Neto, who presided over a phenomenal boom, generating a growth of up to 14 percent a year. Delfim, whose family came from Naples, had a style which was larger than life; with his fat shape, his tireless talk and enormous energy and appetite—he was said to consume five dozen oysters at a sitting —he soon became a superstar on the bankers' scene. He made no secret of his strategy: by borrowing heavily from the banks he wanted to lock foreign capital into the Brazilian system, so that the West would have a vested interest in its success. There was a very dark side to the Brazilian miracle: the desolate northeast, with the decaying rubber towns along the Amazon, was hardly touched by it; the boom city of São Paulo was surrounded by some of the

---

[6]Interview with author, June 13, 1980.

world's worst slums; the government resorted to torture to subjugate the Indians; and the gross inequality outraged many liberals, including Robert McNamara at the World Bank. But this did not affect the assessments of the commercial banks; Citibank had formed close links with the military government, and Rockefeller at the Chase—which was also a big lender—argued against any interference over human rights.

With the oil crisis of 1973 Brazil's future suddenly looked bleaker. The giant industries, the skyscrapers, the highways, and the car plants had been built on the assumption of unlimited cheap oil; and the fourfold increase wrecked the balance of payments and boosted inflation. A new President, General Geisel, sent Delfim into exile to be ambassador in Paris, but continued with expansionist policies, pushing ahead with new steelworks, shipyards, and nuclear power stations, while inflation went over 40 percent. Most bankers found Brazil now much less attractive, but Wriston at Citibank saw the opportunity both to profit from the high returns and to cement the bank's relationship with Brazil. By 1977 Brazil seemed to be on the road to recovery, and other bankers including the Japanese again began piling in, bringing the margins down again. Citibank had been shown to be a good friend of Brazil, and the Brazilians appreciated it. "We feel much safer with Citibank," explained one government economist, "because we know they've got so much at stake."

By 1979 Delfim was back as economic overlord under the new President Figueiredo. He was again bent on high growth, but the new oil crisis and strikes in São Paulo brought new dangers. Inflation was back to over 80 percent, with growth of only 6 percent. Delfim promised that Brazil would become less dependent on oil by financing a vast project to produce alcohol from sugar, on which Brazilians could run their cars; and when the bankers met at their annual meeting of the IMF in Belgrade in 1979, he persuaded them to raise a jumbo loan of $1.2 billion for the new alcohol program, backed by the Brazilian government itself. It was a historic loan, led by Morgan's and three other American banks, with a margin of less than 1 percent above the standard rate of interest, running for twelve years. It was a triumph for Delfim, who had personally persuaded many leading bankers against much of their current advice about country risk. But many big banks, including Bankers Trust in America and the German Big Three, stayed out of it; and the Japanese banks, which had been warned to cut back their foreign loans, only contributed $125 million.

Brazil was still on a tightrope, and in February 1980 Delfim toured America and Europe to try to raise confidence; in New York he breakfasted with Wriston, and saw McNamara, who had flown up from Washington. But most bankers were still skeptical and insisted on high margins or spreads. "I didn't expect to be greeted by a bunch of adding machines," Delfim complained.[7] He was now having to dip into Brazil's precious reserves; and he dreaded that he might have to borrow from the IMF, which would cut back on Brazil's bid for economic freedom. Brazil always showed two different faces to the world: one moment it was the new America, competing overconfidently with the rich nations; the next it was the most vulnerable of all developing countries. By 1980 Brazilians were again talking of being part of the Third World, and suggesting that the world institutions should be restructured for their benefit.

Brazil remained an expensive question mark for both bankers and governments. Would it at last stand on its own feet as a major industrial power? Or would the economic crisis bring about a political crisis which would make it unable to pay off its debts? "If there is a real threat to the international banking system," one veteran London banker observed, "it could well begin in the slums of São Paulo." Had Wriston made his huge profits from Brazil because he understood the country better than others, or because he knew that his government could not let Brazil go down? And who was really taking the risk—the bank, the American government, or the International Monetary Fund?

[7] *Institutional Investor* (August 1980).

TURKEY IN TROUBLE

The bankers faced a more highly charged political scene in Turkey, the traditional "sick man of Europe," which like Iran had been a bankers' nightmare since the mid-nineteenth century, and which stood on the frontier of the Western alliance with the Soviets. In the postwar years, supported by massive aid, Turkey had staggered from one economic crisis to the next, teetering between democracy and military rule. In the early seventies the economy made some recovery with help from remittances from Turkish workers in Germany, but the oil crisis soon hit the country with double severity: the workers were sent home while oil imports further wrecked the balance of payments.

The potential bankruptcy of Turkey now looked like threatening the solidarity of NATO. The Bonn government pressed the German banks to lend money to this traditional sphere of German influence and trade, where the Deutsche Bank had spread itself a hundred years earlier; and American and other European banks were attracted by the high margins. By 1976 the Turkish government was guaranteeing high interest rates through convertible lira deposits, and the big American banks, with Citibank and the Bank of America in the forefront, soon rushed in to take advantage of the quick profits.

By January 1978, when a new Prime Minister, Bulent Ecevit, was elected, the banks were losing their enthusiasm for Turkey as rapidly as they had acquired it. There was mounting violence between extreme left and right, the bureaucracy was corrupt, and the economy showed no sign of recovering. The government had borrowed $3 billion in short-term loans, which had to be renewed, but after one massive rescheduling the banks were reluctant to roll it over, and they were soon cutting off credits, leaving Turkey with little time to adjust. The Turks turned to the International Monetary Fund, which raised two massive loans—the second of which, for $1.6 billion, was the biggest in its history, amounting to 625 percent of Turkey's quota. The Fund hoped that its "seal of approval" for Turkey's austere program would reassure banks; but as the Fund moved in, so the bankers began moving out, stealthily withdrawing more of their interest and part of their capital; in 1979 they made net withdrawals of $340 million.[8] The Bank of America, which had rapidly retreated, became a dirty word in Turkey and changed its name for its remaining operations.

The mandarins at the Fund in Washington were bitterly critical. "The banks overlent when the going was good, and now they show no responsibility," one of them complained to me, for once losing his cool. "The IMF cannot act as the banks' debt collector —we didn't go in to let them get out." The Turks now had a total foreign debt of $16 billion, and half of their exports (including their foreign workers' remittances) went to repaying the debt; while the bankers were resisting the pressures from the IMF to reschedule their loans. Turkey—now once again under a military government —remained a crucial member of NATO; but the bankers, having made their quick profits, were glad to leave it to Western governments and the IMF to cope with as best they could.

THE POLISH PREDICAMENT

Of all the frontiers between banking and politics, the most critical but unmapped were in Eastern Europe, where the bankers moved out of the protective system of the IMF and into the heart of the Communist system. Since the Eastern Europeans had rejected Marshall Aid in the postwar years, they had formed their own self-enclosed economic system of COMECON, and their central banks had been closely interlinked with Moscow. The Soviets underpinned and supervised their lending more strictly than the IMF, with all the rigor of orthodox bankers, with no misgivings about usury, and with large supplies of gold to fortify the reserves. As the Eastern Europeans began to trade more with the West and to buy more Western technology and food, they began to borrow

[8]*Financial Times,* November 13, 1980.

to finance their trade. The first Western bank to open a branch in Eastern Europe was the Crédit Lyonnais, the French bank which had been the chief lender to tsarist Russia in the 1890s, and which Lenin in 1916 had regarded as one of the key imperialist banks.[9] By 1964 the ubiquitous David Rockefeller was visiting Moscow, talking at length with Khrushchev, and soon afterward the Chase became the first American bank to open a representative office, at 1 Karl Marx Square, in Moscow. The relationships between the Communists and Rockefeller were the subject of continual amusement and irony. The Communists regarded him as a king of capitalism, wielding far greater powers than he really enjoyed. "Nobody knows how to revere, blandish, and exalt a Rockefeller," said George Gilder, "half so well as the Marxists."[10] Rockefeller on his side saw the Communists as more reliable and enduring clients than many capitalist democracies. "In terms of straight credit risk," he explained, "the presumption is that there is greater continuity of government in certain socialist states than in nonsocialist states."[11]

From the late sixties the Western banks began lending increasingly to the countries of Eastern Europe, including the Soviet Union itself, reassured by the so-called umbrella theory, which assumed that the Soviet Union would give its economic support to any country in trouble, like the IMF and the central banks in the West. With the great expansion of the Eurodollar market in the early seventies the banks became more interested in lending to Eastern Europe, independently of trading connections, encouraged by the political atmosphere in Bonn and Washington. In West Germany the Ostpolitik, or opening to the East, which Willy Brandt had initiated, encouraged the banks to extend their area of influence into the Communist countries. In the United States Henry Kissinger and others maintained that Western lending

---

[9]See Charles Levinson, *VodkaCola* (New York: Gordon & Cremonesi, 1978), p. 28. See also Feis, pp. 216 ff.
[10]Peter Collier and David Horowitz, *The Rockefellers,* paperback ed. (New York: (Signet, 1977), p. 427.
[11]Mayer, p. 483.

could help to distance the Eastern European satellites from their Soviet masters, while the Polish-Americans pressed for more liberal loans for their cousins. There was a general belief in the West that any economic improvement would have a liberalizing effect on Eastern European policies; and many Marxists were suspicious of Western lending for that reason.[12]

Bankers were inclined to see the whole of COMECON as coming into the same category of risk, assuming that one country would be helped by all the others; and they lent with almost equal confidence to Hungary, Czechoslovakia, and the Soviet Union itself—as the credit ratings (see page 318) suggested. The bankers widely assumed, in the words of *Institutional Investor,* that "Moscow would not allow any COMECON member to default or even reschedule, for economic, political, strategic and image reasons. . . ."[13]

Poland was always a special case. It had the richest resources of minerals of any of the six countries of Eastern Europe, including coal, sulphur, copper, zinc, silver, and lignite. But it also had more headstrong leaders, more determined workers, and inefficient industries. Poland's industrial backwardness had long been the despair of bankers; back in the twenties the young Jean Monnet (later the father of the Common Market) had helped to arrange a loan to Poland and had found Polish industry "only just emerging from medieval conditions."[14] Now the Marxist ideologues had brought their own mismanagement both into Polish industry and agriculture. Poland had, in the words of one distinguished economist, "a combination of wildly over-ambitious, gravely flawed, voluntarist economic policies; incompetent planning and management; and an especially unstable body politic. . . ."[15]

When Gierek took over as Prime Minister in 1970, after food

[12]See *Money on the Move,* p. 104.
[13]See *Institutional Investor* (July 1976). Also Richard Portes, "East Europe's Debt to the West," *Foreign Affairs* (July 1977).
[14]Jean Monnet, *Memoirs* (London: Collins, 1978), p. 103.
[15]Richard Portes, "The Polish Crisis," *Western Economic Policy Options,* London, Royal Institute of International Affairs (February 1981), p. 8.

riots which had led to the fall of Gomulka, he looked to the Western banks to help revive the economy. The Brandt government in West Germany pressed the banks to provide loans, and the American banks, as well as government agencies, followed with loans—many of them into very dubious industrial projects. The First Chicago Bank, in the midst of a Polish-American stronghold, was specially active in Warsaw, and set up its own office there. The Western loans certainly helped to improve the standard of living, and Gierek presided over a boom which was very visible in the form of more cars, TV sets, and consumer goods. But the industrial managers failed to achieve much improvement in industrial production, and behind the outward boom there was economic confusion, about which the bankers were allowed to know very little. The bankers still felt secure under the Soviet umbrella; but, by the same rules, they could do nothing to interfere with national sovereignty.

By 1976 Poland looked much less attractive to bankers: there was a crisis in agriculture, and Gierek raised food prices, which precipitated a new workers' revolt. Some American banks now felt that they had lent quite enough; Alvin Rice, of the Bank of America, testified in 1977 that Poland "would have a difficult time increasing term indebtedness to any American bank that I know of."[16] And some international economists were becoming seriously worried. "We cannot simply continue to ignore the debt, supposing that it will go away as quickly and rapidly as it has accumulated," wrote Professor Richard Portes in July 1977. "We have clearly left it to the bankers for too long already."[17] Yet in the same year the Chase Manhattan was lending $600 million to Eastern Europe, including Poland, to finance a new gas pipeline with little information about how the money would be used.[18] In the following year Poland raised a new syndicated loan worth half

[16]House Banking Committee, *International Banking Operations,* Washington, 1977, p. 721.
[17]*Foreign Affairs* (July 1977).
[18]See Nora Beloff, "The Comecon Bumble-Bee," *The Banker* (May 1978).

a billion dollars. The Western bankers, after all, were short of reliable borrowers; and the Polish government negotiator, Jan Woloszyn, was one of the most respected of all international bankers.

By the beginning of 1980 the Poles were negotiating to borrow another half billion dollars and in April they invited Western bankers to Warsaw to discuss terms, promising that Polish industry was being reformed, and that the banks could monitor it. Then came the crisis of July 1980, with unprecedented strikes, the power struggle between labor unionists and the government, and the capitulation to higher wages.

The Western attitudes were full of paradoxes. American conservatives who abominated labor unions were now boundless in their admiration of the Polish strikers. American labor unionists were refusing to import Polish goods in support of their Polish comrades, while Polish Americans pressed for more credits. The workers in this Communist state were wielding a power enjoyed by few other workers in the world. If Poland had been under the IMF umbrella (as Rumania and Yugoslavia were), the IMF could have been required to be thoroughly stern toward a country with such a huge debt which was now giving in to inflationary wage claims. But it was Moscow, not the IMF, that was the ultimate disciplinarian in Poland; and the Western governments were urging the bankers not to pull back but to make further loans. The bankers' confidence in Eastern European discipline was thoroughly undermined, and they could not be at all sure which side their loans were really supporting. Was it the Communist government or the dissident strikers? "Why should the U.S. or others in the West," asked *The Washington Post,* "pay for the privilege of making Poland safe again for Soviet-style state socialism?"[19]

Poland was now altogether a very doubtful proposition. Yet just as the Polish government was issuing a statement condemning the strikes in Lublin, bankers were meeting in the London offices of

[19]November 23, 1980.

the Bank of America to approve the new loan. By August a consortium, including eleven American banks and the Moscow Narodny Bank, had signed the agreement. The loan had been reduced to $325 million, at a higher interest rate and with strict terms of supervision; the bankers were insisting that the money must be prudently spent, and had at last extracted more economic information from Warsaw. But no one could be very confident about where it would end up. In the meantime, a German consortium led by the Dresdner Bank had raised a new jumbo loan in which other German banks felt compelled to join. "We weren't *forced* to," as one smaller participant told me, "but we knew that if we didn't we would be left out of other good things in the future." The Bonn government encouraged the loan, but could not guarantee it; it only undertook to use all its influence to create political stability in Poland.

The total Polish debt was now alarming—$24 billion, of which more than half was owed to commercial banks, led by the Germans, and followed by the British and Americans. The cost of repayments in 1981 was reckoned to be more than the total value of Polish exports. The commercial banks were now feeling much more aware of their insecurity in Poland, at a time when other big debtor countries like Brazil were also looking more doubtful. For no one could be confident of who would guarantee its debts and enforce its financial discipline. Many bankers assumed that Poland would have to look toward the Soviets for much of its future borrowing; but they could no longer be sure that it was still under the Soviet umbrella, and the West was offering no more than a parasol. Several bankers privately admitted that they would feel much safer if the Russian tanks rolled into Poland.

As for the Poles, they had little to show in exchange for their mountain of debt. The succession of loans had fed their economic expectations and temporarily pushed up their standard of living; but they had done little to improve the basic economy, and had left the Poles apparently still more dependent on their Soviet money masters. As for the theory that Western loans would help to wean the Poles away from their Communist loyalties, it had the most ironic consequence of all: for the Polish strikers had taken the idea of freedom altogether too literally, and the West was now as anxious as Moscow to damp them down.

The Western bankers, having made handsome profits out of indiscriminate loans, now looked to their governments to help them out. They had held long and tense discussions in the Paris Club—the traditional casualty station of international banking—under the chairmanship of the French Treasury, while the Poles had to come to terms with the rescheduling—or, as they preferred to call it, restructuring—of their impossible debt. It was now clearly too dangerous to be left to the bankers. The ultimate country risk lay with the governments who faced the bleak task of trying to bring Polish finances back on the road toward realism, and Washington, London, and Bonn shared the same financial worries as Moscow. While the Polish crisis had created a dangerous political tension between the superpowers, it induced a common interest between their central bankers.

By the end of March 1981 the crunch had come. The representatives of the Polish Central Bank met in London with representatives of twenty-three Western banks, and explained that they could not make the repayments on debts that were due. A week later Warsaw confirmed by telex that they could not repay loans amounting to a billion dollars. The Western bankers appointed a task force of twenty banks—including Lloyds and Barclays from Britain, the Dresdner from Germany, and the Bank of America and Citibank from the United States—to undertake the painful process of rescheduling, while the political situation was constantly deteriorating. "Never before," wrote Peter Montagnon in the *Financial Times*, "has a country on the financial brink in this way also been under threat of invasion from abroad." The European banks, more heavily exposed than the Americans, wanted a speedy agreement to ensure that no single bank called a default and to try to revive the shattered Polish economy. The Americans, more mindful of lawsuits, wanted to freeze all loan agreements to give time for a more equitable agreement; and the Chase, which had been in the forefront, insisted that its loans to copper mines be treated separately. The bankers tried to insist on more information about the Polish economy, while the Soviets accused them of economic blackmail; and at the time of writing (July 1981) the threat of invasion still hung over the negotiations. The unhappy love affair between bankers and the Communists was emphatically over.

Turkey and Poland were both part of the same story. In both countries the bankers' herds had first fallen over themselves to lend without circumspection and then all retreated together. Their interest in both senses had been essentially short-term. Now, as they became more worried about their country risk, they looked again toward the world institutions—which had been left on the sidelines in the great lending boom.

19
THE WORLD BANKER

The parable of the talents is a parable about power—about financial power—and it illuminates the great truth that all power is given
to us to be used, not to be wrapped in a napkin against risk.

ROBERT MCNAMARA,
Washington, September 1968

When international bankers talked about "the world" they usually
meant the thirty to fifty countries which were more or less credit-
worthy where they might be able to do profitable business. Their
map included many risks and uncertainties. Some countries, like
Zaire or Turkey, had long ago ceased to look attractive, but had
trapped the bankers by their previous borrowing. Others, like
South Korea or the Philippines, oscillated between apparent stability and panic. Others, like Poland or Turkey, were on critical
political frontiers where the financial risk was interlocked with the
East-West confrontation. The bankers' globe was more adventurous and interesting than it had been twenty years earlier, but most
of the world's population remained outside it. The 600 million
people of India, the near-billion people of China, and most of the
population of Africa were behind the red line. They might be
eligible for short-term loans for trading deals, or for advice in
return for a fee. But they were too unreliable, too xenophobic, or
too incomprehensible to be worth the commercial risk of longer-
term loans.

But politics did not stop at these frontiers, and the West could
not altogether ignore the rest of the world. Western governments
wanted to maintain their own trading and diplomatic links, even
with the poorest countries, and they each had their own systems
of aid or subsidized loans. It was the World Bank in Washington,

together with its charitable sister IDA, which provided the most important financial link with these nations. During the seventies the World Bank was moving much deeper into the Third World, dealing with a hundred countries with a population of 2 billion. Its character and purpose became closely identified with a single controversial personality, Robert Strange McNamara, who took over the bank in 1968 and was to run it for thirteen years. McNamara became not only the master of an increasingly far-flung global organization; he was also the most vocal champion of those 2 billion people, persistent in arguing that the rich nations must transfer more of their wealth to the poor countries which lay outside their system. "It is inconceivable that one quarter of mankind, moving forward into a self-accelerating affluence, can succeed in walling itself off from the other three quarters, who find themselves entrapped in a self-perpetuating cycle of poverty."[1]

Was he a master banker or a missionary? Was he a messiah or a computer? As he strode across his vast office in the World Bank, slightly stooping but muscular and tense, he still looked like the legendary McNamara of the Ford Motor Company in the fifties or the Kennedy Cabinet in the sixties. His wiry swept-back hair, his steel-rim glasses, his metallic voice, all belonged to the picture of the manager engrossed in corporate strategy. He seemed determined to impose his own rigorous discipline on the rest of the world; he enumerated and classified problems with his fingers; he described the world's poor as "low productivity elements." But then he would give a shy boyish smile which seemed to belong to a much more vulnerable person; or he would suddenly burst out with a sign of angry passion—about the fading ideals of the West, the outrage of poverty, or the dangers of South Africa: "Goddamn it, when South Africa blows up it will tear this nation apart."

As administrations in Washington came and went, many people talked of McNamara as if he were a relic of the age of Kennedy or Johnson who had been left on the lonely rock of the World

[1]Speech to UN Conference on Human Environment, Stockholm, June 8, 1972.

Bank. Since LBJ eased him out of the Pentagon, he had had no obvious domestic constituency: his overriding loyalty had been to the 2 billion poor in the world who had no real constituency. Conservatives in Congress tended to see him as a dogmatic do-gooder; many liberals remembered his record at the Pentagon with anger; to the young his name belonged to the past. Americans became more disillusioned and resentful toward the Third World with which McNamara was associated, and preoccupied with their own problems. Even development experts and Third World diplomats would sometimes depict McNamara as an old-fashioned paternalist.

Yet he remained the central figure in any debate about rich and poor nations; and any argument about the Third World would lead toward him. His analytical mind provided a kind of lens through which one side could focus the blurred shapes on the other side; and his controversial career on the frontier of banking and philanthropy raised new questions about the opportunities and the limitations of bankers in the developing world.

It was a political cliché in Washington that McNamara agreed to run the World Bank as a kind of expiation for the sins of the Vietnam War. It was not an interpretation which he ever encouraged; when he referred to Vietnam—which was rare—it was usually in terms of the failures of information and understanding that led up to the war. "If we'd known that at the time," he once said after reading a historical account of Asia, "we'd never have gone in." Whatever the subconscious effects, he came out of the Pentagon with his self-confidence apparently intact. He never appeared introspective about Vietnam or recent political history. He appeared to live with his immediate problems and with the future.

In fact his own career was rather more continuous than it looked. He made a notable speech about helping the Third World in Montreal in 1966, two years before he left the Pentagon, and he had already been concerned with the blacks in America through his friendship with Bobby Kennedy. He had applied the same managerial skills to each of his giant organizations, whether to the Ford Motor Company, the Pentagon, or the World Bank. The Bank, as one of his veteran colleagues pointed out, was the smallest outfit he had run.

He had always been a loner. Ever since his university days in California he had set himself apart, with his exceptional mind and physique, to work out his own solutions. He had the confidence of the self-reliant skier and camper, exploring the mountains alone, and he had the stoic virtues of self-sufficiency and self-control. But he also had passionate loyalties, and in the crises of his personal friends he showed the qualities of a man who will say little and do everything. With his detachment he clearly felt the need to absorb himself in a single overriding mission—whether to make more cars, to drop more bombs, or to save more people from poverty. "The first requirement of management," he explained, "is to determine your objective." He was often described as a complicated man; but his mind was not often complicated by doubts, and his zeal showed a fundamental simplicity.

When he came into the World Bank in 1968—the year of the peak of the Vietnam War, of students' revolts and Nixon's election —his own mind was clear about his first objective. The World Bank, he knew, had a reputation for arrogance and American domination; from now on he would be damn well sure that there would be no domination by the industrial powers. He was proud of defying pressures from the administration, and he refused for instance to withdraw a loan to India, when Kissinger was "tilting" toward Pakistan. He was never anti-American, he insisted, but simply pro-development.

He recognized that he was the servant of an international political organization, responsible to a board which could accept or reject his proposals. But he was concerned that international bodies were "so goddamned circumscribed" by committees and compromises, and he was determined to give direction and intellectual leadership. The World Bank had always been a fairly autocratic organization since its beginnings under McCloy and Black, but McNamara soon tightened its controls and discipline as he had done at Ford and the Pentagon. And he fashioned his own intellectual instrument in the form of the annual speech to the governors. The speech became his Report on the World, taking a whole year to prepare; it was exhaustively researched, drafted, redrafted, and rewritten by McNamara, occupying thirty days of his year.

He moved into his great office in his shirt sleeves and quickly asserted his authority. He asked to see a list of the Bank's loans alongside a list of the world's population, and was struck by how little they corresponded: hardly any loans went to Africa, to the Arab countries, or (most surprisingly) to Indonesia. "What I found was the sixth largest nation in the world, rich in natural resources, striving in the wake of the most terrible disasters, both economic and political, to set itself straight on the path to development. Without external help Indonesia faces certain disaster."[2] He was convinced that the Bank must rapidly extend its loans over a much wider field; and his first five-year plan doubled the World Bank loans.

He educated himself about the problems of the Third World with the help of his closest advisers: notably Barbara Ward, the passionate English Catholic crusader who was then professor at Columbia; William Clark, his Vice-President for Public Affairs—also English—who had recently spent three years as a correspondent in India; and Hollis Chenery, the Bank's chief economist, whose independence of mind (and of income) McNamara respected. He began traveling the world, with intricate preparations and a tight schedule—flying over an irrigation project, picnicking on a farm, striding through a village, dining with the President. For each visit his secretariat compiled a big black book, briefing him about each member of the government and how to pronounce him, every new project and loan, each newspaper's attitude to the Bank, together with confidential notes about the country's record, prospects, and political hazards. To some people who crossed his

[2]Annual Meeting, Washington, September 30, 1968.

path there was something comic about this tireless American, always looking the same whether in the African bush or the Brazilian jungle, always determined to measure the immeasurable, to keep to his timetable in villages which had never seen a clock, to reduce the muddle of the world into tidy statistics, to make the whole world bankable.

He seemed unassailable, but he was open to influences. He realized how little the grandiose development projects had affected the lives of the poor. He exposed himself to the worries and ideals of the Third World leaders, the Jeffersons and Madisons of Africa and Asia. He came back to Washington demanding that the Bank must work out new answers to the intractable problems of poverty. Always he insisted on statistics and measurement; but behind the numbers he had his own picture of half-starving families in the bush.

He was soon appalled by the most discouraging complication —the galloping increase in population. The 4 billion in the world would soon become 5 billion, and 6 billion by the end of the century, threatening to frustrate any improvement in the standard of living. He faced it with a characteristic directness: he made a speech about it, at Notre Dame University in Indiana, and later in Buenos Aires (where the mayor cut him dead). The world population, he warned, would double in thirty-five years' time; "the first consequence can be seen in the gaunt faces of hungry men." Many ordinary parents, he insisted, wanted family planning far more than their political leaders understood. The enhancement of human dignity, with which the Catholic Church was so concerned, was threatened more by the population explosion than by any other catastrophe.

From population he moved on to the environment. He had already been aware of the problem, he claimed, in his days in Detroit, when he introduced the first relatively small car, the Falcon; and he now saw protecting the world's environment as a crucial part of his duty. He was influenced by his friends, including the Canadian Maurice Strong, the English naturalist Max Nicholson, and his own children. The result was one of McNamara's most radical speeches, at the UN Conference on the Environment in Stockholm in 1972. He attacked the "endlessly spiraling consumer economy" of the richer nations, and he insisted that their real dilemma was not between their domestic and foreign needs but "whether they were going to seek a more equitable balance between private opulence and public responsibility."

He was becoming more preoccupied with the basic causes and cures of world poverty. He had been early persuaded by Barbara Ward and others that the kind of rapid economic growth that was achieved in Mexico or Brazil was not improving the lot of the poorest people; and that the "trickle-down" theory of conservative economists was not working. In Brazil during the sixties, he noted, "the share of the national income received by the poorest 40 percent of the population declined from 10 percent in 1960 to 8 percent in 1970, whereas the share of the richest 5 percent grew from 29 percent to 38 percent."[3] As he explored the rural slums and the destitute shack towns of the Third World he saw the hopelessness and helplessness of people who were not being reached by any sort of aid—the "absolute poor," as he was the first to call them. Even in countries where the middle classes were becoming rapidly richer, it was the poor who were paying for the élite. He was moved by the "do-goodish" attitude to poverty; but do-gooders, as he put it to me, could easily become soft-headed, and he was also outraged by the sheer inefficiency of poverty. He was determined to approach the problem with rational rigor, asking the basic question: why are they poor?

The answer he reached—it seemed simple later but it was quite a jump to him at the time—was that the poor were not producing enough. They were "low productivity elements." These poor communities, he became convinced, could only be helped by becoming much more directly involved with production, particularly in country areas where there was a known technology for growing more food. From then onward he was determined to devote much more of the World Bank's resources to rural proj-

[3] Speech to UNCTAD, Santiago, April 14, 1972.

ects. By 1980 they made up more than 40 percent of the Bank's loans.

His obsession with poverty brought him into collisions. Many governments in the developing world maintained that if they tried to distribute wealth more equally they would diminish their over-all growth; they regarded the miseries of poverty—as in nine-teenth-century America—as the temporary price of rapid expan-sion. McNamara argued at length with Brazilians and Mexicans that there was no long-term conflict between economic and social improvement; that, on the contrary, the projects for rural develop-ment gave a high rate of return. But his plans to redistribute land met with bitter resistance, striking at the heart of traditional social structures. His emphasis on agriculture was shared by many West-ern economists, but it cut across the ambitions of developing countries which wanted to catch up with the industrial powers with their own steel mills or chemical plants. They often suspected that these farming projects were part of a plot to keep the Third World as hewers of wood and drawers of water. This obsession with industry had tragic consequences, particularly in Africa, where harvests were steadily falling, and countries which had been self-sufficient were now having to import their food.

McNamara argued that industry and agriculture must go hand-in-hand, for factories needed markets which could only be pro-vided by more prosperous agriculture. And he insisted that indus-trial efficiency depended on education, which he advocated with utilitarian zeal. He had always been impressed by the example of Japan's educational reforms in the nineteenth century, and he watched with admiration the growing industrial success of coun-tries like Brazil, Taiwan, and Korea, which had provided the right kind of schools and technical colleges. He devoted much more of the World Bank's resources to education, but it was always linked to a utilitarian purpose. "We will not finance," he empha-sized, "any education project that is not directly related to eco-nomic growth."[4]

[4]Address to Bond Club of New York, 1969.

As McNamara had promised, the Bank was now less dominated by the United States; and more senior executives were coming in from the Third World, particularly from Pakistan. But once inside the Bank's fortress in Washington they were apt to lose their national awareness and to acquire the same institutional style, speaking the same language of numbers and judgments with the same World Bank accent. Inside the maze of corridors and lobbies the World Bankers were inclined to talk as if they worked at the center of the only world that mattered, bound round with their statistics and disconnected from other values and ambitions. "McNamara has created a monster," one Middle East banker complained. "It's lost sight of the human side." The confidence of the World Bankers, as they told Buddhists, Muslims, or Hindus how to reform their societies from ten thousand miles away, could be exasperating.

It was becoming less of a bank and much more of a development agency, as McNamara would call it, or even a university of development. It remained very reliable as a bank: while its lending doubled and doubled again it maintained its record of never having a default. Pension funds or insurance companies were much safer buying World Bank bonds than investing in American railroads or real estate; and the Bank always showed a profit. But it also built up a growing staff of experts, not only economists (350 of them by 1980) but agronomists, educationalists, transport experts, health experts, population experts. The old building on H Street stretched over to G Street and across into I Street, and the atmosphere became much less like a club and more like a corporation. By the end of the seventies a thousand projects were going through the World Bank at any one time, ranging from a dam in India to sewers in Ougadougou, each with a long gestation averaging three years between the conception and the first loan or "disbursement."

The World Bankers' confidence was fortified by their knowing that other development agencies were manifestly less efficient. The United Nations Development Program was much less technically qualified, suffering from the need to balance the member nations on its executive. Many Westerners complained that it was made more incompetent by having too many staff from the Third World. But the European Development Fund, which was financed by the European Economic Community, was regarded by many experts as both more extravagant and more incompetent. The staff in Brussels were absurdly highly paid, but they still failed to acquire the technical expertise and efficient accounting which were demanded automatically by the World Bank.

The World Bank was now lending money for all kinds of social projects, from technical schools to health clinics to mass transport; yet McNamara still insisted that it must all be quantified, to show the right return on its capital. Some economists in the Bank thought it undignified, even absurd, to try to calculate these imponderables; who could seriously estimate the economic returns of a lesson in English grammar? Many of them felt that there was an irreconcilable conflict between the quantity and quality of the loans; the more the money was spread out among the murky regions of the Third World, the more impossible it was to keep track of the returns. "Unless we cut down this centralized machine," protested one senior economist, "we'll make aid a dirty word in this city." McNamara still insisted on numbers and more numbers. Did he not know that many of them were really concealed guesses? Or did he have to see the world through statistics, lest he became lost in the immeasurable?

McNamara was always reluctant to discuss generalities at the World Bank. "He stands on his mountaintop," as one of his colleagues described him, "and then brings out, not a telescope, but a microscope." But he could astonish his juniors by the way he kept track of all the Bank's hundreds of projects. "He would go straight to the critical question," one of them said, "as if he were in a helicopter above the trees."

The enigma of McNamara's character was reflected in the staff's uncertainty about their professional identity: were they bankers or missionaries? Some were certainly ambitious and conventional bankers who were gathering useful experience of the wider world before they moved on to Citibank or the Chase. Others were more idealistic men who had become interested in the Third World through the Peace Corps or some other overseas experience. A few of the older Englishmen still belonged to the earlier tradition of colonial service. But in this enclosed world they could all easily lose sight of earlier ideals. The question of identity came to the surface in the recurring arguments with Congress about the World Bank's generous tax-free salaries and expenses. When congressmen or senators complained that World Bank executives were flying around the world first-class, or on a Concorde, most of them felt entitled to some comfort in their arduous journeys. But McNamara took the complaints to heart and let it be known that he would (with a few exceptions) travel economy class, and take taxis rather than limousines. He always resented waste: he would make wry comments on his colleagues' luxury hotel suites and journeys by limousine; and he even became indignant about the extravagance of keeping cars in garages.

To many World Bankers he seemed aloof and disconcerting. He set his own standards, dominating the Bank not so much through face-to-face meetings as through documents, figures, and reports, making pencil notes in the margins which were impersonally translated into action. He was constantly trying to find new ways of ensuring that the Bank did not get out of control—trying new monitoring systems, new manpower budgets, new means of measurement. He arrived every morning at eight o'clock, striding up the twelve stories of stairs to his office, and left at seven. He was jealous of his time, measuring it in minutes, as he had been in the Pentagon or in Detroit. He was impatient at meetings, and as he got older he seemed to retreat more into himself. "His ideal meeting," one colleague observed, "consists of one person, himself." His lunches were brisk and austere. "There was a pad of notepaper laid beside my plate," recalled a British diplomat who lunched with him often, "and as he munched the cottage cheese he produced a big chart which he explained upside down across the table." But he kept his home life with his wife, Margie, strictly separate; and he was always generous with his time for his close friends, like the Kennedys or Katharine Graham, to whom his loyalty was intense.

Outside the citadel of reason in H Street, McNamara realized, the world was a less rational place and its language much more emotional. The developing countries were becoming more impatient at the UN and elsewhere, stridently demanding more generous terms for their commodities and trade; and the more radical critics in the West were complaining that the World Bank was no more than an extension of the capitalist system and American corporate power. One of them, Teresa Hayter, was allowed access to World Bank officials when she was writing her book *Aid as Imperialism*; and she concluded that "aid can be explained only in terms of an attempt to preserve the capitalist system in the Third World."[5] McNamara had a limited sympathy for the demands to restructure the economic system. He testified in 1972 about the need for a new trade regime; but he saw no serious conflict between Western capitalism and the needs of the Third World.

Then in 1973 the victory of OPEC presented a quite new challenge to McNamara. The World Bank was soon bitterly disagreeing with the Nixon Administration about the nature of the change. McNamara was persuaded by Hollis Chenery that the oil price was unlikely to go down, and that the Western nations could cope with the crisis by organizing loans from OPEC and emergency aid for the Third World; Chenery compared the OPEC surplus to the American surplus at the time of the Marshall Plan.[6] But Henry Kissinger and William Simon, whom Nixon had appointed as his "oil tsar," were both determined that the oil price could and should be forced down. The World Bank made alarming predictions about the huge surplus funds which would accrue to OPEC, but the administration regarded any plan to recycle these funds as conniving with the OPEC cartel. As one World Bank economist recalled, "It was almost a kind of treason."

[5] *Aid as Imperialism* (New York: Penguin Books, 1971).
[6] *Foreign Affairs* (January 1975), p. 255.

McNamara quickly saw the possibility of using part of the OPEC surplus to help to finance the Third World countries which were hit dangerously by the higher oil price; and within a month he had gone to the Shah and persuaded him to join in financing a new $3 billion fund. It would be a new kind of World Bank, with a voting system weighted toward the oil producers, the new rich. If it had succeeded it could have generated new relationships between OPEC and the West. But Bill Simon was adamant against the plan, and for the rest of 1974 the administration continued to try to break OPEC and push the oil price down.

It was a difficult time for McNamara. He was saddened by the feeling that Americans were betraying their historic tradition of generosity and optimism toward the rest of the world, the tradition of the Marshall Plan. When Bill Simon moved into the Treasury in April 1974, he was thoroughly opposed to McNamara's attitudes, which he regarded as dangerously socialistic; he wanted to cut back the World Bank's expansion, and by the time McNamara gave his speech in Manila in 1976 he was determined that he should not serve a third term at the Bank. But by the end of the year the Republicans were out and President Carter was glad to reappoint McNamara.

He continued to be at odds with the U.S. Treasury, which resented the World Bank's power and was not interested in aid —particularly when it came to replenishing every three years the funds for the International Development Association (IDA), the subsidized section of the World Bank which provided "soft" loans at low interest over fifty years. He was also at loggerheads with many congressmen and senators, who complained about anything from soybean projects in Papua which competed with their own farmers to lending to countries which ignored human rights. McNamara had many enemies on Capitol Hill, and he was forthright in his replies. He insisted that it was the Americans' destiny to be increasingly interdependent with the rest of the world. If they were concerned about their own poor people, they must put their own house in order, cut out waste, and revise their own domestic priorities: "I gave 'em my cat-and-dog-food speech."

His arguments were powerful, but he increasingly lacked a domestic constituency.

Congressmen were slow to realize that the World Bank was becoming less dependent on the United States. Other rich countries, including Japan, Germany, and the OPEC nations, were putting in more capital, and by 1980 the United States had only 22 percent of the voting power on the board. When McNamara wanted to increase the ratio of the World Bank's loans to its capital, all members agreed to the change in January 1980, except for the United States, Fiji, Vietnam, and Kampuchea; but the rest made up the necessary three-quarter majority, and the change went through.

While congressmen criticized McNamara for not being American, many of his Third World colleagues criticized him for being too American and too paternalist, particularly in the more militant atmosphere after 1973. As one of them put it: "He thinks that development is the rich man's burden; that it's his duty to give enlightenment and analysis to the poor countries. He would have been an excellent liberal viceroy of India, in the old days. But he can't make the leap of imagination to other people's aspirations. He thinks inefficiency is really criminal; but what this revolt is really about is not efficiency, but control." It was hardly surprising that McNamara's viewpoint should be different from that of the Third World. The developing countries were increasingly concerned with sharing economic power, and with redressing the long-term political balance between North and South. But McNamara saw efficiency and urgency as the first essentials for eliminating poverty: he dreaded that if the World Bank were decentralized, or if its decisions were muddled by compromises, it would lose the concentration of skills and the "critical mass" (as he called it) on which its dynamic depended.

McNamara did not spend too much time imagining how the world looked from the other side. He drove on with his lonely self-confidence intact, analyzing each problem rationally and honestly with his own kind of mastery. The Third World might complain that he was insensitive to their political ambitions, but there were plenty of American businessmen and politicians who complained that he was not sensitive enough to *them,* and they looked forward to the conservative and realistic attitudes of his successor, Tom Clausen (see page 392).

On his uneasy checkpoint between skeptical Western capitalists and Third World ideologues McNamara was attacked from all sides—for being too messianic, too tycoonish, too much a computer, too much a missionary. The intellectuals of the New Right would depict him as a leftover from the discredited and woolly idealism of the sixties, frustrating dynamic free enterprise through his obsessions with social change, and muddling the national interest with his overblown multilateral bureaucracy. But he was not much influenced by intellectual fashions; and he saw no contradictions within himself. He was quite able to talk as a computer *and* as a missionary. He had the self-confidence of a Victorian viceroy or a Kipling hero, stoically enduring the "blame of those ye better, and the hate of those ye serve." Yet his preoccupations —about poverty or population, about international taxation or interdependence—were concentrated on the future. With all his statistics he had the kind of imagination which belongs to few bankers. He only embarrassed his banking friends when he concluded his last emotional annual speech, in the old Kennedy style, by quoting from Bernard Shaw: "I dream things that never were —and I say "why not?" "

20
A NEW ORDER?

It seems to be a permanent task for man to shape order out of
contradictions.

WILLY BRANDT, 1980

How did the rest of the world see their place in the new balance
of power? As the richer countries became more preoccupied with
their own problems after 1973, and as the bankers and world
agencies extended their much-needed loans, they could easily
assume that the leaders of the Third World were merely passive
actors on the receiving end, grateful for any help they could get.
But the crisis of 1973 had changed their view of the world, as
much as it had changed that of the richer countries. It brought
greater hardship, but also a new sense of opportunity.

The oil crisis had caused evident suffering to people in the Third
World. They had to cut down on fuel and transport or do without
fertilizers, which were essential for daily survival. They were
caught in a historical trap: they had built their towns, industries,
and transport systems on the basis of this fuel which was cheap
and easily available, only to find that it was suddenly out of reach.
For the rich countries it was a setback; for the poorest countries
it was a disaster. It was hardly surprising if they looked with some
resentment at the Arabs and others who had helped to cause it.

Yet OPEC also provided an exciting success story for others,
and the population of OPEC countries—including 130 million
Indonesians and 80 million Nigerians—made up a sixth of the
Third World. Twenty years ago many of the oil producers had
themselves been semicolonial territories exploited, as they saw it,
by a few giant Western companies. The achievement of OPEC in

nationalizing their oilfields and fixing their own oil price in defiance of their industrial customers looked like changing the whole balance between the two sides of the world. The poor countries which for years had been trying to extract higher and more stable prices for their coffee, sugar, bauxite, or tin were stirred by the triumph of OPEC, and saw the chance to line up their own Pecs to dictate their own terms.

The more militant leaders of OPEC, who had really helped to impoverish the Third World, could thus with some sleight of hand depict themselves as their champions. Even the Shah of Iran, who more than anyone had achieved the quadrupling, soon presented himself as a more effective benefactor than all the petitioners at the UN. "We have had twelve years of UNCTAD now," he said to me in 1975. "What have they done in those twelve years for the poor countries of the world? Nothing at all."[1] Now he was showing the way toward much bolder action. The more radical oil producers, like Iraq, Libya, and Algeria, proclaimed their victory as part of a crusade. Oil was no longer simply a fuel or a means of locomotion; it was a symbol of power, a banner in the vanguard to rally other nations.

And the boldest initiative for unity was no longer coming—as it did in the sixties—from the relatively rich Latin Americans, whose common cause with the other developing continents was always in doubt. It came from Africa.

The chief prophet of the new crusade was the President of Algeria, Colonel Houari Boumedienne, who was well placed to build some kind of bridge between the haves and the have-nots. His country, stretching from the Mediterranean to the Sahara, had its own rich oilfields; but it also had widespread poverty. With the memory of its own grim war of independence, Algeria had maintained a special militancy which asserted itself in harboring terrorists and hijackers and rejecting any agreement with Israel. Boume-

[1]Interview with author, February 4, 1975.

dienne was a master of both French philosophical rhetoric and Arab demagogy. Already before the oil crisis he had been demanding a new world order to redress discrimination against the Third World. Now his ambitions were backed by power.

Four months after OPEC had quadrupled the oil price, Boumedienne presided over a special session of the United Nations in New York. In the corridors and in the delegates' lounge, which had witnessed so many ineffectual resolutions and rejected demands, the diplomats from the Third World now exuded a new sense of expectation. In his marathon speech Boumedienne made the most of it, advising others to organize their own commodity cartels: "For the first time in history developing countries have been able to take the liberty of fixing the price of their raw materials themselves." And he expounded the grand outlines of what he called the New International Economic Order, which proposed to transform the economic balance of the world. It would reorganize commodity prices and trading agreements, reallocate the money and loans from the IMF and the World Bank, and promote massive industrialization in the developing countries, to liberate them from their neocolonial oppressors. The New International Economic Order (NIEO) was proclaimed in the language of international Marxism; but it was an appeal for unity and organization (like the appeals of labor unions in the mid-nineteenth century) which went far beyond the Communist bloc.

A year later Boumedienne was host to another triumphal occasion, when he invited the princes of OPEC to their first summit at the Palace of Nations outside Algiers. It was a bizarre mixture of oil leaders—including the Shah, the Sheik of Abu Dhabi, the President of Venezuela, and the dictator of Iraq, Saddam Hussein—representing every kind of political philosophy. But Boumedienne, addressing them as "Your Majesties, Brothers," took the opportunity to promote his New Order and his theories about oil, which he insisted was not only a fluid, but the source of life itself. He even stage-managed a dramatic reconciliation between those unfriendly oil neighbors Iran and Iraq, with the Shah embracing Saddam Hussein. OPEC, Boumedienne promised, would be the instrument of social justice, the spearhead of the economic recovery of the Third World, the means to escape from capitalist exploitation.

Boumedienne was actually never as straightforward an enemy of capitalists and bankers as he appeared. His domestic policies were much more pragmatic, and two years later I chanced to witness another side of his policies. It was at the ceremonial opening of the great new port and industrial complex of Arzew, near Algiers, where the pipelines carried natural gas from the Sahara, to be liquefied before it flowed on to the refrigerated tankers, which transported it across the Atlantic to Florida. Boumedienne arrived in his theatrical black cloak to inspect the glittering brand-new installations, to take part in the banquet of whole roasted sheep, and to make a long speech to the guests. But they were not only Algerian functionaries and ambassadors: there were American engineers, oil company executives, and an army of bemused American bankers from the Chase, Citibank, and elsewhere who had raised the loans to make the port possible. They listened to Boumedienne's anticolonial rhetoric and attacks on the former French masters with wry amusement. For Algeria was never as independent of the capitalists as it looked. It was borrowing hectically to finance its own industrialization and was dependent on American markets and American bankers.

NORTH AND SOUTH

The New Order still maintained its momentum. The OPEC leaders —even the most conservative, like the Saudis—saw merit in aligning themselves with the rest of the Third World. They realized that the world was now being defined and divided in terms of oil. The poorer countries were now labeled with the bleak classification "oil-importing developing countries" or "non-oil developing countries," while others demoted them to the "fourth world." But at the same time the whole range of developing countries, with or without oil, were determined to maintain some kind of solidarity, which they emphasized by calling themselves the "South," as opposed to the industrialized countries of the "North." The descriptions were inexact, for some industrialized countries like Australia and South Africa lay south of the Equator, while some developing countries like Mexico stretched to the north. Richer Latin American countries like Brazil were reluctant to be bracketed with Africa or India, while the ambitious new industrial countries like the supercompetitors in East Asia had quite different interests from their more somnolent neighbors. But the words were roughly recognizable by both sides, and they suited the militancy of the New Order.

The oil producers, however rich, still insisted that they were part of the South; at UNCTAD and other diplomatic meetings they were part of the negotiating front, the "Group of 77," arrayed against the North. It was crucial to their solidarity that they should not regard oil as separate from other commodities, but as the precursor of a broader victory. The South saw any attempt to single out oil, or to discuss its price, as a plot by the North to split it. The diplomats of the South tried to avoid the very mention of the word "oil"; while the North, particularly the Americans, wanted to discuss oil but nothing else.

It was thus hardly surprising that the North found difficulty in talking to the South. After that flamboyant OPEC summit at Algiers, and after many exasperating negotiations, the two sides came to a Conference on International Economic Cooperation (CIEC) in Paris, to try to continue what was hopefully called the "North-South dialogue." But the North was still interested only in oil, and the South was interested only in its other commodities and terms of trade. At one point the Saudis were close to agreement with the Americans over a formula for the oil price, but the Algerians would not discuss it. "It was their great weapon," as one Western diplomat observed; "they couldn't put it back into the sheath." When they could not reach agreement, the Americans followed a policy of "talk 'em to death," and after eighteen months the talks finally collapsed in the middle of 1977.

ONE WORLD

The South still looked to the United Nations as both its arena and its champion. It was becoming increasingly unwieldy. Its membership had tripled from 51 in 1945 to 152 in 1979, and it had fathered a whole litter of new agencies to deal not just with trade (UNCTAD) and development (UNDP), but with food (FAO), health (WHO), industry (UNIDO), and the environment (UNEP). By 1979 the UN was holding as many as 6,000 meetings a year, and its conferences and secretariats, with tax-free salaries, traveling expenses, and luxurious meeting places, exasperated the richer countries, which paid much of the bill. In fact, the UN was no more extravagant than any other international junketers, like the European Community or the IMF; but the consequences were more visible. The comfortable life-style of the UN lured administrators and experts away from their home countries, which often desperately needed them, and the diplomats from the Third World could develop interests which were quite different from those of their own people and politicians. The "paper war" became more extravagant and more ineffective as delegates hurled more and more documents and speeches into the fray. ("If only there were some way of *eating* paper," a delegate said after a food conference, "we might begin to solve the world food problem.") But the blame belonged not so much to the UN as to its member governments, who (as the Secretary-General Kurt Waldheim complained) indulged in "international escapism." "It is sometimes easier to call a conference, or even found a new institution," said Waldheim, "than to confront a complex problem directly."

To international bankers and businessmen, and to the World Bank, the muddle at the United Nations appeared as a nightmare of incompetence; the absurd consequence of equal votes. The early Western idealism about the UN had almost evaporated, and American politicians, from Moynihan to Kissinger, could easily gain popularity by attacking it. But they often attacked it for the weakness which they had themselves brought about; for the UN was never more nor less than the sum of its members' policies. After thirty-five years it remained the only truly global meeting place which spanned the East as well as the West. In times of real danger its fiercest critics would still run to it for help. And the bankers who were now dealing with one world, stretching from Moscow and Peking to Brasilia and the Philippines, could not afford to ignore the only forum which brought them together.

The South still put faith in the UN, and its chief commercial lobby and rallying point remained UNCTAD, where it now thoroughly outnumbered the North. The Group of 77, which represented the South, still kept its name, but it now numbered 117. The diplomats of the South were still determined to make a common front between nations as different as Brazil and Tanzania; but they had to frame resolutions which were designed more to conceal differences than to state their real interests. Unctalk became still more obscure and heavily coded as it avoided the central issues: to decode it was like trying to guess the shape of a mountain by following the paths round it. And UNCTAD was now facing new setbacks. When it held its first meeting since the oil crisis in Nairobi in May 1976, many countries hoped that they could organize their raw materials as OPEC had done, and they introduced a new Integrated Program for Commodities, to be built round a well-endowed Common Fund. But the fund never got enough money to make it effective. The producers of copper, sugar, and bauxite were less hopeful of following the example of OPEC as the prices of most commodities tumbled in the world recession, while the price of oil kept up.

Yet the New Order refused to go away. The rhetoric, with all its extreme demands, its evasion about the oil price and its blaming of the former colonial powers, exasperated most Western leaders, not least those who were trying hardest to help the Third World. But it still represented a fundamental change of attitude which could not be ignored. The South had a critical bargaining counter. Oil, which was the world's new currency, was nearly all in the South; and the North could not survive without it. The South still saw its other commodities in the same light. It wanted to escape from the humiliations of petitioning for aid, or passing endless resolutions, endlessly ignored. It saw that OPEC presented a chance not only of getting a better deal but of sharing the control of the world's economic system, which it believed was heavily loaded against it.

That was not, of course, how it looked to the bankers—even to the liberal bankers. McNamara at the World Bank was distressed by the attitudes of the ideologues of the New Order. He thought their plans were muzzy and unrealistic, and he did not refer to the New Order at all in his annual speeches in 1974 and 1975. As far as he was concerned, there was only one kind of logic. He was dedicated to efficiency and discipline, and to maintaining the credibility of the Bank to its investors. To the world of H Street the prospect of world finance being run by committees of the UN was intolerable.

But McNamara took the New Order more seriously than most other Western leaders or bankers, and he was worried when the North-South talks in Paris broke down. "The atmosphere today is at best one of regret and disappointment," he said in his annual speech later in 1977, "and at worst one of frustration and disillusionment." He was distressed, too, that the richer countries had failed to live up to the target for aid that the Pearson Commission had set eight years earlier;[2] the level of official aid (ODA), he reported, had been virtually stationary for the past decade, while the incomes of the donor countries had gone up by 40 percent. The United States was giving only 0.26 percent of her gross national product for aid, compared to Pearson's target of 0.7 percent, and both Germany and Japan had reduced their proportion.

McNamara was determined to make another effort to break the deadlock between North and South. He had already earlier in 1977 made a speech at Boston proposing that an independent commission be appointed to report on the problem. By the end of the year he had with some difficulty persuaded Willy Brandt,

[2] See Chapter 6.

the former Chancellor of West Germany, to become chairman of a new international commission, twelve years after Pearson, to "study the grave global issues arising from the economic and social disparities of the world community and to suggest ways of promoting adequate solutions to the problems involved in development and in attacking absolute poverty."

THE BRANDT COMMISSION

Willy Brandt looked at the world from a quite different perspective from McNamara's. He was not an expert on the economic or monetary problems of development, and he distrusted the remedies of economists. Nor was he very familiar with the Third World: when he was Chancellor, he admitted, he gave too little attention to his colleagues who argued for reappraising German priorities. But he believed that the predicament of the Third World now presented a moral challenge to the West and "learning from one's own shortcomings," he said, "sometimes helps in addressing one's fellow citizens." He shared with McNamara an imagination which saw beyond immediate problems and barriers. His own experiences as an opponent of Hitler, as a refugee, and as a young man in devastated Germany enabled him to empathize with Third World leaders; and having witnessed the extraordinary recovery of Europe, he had seen how hopes and visions could turn into realities. As Chancellor he had tried to build bridges between West and East, in his policy of Ostpolitik, with a trustfulness which his enemies used against him; but he was still prepared to be endlessly patient in seeking common interests across the ideological divides. He was determined that any accommodation between North and South should still keep open the possibility of future participation by both Russia and China. He liked to quote the words of the Pope, that "development is another word for peace." For Brandt the priorities of the world were clear: peace, justice, jobs.

He brought his own moral authority to the commission, and sometimes he seemed more a preacher and philosopher than a politician. In West Germany, where he continued to be chairman of the Social Democrat Party, he had been eclipsed by Helmut Schmidt, who had succeeded him as Chancellor. But in Europe he still had a charismatic influence, particularly when he appealed to the young, which put him on a plane above politics. He continually questioned material benefits and was always interested in religious movements; he liked to ask: "Do we all want to be Americans?" His detachment was emphasized by his sense of humor, which often sounded very un-German. There were not many jokes about development, he warned me when he first asked me to work for the commission as editorial adviser; it was still too delicate a question, like joking about trade unions in their earlier days (when I later tried to slip a joke into the report, he carefully excised it). But his own private jokes, told with his naughty-boy look, were able to break across world tensions.

Brandt and McNamara assembled a group of commissioners who were all at least theoretically independent from governments. The Soviets, to Brandt's regret, did not take part; but the eighteen commissioners, with the South in a majority, represented a much wider political spectrum than Pearson's. And the secretariat of development economists was also varied—and frequently split. The commissioners thus provided a kind of personification of the political divisions of the world, reflecting the bitter arguments of the previous years. It was by no means certain, as they soon realized, that they could achieve any kind of consensus. But their different standpoints were significant in themselves as a round-up of world opinion.

Two American commissioners represented different views of global free enterprise. Peter Peterson, the New York banker from Lehman Kuhn Loeb, flew in and out of meetings, scattering outspoken memos, reflecting all Wall Street's skepticism about Third World finances and always stressing the MEGO factor—"my eyes glaze over." But he was well aware of the West's need for secure oil supplies from the Arabs, and for much greater exploration for energy and minerals in developing countries. Katharine Graham, the owner of *The Washington Post* and *Newsweek,* had been persuaded to join the commission by her old friend McNamara. Her conservatism was imbued by her father, the first president of the World Bank (see Chapter 4), who had earlier resigned from the Federal Reserve Board when it went off the gold standard. She was loyal to the World Bank and suspicious of radical ideologies; but she came into the Third World, with all its extremes of poverty, with the open mind of a newcomer; and she developed her own personal relations with members from the South. They were apt to assume that, because she owned two of the world's most famous media, she could tell her editors what to print, which led to misunderstandings. But she could talk with authority about what Americans could or could not take.

Other commissioners from the North revealed how differently they could look at the world. Joe Morris, the burly Canadian Labour leader, was preoccupied with trying to hold back the unions' demands for protection; Edgard Pisani, the French socialist senator, sought to express the world's problems in elegant Cartesian constructs. Jan Pronk, the former Minister for Development from Holland, conveyed the special Dutch commitment to the Third World. Olof Palme, the former Swedish Prime Minister, a close colleague of Brandt on the Socialist International, brought his own poetic style. A special curiosity surrounded the British ex-Prime Minister Ted Heath, who flew in from ocean races or visits to the opera. He had shown his concern for the Third World since the beginnings of UNCTAD, and he was worried about the political insensitivity of the IMF and the fragility of the world banking system. But he was impatient of the clichés of the South, and of OPEC's claims to be acting in the world's best interests. He seemed increasingly doubtful whether the commission could agree on any report.

From the South the most eloquent member was Shridath (Sonny) Ramphal from Guyana, who ran the Commonwealth Secretariat in London and was talked of as a future Secretary-General of the United Nations. He could sound like a Caribbean populist, a London barrister, or a literary diplomat. He and Heath appeared at loggerheads; but he was more conciliatory than he looked, determined to keep links with different sectors of the South. The polished Algerian diplomat Layachi Yaker was a master in three languages of the rhetoric of the New International Economic Order. On the conservative side the Kuwaiti banker Abdlatif Al-Hamad, the director of the Kuwait Fund,[3] had a long experience of lending money to the Third World and provided a bridge between ideologues and bankers. The doyen from the South, Governor L. K. Jha, was one of the founders of UNCTAD and was soon to be Mrs. Gandhi's economic adviser. Amir Jamal from Tanzania came from one of the poorest territories of Africa; while Mrs. Khatijah Ahmad, a Malaysian banker, represented a new mercantile country which was asking not for aid but for reasonable trading terms. The two Latin Americans represented a continent which was moving away from dependence on aid. Rodrigo Botero, the Colombian former Finance Minister, was more concerned with the need for a more stable banking system and more power sharing in the world bodies. Eduardo Frei, the former President of Chile, had the moral authority of an uncompromising opponent of the Chilean dictator Pinochet. Like Brandt he put human dignity and the brotherhood of man at the heart of the North-South debate.

With these contrasts the commissioners showed almost irreconcilable views of the world crisis. They met over concentrated long weekends in Bonn, in Bamako in West Africa, in Tarrytown outside New York, in Kuala Lumpur, and in Switzerland. They listened to everyone from UNCTAD to OPEC, from bankers to environmentalists, from Kissinger to Barbara Ward. But they revealed little sign of a common view or solution. As the secretariat tried to draft a report, they battled over sentences and single words: apparently innocuous nouns like restructuring, multinationals, order, remunerative, basic needs, and even Communist turned out to be booby traps or minefields, bristling with hidden dangers in the war of words.

The verbal battles reflected the opposite historical experience

[3] See Chapter 8.

of two sides of the world—the memory of colonial oppression and helplessness on one side, of self-help and industrial discipline on the other. Militants from the South wanted a kind of manifesto or rallying call, like a UN resolution; while representatives of the North wanted persuasive arguments to convince their own voters, politicians, or bankers of the need for reforms. But other arguments were more fundamental. Was the world's economic crisis of a cyclical kind, which could be cured by judicious reforms and adjustments? Or did it demand fundamental changes in the international system, going back to the roots of Bretton Woods and substituting a quite different sharing of power and control? Yet as the arguments continued against a worsening world economic background, the distinction (it seemed to me) between radicals and reformists became less marked, as the status quo became less and less attractive.

And there were some crossing places between the lines. The role of multinational corporations, which at first looked an explosive question, became much less contentious. The members from the South recognized that the corporations, provided they could be controlled and monitored, could bring precious technology and investment to the Third World without infringing their sovereignty. ("If there's one thing worse than being exploited by a multinational," it was said, "it's *not* being exploited.") When Ramphal put forward a paper describing how developing countries required the safeguards of fair contracts before they welcomed exploration by multinationals, it was Peterson, the Republican banker, who saw its value for the North. As the commissioners became closer and more candid, forced to talk to each other in hotels and castles, they began to see more scope for compromise and horse-trading. "Every time you knock the North," as one of them said, "we'll knock the South." Even the conservative commissioners questioned the structure of the IMF and the World Bank in a world where the dollar was no longer dominant and the new rich of OPEC were becoming increasingly indispensable. And they even began to take seriously a controversial proposal, worked out by Dragoslav Avramovic of the secretariat, for a new World Development Fund to supplement the World Bank and others, providing longer-term loans with extra funds from OPEC and others, controlled equally by North and South.

There were differences between bankers and politicians on both sides, the first talking the language of debits and rescheduling, the second discussing political will and persuasion. But the bankers were as indispensable as the politicians; for the question of aid was now obviously interlocked with the question of debt: and the Special Drawing Right, for all its abstraction, could mean the difference between starvation and rescue. Peterson liked to quote the story about the radical lawyer Clarence Darrow, who was being effusively thanked by a client he had saved from the electric chair. "I can't think how to show my gratitude," said the client, and Darrow replied dryly: "I've never known an emotion that could not be satisfactorily expressed by money."

While the commissioners were meeting with little sign of a consensus the world scene was darkening. The revolution in Iran and the religious confrontation with Islamic fanatics were reminders that economic growth was not, after all, the panacea for the world's ills. The new energy crisis pushed up the oil price again and further undermined the finances of developing countries. The gathering recession in the West brought a new clamor for protection against imports. In the midst of the new oil crisis UNCTAD held a meeting in Manila with 3,000 delegates who achieved almost nothing and produced a communiqué which did not even mention the word "oil."

Four months later the ninety-six "non-aligned" countries had their fifth summit as the guests of Fidel Castro in Cuba, demanding an economic revolution and a worldwide restructuring of industry with a Marxist rhetoric which might have been designed to alienate the North. It repeated the ritual attacks on colonialism, Zionism, domination, and hegemony, and insisted (in the words of the final communiqué) that "the struggle to eliminate the injustice of the existing international economic system and to establish the New International Economic Order is an integral part of the people's struggle for political, economic, cultural and social liberation."

When the Brandt commissioners gathered at the Palais Egmont in Brussels in October 1979 for their last scheduled meeting, they still could not agree. After the fiasco of UNCTAD at Manila Brandt had insisted that they must confront the problem of oil; but the question of OPEC and the oil price still divided commissioners. Speeches rolled on while the deadline approached for agreeing on the report, and even Brandt was losing his patience. Two days before the deadline a committee of four commissioners—Peterson, Al-Hamad, Ramphal, and Palme—managed to put together the basis of a deal: the North would agree to a large transfer of funds, to more power sharing, and to strict conservation of energy, in return for a guarantee of more secure oil supplies and orderly price rises. But others could not agree; the speeches went on, the deadline was passed, and the meeting dissolved gloomily without a consensus.

Then the relationships took an odd twist. The two commissioners who had seemed most at loggerheads, Ted Heath and Sonny Ramphal, agreed to try to negotiate a final text. And as another commissioner put it: "If those two can agree, then we all can. And they will agree, because they're politicians." The scene shifted to Marlborough House, the Commonwealth headquarters in London, and for two months Ramphal and Heath with their aides, coordinating with Brandt in Bonn, thrashed out the report. Ramphal knew that the South must make concessions on energy if it was to obtain more power sharing and aid. Heath was convinced of the need for urgent reforms, whether to prevent mass starvation in the South or to avert a crisis of international debt and the banking system in the North.

Before Christmas the commissioners assembled once again behind the moated defenses of Leeds Castle in England. Thankfully they now felt able to approve with only minor changes the wording of the report; like all verbal battlefields it showed the scars of compromise, but it still retained the basis of a deal, with the forbidden subject of oil at the center. The Brandt Report was published in March 1980, while world tension and recession were still mounting. Would the crisis prevent Western governments from thinking beyond their own borders? Or would it force them to think more seriously about their interdependence? Would the Brandt Report follow the Pearson Report into oblivion?

Certainly it had many similarities to the Pearson Report eleven years earlier, as skeptics pointed out. Brandt too called for "political will" to increase the volume of aid and restated the old target —now still further out of sight—of giving 0.7 percent of the gross national product. Brandt too endorsed many of UNCTAD's demands, including "stable and remunerative prices" for commodities—while cautiously criticizing the wastefulness of UN bureaucracies and the Anglo-Saxon domination of the World Bank. Brandt too concluded that aid was essential but not enough, and that North and South needed a new economic relationship.

But the Brandt commissioners reflected the problems of a more worried and divided world after a decade of turmoil; and their report had two crucial differences from Pearson's. First, they embraced a much more political consensus of people with almost opposite philosophies confronting each other at a time of deadlock; they nevertheless held out some prospect of a global deal, which they hoped could be worked out in a North-South summit. Second, the greater economic confusion in the world had compelled the commissioners to advocate much more fundamental changes to the monetary and economic system. "We face, therefore, not merely one, but several crises," said the report. "The crisis of relentless inflation and increasing energy costs, the crisis of dwindling energy availability, the crisis resulting from mounting financial requirements, and the crisis posed by constraints on world trade and on the growth of export earnings to meet increased debt service commitments. Taken together, they threaten the whole structure of our political, industrial and financial institutions, unless we move urgently and adequately to deal with the basic causes."[4]

[4]*North-South: A Program for Survival* (Cambridge, Mass.: MIT Press, 1980), p. 239.

The commissioners, whether Republican or Marxist, Muslim or Jewish, bankers or moralists, all accepted that they had common interests in achieving basic reforms, without which the crisis was likely to worsen; and that cooperation between North and South was essential to achieve a lasting economic improvement—whether to revive and stabilize world trade, to explore for minerals and oils, to grow more food, to reverse the trend toward protection, or to establish lasting agreements between multinational companies and their host governments.

The concept of "one world," which had been so often advocated by idealists, environmentalists, or statesmen over the past forty years, and which had so often proved premature, had achieved a new reality with the oil crisis. The businessmen needed new markets and new regions of growth for their investment. The Western consumers and industrialists desperately needed oil. The bankers who had been lending so heavily to the developing world needed to be sure of getting back their money. And the developing countries needed more loans and investment, and more markets in the rich countries. To ignore these interdependencies was (as William Clark of the World Bank put it) like saying, "Your end of the boat is sinking."

The Brandt commissioners began by talking about aid, and ended up talking about banking. They realized, as the bleak evidence piled up, that bank lending was eclipsing aid giving in large areas of the Third World: in 1960, 60 percent of the flow of funds to the developing countries had come from concessional aid or "official development assistance"; while by 1977 more than two thirds was commercial—mainly from bank loans, direct investment, and export credits. Of the debts of the developing countries, 40 percent came from loans on the international private markets, compared to 17 percent in 1970, at the time of the Pearson Report. Their combined debts rose from $70 billion at the end of 1970 to an estimated $300 billion at the end of 1979; and in the next five years between $300 and $500 billion might have to be added to their debts to meet their financial needs. In more than half the developing countries (excluding OPEC), debts had grown two and a half times as fast as exports in the previous five years.[5]

The Brandt commissioners accepted that this private lending was crucial, but warned that it could not continue at the same pace, and that the relationship between borrowers and lenders was inadequate. They insisted that the World Bank and the IMF must play a larger role and share more of their power with developing countries. The World Bank could raise more capital, and increase its ratio of loans to capital—which had always been extraordinarily cautious compared to commercial banks—from one-to-one to two-to-one. The IMF should not only increase its lending, but also issue more SDRs, which could benefit the Third World; and sell part of its hoard of gold, devoting the profits to the developing countries.

But bankers could not solve everything. The arguments about mutual interests could never be extended to all countries, particularly to the populations who lived in absolute poverty, with no oil and few raw materials to export. They could only escape from their vicious circle of growing population and declining resources if they received enough effective aid to put them on the road toward self-help and self-sufficiency. Their first appeal had to be to the conscience and morality of the richer countries, rather than to their mutual interest. Yet the two arguments, Brandt insisted, could not be disentangled. A world of desperate food shortages and mass hunger, with the rich nations retreating into themselves and the barriers going up, could not be stable for anyone, whether for bankers or statesmen.

There were always two arguments, as in nineteenth-century Europe, for persuading the rich to share some of their wealth with the poor: the moral arguments about philanthropy and the hardheaded arguments about security, larger markets, and longer-term prosperity. But Brandt insisted that they came together in any

[5]*Ibid.,* pp. 222, 238–40. Detailed studies of debt as well as other background papers are contained in *The Brandt Commission Papers* (The Hague: Independent Bureau for International Development Issues), 1981.

longer-term view. The report recommended an emergency program to provide immediate aid for food and other necessities for the poorest countries, which would cost about $4 billion a year; but it also looked ahead to a system of international taxation, to which all but the poorest countries would contribute, which could provide a more steady source of assistance. "One might argue," Brandt said in his introduction, "that it is hard to imagine international taxation without international government. But we believe that certain elements of what might be called international government are already called for to meet both mutual and national interests, and that by the end of this century the world will probably not be able to function without some practicable form of international taxation."[6]

The most far-reaching claim for mutual interests was the most contentious. Could a massive transfer of resources from the North to the South provide the means not only to make the South more prosperous but to rescue the North from the gathering recession and unemployment? The precedent of Marshall Aid, which had revived postwar Europe while it provided markets and jobs for America, had for long fascinated many development economists. The spectacle of factories lying idle in Europe and America and skilled workers waiting in dole queues, while the poorer countries were in desperate need of goods they could be producing, seemed to defy both common decency and common sense. But the world was now haunted by inflation, and the solution was not so straightforward. If the rich countries were prepared to let inflation rip, they could quickly stimulate their own domestic consumers to buy more cars, houses, or gadgets, thus creating more jobs in the factories. Producing more goods for the Third World would be no less (but also no more) inflationary. The vision of a global Marshall Plan, extending its generosity to India or Africa and reaping its rewards of new markets and jobs, could not offer an easy escape from the West's predicament of inflation and stagnation.

[6]*Ibid.,* p. 22.

But the broader political argument for an accommodation between North and South was much less questionable. As the Brandt
Report put it: "The poor will not make progress in a world economy characterized by uncertainty, disorder, and low rates of
growth; it is equally true that the rich cannot prosper without
progress by the poor. The world requires a new system of economic relationships that acknowledge these mutual needs and
human interests." The extent of this interdependence was becoming much more evident, as the world economy became less stable
—whether to multinational executives, to bankers, or to the mandarins of the International Monetary Fund, who were now finding
themselves on the most exposed frontier of all.

21
THE FINANCIAL SHERIFF

Debts are not the kind of bond that can unite the world.

HERBERT FEIS, 1930[1]

In June 1980 the world's bankers assembled at the Fairmont Hotel in New Orleans for their annual International Monetary Conference, and after the shock of the second oil crisis they were now voicing their worries more openly. Tom Clausen of the Bank of America was more candid and scrutable than usual. "Commercial banks have been and continue to be at the vortex of the recycling process," he explained, "but their role no longer can be viewed in isolation. The task ahead is immense. Its sheer magnitude requires that a greater share of the burden be shouldered by the international financial agencies." Commercial banks, he went on, "are catalysts rather than an alternative to global capital markets, and they cannot be expected to assume the role of insurance companies in providing long-term financing." Clausen proposed that the IMF and other agencies should provide guarantees to the banks to enable them to lend more, and that the OPEC powers themselves must become involved in lending, either directly or through the World Bank and the IMF.

Clausen's speech created a small stir, but many bankers were worried about the implications of closer links with the IMF. As Wriston put it to me: "Tom's idea didn't sell too well. The basic reason is that the IMF is a political institution which would have to decide who got the guarantees and who didn't . . . I don't see the political allocation of the guarantee as a feasible political decision: shall we give it to Mexico? Shall we give it to Zaire?" Al

[1]Feis, p. 467.

Costanzo was likewise critical: "Once you start getting close to any agencies," he told me, "they start wanting to interfere." The bankers' doubts were hardly surprising; with their belief in vigorous free enterprise they looked for official support, but they dreaded intervention. It was an attitude, as one of them put it, of "Help! but hands off!"

Yet they still felt insecure; and wherever they had been in deep difficulties abroad—whether in Zaire or in Turkey or in Peru—they had looked to the IMF as their means of salvation. At the New Orleans conference Wilfried Guth of the Deutsche Bank put the problem more plainly than anyone: "What should happen if, through a combination of unfortunate events, a substantial debtor finds himself in difficulties? In my opinion, there can be no question that in the case of debtor-country difficulties, we have to look at the main "trouble-shooter," the International Monetary Fund."[2]

But the IMF was not so enthusiastic about playing the trouble-shooter—like a sheriff with a doubtful posse in a town full of big-money men. The Fund had a far wider responsibility for the world than the commercial banks, and by 1980 it had 140 member countries. But like any international institution, and like the UN itself, it was as strong or as weak as its controlling members cared to make it; and the Western governments were not in the mood to increase its powers. While the commercial bankers had been hugely increasing their lending, the Fund's resources had remained virtually static.

Since its foundation thirty years earlier the money mandarins had built up their own defenses in their comfortable fortress in Washington. By 1978 the Fund had accumulated a staff of 1,500, of which 30 percent came from developing countries—most of them in relatively junior posts—while the Americans and British occupied a disproportionate number of jobs. A report in May 1979 pointed to some of the recurring complaints. There was too much inbreeding resulting from promotion from below, which

[2]*International Herald Tribune*, June 16, 1980.

caused "a rigid doctrinaire approach"; the middle-level staff, who clung to old ideas and the ancient regime, could prove a powerful force when allied with a few conservative executive directors; most of them had little experience of the problems of developing countries, prescribing their usual "bitter pills"—curtailing the money supply, raising interest rates, and cutting public spending —in an authoritarian way. "It is all right for Fund officials," a former deputy director of the IMF research department, Marcus Fleming, complained, "sitting in air-conditioned offices in Washington, to advise harassed LDC officials to follow these prescriptions. But the heavy price is paid by the people of these countries."[3] The Brandt Report published in March 1980 had been critical of the Fund's lack of political sense. "The Fund's insistence on drastic measures," it complained, "has tended to impose unnecessary and unacceptable political burdens on the poorest, on occasion leading to 'IMF riots' and even the downfall of governments."[4]

OIL DEBTORS

The role of the managers of the Fund had become more uncertain since the oil crisis of 1973. Already their task had been partly undermined by the collapse of the dollar as a world currency. But now they surveyed a world where the dollar was still weaker and where the critical currency was not dollars but oil; while the new rich, including Saudi Arabia, were barely represented round their circular conference table. The commercial bankers were now much more important, and the expansion of the global Eurodollar market, interlocked with the American Federal Reserve system, had thoroughly eclipsed the resources of the IMF. As Martin Mayer described it in 1974:

[3]Paper prepared by S. R. Sen in *The Brandt Commission Papers,* pp. 158–81.
[4]*North-South: A Program for Survival,* p. 216.

Lord Keynes in 1943 dreamed of an International Clearing Union that would give to the growth of international trade and the development of all the world's economies the advantage that unified banking systems had given to national economies. With the linkage of the Fed Funds and Eurodollar markets this dream has been accomplished—the mechanism looks American but in reality it is as impersonal and universal as the gold standard. Unfortunately, the dream is beginning to look more and more like a nightmare, a phantasmagoria of perpetual high interest rates and an inflation geometrically expanding until it bursts the taut skin of international enterprise and international civility.[5]

Just before the first oil crisis a new managing director, Johannes Witteveen, had taken over at the Fund; he was a strong personality, a Dutch professor of economics and former Minister of Finance, and he realized that the Fund must do what it could to help the countries which had been most hit by the high oil price. The IMF agreed to open temporary new "windows" to provide relief, with the help of loans from the OPEC countries, called (in the usual snappy style of the Fund) the Oil Facility, the Extended Facility, and the Witteveen Facility. But these new windows opened under fairly harsh conditions, which scared away most developing countries; and a large proportion of the new loans went to the richer countries, particularly Britain and Italy, which were themselves feeling the pinch of the oil crisis.

The British, who had often been severe in their treatment of IMF debtors in the past, were now getting a taste of their own medicine, beginning to learn how it felt to be in the Third World. In September 1976 the Labour government, after desperately trying to rescue the falling pound while maintaining the welfare state, was forced to apply to the IMF for the biggest loan in its history, of $3.9 billion; and the IMF team, including a senior Englishman, Alan Whittome, arrived in London for the customary inspection in an atmosphere of angry suspicion from the left. The Ford Administration in Washington was determined that Britain must cut

[5]Mayer, p. 503.

her welfare spending, and Bill Simon and Edwin Yeo at the Treasury saw the British extravagance as a kind of morality tale, like the concurrent crisis in New York. "Our role," said Edwin Yeo (then Undersecretary for Monetary Affairs), "was to persuade the British that the game was over. They had run out of string."[6] The IMF team soon proposed its usual remedies, including drastic deflation and cuts in public spending while the Labour cabinet under James Callaghan bitterly debated the cuts. The leader on the left, Tony Benn, warned that the international bankers were entering the citadel of power; and Anthony Crosland, the chief theorist of social democracy, agonized over the destruction of his hopes. Eventually Witteveen himself flew to London, making some concessions and reaching agreement with the chancellor, Denis Healey. Crosland finally gave way, the left was outvoted, and Callaghan persuaded the cabinet to accept the deflationary package, including heavy cuts in public spending and selling off some of the government's shares in the oil company BP. It was an experience, some left-wing MPs maintained, that broke the heart of the Labour Party.

But the British ordeal, in spite of talk about rioting in the streets, was much less harsh than that of most developing countries which confronted the IMF; and Britain was now developing her own oil reserves, which enabled her to borrow easily from commercial banks. The poorer governments with people close to starvation could not cut spending or put up prices without causing genuine riots; the "IMF riots," whether in Ghana, Peru, or Egypt, had become part of the demonology of the Third World. The higher oil bill made it still harder for them to turn round their economies without violence. The IMF would have to become a much more sensitive animal, much more concerned with the politically possible, if it was to regain the trust of the poorer countries.

[6]See Stephen Fay and Hugo Young, "The Day the Pound Nearly Died," *Sunday Times,* May 14–28, 1976, which gives an authoritative account of Britain's dealings with the IMF, though without the cooperation of Denis Healey.

THE DEBT COLLECTOR

The commercial banks in the meantime had created a very different perspective, for the IMF now controlled much less of the world's money. In 1966 the quotas which made up its capital amounted to 10 percent of the total world imports; but by 1976 they made up only 4 percent. Between 1971 and 1973 the world's annual deficits had averaged about $15 billion; but between 1974 and 1976 the deficits had gone up to $75 billion. Only 7 percent of these deficits had been financed by the Fund; another 18 percent was financed by other official bodies, including governments and the World Bank. The remaining three quarters was financed through the banks.

The arrival of the bankers in the Third World, however preoccupied with their profits, was much more welcome than the dreaded visitations of the men from the Fund. The bankers talked very little about conditions, deflation, or devaluation. Provided the country had a reasonable credit rating they would sign their checks without much inspection or cross-examination; and since they were competing with other bankers, who were all anxious to lend, a shrewd Minister of Finance could play them against each other. For the first years after the oil crisis the bankers with their casual pragmatism looked more attractive than the official busybodies, and the developing countries looked with relief at the decline of the Fund.

Yet the Fund still had great influence—perhaps more than before—behind the scenes. For as the bankers lent to the more perilous countries they began to look more anxiously over their shoulders toward the Fund; partly because it was their best source of information, but also because it could reassure them about financial discipline by providing its "seal of approval." The developing countries on their side became more worried that the IMF, after probing their innermost secrets "with their trousers down," would then pass the secrets on to the bankers. They dreaded the "Financial Sheriff." If the sheriff did not give his approval, they knew, the posse of bankers would all stay away. It was the old nightmare of every debtor—the creditors all closing in together, with the police in the background.

The bankers knew that they could not by themselves force foreign governments to cut their spending and increase their taxes to enable them to pay their interest; they still faced the old problem of the Medicis trying to control their spendthrift foreign princes. They had learnt that lesson in Peru in 1976; the American banks had lent $2 billion to the left-wing military regime, while Peru was suffering from falling copper prices, and from a shortage of anchovies, which provided its exports of fishmeal. The Peruvians refused to go to the IMF, dreading its harsh terms. The bankers, once again led by Irving Friedman of Citibank, tried to impose their own terms, including immediate devaluation and higher taxes. There were riots, resignations, and furious attacks on the bankers, while Peru sank still farther into the debt trap. The bankers now insisted that Peru must go to the IMF, which sent out a team led by a woman, Linda Hornig, who had to bear the full brunt of the Peruvians' fury. The team prescribed further austerity and cuts; there were more riotings and shootings; two finance ministers resigned, and the IMF became virtually a temporary ministry of finance. It was not until a year later that the IMF was at last able to reach a stand-by agreement with a new Minister of Finance, which persuaded the banks to lend more money.

The Peruvians' fortunes soon improved as the price of copper and silver went up and they began exporting oil. But the IMF did not forget that it had become the debt collector who was blamed for the shooting. And the banks did not forget that they had failed to impose discipline until the IMF had arrived. The rules of the financial Dodge City were becoming clearer. "There is no way in which the private banking community can lay down economic policy conditions to a government as part of a lending package," as one bank economist put it. "There can only be one financial policeman."[7]

[7]Richard O'Brien (senior economist, Amex Bank), "Should Banks' Lending to Developing Countries Be Underpinned by International Institutions?" *Financial Times* Conference, January 22, 1981.

Where then did the ultimate responsibility and risk really lie? If the Fund, or the Western central bankers, were prepared in the end to impose their own inescapable discipline which would rescue the bankers—as in Turkey or Peru—what kind of risk were the bankers really running? And if they were running no risk, how could they justify their spreads and high profit margins or, for that matter, their high salaries? "If we're just intermediaries without any risk taking," said one senior bank economist, "then we must admit to being overpaid." It was a far cry from the grand simplicity of the nineteenth-century free market, when Barings would put up the interest rates for the shakier American states knowing that if they defaulted the bank would be liable. There was now much more doubt about the real risk to the bankers. Yet the bankers still behaved as if they were quite independent. As the Senate Report of 1977 put it: "If the U.S. Government will have to bear ultimate responsibility for foreign loans of U.S. banks, should it have more say than it now does over the direction of these loans before they are made?"[8] In the great game of chicken the bankers were beginning to call the governments' bluff: they dared not risk letting a bank go down.

The apparent collusion between the Fund and the banks increased the sense of persecution in developing countries. Julius Nyerere, the President of Tanzania, one of the poorest countries in the world, was one of the most eloquent critics. "When we reject IMF conditions," he said in January 1980, "we hear the threatening whisper: "Without accepting our conditions you will not get our money, and you will get no other money" . . . When did the IMF become an International Ministry of Finance? When did nations agree to surrender to it their power of decision-making?" Six months later Nyerere was the host at a meeting of developing countries which put forward the Arusha Initiative, denouncing the Fund's policies and calling for a special UN conference on international money: "The IMF's medicine," it declared, "systematically favors the more conservative sectors of

[8] *International Debt, the Banks and U.S. Foreign Policy,* Senate Foreign Relations Committee, 1977.

society and traditional centers of power. . . . The Fund's policies, conceived to achieve 'stabilization,' have in fact contributed to destabilization and to the limitation of democratic processes."[9] But Tanzania itself could not avoid treating with the Fund; and later in the year Nyerere announced an agreement for an IMF loan.

SHOCK TREATMENT IN CHILE

The IMF always insisted that it was politically neutral; it only insisted on "adjustment" and economic stability, to enable a country to repay its loans. But this stabilizing could have fatal implications for democracy. The usual recipe was to devalue, force down wages, and open up the country to foreign trade and investment. Any democratic government with strong unions and spokesmen for the poor found this adjustment hard to enforce; it was much easier for a military dictatorship, working with economic technocrats. It was in Chile, the unhappy laboratory of political and economic theorists, that the IMF faced a caricature of the problem.

When the Marxist President Allende was elected in 1970 the IMF tried sincerely to help him, while he confronted an economic crisis and inflation galloped up to 700 percent a year. The banks, including the Bank of America and the Chase, resisted the example of the conglomerate ITT, which was trying to "destabilize" the country in connivance with the CIA.[10] But after Allende had been overthrown and killed in 1973, the IMF felt obliged to help the new dictator, General Pinochet, to restore economic order and to cut back inflation; and the bankers watched expectantly.

In November the Fund sent out a mission led by Carlos Sanson, who was impressed by the junta's effectiveness; though with qualifications. He reported confidentially when he returned that the

[9]See Development Dialogue, Dag Hammerskjöld Foundation, Uppsala, 1980: 2.
[10]See for instance the testimony of Ronald Reddatz of the Bank of America, Multinational Hearings, Part 1, pp. 392 ff.

junta "seems to be in full control of the country. However, its rather efficient approach in the handling of the military side has led to difficulties in the political sphere. Because of fears of subversion and retaliation, it continues to relentlessly pursue the leaders of the left who are in hiding, and to keep the principal leaders of the Allende regime on Dawson Island (near Antarctica). . . ." But the new regime (Sanson went on) "is a welcome change from the chaotic conditions prevailing during the last part of the Allende government . . . we were truly impressed by the Minister of Economy, an intelligent dynamic member of the right who nevertheless showed certain sensitivity for social issues."[11]

Sanson and his team easily persuaded the new government to reduce real wages and to devalue the escudo, for Pinochet was eager to earn the Fund's seal of approval as the first step toward re-establishing Chile's financial credentials. Unlike most Third World clients, he positively wanted to have strict conditions—to reassure international bankers and to underwrite his own drastic policies.

The Fund's first loan, in January 1974, allowed for relatively gradual stabilization, enough to encourage Western government creditors, who soon agreed to reschedule their large debts at the Club of Paris. But the junta soon found that this was too gradual, and they were supported by the high priest of monetarism, Milton Friedman, who visited Santiago in March 1975 to advise them and pronounced that "in Chile, with an inflation rate higher than 10 percent a month, gradualism seems to me impossible." In the meantime, the methods of General Pinochet and his secret police in suppressing opposition with torture had disgusted many Western democrats, and the British and Scandinavians refused to attend the next meeting of official creditors. But the IMF was worried that wages were still too high and called for "a much greater degree of austerity." The Pinochet government needed the Fund more than ever, now that Western governments were withholding

---

[11]IMF Confidential Memorandum from Carlos Sanson to Acting Managing Director, December 11, 1973.

official aid; it agreed to the Fund's new conditions and quickly appointed a new economic team of monetarists to enforce them, led by the Minister of Finance, Jorge Cauas, who had worked in the World Bank.[12]

The "shock treatment" of Cauas had its shocking effects: in 1975 the gross domestic product fell by 16 percent, unemployment went up to 20 percent, industrial output went down by 23 percent. Workers' wages went down further, and many small businessmen went bankrupt. But the IMF welcomed the policy of lowering import duties and opening up Chile to the rest of the world as a "major achievement of Chilean economic policy."

In 1976 the Chilean government went again to the IMF for a loan; but the Fund now insisted that wages should be lowered still *further*. This was now too much even for the junta, which actually complained that it would "create political difficulties." And the junta could now do without the IMF's full support, even though Western governments were still holding back aid because of the systematic torture and suppression of human rights. For by May 1976 the junta had got its first major loan from a consortium of North American banks, led by Bankers Trust, lending $125 million to the Chilean Central Bank. The bankers, coming in the wake of the IMF, were enthusiastic about the new Chilean economic team, who were in turn fortified by the bank's loans; and a succession of loans followed, culminating in the loan of $210 million led by Morgan's in April 1978, which was thought to be the biggest in Chile's history.

The Chilean élite had been enriched by the opening up and the inflow of funds, and the new prosperity of the city centers looked spectacular to visitors; but the internal conditions were more wretched than ever. Cauas, the Minister of Finance, told New York bankers in February 1978 that "the private sector is the key to the renaissance of relations between Chile and the United

[12]See Stephanie Griffith-Jones, "The Evolution of External Finance, Economic Policy and Development in Chile, 1973–1978" (Sussex: Institute for Development Studies, 1981), to which I am indebted in this section.

States." But the critics of the regime insisted that the rush of bank lending had made it possible for the junta to defy pressure from Western governments to restore human rights. In the words of Isabel Letelier, the widow of the murdered former Chilean ambassador to Washington: "Repression in Chile can continue precisely because the military junta can rely on private sources of financing ... The large multinational banks have become inextricably linked to the Chilean junta's struggle for political and economic survival."[13] And the IMF and the World Bank could both congratulate themselves on the success of the Chilean experiment: "Under extraordinarily unfavorable circumstances," said the World Bank Report on Chile in January 1980, "the Chilean authorities have engineered an economic turnaround without precedent in the history of Chile."

ENTER DE LAROSIERE

In 1978 a new managing director, Jacques de Larosière, arrived at the International Monetary Fund, and soon found himself in the midst of the crossfire of argument about its role. The managing director was always less visible and comprehensible than the president of the World Bank, with less freedom from his executive directors. He usually only talked publicly to fellow specialists; interviews were traditionally never attributed, unless to "sources close to the managing director," and his arguments with his board were only rarely revealed by leaks from other offices. But a new chief could nevertheless have a far-reaching influence.

After his powerful predecessor, Johannes Witteveen, De Larosière gave a much milder impression. He had spent his career as an inspecteur des finances in the French Ministry of Finance. His precise style—neat owlish head, wire spectacles, enunciated phrases—was inevitably called typically French. He seemed almost lost in the office, with its small garden of indoor plants and

[13]Isabel Letelier and Michael Moffitt, *Human Rights, Economic Aid and Private Banks* (Washington: Institute of Policy Studies, 1979).

its dominating bust of Lord Keynes. But he had his own clear view of the world, and he saw it as a whole. He had already been exposed to the poorer countries as an international negotiator; and his Frenchness was most evident in his concern for structures and systems, rather than perpetual pragmatic adjustments. He arrived with his own ideas about the IMF's role. He believed— sources close to him said—in Keynes's original conception of the IMF as a genuine international bank, with freedom to build up its own deposits and overdrafts and to issue its own currency—rather than the more limited legacy of Harry White. And he believed, as did the Brandt Report, that more financial aid to developing countries could contribute to the world's economic recovery. "It is paradoxical," he said at the UNCTAD meeting in Manila in 1979, "that industrialized countries, most of which are not using their productive potential to the full, are hesitating to increase their financial aid to poor countries. This is despite the fact that such aid could result in increased global demand and thus contribute to reactivation of world trade in a recovery of production."

De Larosière faced a whole new set of problems in the summer of 1979, when the second oil crisis again wrecked the balance of payments of developing countries. It was now still harder to argue that the countries in difficulties only needed a short sharp shock to "adjust" or pull themselves together. He was convinced that the Fund must adapt its character to provide longer and more lenient loans; and he wanted to encourage multilateral investment in the Third World, rather than more lending. But he was up against opposition from executive directors and from many of his staff, who saw any relaxing of discipline as encouraging inflation and irresponsibility.

There was an early test case when the small African country of Sierra Leone, with 3 million people, asked the IMF for a loan to rescue it; it depended heavily on exporting bauxite and diamonds and on iron ore, which had run out, and the higher oil price was the last straw. The more conservative directors insisted on the usual medicine; but the Sierra Leonians pleaded that the increase of domestic prices would cause dangerous hardships. De Larosière favored a less drastic program of cutting public spending and restricting credit. The directors fought back, but Sierra Leone eventually got its loan without having to devalue.

In March 1980 the executive directors met with De Larosière to discuss the full damage of the higher oil price. Each of them expressed his own regional viewpoint with an appearance of detached objectivity. Alexandre Kafka, the Brazilian, spoke for countries which needed the greatest possible help from the international banks. Mohammed Finaish, the Libyan who represented most Arab states, stressed that the oil producers were increasingly worried about how to invest their oil money without losing its value. Bernard Drabble, the Canadian, stressed the role of private investment. Paul Mentré de Loye, the French director, distinguished between the different categories of problem countries. But they all agreed that this new oil crisis was creating more serious deficits for developing countries than the first one and would not soon disappear. There were warning signals, De Larosière said; the banks were lending more cautiously, with wider spreads for shorter periods. The banks (the directors agreed) would still play the chief role in recyling, but the Fund should be prepared if necessary to do more recycling itself, imposing its own conditions. Several directors said that the Fund should be ready to borrow money from the market.

The board was beginning to take a longer-term view of countries in trouble. They still insisted that they must cut down consumption, prevent inefficiency, and stop wasting resources; but they put more emphasis on the supply side, and on encouraging greater production to help them pay for their oil; they accepted that the Fund's programs might take more than a year. They had already been given a paper, the day before this March meeting, by Ernest Stern of the World Bank, about the Bank's own proposals for "structural adjustment," which began to overlap with the IMF. All the directors now agreed that they needed to collaborate more closely with the World Bank.[14] In fact, the Bank and the

[14]Chairman's summing up: IMF Confidential Document, March 21, 1980.

Fund, though they communicated very little, were beginning to converge in their plans to help developing countries.

De Larosière himself kept stressing the need for a "substitution account," which would enable countries with surplus dollars to convert them into SDRs, which would thus take a further step toward becoming a world reserve currency. It would provide an answer, he said, to "the fundamental question of what surplus oil-producing countries can do with their surpluses." Soon after the meeting he toured the Middle East to canvass support for the idea. But when the policy-making group of the IMF, the interim committee, met in Hamburg the following month, the Americans and West Germans poured cold water on the substitution account and postponed agreement for at least a year.

TOMORROW ME BORROW SOME MORE

De Larosière and his directors faced a difficult test of their tolerance in the case of Jamaica—which had long been a nightmare for the money mandarins. The beautiful Caribbean island had only 2 million people, but it was politically highly visible, as the Fund was all too well aware. It was a rumbustious democracy with an outspoken free press—a rare phenomenon in the Third World—surrounded by autocratic neighbors. To the north was Communist Cuba, which tempted many young Jamaican students; to the west was the dictatorship of Haiti; to the east was the tiny capitalist colony of the Cayman Islands. Since its independence in 1962 Jamaica had been loud with demagogy, while its problems worsened and its exports of sugar, bananas, and bauxite, bedeviled with mismanagement, were at the mercy of the erratic world markets. American tourists flocked to the north shore of the island, but their presence only underlined the poverty of the rest. It was a noisy microcosm of the Third World's problems.

In 1972 Jamaica had acquired a new Prime Minister, Michael Manley, an eloquent intellectual from the London School of Economics, known on the island as Joshua, with a fine profile and a charismatic style. He promised much more housing and welfare,

nationalized public utilities, raised a levy from the bauxite companies, and tried to form the bauxite equivalent of an OPEC cartel.
Foreign companies took fright; banks stopped making new loans;
capital and professional men fled; tourists were scared away by
the reports of violence.

At first Manley's government kept away from the IMF, but by
1977 they had to ask for help. The Fund offered them the biggest
loan (per head) in its history, but the conditions as usual were
strict. After drawing the first loan Jamaica soon failed its "performance test" and had to negotiate again. The Finance Minister
resigned, the Jamaican dollar was drastically devalued, and in
1978 average wages fell by 35 percent. Wherever these drastic
remedies had been applied (one Fund official was quoted as saying) they had led either to the death of democracy or the overthrow of the government. There were riots and demonstrations (or
"social tensions," as the IMF called them), while new disasters
visited the island, including floods and the higher oil price. The
only really thriving industry was marijuana. The government
showed no signs of being able to meet its next test, and it had to
go back to the Fund.

The Fund was now divided, and two of its senior men, Walter
Robichek and David Finch, described their differences in a confidential memo to De Larosière in November 1979. More lending,
they reckoned, would have doubtful results: "We are agreed that
if Jamaica was to be considered on its own merit the program
outlined would not deserve our support. However, we are also
agreed that Jamaica cannot be considered on its own merit." They
knew that if the Fund stopped lending to Jamaica the Third World
would blame it for being too inflexible toward countries suffering
under the new oil crisis. But they disagreed about the next step.
Finch insisted that to weaken the strict program would seriously
undercut the Fund's technical reputation. Robichek still thought
there was a fighting chance that Jamaica's situation could improve.[15]

[15]IMF Confidential Memo to Managing Director, November 14, 1979.

De Larosière then sent out a mission to Jamaica, headed by Omar Albertelli, armed with a detailed briefing. The briefing admitted that some of the difficulties like the floods were "unforeseen and outside the control of the authorities," but it was skeptical about the seriousness of Manley's government—the "political directorate," as the briefing discreetly called it. The mission was told to stress "the deeply entrenched suspicion that the government is not seriously committed to its economic program," and to insist that "the number of ministries, departments, statutory boards and government enterprises will need to be reduced sharply."[16] It was sound advice, but it came dangerously near to usurping the government's job.

Albertelli's team—the "night visitors"—began inspecting the island, retaining their professional *sang froid* in an atmosphere of political frenzy. Walls were scrawled with THE POOR CAN'T TAKE NO MORE and splashed with the initials IMF, the symbols of the hated neo-imperialism. The Prime Minister's militant wife, Beverley Manley, added her own invective: "The IMF is not here as any friend in need for developing countries. All over the world people are speaking out against the oppressive terms and conditions of the IMF loans." But when I visited the Prime Minister, just at that time, he complained sadly that the Fund was being used as a political football, and seemed confident that he could reach a new agreement with them. A witty musical by the Jamaican playwright Barry Reckord was running in Kingston, called *Joshua and the Spiderman,* making fun of Manley's optimism. It had the refrain: "Tomorrow me borrow some more."

Manley was soon the victim of his own party's rhetoric: the left wing refused to agree to the IMF's terms, and another Finance Minister departed. Manley prepared for a new general election, with the IMF as the chief issue, fighting against his ice-cold opponent, Edward Seaga, who was committed to new negotiations and welcomed free enterprise: the "Puerto Rico solution." The Jamaican voters were now very skeptical of Joshua, and after a bloody

[16]IMF Confidential Briefing, November 14, 1979.

campaign with 500 estimated deaths, Seaga won a spectacular victory. He faced the daunting task of trying to rebuild Jamaica's finances and negotiated a record new loan.

The IMF, in its own confidential report after the breakdown of negotiations in March, decided that the only possible fault of its staff was that they had been too optimistic in assessing Manley's commitment to their program. "An objective evaluation of the Fund's role in Jamaica," the report explained with eloquent self-congratulation, "must conclude that the Fund has been generous in terms of financial and technical support; cooperative in efforts to mobilize assistance for other external sources; liberal as regards the time allowed for the adjustment of demand; mindful of the external shocks and mishaps over which Jamaica has had no control; and sensitive to the social and political realities of the country."[17]

Certainly the Fund had shown itself more sensitive in this exposed island than in earlier test cases. Certainly Manley had been exasperating in his unrealism, while his government had used the ritual game of Hate the IMF as a distraction from its own mismanagement. The IMF had become accustomed to patiently suffering this hate-ritual, whether in Jamaica or in Britain. But it was a dangerous game on both sides, for it concealed the real truths and responsibilities. The IMF's aloof style, its white face and obscure language, had not helped to educate public opinion and had made it an easy target for demagogic attacks. It was like a replay of the old nineteenth-century battles between populists and federal bankers in the United States, but played in a much more emotional style: the IMF was now a prime target in the war of words from the South.

The underlying tragedy of Jamaica, as of many other debt-ridden countries, required more fundamental remedies than the IMF could provide. It could only escape from its debt trap if it were to increase its exports and earn foreign currency; and that

[17]IMF Document: *Jamaica—Role of the Fund in Recent Stabilization Efforts,* April 18, 1980.

required not so much loans as productive investment and management—which begged the whole question of distrust between North and South.

THE MONEY JIGSAW

By the time of the annual meeting in Washington in September 1980, where this book began, the International Monetary Fund was in the center of the world's money maze, surrounded by dependants, each with its own insecurities.

The big commercial bankers were becoming more concerned to share their political risks. Turkey had already borrowed a record sum from the IMF when the banks refused to lend more; Brazil looked like having to approach the Fund; Poland, though outside the IMF system, was rapidly becoming the responsibility of Western governments. A whole row of developing countries, from the Philippines to Jamaica, were near their limits of commercial borrowing. Many bankers were looking, like Clausen and Guth, toward the IMF as a collaborator or a safety net, and most were reluctant to lend any more to developing countries. "There's no way," Felix Rohatyn of Lazards told me, "that the Western banking system can be responsible for funding the balance of payments of the Third World. Recycling means lending more and more to less and less credit-worthy countries; they borrow to pay the interest on the interest. We can't pretend that we can take the risk. All we can do for the Third World is to give them Mr. Yamani's telephone number."

The developing countries, on their side, were becoming more desperate as they felt the pinch from the second oil crisis. They had organized a special session at the United Nations in the summer of 1980 to prepare for "global negotiations" toward a new order, but the session had petered out in disarray. With the higher cost of oil, they found it still harder to keep pace with their debts, as interest rates were rising. "The end of cheap oil," Morgan's warned in its monthly report, *World Financial Markets,* in January 1981, "is being followed by the end of cheap money." The developing countries' honeymoon with the bankers was now finally over: they looked more anxiously toward the IMF as their savior, and they pinned some of their hopes on the Brandt Report as a blueprint for a new order.

At the IMF De Larosière was clearly concerned to enlarge the role of the Fund, to play a bigger role in relending the oil money. At the annual meeting in 1980 he announced that the IMF would set about borrowing large funds, either directly from the OPEC countries or from the commercial market; and six months later the Saudis lent $10 billion to the Fund. It was a step further toward Keynes's concept of the international clearing union, as a genuine global bank ("when one chap wants to leave his resources idle, those resources . . . are made available to another chap who is prepared to use them").[18] But the IMF, like the commercial banks, was still an upside-down pyramid with too little capital in proportion to its loans; and more capital was only likely to be found in the OPEC countries, particularly in Saudi Arabia.

The Arabs remained the jokers in the pack, and the annual meeting had dramatically revealed the political tensions in the heart of the economic system. The richer Arab states had been pressed by the Palestinians to get them a place as observers at the meeting; but McNamara, appalled by the prospect in the midst of President Carter's election campaign, mobilized all America's allies to defeat the proposal. The Arabs were furious at this manipulation, as they saw it; for them it was an issue, not so much of Palestine, as of power sharing. "We thought that McNamara was an internationalist," one of them said to me; "now we know he's an American." They refused to put up money for McNamara's pet new project of an energy affiliate. It began to look as if the whole future of international lending would depend on the strip of land alongside the Jordan River. The Arab "money weapon" had not shown itself, as the Israelis had feared, in threats to pull out their deposits from the big banks; but the Arabs were understandably reluctant to support world institutions unless they had more political say.

The Saudis were partly placated, and the next year there was

[18]See Chapter 4.

agreement to increase their quota to the IMF. But in the meantime they had their own ideas about spending their surplus. In 1980 they had embarked on a new five-year plan which would cost no less than $250 billion—or $32,000 for each Saudi. And four months after the IMF meeting they presided over the Islamic Summit at Taif (see Chapter 1), where they proclaimed a *jehad* or holy campaign to regain Jerusalem, and promised billions to the Muslim nations of Africa and Asia. Would the Saudis, if they could not share economic power in the West, build up their own Islamic power in the South?

In the West, in the meantime, there was now a much meaner and more skeptical attitude toward the world institutions and developing countries. At the annual meeting in 1980 McNamara had delivered a passionate last annual speech describing the plight of the absolute poor and the deteriorating economic prospects. He deplored the declining aid from the West, which was "shockingly small" and insisted that the World Bank "had only barely begun to develop its full potential for service and assistance." But the era of McNamara was drawing to an end. McNamara himself had recommended his successor, Tom Clausen from the Bank of America, believing that a respected and cautious banker would carry weight with Congress and the Republicans. Clausen had his own kind of dedication. He was aware of the problems of the Third World, to which his own bank had lent $8 billion, and he realized that the World Bank must take a long-term view: "Where people are desperate, you have revolutions. It's in our own evident self-interest to see that they are not forced into that." He explained that bankers need to keep their clients above water: "You must keep the patient alive, because otherwise you can't effect the cure."[19] But he did not reveal McNamara's idealism or imagination, to visualize a different kind of world. The World Bank was back in the hands of an orthodox banker.

When the Reagan Administration moved into Washington, it was preoccupied with cutting public expenditure and inflation

[19]*Sunday Times,* London, November 23, 1980.

within its own country; it saw world institutions in the same light, and it was distrustful of multilateral agencies which limited American influence. It wanted to cut back the American contribution to the World Bank's capital, postponed any American contribution to McNamara's new energy affiliate, and reduced the contribution that it would ask Congress to approve for IDA, the soft-loan agency of the World Bank. The American executive director, Colbert King, who had been appointed by Carter, resigned before his term expired, protesting that "now is not the time to undermine our influence in the World Bank and global economic development."

The new policies in Washington were part of a much broader Western retreat. The captivity of the hostages in Iran had helped to sour the Americans' view of the Third World. The invasion of Afghanistan and the threat to Poland had increased fears of Soviet aggression, and made Washington much more interested in the East-West conflict than the North-South divide. Both Europeans and Americans were showing signs of turning inward as the recession, inflation, and high unemployment increased their problems at home; and their withdrawal had shown itself in the reception of Brandt's Program for Survival, which had been published in early 1980. In Britain Mrs. Thatcher's government dismissed the report as alarmist, and the Foreign Office insisted that the international capital market could cope with the recycling problem. Germany and France were preoccupied with their internal political conflicts; and even Sweden, with its long interest in aid, was engrossed in its own economic crises. In the United States the report was little noticed in the tumult of the election campaign and was relegated to page 26 of *The Washington Post*; when Brandt came to Washington he was regarded by White House advisers as being too soft on the Soviets, and President Carter was only with difficulty persuaded to see him. Brandt had put his hopes on a North-South summit, scheduled for October 1981, which could bypass the fruitless confrontations between diplomats on both sides and work out the real mutual interests. But the inward-looking mood of the Western nations was not conducive to its success.

Yet the arguments for much bolder initiatives, whether based on morality or on mutual interests, remained inescapable. It was left largely to development experts, to churchmen, and to radical politicians to argue the need for fundamental changes in the world system—and to the younger generation, who were more worried about living their lifetime in a world so divided between rich and poor. But the commercial interests for creating a more stable economic framework were equally pressing. Multinational executives and bankers were as involved as anyone in the interdependence between nations; for their own business, of manufactures or loans, had locked them into other parts of the world which could not survive if the West closed its doors. However much they saw themselves as champions of free enterprise, it was becoming much harder to believe—after the oil crisis, the debt crisis, and the growing political tensions with developing countries —that the world's problems could be solved by free enterprise alone.

22
THE DANGEROUS EDGE

Our interest's in the dangerous edge of things.
ROBERT BROWNING
Bishop Blougram's Apology

The Western nations, in their new mood of withdrawal, were much more skeptical about all aid to developing countries, unless it was linked to military alliances or direct advantages to the donors. Conservative politicians and academics in America complained about the wastage and corruption of aid projects which were "pouring money down the rathole," and were much more concerned with the East-West conflict than the North-South divide. They saw themselves returning to realism and discipline after the years of liberal softness. But to many liberals, including McNamara, this was a tragic rejection of the American history of involvement and generosity toward the rest of the world. Certainly the protests about waste and corruption seemed to come oddly from a country which in the previous century had been through such vicissitudes of extravagance and default. The United States had after all been the most spectacular example of a developing country which had rapidly graduated to unparalleled prosperity.

There was a comic irony in the eagerness with which the new champions of free enterprise attacked the wastefulness of aid. For the commercial bankers—the high priests of private enterprise—were now responsible for far greater flows of money to the Third World than all the aid agencies put together. Ever since the oil crisis of 1973 had built up the OPEC surpluses, these flows had been drastically "privatized," until over two thirds of the money now came through the banks. And these bank loans had ended up in wastage on a far greater scale than the most incompetent aid agency could have dreamt of—whether they went to the private coffers of President Mobutu in Zaire, to bribes to Indonesian officials, or to the Communist Party funds in Warsaw. Most official givers of aid at least had people in the field who tried to see that the money reached its destination; and the loans from the World Bank were subject to rigorous local supervision. But the commercial bankers' loans, as we have seen in earlier chapters, could all too easily be deflected from concrete projects into private bank accounts or government treasuries without any foreigner noticing.

Much of the bank lending in fact was beginning to look very much like a form of aid. In many countries the bankers saw little prospect of getting back their capital; as Professor Jonathan Aronson puts it, the "classic definition of banking as 'lending money and getting it back' was no longer accurate."[1] Whether in Zaire, Brazil, or Poland, the prospects looked increasingly remote as the debts were piled higher. Bankers were accustomed to countries like Canada or Australia remaining in debt over the decades; but those countries had high credit ratings with little danger of revolutions or default. Now, in their search for new customers and profits, they had ventured much closer to the frontiers of chaos. It was true that the developing countries only accounted for about 5 percent of their total lending, and the bankers concentrated on the twenty to thirty countries which they regarded as most creditworthy. But the red line of the bankers was always shifting, as yet another country found oil or began exporting to the world markets; and even India and China had their attractions to bankers who needed to balance their portfolios and find new markets.

The bankers approached the Third World with an almost opposite viewpoint to that of the do-gooders—the development economists, the UN experts, the Oxfam workers, or Christian missionaries. They could never forget that they had to earn a return on their capital and that their shareholders and supervisors

[1] *Money and Power* (Beverly Hills: Sage Publications, 1977), p. 165.

were watching them. While the development experts wrote their papers on poverty and famine the bankers read *Euromoney* or the *Institutional Investor* and argued about an extra ⅛ percent on the interest rate. But they could still find themselves on the same plane to Delhi or Sri Lanka, concerned about the same problems of growth rates and country risk; and their funds might even end up in the same place.

Few bankers like to admit that they are in the business of aid; it goes against their whole professional self-image of caution and custody. But their foreign lending always depends on more political and philosophical assumptions than most of them care to admit. So long as the merry-go-round of borrowing and lending continues to turn, through less and less credit-worthy countries, they can continue to collect their interest and profit without worrying too much about getting their capital back. But the carousel depends on everyone accepting that the loans are basically sound, representing real assets; and the whole game is threatened if a bank calls a country in default. The bank supervisors—who are the real judges of the bank's stability—know well enough that these precise and elaborate structures depend in the end on almost mythical assumptions about the reliability of sovereign states. The assumptions strain the bankers' concept of credit to its limits; but if enough people share that trust it becomes a kind of reality. Bankers, together with their clients, always have a vested interest in hope. And it was on hope that the fortunes of much of the world were depending.

After the first massive increase in bank lending Lord Lever, the former Labour cabinet minister, addressed a large lunch of international bankers in London. "I have never been so sumptuously entertained," he began, "by such a distinguished collection of *bankrupts.*" There was much laughter, but afterward a Swiss banker came up to Lever and said: "They thought you were joking. But I know you were being serious." Lever *was* being serious: he insists that banking is a kind of charade which depends on pretending that loans to the Third World are much safer than they really are. It is not an argument, he insists, for stopping the lending, but for supervising loans more closely, and recognizing the reality: that many countries will never be able to repay their loans; they can only borrow more to repay their immediate debts. The charade must go on, because it has become essential to the world's survival; it is in fact a gigantic system of aid. "It makes the Marshall Plan look like peanuts," Lever says, "but because it's concealed as businesslike banking, it's much more acceptable to voters."

Whether the bankers saw it as aid or hard-headed business, they were caught up in the complex and bewildering process of development, together with the aid givers, the world agencies, and the United Nations. They could not now escape from it if they wanted to. There was nothing new, as we have seen, in the link between bankers and development: it was only a return to the historic pattern, in which bankers had been interlocked with developing nations since the Middle Ages. As they began lending their surplus funds—first from Italy to Britain or France, then from Europe to America or Asia, then from America to the rest of the world—they faced recurring disasters, with greed and fraud on both sides, punctuated by defaults, gunboats, and occupations. Marxists would still maintain, following Lenin, that international bankers represented the highest stage of capitalism, which led inevitably to wars; but the Communist states had not devised a better system for transferring wealth, and they were themselves deeply in hock to the capitalists.

The bankers, whatever their faults, had played a historic role in building up the economies of developing nations, including the United States, Russia, and Japan. There had been disaster areas where their money never took root or where the conflict of cultures was too extreme. The row of Islamic countries on the old route from Europe to India—through Egypt, Turkey, Iran, and Afghanistan—became a bankers' trap in the nineteenth century, and remains so: the conflict between Western capitalism and Islamic extremism is now once again explosive. But after the bleak interim between two world wars, with depression, protection, and nationalism, the bankers were back in the development business, extending themselves still farther with the spread of the Eurodollar billions. They made some huge mistakes in their shortsighted pursuit of profits, as in Iran, Indonesia, and Poland. They helped to underpin some of the ugliest regimes in the world, including Chile and South Africa. They followed the vagaries of the global money market, which allowed too many loans one moment and too few the next, providing a wobbly basis for any country's steady development. But they were nevertheless helping to transform the economic map of the world as they lent to the new industrial countries in East Asia or Latin America; or opened up new trade and prospects in India or China; or ventured into the least creditworthy countries in their restless search for profits and fees.

They could claim to be the most global profession of all, as they sat in the middle of their web of credit stretching from Moscow to Brasilia, from Sweden to Tanzania. They had created their own version of One World, speaking the same language of interest rates, maturities, margins, and roll-overs. But debts (as Herbert Feis wrote) were still not the kind of bond that could unite the world; they generated insecurity and unease on both sides. As the Third World went deeper into debt, the bankers were less confident of the stability of their upside-down pyramids. It had always been possible for a country in difficulties to bankrupt a bank, as Britain had brought down the Medicis, or Argentina had brought down Barings. However watchful the central banks and the supervisors, there was always the danger that a foreign demagogue would repudiate his debts; that the merry-go-round of lending would stop and the banks would fall like the proverbial dominoes.

The bankers were reluctant to accept their need for official support, for the whole psychology of risk depended on assuming their self-sufficiency; while the central bankers and supervisors had to *appear* not to be ready to rescue them, in their constant game of chicken. But the game could also conceal a real reluctance of central bankers or international institutions to face up to the danger, and to the responsibility for rescue. No one was sure whether there was really an international "lender of last resort." As Charles Kindleberger asked in 1977: "How is self-reliance preserved in the system? Is it possible artistically to threaten no rescue, while actually rescuing at the last minute, as in the New York crisis—that is, to keep the others honest but not to suffer the spreading collapse of a major failure or failures?"[2]

In the meantime there was mounting evidence, whether in Zaire, Turkey, or Jamaica, that the commercial bankers could not go it alone. They had to look to the International Monetary Fund to take over more of the role of lending; and the IMF in turn had to look toward the Saudis and other OPEC countries for both loans and capital. Further loans to the Third World would have to come either directly from the OPEC powers who would lend with their own political or religious motives, or from world institutions using more money from OPEC. It was the expansion of the world bodies which offered the more stable and less politically influenced alternative.

ONE WORLD?

Many developing countries were now facing the kind of nightmare that afflicts many debtors: they were spending more and more of their available money on repaying the interest, or even the interest on the interest. Some of them owed so much to one lot of bankers that they needed other bankers to find ways to repay. They were borrowing not for the kind of capital projects that could help to pay off their debts but simply in order to keep their people from penury or starvation—with no real end in sight. "It reminds me of the Chinese proverb," said Bailey Fiedler of Bankers Trust: "If you want to help a starving man you don't give him a fish, you give him a fishing rod. But we're only giving him fish."

Their impossible debts were signs of a much deeper difficulty: that these countries were not able to pay their way in their world with their exports. Even the most productive and well-managed

[2]Charles P. Kindleberger, *Manias, Panics and Crashes* (New York: Basic Books, 1978), p. 209.

developing countries like Korea or Taiwan faced a dangerous prospect; they had based their borrowing and expansion on being able to sell shoes, cameras, and radios to customers in the West, but now they saw the doors of protection closing against them. The less efficient countries faced a more fundamental problem; for they lacked the management or organization to provide enough exports. The bankers had lent to countries like Jamaica, Zaire, and Poland on the basis of their mineral or agricultural resources; but those countries could only extract their wealth by organizing human resources—whose difficulties the bank economists were inclined to forget.

In the nineteenth century the Western bankers and investors were interested not only in lending but in investing, helping to build railroads, steel mills, and factories in developing countries like the United States and Russia: the investments could pay dividends, while building up those countries' productive strength. But now the bankers, except in a few more developed countries, were more interested in lending than investing. It was the multinational corporations which had taken over the direct investment, providing money, management, and technology on their own terms, within their own complex organizations. The corporations saw profit and security for their investments in a few developing countries like Brazil or Singapore, but elsewhere they faced the fierce political resentment of young nations, insistently demanding Africanization, Asianization, or total nationalization, which made their task difficult or impossible. Yet these countries were painfully learning that they could not easily maintain or increase their exports without the help of the multinationals, which could provide not only management and technology but distribution and markets; and Lee Kuan Yew had shown how Singapore could succeed by "plugging in," as he put it, "to the world grid of industrial power houses." The new nations began to realize, not without some bitterness, the truth of that saying: "If there's one thing worse than being exploited by multinational corporations, it's *not* being exploited."

The problem of world debt leads ineluctably to the problem of world management, which in turn depends heavily on the multi-national corporations. These corporations, even more than the banks, were caught up in the political tensions of the North-South divide. They needed to extend their development and investment in the Third World, particularly in oil and minerals, on which so much of the Western economy depended; but they could only be secure if they could obtain the trust and confidence of their hosts. The hosts had good reasons to be suspicious of some of the multinationals, after the history of exploitation by the oil companies in the Middle East, or of political interference by the less scrupulous corporations like ITT. They had longer memories than the corporate managers. But they became more aware of their need of help, as their debts mounted and the failures of local management became clearer; and already by the late seventies they showed indications (it seemed to me) of having passed the peak of their resentment of Western investment—whether in Mozambique or Angola in Africa, or in Jamaica in the Caribbean, or in India. There were strong interests on both sides, as the Brandt Commission had reported, to achieve mutual bargains which would allow for development without exploitation. It is a historic challenge for the multinational managers: to forge relationships with these countries which are genuine partnerships, which do not bear the marks of neocolonialism or Western arrogance, and which are sensitive to the needs and ambitions of their hosts. Their response to that challenge will affect the prosperity of large areas of the world.

But the bankers could not dodge their own responsibility for the world's future. They were now hostages in the Third World, in the classic trap in which the banker is owed so much by his client that he has to keep lending him more to keep him alive. Some countries like Brazil had laid the trap deliberately, to ensure that the West had a vested interest in their future, while others had found it by accident; but in either case creditors and debtors were bound together by their chains of gold. The bankers often succeeded in passing the buck, as in Turkey and Poland, to their governments or to the IMF; but in any long-term perspective they could not ignore that their borrowers needed bold reforms in the world system to enable them to become economically stable. The new industrial countries had to be able to sell their goods to the West without discrimination; the countries with valuable raw materials needed more stable prices to plan their development; and all developing countries wanted to participate more fully in the running of the world institutions. The bankers, whether they liked it or not—and many did not—were implicated in the whole tense relationship between North and South.

But the world's economic future was too dangerous to be left to bankers alone. That great shift of wealth after 1973 had hugely increased their expansion into the Third World, leaving the IMF and the World Bank panting behind. But as their debts mounted and their insecurities grew, bankers could not take all the burden of this tricky process of lending the money from one part of the Third World to another. The unbalanced state of the world after the oil crisis called for much more fundamental changes in the economic arrangements. The OPEC countries had capital without technology; the industrial countries had technology without enough capital and markets; the developing countries had potential markets without capital or technology. Each group suffered its own insecurity in this triangle of distrust, but they could not overcome it by retreating into self-sufficiency and self-help, for they were made still more interdependent by the necessity for oil, which connected the most disparate parts of the world; and as oil turned into money the relationships deepened. The industrial nations in their new mood might long to ignore developing countries which did not have oil; but the OPEC countries still insisted on aligning themselves with their poorer neighbors, co-religionists, and allies. The South still had minerals and raw materials which the North could not do without, and three quarters of the world's population. With all their difficulties the developing countries offered more exciting prospects than the old centers of the North.

The reconciliation of this uneasy triangle could not be achieved by the workings of free enterprise alone, even by the most farsighted bankers and businessmen; for it calls for political accommodations which can only be reached by governments and world institutions. The development of a truly international bank backed by the resources of all the major nations, which was in the minds of Keynes and others at the end of the Second World War, was never more necessary than now, thirty-five years later. It would be a tragic irony if Western nations were to turn against the existing world bodies at the time when they needed to expand their role rather than contract it: to serve not only as the intermediaries for loans between rich and poor nations, but as the channels for productive investment; to provide not only the fish but the fishing rod. World institutions, with the resources of OPEC behind them, are much better able to deploy these new funds for the benefit of the Third World than the Western bankers or governments acting individually. The creation of a more stable economic system can only be achieved by cooperation between nations. In the words of the Brandt Report: "Change is inevitable. The question is whether the world community will take deliberate and decisive steps to bring it about, or whether change will be forced upon us all through an unfolding of events over which the international community has little control."[3]

It has been the bankers' destiny, as they carried their briefcases and deadpan style into the jungle, to find themselves on the dangerous edge of the world, pointing up the contradictions and cross-purposes. They are not often loved for it. They may leave behind them impossible debts, disillusion, or default. Their view will always be incomplete. But they show the way to the real needs of a world which can only be brought together, not by credit in the bankers' sense, but by a more fundamental trust.

[3] *North-South: A Program for Survival,* p. 269.

INDEX

attitude and generosity to developing countries, 28–9, 352–3; but no cheaper oil, 28
Brandt Commission and, 366
deposits and investments in West, 152, 176, 269, 315
involvement with and contributions to IMF and World Bank, 348–9, 372, 375, 391, 400
1973 oil crisis and after, 8, 149–60, 317
total deposits in U.S. banks (1976), 157–8
Oppenheimer, Sir Harry, 200–1, 206, 214
Osgood, Colonel Samuel, 57
OTRAG (West German missile company), 193
Overseas Development, Ministry of (G.B.), 123
Overstone, Lord, 40, 161

Pahlevi Foundation, 295
Palais Egmont, Brussels, Brandt Commission meeting at, 366
Palestinians, the, 16, 391
Palin, Ronald, *Rothschild Relish*, 62
Palme, Olof, 362, 366
Palmer, Arnold, 186
Pao, Sir Y. K., interview with author, 226, 227
Paper Money, "Adam Smith," 195
Paribas, *see* Banque de Paris et des Pays-Bas
Paris Club, 191, 335
Park, President (South Korea), 222
murder of, 223
Partners in Development, see Pearson Commission and Report
Pasha, Ismail, 52
Patel, I. G., 236
Patterson, Ellmore, 155, 170, 171
Patterson, Herbert, 103, 104

PDL (Poverty Datum Line, S. Africa), 205, 206
Peabody, George, 61
banker and philanthropist, 63
Peace Corps, 114, 347
Pearson, Hesketh, *The Smith of Smiths*, 61
Pearson, Lester, chairman of Pearson Commission, 124
Pearson Commission and Report (1968/9), 110, 116, 359, 367–9
project of World Bank, 123–5
Pearson, Group (conglomerate), 272
Pecora, Ferdinand, 74
Penguin Books, 272
Penn Central Railroad, collapse of, 108, 109, 190
Pentagon, the, and foreign sales of arms, 153
Percy, Charles, 157, 172–3
Perkins, James, 74
Pertamina, Indonesia state oil company, 185–7, 274
Peru, 378
Peterson, Peter, 10, 273, 361, 364, 365, 366
Petrodollars, 153
Phillips, Sir Frederick, 83
Pieske, Eckhard, 213
Pierpont Morgan, Francis Henry Taylor, 65
Pindling, Lynden, 281
Pinochet, General, 363, 380–1
Pisani, Edgard, 362
Platten, Donald, 95, 211
Player, Gary, 186
Poland, 329–36
huge foreign debts, 25–6, 146, 184, 334–6
strikes in, 333, 335
Polynesian Studies, Journal of, 288
Portes, Richard, 331, 332
POS (point-of-sale terminal), 247

For a complete list of books available from Penguin in the United States, write to Dept. DG, Penguin Books, 299 Murray Hill Parkway, East Rutherford, New Jersey 07073.

For a complete list of books available from Penguin in Canada, write to Penguin Books Canada Limited, 2801 John Street, Markham, Ontario L3R 1B4.